Large businesses can no longer afford to remain isolated. Transnational Expansion is in most cases, the key to survival. One of the methods is to enter foreign markets to ensure movement of capital and ghouls through transactional mergers and acquisitions.

Dr Ramesh has covered the subject from all angles including the synergies emerging from such mergers and acquisitions. He has dealt with the subject from a broad prism of statutes of the USA, UK and the EU and has analysed them from the Indian perspective. He has dealt with all the vital areas including law, purpose and practical issues, relevant for and to be borne in mind, while venturing into CBMAs.

The book would be useful to lawyers, law students, industry professionals and chartered accountants alike. It should be a fine guide to those who wish to acquire basic knowledge on the subject.

- **Justice Raja Shaker Mantha**, *Judge, High Court at Calcutta*

Having Obtained a Doctorate of Philosophy (Ph.D) in law for his thesis on Cross Border Mergers and Acquisitions, the author has mastered the intricacies of the subject while making a Comparative Study of the Legal Framework and Procedure in India and the USA. Moreover, the author has put immense effort to simplify the subject so that even a layman can understand well the world of cross-border mergers and acquisitions.

In dealing with impact on CBMA and prevention of fraud in CBMA, the author made a very detailed analysis and a laudable explanation which will surely give the reader more insights about the subject

- **Justice B. Krishna Mohan**, *Judge, High Court of Andhra Pradesh, Amaravati, Guntur*

Coming to the present research work, I can say this is one of the novel topics which has contemporary relevance though titled as legal framework but interdisciplinary approach a combination/blend of Management and Business Studies too. The theoretical presentation of the choppers is a lucid and very much information, interesting, the terminology of the International business is very well explained, and the linkage between the chapters is apt and convincing. The research design and development is well articulated and addressed the gaps with the detailed justification by citing suitable research studies. The construction, flow and uses of English language appear at the free and hence appreciable.

- **Justice Dr. Bulusu Siva Sankara Rao**, *M. Com., LL.M. Ph.D., LL.D.(Post-Doctoral Fellow), Judge-Judicial Preview, Andhra Pradesh*

It is remarkable that a seasoned Senior Police Officer of the Indian Police Service has been able to find time, energy and inclination to do an incisive study of such diverse topics as security of state and an important aspect of the corporate ladder such as "Cross Border Mergers and Acquisitions". It shows his thirst for knowledge and urge to share it with others by publishing his work.

- **JUSTICE M. S. RAMA CHANDRA RAO**, *JUDGE, HIGH COURT FOR THE STATE OF TELANGANA*

This book gives a comprehensive and lucid presentation on cross-border mergers and acquisitions framework in India, including a good insight into the interplay between the Companies Act, FEMA, SEBI Regulations, etc. It also makes an in-depth comparative analysis of the CBMA framework obtaining in India and the US. It should serve as a useful reference book for students, practitioners and policymakers.

- **SRINIVAS INJETI**, *IAS*

CBMA is particularly interesting because it is one such topic that is multidisciplinary nature and brings out the disciplines like economics, management (finance and strategy, in particular) and law together. Therefore, who but a scholar in all the three fields—Dr. B. N. Ramesh, can address this topic more eloquently!! As an Indian Police Service Officer, and a double PhD holder, Dr. Ramesh is uniquely placed to address this topic from multiple perspectives. Dr Ramesh starts with the historical perspective of the CBMA, and extends his analysis to the current day laws and regulations that govern CBMA, especially in the US India relations…. Another nice feature of the book is, it provides a comprehensive perspective on how various laws—competition law, intellectual property law, etc. —play a role in CBMA. Both for personal and professional reasons, I have the privilege of knowing Dr B. N. Ramesh for a while. In fact, I had the opportunity to have several in-depth conversations with him on several matters relating to economics, statistics, politics, national security, etc. In all these interactions, if there is one thing that catches my attention, it is his erudition—the same erudition that comes across in his book as well.

- **VISVANATH PINGALI**, *Associate Professor, Indian Institute of Management, Ahmedabad*

Cross Border Mergers and Acquisitions

This book presents a comparative analysis of cross-border mergers and acquisitions (CBMA) in terms of competitive framework and procedures between India and the United States of America.

It discusses themes like statutes, regulations, rulings, legislations and analysis of CBMA; competition law, antitrust, and demerger; new legal initiatives by India like New Economic Policy (NEP), Goods and Services Tax (GST), demonetisation and amendments in the Foreign Exchange Management Act (FEMA); and the impact of COVID on CBMA, to showcase the challenges and opportunities of specific CBMA experience in India in a global framework.

This book will be an essential read for scholars and researchers of law, corporate law, company law, international company law, corporate governance, international relations, public policy, international trade law, economics, and for practitioners, policymakers and consultants working on the subject.

Boppudi Naga Ramesh belonged to the Indian Police Service (1988 batch), and worked in West Bengal cadre and in different parts of India, fighting anti-insurgency forces and left-wing extremist forces in the Kashmir Valley and in central Indian states. As a civil engineer, he worked for TATAS and earned an MBA degree from the Indian Institute of Management, Calcutta. A triple PhD, his first PhD was from the Indian Institute of Technology, Kharagpur; his second PhD was from the National Police Academy, Hyderabad; and the third PhD was from National Law University, Delhi, India. He is MA Psychology, LLB, LLM and Post-Doc Fellow from JNU, New Delhi. He retired as a DGP, in West Bengal, and presently is a Professor of Law and Management at Maharashtra National Law University, Aurangabad, where he pursues a postdoctoral fellowship in LLD. He won the President of India Police Medal for Meritorious Services and many other medals which include the distinguished alumni medal from IIT Kharagpur. He has participated in many marathons and is an international cyclist as a commando trainer.

Cross Border Mergers and Acquisitions

A Comparative Study between India and the USA

B. N. Ramesh

LONDON AND NEW YORK

First published 2023
by Routledge
4 Park Square, Milton Park, Abingdon, Oxon OX14 4RN

and by Routledge
605 Third Avenue, New York, NY 10158

Routledge is an imprint of the Taylor & Francis Group, an informa business

© 2023 B. N. Ramesh

The right of B. N. Ramesh to be identified as authors of this work has been asserted in accordance with sections 77 and 78 of the Copyright, Designs and Patents Act 1988.

All rights reserved. No part of this book may be reprinted or reproduced or utilised in any form or by any electronic, mechanical, or other means, now known or hereafter invented, including photocopying and recording, or in any information storage or retrieval system, without permission in writing from the publishers.

Trademark notice: Product or corporate names may be trademarks or registered trademarks, and are used only for identification and explanation without intent to infringe.

British Library Cataloguing-in-Publication Data
A catalogue record for this book is available from the British Library

ISBN: 978-1-032-07796-3 (hbk)
ISBN: 978-1-032-50122-2 (pbk)
ISBN: 978-1-003-39698-7 (ebk)

DOI: 10.4324/9781003396987

Typeset in Sabon
by SPi Technologies India Pvt Ltd (Straive)

Contents

Foreword   xvii

1 Meaning of Mergers and Acquisitions   1

   The Matrix of the Global Economy 3
   Types of Mergers and Acquisitions 3
   Meaning of Cross-Border Mergers and Acquisitions (CBMA) 4
   History of the CBMA in India 5
   The CBMA and RBI 6
      Mandatory Prior Approval 7
      Central Government Responsibility of Framing of Rules in
         Consultation with the RBI 8
      Approval by the National Company Law Tribunal (NCLT) 8
      Permitted Jurisdiction for an Outbound Merger 8
      Penalty 9
      Types of CBMAs 11
      The Magnitude of CBMAs 11
      The CBMA and Competition Law in India 15
      The CBMA and Indian Tax Reforms 15
   The CBMA and Financial Sector 16
   CBMA and the Legal Provisions in India 17
   Rules and Regulations 17
      The CBMA and Indian Experience in Implementation 17
      Indian Experience 18
   The FDA and Emerging Markets 21
      The Case of India 21
      Economic Policy Reforms and the CBMA 22
      Major Legal Reforms of the CBMA in India 23
      Demonetisation and the CBMA 24
      Impact of Demonetisation 26
      The CBMA and Growth in Business 26
      The CBMA and Jan Dhan Accounts 28

People's Inclusiveness and Economic Reforms 28
   Finance Banking Governance Reforms 29
   IT Act and the CBMA 30
   The CBMA and FEMA 31
   Issuance of Shares in the CBMA 31
   The Framework to the IBC Process—Opportunities 31
   Start-ups and the CBMA 32
   Kaizen and the CBMA 33
   The CBMA and Domestic Experience of Learning Importance 34
   The CBMA and Prevention of Corruption Act, 1988 and Foreign
      Direct Investment Rules 34
   The CBMA and SEBI 35
   SEBI and the CBMA 35
   Motives for the CBMA 37
   CBMA: Culture and Corporate Governance 37
   The CBMA and Emerging Countries 37
   The CBMA and Specific Types of Mergers 37
   CBMA and the Competition Law, 2002 37
   CBMA and the Stamp Duty Act 37
   CBMA and the Judicial Infrastructure 38
CBMA and the USA 38
   Securities and Exchange Commission 38
   FTC (The Federal Trade Commission) 39
The CBMA and USA Tax Reforms 40
   The CBMA and Tax Reforms in the USA, CFC, TIPRA 40
      Controlled Foreign Corporation (CFC) 40
      FIRPTA, 1980 and THA-2015 41
      Internal Revenue Service (IRS) 41
   CBMA and Legal Due Diligence 43
      The Doctrine of Successor Liability and Department of Justice,
         USA 44
   CBMA and Legal Due Diligence in Antitrust/Competition
      Matters 45
The Sarbanes–Oxley Act, 2002 46
   The Dodd-Frank Act 48
   National Security in USA and CBMAs 49
   CIFUS and the CBMA 50
   Clayton and the HSR Acts and Amendments 51
   Specific Examples 55
Comparison between the USA and India 56
   International Law 58

CBMA and BRICS (Brazil, Russia, India, China and South
  Africa) 59
CBMA and International Trade 60
Indices and Ratios 62
CBMA Emerging Economies, India and BRICS 65
CBMA in Emerging Economies and Developed Economies 67
  LDC and EM in the CBMA Environment 67
  Emerging Opportunities and CBMA 69
  Comparative CBMA in Various States of the USA 70
Upheavals in Global Economy 71
CBMA and Cyber Business 72
Conclusion 72

2 Cross-Border Mergers and Acquisitions: Statutes,
  Regulations, Rulings, Legislations and Analysis   79

Introduction 79
Culture and the CBMA 79
CBMAs 80
CBMAs: Ease of Doing Business 84
Ease of Doing Business Index (EDBI) 84
Solvency and Ongoing Concern 84
IBC (The Insolvency and Bankruptcy Code) 86
  Cross-Border Insolvency; India and the USA 91
  Pre-Packs 91
  The Pre-Pack in the USA 92
CBMAs and GST 92
CBMAs and Real Estate Regulation Act (RERA) 93
Impact of RERA on the Functioning of Real Estate Developers and
  Other Stakeholders 93
CBMAs, RERA Priorities Present, and Future 93
Amendments to PC Act, 1988 and FDI Rules 94
The CBMA and Insider Trading 96
The CBMA and Hostile Takeover 98
The CBMA and Warranties 98
The CBMA and Industrial Dispute Act and Essential Acts 99
The CBMA, Specific Relief Act, and Corruption 100
Corruption and IBC 2016 100
The CBMA and FDI 100
Gaps in the CBMA Domestic and International Learning
  Experience 101
Purchase and Sales and CBMAs 103
CBMAs and Influencing Factors 103
Enabling Factors of the CBMA 103
Foreign Investors 106

Motives for the CBMA 107
The Benefits of the CBMA 107
Challenges and the CBMA 107
Synergy—CBMA 109
Corporate Governance 109
The CBMA Culture Governance and Corporate Governance 110
Employee Attrition and the CBMA 111
Comparative Factors, International versus Emerging Countries, and the CBMA 111
Implementation in Developed Countries—CBMA 112
Emerging Markets and the CBMA 112
Example of the CBMA in Intra-emerging Developing Countries 113
The CBMA and Specific Types of Mergers 114
Fraud and the CBMA 115
   Insider Trading 115
Provision of Section 195 of Companies Act, 2013 116
Competition Law and the CBMA 116
Provisions and Implementation of the Stamp Duty Act (1899) 116
Judicial Review 116
Innovation and the CBMA 117
Integration and the CBMA 119
Technology and the CBMA 119
Research and the CBMA 120
The Effect of Synergy 121
Culture and CBMAs 121
The CBMA and Corruption 122
Lawyers and the CBMA 123
Reasons for Failure of the CBMA 123

3 CBMA, Competition Law, Antitrust and Demerger   127

Introduction 127
Competition, Antitrust and the CBMA 127
The CBMA and Antitrust Laws 128
The CBMA and US Antitrust Experience 129
Case Study 131
Antitrust Matters and Global Enforcement Guidelines 132
Antitrust Litigation in the United States 134
Frivolous, Bad Faith and Sham Commercial Litigation and CBMA 135
Competition Policy and CBMA in India 136
Competition Commission of India, Recent Developments 136
   Coordination among Various Regulators 137
Competition Act, Competition Commission, Mergers, Amalgamation Enforcement, Suggestions 137
Recent Experience in CBMA and Ease of Doing Business Index 138

Gaps, Tribunals, Scope for Correction 140
The Concept of Demergers in India and the USA 141
Legislative Initiatives in India and Jurisdiction of Ministry of Corporate Affairs 143
  Ministry for Corporate Affairs, Government of India 143
Inbound Mergers 145
Out Bound Mergers 146
Companies Compromises and Agreement or Amalgamation Rules, 2016 146
Bilateral Agreements and CBMA 148
  Nokia's Case 149
Stamp Duty and CBMA 150
  Stamp Duty Act and Its Implications on CBMA 150
Stamp Duty Law in India-Legislative Provisions 150
Maharashtra Stamp Act, 1958 151
Karnataka Stamp Act 151
Controversy 151
Li Taka Pharmaceuticals vs State of Maharashtra (1997) 151
Hindustan Lever vs State of Maharashtra (2004) 152
Delhi Towers Ltd vs GNCT of Delhi (2009) 152
Delhi Towers Ltd vs GNCT of Delhi (2009) 152
Specific Relief Act, 1963: The Amendment Bill, 2017 Implications on Business Transactions and CBMA 153
  Specific Relief Act, 1963 153
The Implications of the Amendments to the Specific Relief Act, 1963 (SRA, 1963) 153
The Proposed Changes 153
General Rule, Specific Performance and Changes 154
Discretion Given to Courts and Committees 154
Rights of Third Parties 154
Separate Class for Public Contracts 155
Implications 155
Effects of the Specific Relief (Amendment) Bill, 2017 on the Law of Remedies for Breach of Contract 156
Limited Liability Act, 2008 and Its Implications on CBMA 157
LLP Act in India 158
Benefits 159
CBMA and CAG 160
Corruption Transparency Issues in Cross-Border Mergers and Acquisitions, the USA and India 161
Corruption 161
FCPA in the USA 162
Example of Major Cases 163
Enforcement in the USA 163
Control Framework and Structures 165

xii *Contents*

Compliance Programmes 165
Scope of Improvement 166
Vicarious Liability/Responsibility and CBMA 167
Anti-corruption due Diligence and Critical Examples 167
Effectiveness of FCPA Implementation 168
Critical Examples of Anti-corruption Prosecution in CBMA 169
Transparency and Evaluation of Indian CBMAs 172
Conclusion 173

4 New Legal Initiatives by India in CBMA Environment   180

Introduction 180
Money Laundering and CBMA 180
SFIO and the CBMA 182
The Importance of Credit in the CBMA 184
SARFAESI and the CBMA 186
The CBMA and Banking Reforms 187
The CBMA and Banking Sector Reforms 188
RBI Reforms and the CBMA 189
Tax Havens and the CBMA 190
Banking Sector and the CBMA 190
Banking and New Initiatives 190
Stamp Act and the CBMA 193
Latest Developments 194
Improvement in Ease of Doing Business Index 198
Efforts for Modifications of Law 199
Conclusions 201

5 COVID and the CBMA   205

The Impact of COVID-19 Pandemic Crisis on Mergers and Acquisitions 205
COVID-19 Pandemic and the CBMA Trends 206
Logistics, Transportation, Supply Chain Management and COVID-19 Pandemic 207
Government Regulators 208
Scope for Increases in FDI and FPI through CBMA during COVID-19 Pandemic 208
Travel and Tourism 209
Regulator Dilemma 209
COVID-19 Pandemic and the Changes in the Structure of Business in the Context of the CBMA 210
Investment Funds and SEBI 210
Letters of Intent 211
Non-Uniform Impact of the COVID-19 Pandemic 211
The MAE/MAC Impact on the CBMA vs. COVID-19 Pandemic 211

The Strategic Outlook of the Global Economy Due to the COVID-19 Pandemic 211
Resilience and COVID-19 Pandemic 212
Flattening of the Pandemic Graph 212
Lockdown and COVID-19 Pandemic 213
Impact of COVID-19 Pandemic on International Business Law 213
  Accountancy Issues 213
    Accounting-Related Issues 213
Long-term Stability vs. Short-term Crisis 213
The Response of Major Centres and Industrial Sectors 214
Prevention is Better than Perishing 214
  Anticipation Is Better than Precipitation 214
  International Rules on the CBMA Restructuring 214
RCEP and the CBMA 215
COVID-19 Pandemic, the CBMA and Corporate Fraud 216
Risks and Threats to the CBMA 217
  Mergers and Acquisitions and Distressed Assets 217
  Protective Measures and Impact of COVID-19 Pandemic 217
  Law Business Strategy, the CBMA and COVID-19 Pandemic Impact 217
  Economy and Cross-Border Mergers and Acquisitions 218
Litigation and Cross-Border Mergers and Acquisitions 220
Due Diligence and Emerging Technology 220
Legal Implications and Labour Law 220
Impact, Short- and Long-Term of COVID-19 Pandemic on the CBMA 221
Legal Implications of Failed Negotiations on Price Front 221
Revenue and Solvency Issues 221
Date-line Compliance 222
Legal Position of Merger Law and the Changes in the USA 222
Regulatory Law in the USA 223
Pandemic COVID-19 and Lessons 223
Attempts to Amend the Merger Law in the USA 224
Work from Home and Quarantine Care and COVID-19 Pandemic 224
Global Economic Distress and COVID-19 Pandemic 225
Business during COVID Era 225
Innovations in Administration 226
COVID-19 Pandemic and Govt. of India's Response 227
Opportunistic and Predatory Takeovers 227
Effects of Timelines and Antitrust Review Mechanism by the State 228
T-Mobile Sprint Case 228
  Introduction 228
  The Verdict of DOC, the USA 229

Conclusions of Law 230
FTC and COVID-19 Pandemic 230
Employee Attrition and Precautions in the CBMA Environment due to COVID-19 Pandemic 230
Post-COVID-19 Pandemic Strategies in the CBMA 231
Proper Due Diligence 231
Evaluation of Business Worth in the Post-COVID-19 Pandemic 232
Post-COVID-19 Pandemic Regulatory Aspects by Government and Autonomous Agencies 232
Compliance to Legal Provisions and Documentation 232
IBC, CBMA, COVID-19 Pandemic, India and the USA 232
Insolvency and Bankruptcy Code and Its Effectiveness 233
Resolving Insolvency 234
Banks, Non-Performing Assets, Insolvency and Bankruptcy Code 235
NPA and IBC 236
Non-Performing Assets 237
IBC vs Insolvency Proceedings in the USA 238
Timelines and IBC 239
The Similarity between IBC and USBC 239
International Opinion about IBC 239
Effect of IBC in India 239
Banker's View on IBC 241
The US Bankruptcy Code, 1978 242
Comparison of Bankruptcy Regulations between India and the USA 243
Post-Bankruptcy and Reconstruction 244
Composition of Creditors Committee and the Law 245
Historical Evolution of Bankruptcy Law in the USA and India in the Context of the CBMA 245
Impact of Current Pandemic Wave-II in India 246

6 Pandemics, Business Response, Law and the CBMA 248

Supply Chain Logistics and COVID-19 Pandemic 248
Insurance and COVID-19 Pandemic 248
Case Study of Start-up and Acquisition during COVID-19 Pandemic Era in India 249
Case Study Example of the Law Enforcement in India as the Cause of Ease of Doing Business in India 249
New Technology Banking Reforms and COVID-19 Pandemic 249
Industrial Labour Reforms and Ease of Doing Business Index 250
Legal Innovation 251
Online Dispute Resolution and Ease of Doing Business 251
Digitalisation and Cross-Border Mergers and Acquisitions 252
Fraud Prevention 253

Whistle blower Protection and Rule of Law as a Tool for Ease of
  Doing Business in CBMA Environment 253
Ultimate Suggestions 256
COVID-19 Pandemic and Cybersecurity and the CBMA 257
Cybersecurity, CBMA, and DSCI 258
National Company Law Tribunal 259
  COVID-19 Pandemic and Resolution for Liquidation 259
NCLT, COVID-19 and New Electronic Initiatives 260

7 Fairness in Acts and Activity   262

Competition Commission of India 262
IBBI Initiatives and Accountability 264
The Federal Trade Commission of the USA and Its Performance
  Snapshot for the Year 2019 266
Security Exchanges Commission and Mergers Acquisitions Joint
  Venture Guidelines, an Update in the USA 267
FDI and Its Links with Foreign Trade Growth in India 267
Banking Sector Reforms and the CBMA 267
Start-Ups and New Technologies 269
Suggestions 271
The Non-Last Word 277

8 Recent Reforms in Law in India   278

CBMA and UNICORNS 280
  One-Person Company Framework (OPC) 282
MCA 282
  21 Version 3.0 282
  NCLT Framework Strengthening 283
  Foreign Direct Investment in Insurance Companies 283
  Securities Market Code 283
  Exemption of Stamp Duty in Government Sale Transactions 283
  Mergers—Acquisitions Vis-à-vis Budget 2021–2022 284
  Latest Developments (till June 24, 2021) 284
Prevention of Scams/Frauds in CBMAs 285
  Role of NFRA (India), PCAOB (USA) 285
    Comparative Infrastructure in the USA and Lessons to Be
      Learned 285
  PCAOB 286
    Cross-Border Mergers and Acquisitions and Jurisdiction 288
United States and the Doctrine Effect 289

9 Kaizen for Global Excellence — 290

Recent Examples of Implementation of Legal Provisions in India 291
Post-COVID Pandemic Changes, Threats and Opportunities 291
IBBI Regulatory Framework Changed Mandate 292
Evaluation of Initiatives and Implications for Further Action 293
Suspending a Tiny Part of IBC 294
  Lessons of the Pandemic—2nd Annum in the Year 2021 295
Role of AI (Artificial Intelligence) and ML (Machine Learning) in the Corporate Sector 295
Exposure of New Sectors to Competition and Predation 296
The Dangers of Living with Obsolescence 296
Disruptions, Hacking, Cyber Threats and Fraud 297
Cost of Repetition and the Question of Legitimacy and Intention of Enforcement 297
Kaizen in the Economy, Law and Integration of Technologies vs Increasing Redundancy of Differentials 298
Current Reforms in India 298
Non-Performing Assets and the Banking Law 299
IBC, IBBA and Specific Law for the Prevention of Insolvency 299
The Role of Enforcement 300
Lobbies, Pressure Groups, Publicity and Public Interest Litigation Policy 300
Indexes of Governance—Ease of Doing Business, Arbitration, Redressal of Disputes, ADRs 300
Regulatory Authorities and Enforcement 301
Credibility of the State through Performance of Government 301
Seamless Connectivity from Military, Medicine and Management (M^3) for Diagnosis, Delivery and Diligence (D^3) 301
Law as a Link from the Past, through Present for Future and Perspectives of Law 302
Law as a Fair Elixir of Tri Virtues—Equality, Freedom and Justice 303
Corporate Justice, Civil Justice, Criminal Justice and Governance 303
Global Trade, Export Import 2021 and International Trade in Goods and Services in India 303
  Domestic Trade Policy 303
  Financial Services 304
Suppliers of Financial Services Must Comply with the Requirements Set Out in the Relevant Legislation 304
  Banking 304
  Securities 304
  Insurance 304
  DIPP and FDI 305

Index — 307

Foreword

A corporate entity would always like to have maximum return on its capital in selling its wares (or services) whereas consumers would demand best value for the price paid by them for such wares or services. In classical capitalist economy, interplay of these two factors would ultimately determine the optimum value for money and make the individual transactions just and fair. But market place does not operate in a vacuum with only two categories of players—buyers and sellers interacting with each other. There is tax to be realised, which according to the American jurist Oliver Wendell Holmes, "is the price we pay for a civilized society." Intellectual Property Rights limit the entry of producers in a particular field of commerce. Sometimes, the government itself may confer monopoly grants. In an extreme situation such grant could extend to delegation of sovereign powers as well, as was in the case of East India Company. The regime of intellectual property is also built up on such monopoly grant, often with a time limit (as in the cases of patent and copyright). Conversely, from the middle of the 20th century, there has been substantial control over direction of private capital flow imposed by the State itself. This has been done sometimes by blocking the entry of private capital itself in certain core sectors and rigid regulations of the market by price control. In areas involving essential services like public health, free competition for private players has been restricted in public interest. These restrictions still exist in Europe as also in our country, particularly in the healthcare sector. In the crisis period of COVID-19, such state involvement became a necessity.

The context I have referred to in the preceding paragraph largely relates to the period prior to the 1990s, and in this book on merger and acquisition in a global perspective, the author has dealt with a subject which has direct impact on the pricing mechanism in current times. A historical perspective, of course, has been given. As many barriers on capital migration from country to country are being systematically dismantled (as opposed to migration of workforce), cross-border merger and acquisition (CBMA) have become potent tools for large corporations becoming larger. Communication technology also has come to the aid in such pursuit—one does not have to be in a location physically to conduct activities from there. The two countries primarily chosen for analysing the subject of merger and acquisition would help the readers comprehend the issues well. For little over hundred years back, the pitfalls of anticompetitive activities were realised in the United States, which prompted antitrust action against Standard Oil. Now some of the supersuccessful technology companies are being subjected to scrutiny on the same count in the United States as well as Europe. The common law principle of invalidating agreements in restraint of trade was the precursor to anti-competitive legislations in England in early 18th century. And in our own country also, when many public utility services are in the process of being opened to private capital, the subject of enquiry becomes all the more relevant.

Most of the publications on merger and acquisition available in the market focus on the issue from the lens of those handling such exercise. They are mostly lawyers, accountants, investment bankers and regulators. The author of this book, who is a very senior policeman in real life, however, has expanded the scope of enquiry much wider and has given an overview of the subject from every conceivable discipline. It deals the subject from the perspective of competition law, tax reforms, information technology apart from detailing the legal issues involved in merger and acquisition having international character. The other feature which I found interesting is correlating the subject with certain contemporary financial decisions of the Indian authorities—like demonetisation or the COVID-19 pandemic. One interesting area dealt with by the author is the anti-corruption actions connected to CBMA. Now that big economies are making overseas corrupt activities actionable in the home countries of the corrupt corporate citizens, sections of this book dedicated to this feature is a valuable addition to the existing publications on CBMA. Add to this the rights of whistleblowers and workers, this book becomes a unique compendium.

This is a book not meant for a lawyer, if the latter has in mind a statute-based legal text meant to help him or her in legal disputes. But it is meant for lawyers, legal academics, economists, policymakers, activist shareholders and trade unionists to enable them to get an overview of international mergers and acquisitions and the potential impact of such cross-country corporate communions in their respective area of action. The author has put in hard work to collate such multidisciplinary materials on mergers and acquisitions with international dimension to give a comprehensive view on the subject in this work. In the process, he has also taken up the onus on himself to continue updating the content in subsequent editions. The book is based on historical legal and economic events blended with contemporary developments in the fields of politics, economics, business and law. In these fields, the policies are ever-evolving.

JUSTICE ANIRUDDHA BOSE,
SUPREME COURT OF INDIA

1 Meaning of Mergers and Acquisitions

Mergers and acquisitions are set to become a vital feature of the future planning of corporates globally. Many commercial goals like growth synergy, profit and survival are all there for the corporates to achieve in the near and far future. Mergers suggest the consolidation of two or more companies. The word 'acquisition' conveys that one company has been either acquired or sold to another. Mergers and acquisitions in the international context consume a lion's share of direct investment of cross-border funds. They are an important influence on the evolution of the space economy. All major queries engaging the minds of senior researchers in cross-functional studies of investments, better returns and the dynamics of market–money–mind in terms of value addition for the new product–process–performance invention are within the domain of Cross-Border Mergers and Acquisitions (CBMAs) across the world, more in the developed world and making the footprint in the developing world. On March 20, 2021, the CBMAs, according to the Ministry of Corporate Affairs, Govt. of India data, as presented by the M&A report, 2021, stepped up to $ 82 billion, registering a jump of 23% from the year 2019. The coronavirus pandemic, while creating depressions somewhere in the economic landscape, scaled up CBMAs in the technical world. For instance, Facebook (FB) went for a 10% stake in the Jio platform to the tune of $ 5.7 billion. Jio hit $ 20 billion, including Google's 7.7% stake of $ 4.5 billion. The 1980s witnessed Chinese aggression in globalising its economy and causing a huge impact on the cross-border merger business process in the entire world. In the 1990s, India also witnessed a liberalisation regime under the leadership of the late P.V. Narasimha Rao's government. It is often argued in the light of the above facts about China and India globalising their economies that companies from developing markets are often forced to undertake and explore the possibility of cross-border mergers to face the challenges of liberalisation domestically because of the increased competition and removal of protectionism.

The pandemic COVID-19, which started in the State of Wuhan in China, registered a tectonic shift in the entire world, in as much as entire Europe and USA became the worst victims in the 21st century. At the time of writing this chapter, already six months after the spreading of the virus and its death dance have become globalised. Experts suggest that India can be an

DOI: 10.4324/9781003396987-1

immediate beneficiary of shifting the base of industries from China, in essence, of the companies from Europe and the USA.

"Firms from emerging markets are compelled to undertake cross-border acquisition to survive liberalization."[1] In the USA, a merger is a combination question in which only one corporation survives and the merged corporation goes out of existence. In a merger, the acquiring company acquires the assets and liabilities of the merged company. The statutory merger also refers to this type of transaction of business. The process has to be completely in compliance with the rules and regulations mentioned in the specific law. The most common law is the Delaware law, and many companies follow both state and foreign laws. The importance of mergers and acquisitions of a specific company in different parts of the USA under different state laws is different from the law relating to CBMAs. It is to be noted that a subsidiary merger is different from a statutory merger in which the substitute merger of the targeted company becomes a subsidiary or part of the subsidiary of the parent company. For instance, General Motors of Electronic Data Systems is an example of its subsidiary merger. There is also a provision for reverse subsidy mergers. Generally, a company can expand its activity by acquiring the shares of another company or by taking control of the affairs of the company.

Acquisition of another company, if such a company is a listed company, is referred to as a takeover or substantial acquisition. In India, the Competition Act of 2002 and the erstwhile Companies Act, 1956 recognise such takeovers, subject to specific regulations through the Security and Exchange Board of India (SEBI), substantial acquisition and shares and the takeover regulations of 1997. Once a company takes over or acquires another company, the natural process would be to amalgamate such acquired company with itself or with another company to form a new company. Thus, amalgamations and takeovers are different from others because here mere taking over by purchasing the shares happens. While in mergers, there is enough of the organic synergetic–oriented integration process of two entities which are different both in space and time across the globe. The SEBI takeover regulations do not apply to the acquisition of shares of an unlisted company. The guidelines issued under the new Companies Act, 2013 address this issue.

The word "merger" has been defined neither in the erstwhile Companies Act, 1956 nor in the Companies Act, 2013. However, this term has been defined under the Income Tax Act, 1961. The Companies Act, 2013 refers to amalgamation and the National Company Law Tribunal (NCLT) also refers to it. Amalgamation is to compound, consolidate or combine the business interests of firms. In England, according to Halsbury's laws, it is mentioned that "neither reconstruction nor amalgamation has a precise legal meaning."[2] Amalgamation is a fusion of two or more companies in vogue into one origination. Post-amalgamation, the shareholders of the newly amalgamated company. Section 394 of the previous Companies Act, 1956 of India has many similarities with its corresponding parallel section in England's Companies Act, 2006, i.e. Section 900 of the Companies Act, 2006 of England[3] provides that an application is made to the court for sanctioning a compromise agreement arrangement but the members are creditors for the amalgamation of two or more companies or the whole or any part of the undertaking or property is to be transferred to another company the court has specific powers to enable the reconstruction of the companies generally.

In India, the terms "amalgamation" and "merger" are used interchangeably. According to accounting standards and also the tax laws, we have two types of amalgamations, namely first, through merger and, second, through purchase. Section 21(b) of the Income Tax Act, 1961 of India concerning companies mentions that the merger of one or more companies with another company, or the merger of two or more companies to form amalgamation, becomes the property of the amalgamated company under amalgamation. Specific procedures exist in the post-amalgamation shareholding process as per the I.T. Act, 1961.

The Matrix of the Global Economy

CBMAs are influenced by the global economy matrix, the worst example being the 2008 global financial crisis and the Y2K problem combined into the 2001 global economic crisis. The present COVID-19 is an extension of the same recurring tsunami.

"Emerging market companies pushed for legitimacy in foreign markets by conducting cross-border acquisitions."[4] For 12 years after 2008, the CBMA landscape was significantly pushed towards larger companies. Young companies and overvalued companies with higher industry-adjusted ratings are more likely to acquire companies with the highest stakes by a single promoter. "Competition in the domestic industry as measured by Herfindahl-Hirschman Index (HHI), increases the probability that is consistent with the results as reported in the various research findings."[5] Worldwide CBMAs' evidence informs that large multiproduct companies with many specialised boards working at the global level are proving CBMAs across continents when the boards see an opportunity in a distant land for benefits in any or all of the three criteria mentioned by Harvard Strategy professor Dr Micheal Porter. Dr Porter maintains that ultimate success happens when there is a cumulative gain in (a) cost, (b) leadership and (c) differentiation. Competitive analysis inspires due diligence in CBMA activity.

Global trade is hierarchically dynamic and chaotic. Foreign investment rules and taxation rules coupled with fluctuating currency markets influence CBMA decisions. Periodic elections, demonetisation and GST (goods and services act tax) also impact CBMA decisions.

Types of Mergers and Acquisitions

Mergers are subdivided into horizontal, vertical and conglomerate types. A horizontal merger occurs when two companies inorganically combine. Competition law in India and the antitrust law in the USA, respectively, deal

4 Meaning of Mergers and Acquisitions

with a post-horizontal merger entity, threatening competitive spirit. The 1998 merger of two petroleum giants, EXXON and MOBILE, who created a merger of US $79 billion, is a classic example of a horizontal merger.

Vertical mergers are conjunctions of companies having chronological vendor–supplier or buyer–seller relationships.

The best example of a CBMA vertical merger is the 1993 pharmaceutical giant MERCK's acquisition of the containment services corporation MEDCO for US $ 6 billion

Acquirer	Name(s) of acquired company	Year of acquisition	Specific Area of operations
General Electric	Many different companies	Continuous event	Industrial Products
Procter and Gamble	Gillette	2006	Household products
Oracle	People Soft,	2004	Software
ESBC	Ameritech	—	Communications
Nations bank	Bank of America,	1998	Commercial banking

The corporate value chain involves logistics, which are inbound, operations-related, marketing, distribution-sales and customer support. Forward integration signifies the flow of integrating efforts from inbound logistics to customer support. A similar activity that reverses the direction of the flow, namely from customer support towards inbound logistics, is termed Backward integration. The 2003 acquisition of OfficeMax by ICSC ID for $ 4.01 billion is the best illustrative instance of forward integration. America Online backwardly integrated with Time Warner in the year 2000.

Meaning of Cross-Border Mergers and Acquisitions (CBMA)

Section 394 of the Companies Act, 1956 deals with CBMAs. However, it is silent about how the consideration would be discharged. CBMA is emerging as an important aspect of the general merger and acquisition activity. The new Act of 2013 introduced pragmatic reforms for M&As in making the process easier, faster and cleaner for companies. Some of the highlights include the setting up of the National Company Law Tribunal (NCLT) to hear and decide on M&A proposals, cutting down on the probability and scope of objection to M&As and easier as well as wider participation of shareholders through postal ballot approval. "These along with others, more creative and hurdle-free approaches are there towards M&As."[6] "Cross-border M&A supported by technological advancements, low-cost financing arrangements, and robust market conditions, have made dealmakers confident and think more creatively about their growth strategies."[7] CBMA, in essence, means controlling the transactions of entire or a substantial practice of another enterprise, irrespective of the place of operation or the nationality of the personnel of the company.

"In short Cross-border M&A is more difficult than domestic M&A, a lot to think about due diligence process, a qualified, experienced due diligence team can help ensure that you have thoroughly considered all relevant factors, understand the legal requirements associated with your proposed transaction."[8] "CBMAs have become topics of interest mainly because they help a firm to enter new international markets and thereby enhancing their ability to compete in global markets."[9] Reducing cost in terms of land, labour and capital is for the essence of profit even before sales. This is the essence of cost accounting. CBMA with a well-operating company obviates the hard work in establishing a new enterprise from scratch. CBMAs result in saving cost and time and enhance quality and quantity. Time as a resource is involved in the choice of land, labour and in obtaining a licence from government authorities. Saved becomes earned money when CBMAs result in taking over an existing facility. "Synergy is important as it signifies teamwork, coactions, harmony, and alliance. CBMAs are synergetic for combined sales offices, staff facilities, plant management, etc, which lower the operating costs."[10][11]

"Synergies are of different types such as manufacturing synergy, operations synergy, financial synergy, managerial synergy, marketing synergy, etc. As an illustration, Mahindra & Mahindra Ltd (M&M) acquired Jiangling Motor Company Group (JMCG) that will make the company's entry into tractor manufacturing synergy."

"To gain access to new markets a foreign company prefers to merge with a local established company which knows the behavior of the market and has established customer base."[12] "In a free competitive and globalized world, a company must be placed in such a manner that it is in a position to compete with the best in the world."[13]

History of the CBMA in India

In India, the first company legislation is the Joint Stock Companies Act, 1850, which was based on the English Companies Act, 1844. This act recognised companies as distinct legal entities but did not introduce the concept of limited liability. It was recognised for the first time by the Companies Act, 1857, but the concept was not extended to banking and insurance companies. This right afterwards was extended to the banking companies also in the year 1858. This act was replaced by the Companies Act, 1913, which was based on the English Companies Consolidation Act, 1908. By the end of 1950, the Government of independent India appointed a committee under the Chairmanship of Sri H.C. Bhalla for the revision of the Indian Companies Act. This committee submitted its report in March 1952. On the recommendation of the committee, the Companies Act, 1956 was enacted which came into force on April 1, 1956. This act, consisting of 658 sections and 14 schedules, was the largest of all the legislative enactment passed by the Indian parliament so far; once again, this act largely followed the English Companies Act, 1948. India's Companies Act, 1956 was a legal instrument of the licence permit raj vintage and was mainly responsible for

6 Meaning of Mergers and Acquisitions

the lower growth rates of economy, in general, and industries, in particular. Prof. Raj Krishna, in the year 1978, coined the word "Hindu rate growth." This so-called Hindu rate of growth is 3.00%. Therefore, the act was amended several times; the major amendments were introduced in the years 1960, 1962, 1963, 1964, 1965, 1966, 1967, 1972, 1974, 1977, 1985, 1988, 1991, 1993, 1996, 2000, 2001, 2002 and 2006. The enactment of Companies Act, 2013 is one of the most significant legal reforms in India in the recent past, aimed at bringing the Indian Company law in tune with global standards, incorporating recommendations made by various committees such as the J.J. Irani Committee, the Naresh Chandra Committee and Vepa Kamesam Committee. The Company Bill, 2008 was first introduced in the Lok Sabha on October 23, 2008, to replace the existing Companies Act, 1956. Due to the dissolution of the Lok Sabha, the bill was re-introduced in the Parliament in 2009 and subsequently sent to the Standing Finance Committee. The Committee presented its report in August 2010. Again, the bill was referred to the Committee in 2011 with the inclusion of certain new provisions. The bill was passed by both houses, in Lok Sabha on December 18, 2012 and in the Rajya Sabha on August 8, 2013, and became an act called the Companies Act, 2013. It received the assent of the President of India on August 29, 2013 and was made effective from April 1, 2014. This act comprises 29 chapters, 470 sections and 7 schedules. The enactment of the new Companies Act, 2013 is a historically correct step in the right economic direction for India. The Companies Act, 2013 again was amended by the Companies (Amendment) Act, 2015 which received the assent of the president on May 25, 2015. It was notified in the Official Gazette on May 26, 2015. The Companies (Amendment) Bill, 2016 was introduced in the Lok Sabha on March 16, 2016. The Finance Standing Committee of the Parliament recovered on April 12, 2016 the Companies Act (Amendment) Bill 2016. "The Cabinet Committee and Economic Affairs (CCEA) approved the amendments. Lok Sabha (People's House) of India on July 27, 2017, passed the Companies (Amendment) Bill 2017. The Rajya Sabha (Upper House) gave its asset on 19th December, 2017."[14]

The ease of daily business in India became a benchmark for attracting investments both domestically and from the foreign direct investment (FDI) route. The Companies Act (Amendment) Bill, 2017 was passed and became a part of the Companies Act, 2013. This amendment covered the vital aspects of strengthening the standards of corporate governance (CG) and mentions tangible corrective penal actions for wanton culpability by corporates. By means of the amendment of the Companies Act, 2013, more than 40 changes were brought.

The CBMA and RBI

The banking regulation act of India and the industrial policy of the Government of India empower the Reserve Bank of India (RBI) to lay the groundlines for any merger-related procedures which include the share capital swap ratios and disclosures. Mergers here also include cross-border mergers. RBI adopts a prudential perspective to estimate the welfare and suitability of the financial condition when such cross-border mergers become a reality. RBI, in its role as a regulator, ensures the implementation of the rules and the laws passed by the government and, at the same time, as it is entrusted with the task of regional development and the social corporate responsibility of impact on the society, examines the logic of the post-merger financial benefits, employment and local area prosperity issues that such mergers will eventually bring in to India. Being a banker to the Government of India, RBI checks the risk profiles and risk management systems of merger applicants, the purpose being to check the three vital aspects of measuring, monitoring and managing such risks.

RBI, SEBI, Competition Commission of India, IBBI and other regulators need to work in tandem and as a single harmonised system in full coordination and synchrony. It is expected of the above regulators that they examine:

a   The objective.
b   The impact of the merger on financial markets.
c   The impact of the mergers on the monetary policy and the interest policy.
d   The impact of mergers on the overall industrial structure.
e   The cost–benefit analysis to the customer and small and medium scale businesses.
f   The impact on bank branches which includes the price quality and availability of services to different branches.
g   The impact of mergers on the timing and the socio-economic aspects of the banking industry.

The regulators may look at how the CBMA will contribute to the global competitiveness of the sector of financial services. The employment and the quality of the jobs in any sector as well as the differentiation that such a merger will bring with it in the transitional and permanent aspects of the industrial environment are other important issues. RBI, being the bank to the government, is expected to look into the positive impact of mergers on adopting new technologies for the banks and to minimise and mitigate the adverse effects of mergers on the banks. RBI's role in regulating the safety insurance of the funds of depositors and monitoring the role of the banks in economic growth is of paramount importance.

Mandatory Prior Approval

RBI accords approval for merger under Sec. 234 (2) of the Companies Act, 2013. Among other things, mergers are akin to agreements under the Indian Contract Act, 1882 and the consideration aspect is taken care of partly or wholly by cash or depository receipts. The provisions under the Income Tax Act, 1961 and the guidelines of the Securities Exchanges Bureau of India

8 Meaning of Mergers and Acquisitions

(SEBI) and the Competition Commission of India are also mandatory in making a major proposal becoming a reality. Sub-section (2) under Sec. 234 (2) of the Companies Act, 2013 mentions the word "Foreign Company." It essentially means any corporation/company established outside the country of India and such a foreign company may or may not be conducting business within Indian Jurisdiction.

Central Government Responsibility of Framing of Rules in Consultation with the RBI

"Section 234(1) provides that the Central Government may make Rules, in consultation with R.B.I in connection with mergers and amalgamations provided under this section."[15] The coverage, consistency (both within and with other existing laws) and clarity of such rules will be important criteria.

Approval by the National Company Law Tribunal (NCLT)

The Companies Act, 2013 created a new regulator, the National Company Law Tribunal (NCLT) which upon its constitution will assume the jurisdiction of high courts for sanctioning mergers. The tribunal will consider a merger application; thereafter, the company concerned has to obtain approval from the RBI and comply with the provisions of Sec. 230 to 232 of the New Act and the rules.

Permitted Jurisdiction for an Outbound Merger

The Companies Act, 2013 has now opened its doors for outbound mergers. Outbound mergers are only permitted with a foreign company incorporated in the following jurisdictions:

1   A jurisdiction whose securities regulator is a member of the International Organization of Securities Commission's Multilateral Memorandum of Understanding (MOU) or a signatory to the bilateral MOU with the Securities and Exchange Board of India (SEBI),
2   Whose Central Bank is a member of the Bank for International Settlements (BIS),
3   A jurisdiction that is not identified in the public statement of the Financial Action Task Force (FATA) as:
   3.1   A jurisdiction hearing of strategic anti-money laundering.
   3.2   A jurisdiction combating the financing of terrorism deficiencies to which countermeasures apply.
   3.3   A jurisdiction that has not made significant progress in addressing the deficiencies.
   3.4   A jurisdiction that has not committed to an action plan developed with the FATF to address the deficiencies.

4 Valuation
On issues relating to valuation in the matters of the outbound merger, the foreign company concerned must guarantee that such valuations are performed by an authentic professional member of a recognised body with the accredited reputation of compliance to the strict international standards of the principles of valuation and accounting, acceptable universally.

A declaration to this effect is required to be attached with an application for obtaining RBI approval for an outbound merger but the law remains silent on such a requirement for an inbound merger.

5 Fast-Track Merger
Fast-track mergers, as a process, are a result of simplified procedures for a specific category of companies under the broad head of mergers, acquisitions and amalgamation. Fast-track mergers are applicable to tiny companies holding/wholly owned second-tier organisations/companies.

Provisions under the Companies Act, 1956 which deal with traditional mergers and amalgamations are time-consuming and costly processes as they include clearances from many regulatory bodies and every type of company must go through this route. A better score in ease of doing business in India demands a simplified and expedited process for cross-border or other mergers of companies of various sizes—small, holding, subsidiary and special category company—with negative consideration for third-party interest(s). The present act enables companies to undergo mergers and amalgamation procedures quickly, simply and within a fixed time duration. Cross-border mergers are regulated by the RBI under the Foreign Exchange Management Act 1999 (FEMA) to harmonise the scope of cross-border mergers. RBI has released (as of April 26, 2017) the Draft for Foreign Exchange Management (Cross-Border Merger) Regulations 2017 (Draft Regulation) that prescribe certain guidelines to be followed in case of both inbound and outbound mergers.

Penalty

"Every offense under the new Act [except those referred to in offenses under Sec212(6)] shall be deemed to be non-cognizable."[16] "Within the meaning of Sec-439(2), Criminal Procedure Code, 1973, no court shall take cognisance of any offense under this Act which is alleged to have been committed by any company or any officer thereof, except on the complaint in writing of the Registrar, a shareholder of the company, or a person authorized by the Central Government."[17] "For violation of the proceeding relating to sanction of Reconstruction and Amalgamation of Companies under section 232 of the Companies Act, 2013, the transferor company or a transferee company, as the case may be, shall be liable to a fine, not less than one lakh rupees but which may extend to twenty- five lakh rupees and every officer of such transferor or transferee company who is in default, shall be punishable with imprisonment for a term which may extend to one year or with fine which shall not be less than one lakh rupees but which may extend to three lakhs rupees or with both."[18]

The Companies Act, 2013 under Sec. 234 allows the merger of a foreign company with an Indian one. There are two types of mergers here. One is the inbound merger with one other. The second one is an outbound merger. Notified jurisdictions have also been added recently in the April 2017 notification.

The Company Act, 2013 lays down the criteria for mergers and acquisitions with a foreign company. Indian companies can make payments to shareholders of a foreign company by way of cash or depository receipts subject to the requisite guidelines and approval of the laws about CBMAs as mandated in the Companies Act, 2013. There was an interesting case recently involving MOCHIP Semiconductor Technology Limited, a California-based company that merged with an Indian company in Hyderabad. Practical experience around the world after correct observation needs to be made in the form of law in India so that the merger and acquisition process across countries and continents will be smoother and will not be repetitive in terms of the mistakes that happened elsewhere. Bloomberg's DNA report on mergers and acquisitions (in their law report) makes the above issue clear when the law report mentions that,

> This is not the time for a quick and dirty decision-making process, as there is no one size fits all solution available. Chief among the factors influencing the decisions are, the long term strategy of the company, its degree of international exposure and the familiarity with the new market, the extent of resources that it can commit, the degree of risk it is willing to incur, a network of existing relationships, the general industry environment in which it operates, and the particular characteristics of its products and services.[19]

The transferee company filed the petition for amalgamation and the name of the transferor organisation was not added as a party to the writ. The point that was discussed was whether the Indian Court has jurisdiction to pass an order of acquisition in respect of a company incorporated outside India which winds up as a foreign company. The notification on April 2017 shed light on this and there is no longer any requirement for ambiguity in this connection. In 2018, most of the cross-border mergers and acquisitions took place in the technology and information communication fields. E-commerce giant Walmart was in the news for taking over the Indian e-commerce company Flipkart. Both Walmart and Flipkart use e-commerce platforms and software innovations daily. Mergers and acquisitions strategy for technology-specific companies in taking over either by outright purchase or in partnership agreement involves benefit accrual not merely from

IP (Intellectual Property) assets but mainly from domain advantage, including people, terrain skills, experiential wisdom, goodwill, customer base and acceptance. Venturing into unknown terrain, an unknown legal environment, the politico-economic culture of the host country is risky. The host country, if not handled optimally, may become a "hostile" country and taking over a well-run tech company is a better option than the strategy of ground zero. The Companies Act, 1956 does not permit Indian companies to merge with a foreign one. Section 234 of the Companies Act, 2013 mandates the mode of mergers and amalgamations between companies registered under this act, incorporated in the jurisdiction of other countries. With the prior approval of the RBI, they come under the provisions of the Companies Act, 2013, and as per the terms and conditions of the scheme of merger, amalgamation can provide for the payment of consideration to the shareholders of the merging company in cash or partly in cash and partly in Indian Depository Receipts (IDRs). The Companies Act, 2013 especially allows for both inbound and outbound mergers, post-April 2017.

Types of CBMAs

According to the notification released on April 2017 by the Ministry of Corporate Affairs, Government of India, there are two types of CBMAs: inbound CBMAs and outbound CBMAs. Some are efficient and some are not.

The Magnitude of CBMAs

It is a well-known consensus that there are different categories of mergers and acquisitions, in both quantity and quality, often akin to waves of an ocean. The USA witnessed such waves of M&A activity, prominently for five times. "The following diagram depicts the surges in the activity of CBMAs till 2015. Enforcement system capability is important. The probability of deal completion is positively associated with levels of economic freedom of countries of the acquirer and target." (Figure 1.1).[20]

An important theme for the year 2014 is the return of big deals in CBMAs, with 95 deals having a value of over US $5 billion, more than double of what happened in the year 2013. The same was reflected in the years 2015, 2016 and 2017 comparatively. Private equity investors and cash-rich investors have access to liquid cash and hence there has been a surge in the availability of credit for highly rated takeovers. This provides an opportunity for big-ticket transactions.

Cross-border mergers entail several complexities linked by the overall outlook of a specific market, government stability, ease of doing business, in the region and availability of financing options, regulatory framework, etc. Industry characteristics are of great importance in cross-border mergers and acquisitions. The effect of these distinct characteristics on value creation is also dependent on the bilateral cross-country relations in terms of the

12 Meaning of Mergers and Acquisitions

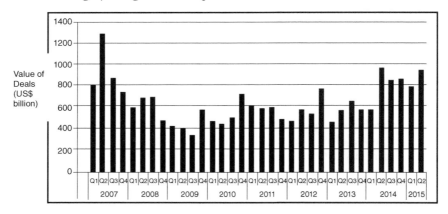

Figure 1.1 Cross-Border Mergers and Acquisitions Values in 2015.
Source: Merger market Global and Regional M&A: First Half 2015.

institutional distance, variations in language and diplomatic connections. Digitalisation rules the world in uniting the communication channels, lessening the atrophy and customising global clientele to a sander platform of usage. Information Technology (IT)-enabled Service (ITeS.) industries are on the wanton list for the CBMA activity due to the perfect accumulated advantage of post-facto autonomy. Value addition and new value creation are seen in monetising such acquired autonomy after the CBMA. Investible funds of global conglomerates tend to move towards ITeS digital companies when compared to integration benefits resulting from the CBMA activity in manufacturing industries. Digital scriptures annul institutional distance and dichotomies of lingua franca across the nations. The languages Python and R are as universal as zero and one. Diplomatic dynamics too takes a backseat when opportunities for multiplication outperform a mere arithmetical addition. In the year 2014, cross-border mergers and acquisition deals for value in India stood at US $139.9 billion. Representing an 82.6% increase in the value compared to 2013, the average deal size for cross-border varied from US $453.9 billion in 2014 compared to US $291.4 billion in 2013 and also crossed the record figure of US $ 437.7 billion in the year 2007 (Figure 1.2).

Will Martin of the University of Minnesota made an interesting observation in that CBMA transactions amplified issues that arise in domestic merger and acquisition transactions. The reciprocity among different statutes, both national and local, has the potentiality of inept and ill-bred contradictions. Unresolved contradictions confuse and become costly due to compliance with exceedingly strainful regulations over seemingly simple transactions. Apart from issues like corporate governance, regulatory approval by the Federal Trade Commission (FTC) and the Department of Justice (DOJ) and the securities and tax issues also are of primary importance in the case of the United States of America. The scrutiny of the Internal Revenue Code (IRC) is much more impactful in the case of the

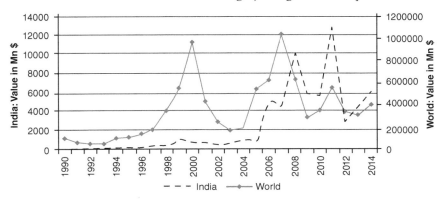

Figure 1.2 CBMA in India and the World.
Source: UNCTAD, 2014.

CBMA. Non-exempt securities issued as per merger consideration also need to undergo the compliance requirements of the 1933 and 1934 acts and the state blue sky laws. In the USA, the tax considerations are very stringent in the case of the merged entity rather than the tax considerations on the merger of subsidiaries. Hence, it is felt that it is better to plan for better tax savings merger of subsidiaries than a merger of companies. Martin affirms,

"The US corporate tax rates exceed the rate of all other industrialized countries. Accordingly, foreign companies seek to minimize the assets that become subject to tax in the USA. The greater tax eats away at the profits from the transaction. A direct merger subjects the entire merged entity to the US corporate tax. Moreover, the direct merger gives dissenting shareholders significant veto power because their approval is required to approve the merger and amend the organizational documents to resolve any contradictions between National Laws. The merger of subsidiaries presents a more workable option. This structure circumvents the United States' higher tax by allowing the foreign Corporation to isolate their non-merger assets. This structure also prevents dissenting shareholders from blocking the deal because the parent company is no longer a party to the Merger. Finally, the merger of subsidiaries allows the acquiring company to cherry-pick certain assets without giving the acquiree undue influence over operations of the parent." (Figure 1.3).[21]

One point to keep in mind, according to the report of *Financial Express* published on January 1, 2018, is that in the year 2018, India was likely to witness CBMAs worth US $50 billion only because of plenty of stressed corporate assets on offer, attempting a valuation quantum jump of 170%. Over 70% of the number of transactions in the year 2017 was witnessed there. There were 944 transactions, out of which 280 were of the cross-border type in the year 2017 and US $32.4 billion because of CBMAs. According to the Chamber of Commerce, this is an improvement compared to only

14 *Meaning of Mergers and Acquisitions*

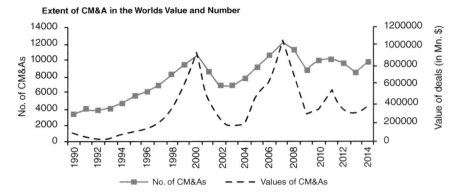

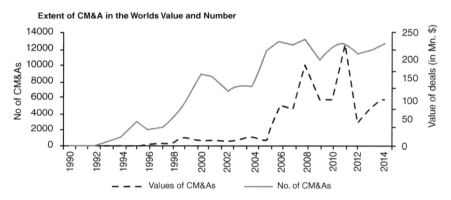

Figure 1.3 Extent of CBMA in the World: Value and Number.
Source: UNCTAD, 2014.

195 cross-border transactions in the year 2016 with a value of US $ 10.3 billion. Thus, one can see a jump of three times in value and a 60% jump in terms of transactions from the year 2016 to 2017.

> The Chamber identified the following sectors in which there is a quantum jump namely firstly, healthcare, secondly telecom, thirdly energy, fourthly real estate, fifthly, media and entertainment, sixthly banking, seventhly insurance, eighthly oil, ninthly cement, and lastly consumer products. Secretary-General, D.S. Rawat, of Associated Chambers of Commerce, felt, the CBMA opportunities in the year 2018 would remain robust given the fact a lot more assets continue to remain under stress.[22]

Big-ticket projects referred to the National Company Law Tribunal under the Insolvency and Bankruptcy Code (IBC) would see a change in the promoters in areas like real estate.

The Chamber of associate commerce also suggests using the guidelines and legislative support in the Income Tax Act, 1961 and the Competition Act, 2002 to boost mergers and acquisitions activity in India. Mr. Rawat further maintains that amendments in the Stamp Act 1899, to bring uniformity of stamp duty in all India states particularly to all transactions can prove to be a catapult for the future CBMAs in India.[23]

The CBMA and Competition Law in India

The Foreign Direct Investment (FDI) policy adopted post-1990 in the liberalisation arena in India was mainly intended to work for the transfer of sophisticated technology and marketing and managerial capabilities, employment creation, export promotion, etc. The Monopolies and Restrictive Trade Practices Act, 1969 (MRTP ACT) was replaced by the Competition Act, 2002, while the Competition Commission of India (CCI) replaced the three-decade-old MRTP Commission. The CCI resulted in inbound transactions increase, but it also ensures that there is fair play and there is no return of monopoly.

The CBMA and Indian Tax Reforms

Deng Xiao Ping is considered the father of reforms in modern China. In India, the credit for similar work goes to the late Prime Minister Shri P.V. Narasimha Rao. Shri P.V. Narasimha Rao became the Prime Minister in 1991 when India was facing the biggest economic crisis in its history.

> The year 1991 is quoted as the year of radical change in entire world structure - a year which led to phenomenal reforms in the spheres of politics and economy. This is the year when the cold war between the two superpowers came to an abrupt end; a year where Gorbachev decided to realign Russian policies to suit a world order- built on cooperation and support.[24]

The year 1991 witnessed fundamental modifications by the government in terms of financial policies as well as tax reforms.

> Initially the rigors of the Indian Income Tax legislation were sought to have tampered and fundamental changes in the Income Tax Act, like taxation of companies as an entity by themselves were introduced. Changes in the regulatory atmosphere were also embarked on. Capital market reforms were brought in by strengthening the Securities and Exchange Board of India (SEBI). Reforms in the Insurance sector initiatives with the setting up of the R.N. Malhotra committee which was followed by the setting up of an insurance regulatory body in 1996. Banking reforms had also been carried out alongside. All these are significant indicators of the attempt of the nation to position itself as an integral part of a global system - dictated by a feeling that India cannot isolate itself in an otherwise converging world economic situation.[25]

16 *Meaning of Mergers and Acquisitions*

The history of income tax in India during the British regime starts with the Income Tax Act, 1922. Till the year 1991, the Indian Income Tax system is a continuation of the principles enshrined in the Act of 1922. The case-law of the British courts influenced the tax tribunal's interpretation of the Income Tax Act and that of including the High Courts and Supreme Court. Chapter VI-A was added to the Income Tax Act during the 1970s after the famous Garibi Hatao program of the then Prime Minister, Shrimati Indira Gandhi. Even though the industrial resolution policy took place in the early 1950s, with the public sector expected to take the commanding heights of the economy, suitable modifications to the Income Tax Act were only made in the 1970s with the introduction of chapter VI-A.

> Until 1991, the Indian tax system was a mixed bag. On the one hand, the government had offered tax sops concerning industrial undertakings/export activities while, on the other, there were income tax levies even on undistributed income of certain companies - much like the Controlled Foreign Corporations regulations prevalent in the USA.[26]

The CBMA and Financial Sector

"The financial sector witnessed convergence throughout the world. The financial sector promotes interdependence among institutions and to work seamlessly and flawlessly it needs to adopt global standards so that financial sector institutions will function smoothly throughout the world. Globally, the financial sector works through the three following tripartite interceptors namely- a) banking b) insurance c) capital market. Free flow of capital has been and universal reality from times immemorial. The Reserve Bank of India (RBI), Securities and Exchange Board of India (SEBI), Insurance Regulatory Development Authority (IRDA) are discharging these roles. The regulatory bodies are part of a universal setup that has persuasion powers on the national bodies. These regulatory bodies have set up almost common regulations regarding the establishment, management, functioning, accounting, policies to be followed, and solvency measures of the integral bodies with the result that there exist today, in the financial sector, a regime of close association and congruence. A similar common approach emphasizes the need for the adoption of a common account standard, to be adopted by all those countries that want to come together. Every one of us knows for a fact that this is still a dream to fructify. Amongst developed countries, basic differences in the fundamentals of the accounting standards to be followed. The UK has a system of accounting standards; so is the USA. We have a set of standards that keeps evolving and tries to synthesize what is good for the local conditions. An enterprise that has raised capital in different markets is now called upon to file statements and disclosures in each country based on the individual requirements of law and regulations followed in that country."[27]

CBMA and the Legal Provisions in India

The following are the legislative acts in India regarding the topic of CBMAs.

Sl.No	Year	Name of the Act.	Section
1.	1872	The Contract Act	
2.	1897	The Stamp Duty Act	
3.	1934	The Reserve Bank of India Act and Reserve Bank of India Rules	
4.	1947	The Trade Union Act	
5.	1955	The Pollution Control Act	
6.	1961	Income Tax India 1961 and Amended Rules, thereafter.	
7.	1986	The Environmental Protection Act	
8.	1988	The Prevention of Corruption Act	
9.	1992	The Security Exchanges Board of India Act and Takeover Rules	
10.	1993	The Human Rights Act	
11.	2002	The Competition Act of India	
12.	2002	The Foreign Exchange Management Act	
13.	2002	The Prevention of Money Laundering Act	
14.	2003	The Competition Controller of India Rules	
15.	2008	Rules regarding Prevention of Sexual Harassment at Workplace	
16.	2008	The Limited Liability Partnership Act	
17.	2013	The Companies Act	Section 234
18.	2016	The National Company Law Tribunal Act	
19.	2016	The Insolvency and Bankruptcy Code	
20.	2016	The Compensatory Forestation Act	
21.	2017	The Goods and Services Tax Act	

Rules and Regulations

The following rules of various important organisations in the Finance Ministry and the Corporate Affairs Ministry of the Government of India also apply to the transactions of CBMAs and have to be taken care of during the pre-integration and the post-integration processes of the implementation of CBMAs.

The CBMA and Indian Experience in Implementation

Antitrust de-merger matters, legislative initiatives and establishment of the Ministry of Corporate Affairs aspects were discussed. Chapter 4 aims to find out answers to research questions in terms of identifying the gaps in the CBMA environment in India and the light of the Insolvency and Bankruptcy Code and RERA.

18 Meaning of Mergers and Acquisitions

Indian Experience

Insolvency and Bankruptcy Code, modifications in FEMA, execution of demonetisation and issuance of a gazette by RBI coupled with the Goods and Services Tax Act are the most impactful initiatives taken recently in India.

Captivating investment opportunities await the informed investors in Emerging Markets (EMs). However, inbuilt risks and intricacies accompany these opportunities. Returns from these EMs vary momentously. The EM is a nation-state that endures certain qualities of a Developed Market (DM), but may not fulfil all the required criteria of a developed market. The economies of China and India are considered to be the largest emerging markets."[28]

India has a very tragic colonial experience and the national movement of freedom struggle made many inputs in the economic policy formulations which are suspicious of free trade and the philosophy of laissez-faire. Like many past colonies, India also inaugurated the economic innings in the so-called Licence-Permit raj with draconian regulations, resulting in the Hindu Rate of Growth at 3% per annum. The Emerging Markets (EMs) suffered the double jeopardy of least sophistication coupled with a truncated rent-seeking regulatory system.

CBMAs require a conducive international environment of privatisation, liberalised trade policies, free flow of capital, adequate safe financial markets and a receptive mentality for technological change. The liberalisation of the Indian economy was led by Prime Minister Shri P. V. Narasimha Rao after June, 1991. "According to Forbes, there are major four trends in mergers and acquisitions in India, namely, an abundance of liquidity, slowly rising that cars, energy and technology leading the way, and political factors to watch for in the year 2017."[29] "The major reason behind this is strong government and meaningful support for the growth of the business; the desire to reduce dependence on supply chain uncertainties by backward or forward integration, taxation, and distressing sales and marketing department by the horizontal integration (Figures 1.4 and 1.5).[30]

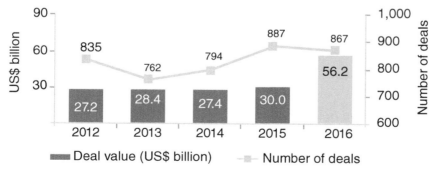

Figure 1.4 Recent M&A Activity in India.
Source: Earnest & Young, Transaction 2017.

Meaning of Mergers and Acquisitions 19

	2015		2016	
	Count	Value(US$ million)	Count	Value(US$ million)
Domestic	483	16,360	505	25,141
Inbound	258	9,949	204	21,396
Outbound	146	3,708	158	9,650
Total	887	30,017	867	56,187

Figure 1.5 M&A Recent Behaviour in India.
Source: Earnest & Young, Transaction 2017.

According to Economic Times Intelligence, in the year 2017, India saw more than 1000 mergers and acquisitions, the highest in the current decade. The deal-making happened on the back of a record year in terms of raising equity. A total of Rs. 181,605 crore was raised in the year 2017.[31]

"A record $ 25 billion was invested by the private equity players and an equal amount was also taken out as exit from India."[32] The number of CBMA deals also maintained almost parity with the figures in 2016 all while there were 368 deals in 2016 there were 340 deals in 2017 in India. This small loss in CBMAs was more than compensated by the domestic deals which increased from 528 in 2016 to 682 in 2017. The following graphs (Figures 1.6 and 1.7) pictographically depict the cross-border and domestic mergers and acquisitions scenario comparatively for the years 2016–2017. The inference is clear in that while CBMA registered a minor deceleration the domestic mergers saw a growth phase.

The following graphs indicate the deal summary both in terms of numbers and values for the years 2016 and 2017 and part 2018 (for the two months of January and February). The fundamental basis of doing business in India is changing.

The round of mergers and acquisition activity will be around consolidation of business and other factors promoting the CBMAs include that reduction, sectorial consolidation, static and challenges of succession planning in a family run business and also harvesting by private equity funds. According to one analyst, the sale of stressed assets under the Indian bankruptcy code is a new chapter in the Indian context.[33]

The graphs in Figures 1.8 and 1.9 are relevant proving the impact of value and volume figures both domestic and cross-border in all three previous financial years. It is clear that the financial year 2017–2018 registered impressive growth in CBMA both in volume and value from which it can be inferred that the legal initiatives started yielding results.

20 *Meaning of Mergers and Acquisitions*

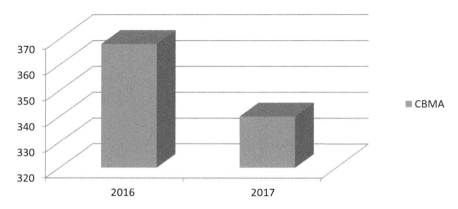

Figure 1.6 Chronological Comparison of the CBMA.

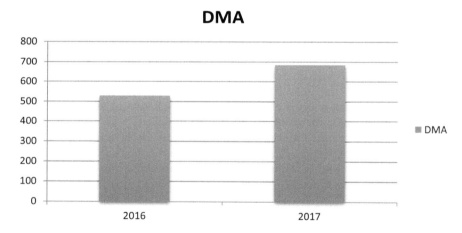

Figure 1.7 Chronological Comparison of DMA.

In 1991, the Indian economy was valued $ 1 trillion. Over a decade, the economy touched the size of $ 2.2 trillion. This was achieved through many measures both structurally and by taking on new initiatives, within the economy. Despite the above, reforms are required in important sectors such as natural resources, roads and electricity, mining and shipping and areas like intellectual property rights.

Meaning of Mergers and Acquisitions   21

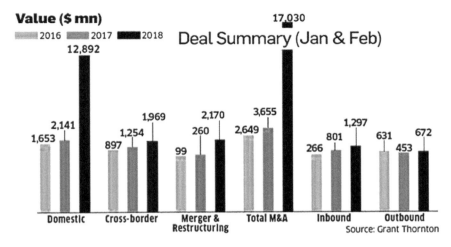

Figure 1.8 Chronological Comparison of Deal Summary Values.
Source: Great Thornton, 2018.

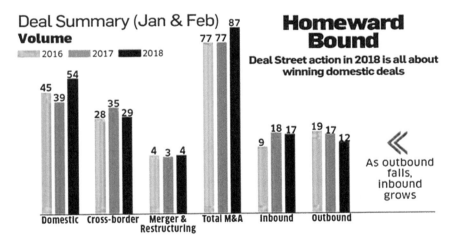

Figure 1.9 Chronological Comparison of Deale Summary Volumes.

The FDA and Emerging Markets

The Case of India

The FDI inflows into Asia were down by 15% to US $43 billion in the year 2016 which is a decline for the first time in six years. India witnessed an inflow of US $ 44 billion in 2016 remaining as the most favoured destination

22 Meaning of Mergers and Acquisitions

due to its attractiveness among multinational corporations for CBMAs according to the United Nations trade report.

> Flows to India were stagnant at the US $ 44 billion in 2016. CBMAs deals have become increasingly important for foreign multinational enterprises to enter the rapidly-growing Indian market according to the United Nations Conference on Trade and Development World Investment Report 2017.[34]

Economic Policy Reforms and the CBMA

The economic policy reforms are as follows:

a   The privatisation of public enterprises.
b   Removal of controls and permits.
c   Easing industrial licensing.
d   Elimination of trade barriers.
e   Regulating the industrial policy.
f   Establishment of development banks.
g   Reduction and statutory minimum levels of reserve ratios.
h   The gradual dismantling of that administered interest rate structure.
i   Liberalising foreign investment.
j   Foreign trade.
k   Outward investment policies.
l   Technology imports.
m   Reforms in foreign exchange policies.
n   Easing of foreign ownership ceilings.
o   Access to global markets.

It also included, among others, the creation of an efficient and profitable financial sector whose aim was to provide operational and functional autonomy to all the institutions including SEBI, RBI, DRI, ED, etc. Further key measures include political reforms, re-engineering the rule of a government through the following initiatives

a   Political reforms.
b   Re-engineering government.
c   Administrative and legal reforms.
d   Agriculture sector reforms.
e   Industrial structure reforms.
f   Financial sector reforms.
g   Substantial deregulation of the stock market with the new issues market being introduced in the year 1992.
h   Controls on the lending rates of the banks.
i   Long-term institutional reforms.

Meaning of Mergers and Acquisitions 23

The differential capital market is also reformed by the following initiatives

1 Establishment of the statutory regulator for the security market through the establishment of SEBI.
2 Introduction of electronic trading to improve transparency.
3 Dematerialisation of shares.
4 The diversity of market intermediaries.
5 Bringing reforms in the role structure and functioning of:

    a   Mercha3nt bankers.
    b   Underwriters.
    c   Share register.
    d   Rating agencies.

6 Reforms in the takeover code, etc.

Major Legal Reforms of the CBMA in India

The GST (Goods and Services Taxes) Act, which came into effect on July 1, 2017, is the biggest tax reform being undertaken since the Independence, of India in 1947. The GST absorbs every possible indirect tax to beget one single/unique/uniform rate and that process harmonises the whole of India into a united marketing entity. It replaced at least 17 state and federal taxes and brought them under a single tax state.

The GST is an all-embracing indirect tax levied on processes comprising of making, selling and consuming of services as well as goods in the entire country of India. It replaces the existing taxes levied by the union and provincial government authorities. GST is both a qualitative and quantitative forward step. GST reduces the tires of taxation and brings in an equitable level playing the balancing field of taxation in both the industrial and service sectors.

The Modi government first came to power in the year 2014 and was re-elected with an enhanced mandate in the year 2019. The new National Democratic Alliance Government, in implementing its election manifesto of both the 2014 and 2019 elections, is insistent upon striving for effective international cooperation, conducive trade with countries abroad, invitation of FDI, and emphasis on the development of suitable infra- and supra-structure. To translate the above manifesto promise into manifested delivery, the NDA Government devised plans like "Make in India," Start-ups India, Make for India and promotion of experts. Matching domestic economic policy initiatives were taken through the slogan "Sab Ka Sath, Sab Ka Vikas" (togetherness with all India, devolvement for all Indians). The main focus continues to be integral human development, better India for ease of doing business for better happiness for Indians.

According to Sivertsen,

there were 7700 deals of mergers and acquisition in the cross-border arena worth the US $ 2.7 trillion which was an increase of around 3% from the 2010 comparative year. The market for 2010 was slowed down and in the year 2011, due to the European sovereign debt crisis which continued to affect the global economy on the wrong side during the comparative period of two decades from 1991 to 2000. One can say that the share of India in the developing economies has notably improved from 1.53 %in the CBMAs in 1991 to 8.9% in 2010 and the growth rate in between these two periods on an average of 6%, shows that when the economy grows, the propensity of the CBMAs'" contribution to the overall economy and GDP also grows.[35]

The study of CBMA in a comparative manner for two decades from 1991 to 2010 is essential for the following two reasons, namely, that 1991 saw the liberalisation in India although belatedly, and second, India undertook many reforms resulting in utilising the opportunities that globalisation as a wave offered to all countries.

Demonetisation was not a merely bold step by the Prime Minister of India on November 8, 2016, but it is a step in the right direction to digitalise the Indian consumer and empower the Indian tax collector (Figure 1.10).

Demonetisation and the CBMA

The Prime Minister, on November 8, 2016, demonetized large currency notes which was later termed "the single most economic reform in the history of independent India."[36] At 2000 hours on November 8, 2016, in a televised live speech, Shri Narendra Modi suddenly announced the scrapping of high-value currency notes (Rs 500 and 1,000) of India. The purpose ostensibly was to check the tax evasions and to eliminate the security target to the sovereignty of India through fake currency printing and circulating resorted to by inimical powers to India. A review after six months by experts found that "the move could not achieve the desired results."[37] Instances of circulation of fake currency notes were observed and corruption too was not evidently controlled. The positive outcome of demonetisation according to the informed observer was the knowledge about the actual flow of currency and the undeclared quantity of currency.

In FY 2016–2017 year, only 5.5 lakh people, out of the 3.65 crore individuals who filed returns, paid income tax of more than Rs 5 lakh and accounted for 57% of the total tax collection. This essentially means that only 1.5% of those filing tax returns (3.65 crores) were contributing to 57% of the tax kitty. The Prime Minister wanted to address this issue by bringing the unaccounted money into the banking channel. The United States and the United Kingdom are the most influential developed states among the comparative group. The United States has been a market leader followed by the BRIC group since the year 2002. One would realise that the BRIC group has surpassed the UK in the year 2002. The US curve

Meaning of Mergers and Acquisitions 25

	Number of deals							Value of deals (US$ millions)					
Year	World economy (1a)	Rate of growth (%) (1b)	India⁴ (India/ World) (2a)	Rate of growth (%) (2b)	India/ Developing (%) (3)	India/ Asia (%) (4)	India/ S.Asia (%) (5)	India/ BRICs (%) (6)	World economy (7a)	Rate of growth (%) (7b)	India⁴ (India/ World) (8a)	Rate of growth (%) (8b)	India/ Developing (%) (9)	India/ Asia (%) (10)	India/ S. Asia (%) (11)	India/ BRICs (%) (12)
---	---	---	---	---	---	---	---	---	---	---	---	---	---	---	---	---
1991	1 582	-23.65₂	2₍₁₃₎	-33.33₂	1.53	2.53	50.00	4.44	21 094	-78.67₂	-	-	-	-	-	-
1992	2 132	34.77	3₍₁₄₎	50.00	1.57	3.66	42.86	5.45	48 106	128.06	34₍₀₇₎	-	0.45	1.55	66.45	2.01
1993	2 179	2.20	8₍₃₇₎	166.67	2.39	4.10	44.44	6.25	43 623	-9.32₂	81₍₁₉₎	135.86	1.78	5.65	58.54	6.84
1994	2 774	27.31	15₍₅₄₎	87.50	3.43	6.98	71.43	10.42	91 769	110.37	90₍₁₀₎	11.34	0.86	2.48	84.33	4.07
1995	3 404	22.71	32₍₉₄₎	113.33	5.87	12.50	84.21	16.58	112 527	22.62	209₍₁₉₎	132.45	3.11	11.45	89.99	14.78
1996	3 650	7.23	24₍₆₆₎	-25.00₂	3.37	7.74	68.57	11.32	142 557	26.69	141₍₁₀₎	-32.80₂	0.70	2.12	10.23	2.91
1997	4 132	13.21	32₍₇₇₎	33.33	4.34	9.55	76.19	13.06	180 751	26.79	396₍₂₂₎	181.07	1.09	2.50	60.24	1.84
1998	4 942	19.60	52₍₁₀₅₎	62.50	4.99	11.13	85.25	14.90	406 427	124.85	334₍₀₈₎	-15.64₂	0.66	2.05	67.49	1.32
1999	5 449	10.26	49₍₉₀₎	-5.77₂	4.73	9.18	92.45	13.92	630 807	55.21	805₍₁₃₎	141.08	1.19	2.59	97.79	3.97
2000	6 280	15.25	80₍₁₂₇₎	63.27	7.43	14.08	90.91	16.39	905 214	43.50	1 064₍₁₂₎	32.22	2.03	7.51	99.07	5.22
2001	4 368	-30.45₂	53₍₁₂₁₎	-33.75₂	7.07	11.91	98.15	18.66	429 374	-52.57₂	683₍₁₆₎	-35.83₂	1.10	2.83	99.83	4.00
2002	3 114	-28.71₂	26₍₈₃₎	-50.94₂	4.68	6.28	74.29	9.12	248 446	-42.14₂	542₍₂₂₎	-20.64₂	1.29	1.70	61.90	2.69
2003	3 004	-3.53₂	50₍₁₆₆₎	92.31	7.82	10.18	94.34	16.72	182 874	-26.39₂	693₍₃₈₎	27.86	3.42	5.40	57.47	5.17
2004	3 683	22.60	56₍₁₅₂₎	12.00	6.95	8.86	86.15	13.49	227 221	24.25	1 034₍₄₆₎	49.27	4.20	6.78	46.98	6.96
2005	5 004	35.87	94₍₁₈₈₎	67.86	8.85	11.30	93.07	17.03	462 253	103.44	526₍₁₁₎	-49.10₂	0.82	1.30	71.28	32.34
2006	5 747	14.85	130₍₂₀₂₆₎	38.30	10.66	15.22	93.53	20.70	625 320	35.28	4 424₍₇₁₎	740.50	4.96	6.78	56.12	13.10
2007	7 018	22.12	147₍₂₀₉₎	13.08	9.47	14.71	92.45	19.17	1 022 725	63.55	4 405₍₄₃₎	-0.42₂	4.39	6.17	82.02	8.83
2008	6 425	-8.45₂	136₍₂₁₂₎	-7.48₂	9.06	13.45	86.08	17.85	706 543	-30.92₂	10 427₍₁.₄₈₎	136.69	9.95	15.13	82.40	22.87
2009	4 239	-34.02₂	104₍₂.₄₅₎	-23.53₂	10.67	15.01	92.86	19.19	249 732	-64.65₂	6 049₍₂.₄₂₎	-41.99₂	15.48	15.80	99.26	25.54
2010	5 405	27.51	115₍₂.₁₃₎	10.58	8.91	14.23	94.26	14.01	338 839	35.68	5 537₍₁.₆₃₎	-8.46₂	6.69	15.09	99.67	15.68
AVG	4226.55	7.33	60.4	31.55	6.19	10.13	80.57	13.93	353810.10	24.78	1873.67	67.55	3.21	5.74	69.55	9.01

Figure 1.10 Number of Deals and Value of Cross-border M&As by Region/Economy of the Seller, 1991–2010.

Notes: AVG—Average; India/Developing signifies the percentage of India's share in developing economies, similarly for India/Asia, India/South (S.) Asia, and India/BRIC group. (a). Columns 2a and 8a parentheses signify India's share as a percentage of the world economy.
Source: Data extracted from UNCTAD – —World Investment Report 2011, spreadsheets.

represents a mountain shape and it justifies the theory of business cycles. One can reasonably say here that there is moderate competition between multinational corporations from the developed markets and the multinational corporations for emerging markets in adopting.

Impact of Demonetisation

While many top-notch economists were divided over its impact on the economy, former UIDAI Chairman hailed Hon'ble Prime Minister Narendra Modi's demonetisation move and said that it would see an enormous increase in the use of digitalised services of transaction involving buying, selling, expenditure and investment. He also explained how India's over 80% workforce will come into the formal channels. The chairman of UIDAI asserted that digitalisation of transactions means a formal economy and accountability would result after correct accounts.

> India is going to go from data-poor to data-rich and that will make it more and more difficult for people to do dishonest things or to be outside the system. You will reduce the amount of black money in the system.[38]

India got an opportunity in the year 2008 to get assets at every undervaluation level; it was correctly utilised and debt financing was also done by Indian investment bankers themselves because of the possibility of the following interesting aspects.

1   Regulatory and legal reforms that happened over some time.
2   When a crisis happens and if such a crisis becomes an opportunity for the domestic industry, then, companies do take initiatives to expand their business activities abroad.

The International Monetary Fund officials observed that financial sector reforms need to be implemented to enable stable growth in an otherwise stagnant economy. They officially used the metaphor of elephants running in describing the reforms that led to the growth of the Indian economy. "The Director of the Asia and Pacific Department at the International Monetary Fund (IMF), also praised the Modi government for doing well in the area of reforms."[39]

The CBMA and Growth in Business

This also proves that many Indian parent companies have been acquiring foreign multinationals through their affiliates and there were established. Bharti Airtel acquired Kuwait-based Jain Telecom for US $10,700 million in the year 2010. Adani Enterprises and GVK Power bought Australians based on US $1909 million and Hannah Cool for US $1260 million respectively in the year 2011. Besides, one can find a number of Indian firms that became the targets for the Australian MNCs. For example, British Petroleum acquired some percentage of equity shares in Reliance Petroleum for US $7200 million in the year 2011 (Figure 1.11).

The most important trend we can observe is that till 2007, the sales of the CBMA were in an increasing trend from 1991 to 2002 and then also from 2000 to 2006. However, from 2007 onwards the purchases had a surplus than the sales from 2007 to 2010. In other words, some Indian companies have become targets for foreign parent firms in light of the foreign market entry or other international venturing business models. This happened because further liberalisation and globalisation was a trend that continued right from 1991 irrespective of who occupied the chair in the centre of economic administration of the country.

One can see a gradual growth of the liberalisation process resulting in the figures that reflect the overall trend. The Indian firms have been trying to tap international markets through diverse inorganic strategies such as

a   Joint ventures.
b   Alliances especially from the year 2003.

However, from the year 2007 onwards, Indian MNCs have invested the highest amount of equity and cash to buy global entities in various developed and developing markets.

Dr Y.V. Reddy, the former Governor of the Reserve Bank of India, is an acknowledged expert on monetary and fiscal policies and has authored critical reports on the financial crisis of the year 2008 and how India escaped the crackdown of its economy. This was made possible through institutional intervention by watchdog agencies like the SEBI, DRI and Economic Intelligence Bureau.

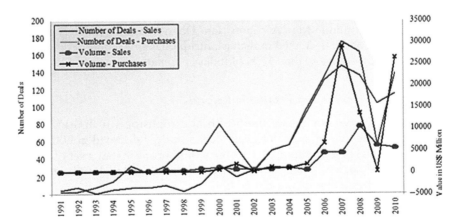

Figure 1.11 India's Cross-border M&A Sales and Purchases, 1991–2010.
Source: Great Thornton, 2018.

The CBMA and Jan Dhan Accounts

Jan Dhan accounts were aimed at bringing 70% of the Indian population which remained unbanked for 70 years to the banking network to use the rural purchasing power becoming a point of the national economy. Tractors, fertilisers, automobiles, agricultural marketing societies and Food Corporation of India are active players in rural India, and bringing the transactions into the banking accountancy makes the hitherto unmentioned consumerist activity tangible. It is relevant for CBMAs as many sunrise industries are located in rural areas, the biggest examples being mobile phones and solar energy. In both the above fields, global business houses through CBMAs are the major players.

On the occasion of the first Independence Day (August 15, 2014) celebration of India after becoming the Prime Minister of India for the first time, Shri Narendra Modi brought out the Pradhan Mantri Jan-Dhan Yojana (Prime Minister's plan for people's money). Indians lacking access to banking services and farmers committing suicides due to usurious interest rates from private money lenders were not uncommon. This national mission, the first of its kind, was aimed at ensuring access to deliver financial services, including bank savings accounts, credit assurances, insurance plans, ease in remittances and direct receipts of subsidies from government and pensions to all Indians. An unbanked India was targeted to become fully banked.

The effort of Prime Minister's plan was to implement the target of making banking services available to more than 15% of India's population.

The *Economic Times* reported that in the financial year 2013–2014, over 1.9 million account holders utilised the overdraft facility to the tune of Rs 2560 million. The Common-Man Account (Jan-Dhan Account) holders claimed insurance coverage to the tune of Rs 10,00,000. The account also provides for life insurance cover to the tune of Rs 30,000 paid directly to the nominee in case of the death of the account holder. With more than 278.4 million account holders under Common Man Accounts (Jan- Dhan Account), which is almost the population of the USA, the Pradhan Mantri Jan-Dhan Account programme successfully covered more than 15% of India's population.

People's Inclusiveness and Economic Reforms

Eventuality always symbolises the health and robustness of India's economy. Hence, the rate of growth for purchases sharply declined in 2009 and then immediately recovered in 2010. One would propose that a set of political, legal and societal changes affect the strategies of local and overseas forms when competing in and out of India.

From here, it can be concluded that India's economic, banking and financial reforms have attracted many investment bankers and private equity firms in recent years. The economic changes in foreign investment policies and firms motivated Indian multinational corporations to utilise potential

Meaning of Mergers and Acquisitions 29

opportunities in other developing economies, for example, Africa and Middle East regions.

Finance Banking Governance Reforms

This phenomenal growth recognises that India's economic, financial and banking reforms place local multinational corporations on the world map through international processes as has been already affirmed. While China recorded transactions to the tune of 3637 in the 20 years from 1992 to 2010, India's figure for the comparative field was near 1,200, which is one-third of China's figures. In terms of the value of transactions, the figures are 37,473 for India and 167,262 for China; this is also again almost 4.5 times that of the Chinese case. In terms of purchase, the figures are 2,217 for China and 1,008 for India and transactions for 2,220 for China and 830 for India; thus, the Chinese average deal accounts are higher than India's average deals both in value and number and in both sales and purchase.

There is not a single transnational corporation in the non-financial banking world among the first 100 in India for the period 2001 to 2018 in terms of foreign assets. China has got nine such transnational corporations (TNC) having foreign assets ranking among the first 100 in the world in the year 2010 followed by Russia. In terms of developing economies for the first 100, China has got 9 followed by Russia and India has only 7 and Brazil has 3. No Indian transnational corporation was ranked in the top 10 list. Tata Steel was ranked number 14, Tata Motors number 25, public undertakings ONGC 30, Hindalco 33, Suzlon Industries 67, TATA Consultancy Services 69 and Reliance Communication 72. Overall, 28 TLCs rank from the BRIC group and several TNCs are in product industries such as diversified metals, petrol and natural gas and telecommunications.

In the top ten, there are two companies from China and one each from Brazil and Russia and the first rank was given to the Hong Kong divaricate firm Cochin Hutchison Power Limited followed by China's City group. According to Ramamurthy in their 2012 research report,

> one would consider that MNCs from developed countries have to gear up to extract new opportunities in emerging markets and MNCs from emerging markets have had to figure out how to take advantage of opportunities and another part of the world.[40]

Lu Zui and Hen in the year 2010 observed that "Chinese government promotional measures and monetary policies have a significant impact on FDI performance."[41]

> In the world investment report of UNCTAD in the year 2011 which gives country rankings by performance index, India is ranked 80 in the year 2008 and gained to 67 in 2009 and then fell sharply to 97 in 2010. In the case of the FDI potential index, India is ranked 86 and then again

30 Meaning of Mergers and Acquisitions

79 by 2009. In 2017, UNCTAD gave INDIA third rank in an investment destination. India ranked tenth in terms of FDI inflows in 2016, and India would be behind the USA and China only till 2019.[42]

Rankings of India by the World Bank, UNCTAD, Moody's, etc. are extremely relevant for CBMAs and India's biggest competitor for attracting FDI through CBMAs is China. India's efforts are on to fill the gap and to utilise the opportunities (Figure 1.12).

The Competition Act, 2002 is a vast improvement to the negative dysfunctional predatory MRTP Act of 1969. The above figure brings out the scope for attracting the FDI through the CBMA among all the three major players, namely developed, developing and transition economies.

IT Act and the CBMA

Taxation should not be a vexation. The more simplified the tax rules, the more will be compliance and the less will be litigation. Further, attractive tax policies encourage increasing capital flows through FDI and the CBMA.

Without proper reforms in taxation laws and ease coupled with simplicity in implementation, the CBMA environment would be severely

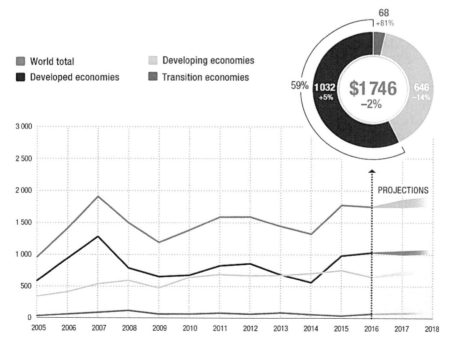

Figure 1.12 FDI Inflows, 2005–2016 and Projections, 2017–2018.
Sources: UNCTAD, FDI/MNE database www.unctad.org/fdistatistics).

constrained. While the Companies Act, 2013 was brought, the Income Tax Act, 1961 remained status quoist.

> The Income Tax Act, 1961, has yet not been amended to be in line with the amended Companies Act and the merger regulations. As per the income tax act, in a scheme of amalgamation, any transfer of capital assets by a transferor company shall be exempt where the resultant company is an Indian company. Again as per Income Tax Act, in a scheme of amalgamation in a transferor of the capital by a shareholder in consideration for the issue of shares in the resulting company shall be exempt.[43]

The CBMA and FEMA

FEMA is a better law when compared to FERA. The draconian FERA was a relic of the monopolistic licence permit raj which made India stagnate at the infamous Hindu rate of growth. FEMA is more facilitative than FERA. Two examples here will illustrate the above point. Despite the new act's facilitation for the CBMA and takeover, worldwide exposure to the Indian industry did not happen. One example is the Vodafone Hutchison Telecom deal which faced tax litigations with the Indian revenue department and tax authorities between 2007 and 2012. But the delay process costs a lot and sends wrong signals to the world.[44]

The Government of India needs to remove the multiplicity of regulations governing product market distortions, the market for an estate and widespread government ownership of businesses so that it would grow as fast as China.

Issuance of Shares in the CBMA

Compliance with regulations regarding foreign exchange law, especially FEMA (the Foreign Exchange Management Act) and PMLA (the Prevention of Money Laundering Act), is existing in the case of issuance of shares in any CBMA transaction. The main regulations governing the issuance of shares of the resultant entity according to a CBMA are the Foreign Exchange Management Act (transferred to security by a person resident outside India) Regulations, 2000 (transfer and issue of any foreign security).[45]

The Framework to the IBC Process—Opportunities

The Insolvency and Bankruptcy Code (IBC) was introduced by the Government of India to aid the process of the cost of doing business in India. Business needs easy entry processes and easier exit processes. Insolvency is a possible event and bankruptcy is the probable outcome for any business. Having realised the need for level playing as per other global competitive systems, especially in the USA, the IBC was introduced. The foreign players through CBMAs can know how to utilise a level playing field in India. The

IBC facilitates better bids for IBC cases so that foreign capital and expertise can move to India. In any business, time is costlier than capital. Time overruns are fatal compared to cost overruns. IBC means adherence to time and it ensures the resolution processes of corporate insolvency (CIR process) well within the announced time schedule. The COVID-19 pandemic compelled the Government of India to suspend this process from April 2020 for six months, and in October 2020, it was further extended. However, pandemics are emergencies and the above execution is normal.

The crucial nature of the economic performance of any country depends not on its intention but on its implementation. Policy administration and planned implementation rather than policy-making are important for any country and the same is true in the case of India. Enhancing India's image requires a lot of restructuring and re-engineering of its public administration tools in terms of the administrative setup that it has established in terms of tax administration, rule administration and plan administration for promoting not only mergers and acquisitions but also all other aspects. Only when India does it, then only it will be able to attract FDI through CBMAs or increase its domestic investors to acquire assets abroad. This entire process involves the following initiatives.

Providing administrative training in the areas of tax administration, tax rule making, consultancy areas with other affecting systems and research areas to make the Indian rules on par with the rest of the countries so that the country's advantage as a destination for CBMAs in terms of inbound logistics will be in favour of India and also constantly be keeping a watch on the global monitoring agencies as to how they are rating Indian efforts and initiatives.

Setting up of economics and business research organisations with infrastructure and resources so that the best talent that is available abroad and India will be there working seamlessly without any troubles and any infrastructural bottlenecks and with synergy and energy. A thorough discussion on IBC will be coming up in the later chapters.

Start-ups and the CBMA

Looking closely into the rural sector, India has to promote economic and financial savings so that the same economic and financial savings can be utilised for plumbing them back into the economy and, thus, unemployment and disguised unemployment in terms of productive unemployment and underemployment issues are not there and people are generally energetic and happy and they are not bothered about their earnings tomorrow.

Designing a comprehensive policy that motivates the younger generation to take up start-up India projects and not to be dependent on government jobs as security is important. Unfortunately, in India, even if it is a job of the lowest level, a job in government is more attractive to even PhD scholars than starting up a training institute to train people like them to be most skilful. For example, in a recent Uttar Pradesh government advertisement for the post of 130 attendants in subordinate courts in Uttar Pradesh, there were more than 1,50,000 applications, out of which thousands of people were PhDs and 1,00,000 were engineers.

Kaizen and the CBMA

Kaizen means constant improvement. Toyota introduced Kaizen in the industry for quality improvement. Controlling higher education universities and institutions was done by establishing fraud search committees so that crony capitalism is not reflected in universities because universities are supposed to be temples of ethics and they are supposed to be promoting ethics among temples and hence fraud search committees must work without corrupt elements and vested interests among universities as the faith in the systems of democracy and establishments starts with universities. Those who administer universities must be men of impeccable character. Indeed, policymakers should develop strategic guidelines to view the financing choices in rural villages and develop minimal infrastructure facilities in backward districts and areas as rural backgrounds and villages offer the greatest catchment area for both investment and talent. Similarly, if neglected the same can follow the most dictum of encircling the towns with villages. Hence, it is suggested that villages, towns and cities should not be like gated communities but instead should be like the place of worship among forest areas so that because of them the forest becomes a tourist place. One can also say the forest becomes a place of rest for all.

There should be greater coordination and control among all the related ministries rather than the ministries working alone. One should never put a lid on public power and control for one's benefit. Any damage to social goods is a public grievance. Banking and financial institution products and services must reach every corner of the country which would bring more savings and investments. The following are the observations of the Mackenzie report. The consultants observed that India is a well-developed equity market compared to the banking sector but the barrier is successive government interventions through the allocation of capital and a consequent holding back of growth.

Besides, the barriers are regulations and governing the product markets, land distortions, licensing and quasi-licensing counterproductive taxations. Suggestions include rationalisation of taxes and excise duty by establishing effective and individual regulators and removing restrictions on FDI, undertaking widespread privatisation and reforming private property and tenancy laws to promote compliance. Developing countries must reduce restrictions on foreign investment, and lower the important streamlined requirements for starting new businesses.

The success of CBMAs in emerging markets like India requires constant learning in a multidimensional managerial paradigm including legal reform, administrative reform, admission reform, best benchmarking practices adaptation and constant training with the practitioners and policymakers within the crucible of emerging trends of the CBMAs across the world. The training needs to cover human resource practices by taking into account differing cultural environments, which are critical success factors if treated well, but become critical failure factors if not considered properly.

Emerging markets differ from developed markets because of their linkages with all three phases of the economy, namely the agricultural economy, the industrial economy and the service economy. Any partial or truncated over-emphasis on any one of the above three sectorial divisions of the economy will ultimately lead to imbalances in the economy and thus derail the entire process of development that is the main goal of any economic policy in emerging economies.

The purpose of any nation being termed as an emerging market is not to remain as an emerging market but to attain the stage of a developed market and all the indicators in this research were pointing out the current effort of India to commit to a developed market.

So far, many important aspects of CBMA in India were discussed and a discussion on India's position among emerging economies in comparison to developed economies will follow.

The CBMA and Domestic Experience of Learning Importance

The scenario of mergers and acquisitions in India as of today is better described as cautious optimism. Although there is a volume-wise decrease, there is a value-wise increase according to the 2017 reports. Cement and energy in inbound acquisitions and oil gas and mining in the outbound acquisitions areas are creating value addition as of today.

The amendments to procedures in relaxing regulations by providing self-certification mechanisms, creating tax exemptions for the promotion of cross-border merger facilitating legal support through fast-track patent examination, digitalising clearances and permission and post portals through proper modification of existing rules are some of the initiatives being undertaken by the government. Insolvency and Bankruptcy Code (IBC), 2016 was introduced for reducing the time limit in the insolvency process and also for realising the Non-Performing Assets (NPAs) of the public sector banks. The introduction of the Goods and Services Tax (GST), 2017, and the initiative of demonetisation also were expected to contribute to the process of liberalisation and process improvement.

The CBMA and Prevention of Corruption Act, 1988 and Foreign Direct Investment Rules

Efforts are being made by the government to bring in changes in the Foreign Exchange Management Act, 1999 through a policy is promulgated by the Department of Industrial Policy and Promotion (DIPP) on par with the best-benchmarked practices in the world to facilitate more investment and also to facilitate a level playing field for the investors from abroad. Similar amendments are also being planned to the FEMA, 1999 and Department of Industrial Policy and Promotion. The Industrial Disputes Act, 1947, is also being looked into. The Banking Regulation Act ,1949 and the RBI Act, 1934 are being amended so that the Companies Act, 2013 and the Banking Acts including the previous Banking Regulation Act, 1934 are all on a similar path.

The CBMA and SEBI

The shares and takeover regulations 2011 code of the SEBI along with the code of the capital and disclosure requirements 2009 and the service code of prohibition of insider trading regulations 2015 are all being brought under one platform to remove confusion and to facilitate convergence. Similar amendments are also on the anvil for sector-specific regulation mechanisms for sectors like pharmaceuticals, civil aviation, robotics, information communication technologies, shipping, rail construction, banking and nanotechnology.

SEBI and the CBMA

SEBI (Securities and Exchange Board of India) Chairman Sri Ajai Tyagi opined that deeper structural and regulatory changes are needed for the development of the corporate bond market to establish coordination between the government and the financial sector regulators. It is no surprise that in the COVID pandemic period between April 2020 and September 2020, nearly 6.3 million depository participate (DP)accounts were added when compared to 2.704 million accounts during the corresponding period last year. Similarly, foreign portfolio investors invested US $11 billion in the equity ma in the year 2020 so far. The Indian financial sector is largely dominated by bank lending. However, there is an emerging necessity for indulging and inculcating diversification by fundraising through capital markets. The equity and debt capital markets were hovering around the bonded range of 9 to 9.5 lakh crore per annum rupees. According to informed sources, the volatility index in the stock market rose from an average of 15 in the three-month pre-COVID-19 pandemic period to 84 in March 2020. However, perhaps the market endorsed the internal strength of the capital markets in India that the volatility index came back from the all-time high of 84 to 25 as of today.

The above feat was made possible due to the structural and supervisory initiatives which among others include surveillance with respect to exposures and margins to curb volatility. There is also a need for strengthening infrastructural facilities like the investor protection fund which is adequate at merely Rs 25 lakh. There is an issue of the derivative market volume being almost 85% of the cash market volumes which converts the markets into markets of gambling. To this dilemma, SEBI intends to act upon the issue of upfront margin so that the upfront margin will be measured 4 times starting from December to reduce speculation of some of the initiatives that the SEBI is expected to take or as follows.

1. RFQ (request for quotation) platform is being worked out and is supposed to have mandated mutual funds to trade a certain percentage of their trade on this platform for transplant discovery of bond prices.
2. PRFDA and IRDAI also agreed in principle to mandate a certain percentage for their entities to come on the RFQ platform.
3. Improving transparency and bond pricing is the need of the hour.

Mr Udai Kotak, the president of the Confederation of Indian Industry, on October 21, 2020, suggested some reforms to SEBI. They are as follows.

1. Capital adequacy-based framework for stockbrokers and a focus on delivery-based estimates.
2. SEBI should consider reviewing open interest limits.
3. SEBI should also consider easing the areas of reclassification of promoters under listing obligations.
4. SEBI should consider a modification to disclosure requirement regulations.

The main emphasis here is to remove the philosophy of one-size-fits-all so that the old blunted instruments will be replaced by fine-tuned guidelines. CAR (capital adequacy ratio) is the measurement of the availability of capital with a bank or lender vis-à-vis its risk-awaited credit exposures. This brings into focus the recent scam in which stockbroker KARVY was caught using the shares of customers and clients to avail bank loans. Stock markets cannot be on credit and they must be based on cash and delivery. Mr Kotak believes that the derivatives market was more of a liquidity provider and a catalyst for capital formation through which investors invest cash into the equity market. SEBI needs to review the open interest limits which were put in place in the guidelines issued on March 20, 2020. Recovery Expense Fund (REF) was established by SEBI. The main goal of the REF is to ensure the legitimate interest of investors in raising funds by issuing Debt Papers (DP) in the stock exchange. This is a positive step in the right direction and makes the Indian financial markets transparent, belief-worthy and investment prone from the point of view of global players. This direction was necessary because defaulting by large incorporates in recent times impact mutual fund investors badly. The main purpose of such funds is that in the event of a default by any corporate house, the debenture trustees may utilise the fund for taking appropriate legal action to enforce the security.

Motives for the CBMA

Growth, enlarging the marketing arena, chasing raw materials, reducing labour costs, leveraging intangible assets and invoicing tax liabilities are some of the motivations for CBMAs.

CBMA: Culture and Corporate Governance

Culture being an important arena, coupled with differences in governance issues of implementation, is an important part of due diligence in CBMA. Administrative law and corporate culture coupled with systems of governance encouraging the rule of law are of vital importance for proper CBMA goals.

The CBMA and Emerging Countries

According to the current practice of apportionment of economies of the world, there are three major typologies: (a) developed countries, (b) emerging countries and (c) developing countries. Emerging countries witness aggression in local government regulations, class of confiscatory tax policies and restrictions on cash remittances. Motivations for work are different in emerging countries when compared to developed countries.

The CBMA and Specific Types of Mergers

In addition to horizontal and vertical mergers, specific CBMAs are congeneric conglomerate mergers, which take care of the special situations in the environment of CBMA.

CBMA and the Competition Law, 2002

The infamous MRTP Act, 1969 was replaced by a just Competition Act, 2002. The Competition Commission of India was created to regulate and implement the law of the Competition Act, 2002. The Competition Commission of India, CCI is expected to regulate combinations and is likely to cause an appreciable adverse effect on monopoly.

CBMA and the Stamp Duty Act

The Stamp Duty Act, 1897 provides for registration and payment of duty to the competent authority. It covers the following legal requirements, namely transfer inter vivos stamp duty to be levied on conveyance deed oblique instrument and stamp duty rate to be prescribed in the schedule of the stamp act.

38 Meaning of Mergers and Acquisitions

CBMA and the Judicial Infrastructure

The Company Act, 2013, the newly created National Company Law Tribunal (NCLT) and the National Company Law Appellate Tribunal (NCLAT), apart from the judicial review of the High Courts and the Supreme Court of India, are part of the vital judicial infrastructure.

CBMA and the USA

Variables such as exchange rates, and stock prices, influence the number and the direction of the CBMA vary between companies in the United States and each of the four European countries: Germany, Italy, the United Kingdom, and France. Research done through logit models suggests that bond yields explain the trends in CBMA, and the multi-regression models indicate that US stock prices to be a good explanatory variable. The results suggest that foreign acquisitions occur more frequently when bond yields in the country of the acquired company are higher than those from the country of the company being acquired. A depressed stock market of the USA relative to the foreign stock markets encourages the foreign acquisition of the US companies.[46]

Securities and Exchange Commission

In the United States, the Securities Acts of 1933 and 1934 form the foundation of the starting of the Securities and Exchange Commission (SEC). The Securities Acts of 1933 and 1934 are also the repositories of regulator regulations related to security administration. For the sake of convenience, the Congress of the United States of America transferred partially certain duties of the SEC to autonomous institutions like the New York Stock Exchange (NYSE). NYSE is an autonomous body and self-recruiting in itself; however, it operates under the overall control of the SEC of the USA.

The SEC, in the glorious traditions of decentralised administrative law, in implementing the principles of delegation, democracy and efficiency, transports some of its workloads for better education through specialised scrutiny after creating institutions of global eminence like the Financial Accounting Standards Board (FASB). Under the Sarbanes-Oxley Act, 2002, SEC is supervising the Public Company Accounting Oversight Board (PCAOB). The main duty of PCAOB is to advance, assert and administer standards that guide auditors in administering and qualifying Corporate Financial Reports (CFRs). The proclaimed objective of the Sarbanes Oxley Act, 2002 was to accomplish increased corporate transparency in connection with financial statements. However, the real estate crisis and the banking crisis in the USA in the years of 2008 and 2009 leave much to be desired. In the case of CBMA, this aspect becomes even further complicated. State legislation has a significant impact on governance practices by requiring corporate chapters to define the responsibilities of boards and managers concerning shareholders.

FTC (The Federal Trade Commission)

The SEC, the Federal Trade Commission (FTC) and the Department of Justice (DOJ) discipline companies with inappropriate governance practices through formal and informal investigations, lawsuits and settlements. The SEC of the USA, as early as the year 2003, approved the transparent plan for new listing standards. The purpose of new listing standards is that any lucrative or action plan of any company had to be put to shareholder vote first. The genuine interests of the shareholders of nearly 6200 companies listed in the New York Stock Exchange (NYSE), the Nasdaq were thus protected. In January 2007, SEC implemented additional disclosure requirements for chief executive officer pay and perks that exceed US $10,000 in value.

> Federal security laws impose several reporting, disclosure, and anti-fraud requirements on acquirers initiating tender offers. Section 14(D) S of the Williams Act requires that any individual or entity making a tender offer resulting in owning more than 5% of any class of equity must file S scheduled 14(D)-1 and all solicitation materials with SEC.[47]

There is a concept of hostile takeover which goes against the management entrenchment theory. Hostile takeovers are positive in one aspect in that as an attempt of effort or threat of an attempt, hostile takeovers will induce self-introspection in the managements, ultimately resulting in weeding out dead wood and removing the bad apples from the cart well within time. In other words, the managers would be removed by external threats at least.

"Indeed, there is evidence of frequent management turnover even if the takeover attempt is defeated because takeover targets are often for financial performers."[48] "An alternative is the shareholder interest theory, which suggests that management resistance to proposed takeovers is a good bargaining strategy to increase the purchase price to the benefit of the target companies shareholders."[49]

At various levels of the government, regulators exercise their legal power to ensure fair play in the business field. All the regulations draw their power of enforcement through the law. Judicial review always guides the regulator's actions. Some regulations are common to all companies while some are specific to industries. In the USA too, there are general and specific regulations. The general regulations include federal security, antitrust, environmental laws, racketeering laws and employee benefit laws. The specific laws include areas of banking, telecommunications, insurance, defence contracting, public utilities, real estate, transportation, pharmaceuticals, chemicals, nanotechnology, etc.

The CBMA and USA Tax Reforms

The CBMA and Tax Reforms in the USA, CFC, TIPRA

Controlled Foreign Corporation (CFC)

Controlled Foreign Corporations (CFC) are special-purpose instruments. They are started to save tax from places of high tax incidence. Corporations can be like onions, with no link in each layer either diametrically or vertically. The parent country firm can achieve an allowed facility of tax deferral, till the kind for a passive income of such overseas CFC is NOT distributed. Law Tax Havens are Bermuda, Singapore, Liechtenstein, etc. The Action Plan on Base Erosion and Profit Shifting (BEPS) of the Organisation of Economic Co-Operation and Development (OECD) has many benchmark rules for detecting and punishing tax avoidance frauds. More than 100 countries are signatories to this action plan.

The rules are needed only concerning the income of an entity that is not currently taxed to the owners of the entity. Generally, taxpayers must include in their income, all accounts correctly, if any. Enacted in the year 1962, in the USA, these rules include most of the features of the CFC rules used in other countries. They were designed especially under subpart (f) rules to prevent US regions and resident individuals and corporations from artificially differing otherwise taxable income through the use of foreign entities. US property specifically includes the obligations of or investments related to related parties, with a physical status in the USA, and the stock of a domestic corporation. Subpart (f) income includes the following Foreign Personal Holding Company Income (FPHCI), foreign-based company sales income, foreign-based company services income, foreign-based company oil-related income and insurance income. Under the US Tax rules, the foreign entity may be classified for tax purposes as a corporation or a flow-through entity somewhat independently of its classification for the foreign purpose. Another law of importance in the CBMA scenario is the Tax Increase Prevention and Reconciliation Act of 2005 which is also called TIPRA. This act prevents several tax provisions from the sun setting shortly. The two most notable pieces of the act are the extension of the reduced tax rates on capital gains and dividends and the extension of the Alternative Minimum Tax (AMT) reduction. A CFC is any corporation organised outside the USA that is more than 50% owned by the US shareholders.[50]

The Foreign Investment in Real Property Tax Act of 1980, also called FIRPTA, 1980, is a tax law of the USA that imposes income tax on foreign persons disposing of the real property interest in the United States. Purchases of real property interests are required to withhold tax on payment. Withholding may be reduced from the standard 15% to an amount that will cover the tax liability, application in advance of the sale. FIRPTA overrides motion-recognition provisions as well as those remaining tax treaties that provide the exemption from tax for such gains. President Obama signed the law of protecting Americans from the Tax Hikes Act (THA) of 2015, on December 18, 2015.

FIRPTA, 1980 and THA-2015

The THA (2015) brought momentous alterations in laws relating to taxation concerning subjects like mutual funds including stakeholders namely investors and fund managers. Often, the vital angle of concern covered includes private equity-related issues. THA 2015 also modified the rules relating to FIPRA, (1980) and the rules applicable to Real Estate Investment Trust (REITs). THA (2015) also covered rules relating to Regulated Investment Companies (RICs). Taxpayers in the United States may face various penalties for values related to federal, state and local tax matters.

Internal Revenue Service (IRS)

At the federal level, the Internal Revenue Service (IRS) charges rules, levies penalties and administers tax machinery. Tax rules vary widely, are administered by the state and local authorities and are not always taken into account in every matter related therein. Penalties may be monetary or may involve forfeiture of the property.

Criminal penalties may include jail terms but are imposed only by a federal judge after a defendant is convicted.

> The most monetary penalty is based on the amount of tax not properly paid. Penalties may increase with the period of non-payment. Some penalties are fixed dollar amounts and others are fixed percentages of some measures required to be reported.[51]

"There are over 150 kinds of civil penalties in the United States Internal Revenue Code (USIRC), using in CBDT which is reflected in the number of applicable files."[52] "Taxpayers and stakeholders of Controlled Foreign Corporations (CFC) must file form 5471 concerning each controlled foreign corporation."[53] Penalties for failure to timely file are the US $1000–50,000 per-form, plus possible loss of foreign tax credits. Intentionally filing material false tax returns is a criminal offense. A person convicted of committing tax fraud, or aiding and abetting another in computing a tax fraud, may be subject to forfeiture of property"[54] "and/or jail term."[55]

> Conviction and sentencing are through the court system. Responsibility for prosecution is on the Department of Justice, United States of America, and not on the Internal Revenue Service (IRS). Penalties may be assessed against cracks, protesters who raise arguments that income tax laws are not valid or those who otherwise file frivolous returns or Court petitions.[56]

"The most relevant penalty for those who commit fraud in the scenario of the CBMA is one of tax advisor penalties. The penalty is applied to the people who promote tax shelters"[57] or "who fail to maintain and dispose of a list of reportable transactions"[58] with their customers and clients or undertakings. The monetary penalty here can be very severe.

While many motivations are driving a company to go for a CBMA, pre-empted competition as a motivator works across many industries. When growth opportunities fly as attractive options, the drive to pounce upon a new company with a significant portfolio and assets is enormous. CBMAs are the best-suited strategy tools in the global context. The best instances in the previous century are dot com and telecom companies. In the present century, the best examples are commodity companies and energy-producing companies. During the previous decade, 2011 to 2020, the best examples are the e-commerce companies like Amazon and during the COVID-19 pandemic that affected 2021, it is the vaccine biotechnology companies. Corporate law firms are popular among companies looking to expand externally through a merger or an acquisition, especially companies with international borders. Such deals are more complex as they involve different laws governed by different jurisdictions and thus require very specialised legal handling. International law firms are best suited for this job with their expertise in multi-jurisdiction matters. Some of them are as follows. "Audit and accounting firms are also required to handle the merger and acquisition deals in auditing, accounting, and taxation. These organizations have expertise in assessing the value of assets, through appropriate audits and also through advice on taxation issues."[59] In cases where cross-border merger or acquisition is involved, the stock taxation part becomes critical and such companies fit well in such situations.

> Audit and account expect these companies have other experts on their panel to manage any aspect of the deal well. Some of the well-known forms from this category with specialized services in the mergers and acquisitions are KPMG, Deloitte, Price Waterhouse Coopers (PwC), Earnest & Young (EY), and understanding these companies together or tagged as the big four.[60]

CBMAs involve many crucial cross-functional domains covering discussions. Proper information collection and scrutiny by consulting experts from different professions and across many countries became the most vital imitating step in CBMA execution. The bigger companies in this business have a global footprint which helps in identifying targets based on suitability in all aspects. The firms work on the acquisition strategy followed by screening due diligence and advising on price valuations making sure that the clients are not overpaying and so on. The most prominent and expert consulting firms include famous brands like the Boston Consulting Group (DCG), McKinsey, Bain and Company, KPMG and A.T. Kearney.

CBMA and Legal Due Diligence

Legal intelligence is a key component of any CBMA deal. It should not be misconstrued as a simple procedural hurdle. CBMAs require, apart from the minimum necessary compliance to regulatory laws, the essential adherence to different demands of corporate governance in both host and parent countries and need adjustment to the political climate in both places and sometimes in a third country vendor area and a fourth country marketing/consuming areas. US anti-bribery and antitrust laws present particularly important issues given the international breach, successor reliability and the US operator's active role in cross-border enforcement. Non-U.S. companies, whether incorporated in Asia, Europe, or elsewhere, must be aware of the issues these laws present and tailor-make their legal due diligence protocols appropriately to assess the risks.

Legal due diligence is about time and timing too. Law is dynamic. In democratic countries, electoral compulsions and accountability through political manifestos, corporate law is as dynamic as corporate profits/losses. M&A deals can create or transfer to the target company's true value cannot be determined without considering all the relevant legal issues, and it makes legal due diligence an essential step in any CBMAs deal.

The rule of law is the cornerstone of the American Constitution Manifestly; this principle becomes a regulatory tool of Governance, covering all aspects- social, economic, political, cultural, philosophical and constitutional angles of an American citizen. In commercial space, this principle becomes paramount across the whole world where and when American Corporations function. CBMAs are no exception to this basic principle.

The rule of law connotes the accountability of all governments, agents, agencies, institutions and all persons towards "The LAW." This "LAW" should be an outcome of the four vital ingredient systems: (1) equality in enforcement, (2) independence in adjudication, (3) transparency in promulgation and (4) consistency and trust in fundamental human rights covenants.

The US corporate laws are all-pervading and interactive. Fraud prevention and anti-corruption/bribery are the tools through which U.S. laws aim to prevent monopoly and manipulation. The doctrine of successor liability is vigorously enforced by the US regulators (SEC, IRS and FCPA). Any CBMA activity with a US company or any other companies within the USA cannot be impervious or blind towards the due diligence in the legal process, ab initio.

> In the Indian context also, knowledge about the anti-bribery and antitrust laws of the United States of America is important because India conducts cross-border mergers and maximum with the companies incorporated in the USA. The US Foreign Corrupt Practices Act (FCPA), 1977 broadly prohibits payments to foreign government officials to obtain a retail business.[61]

"The FCPA applies to any entity listed on a US Stock Exchange, person or business, and certain persons are entities acting within the US."[62] The Department of Justice and the Securities and Exchange Commission ensure the implementation of the doctrine of successor liability in the United States.

The Doctrine of Successor Liability and Department of Justice, USA

The doctrine of successor liability, apart from covering civil or criminal liability, also unexceptionally covers violations under Foreign Corrupt Practices Act. The Department of Justice (DOJ) of the USA enforces the same.

Successor liability is an article of faith among CBMA practitioners as an entity seeking to acquire another entity without being saddled with the liabilities of acquiring such assets. Certain jurisdictions within the USA, for instance, in the state of Massachusetts, prefer to follow a buyer buys assets and liabilities remain with sellers corporations only. However, the word "liabilities" is not an all-pervading generic term. No buying company can escape criminal liability if it takes over the company as a company. Deal making, hence in case the CBMA cannot afford to be ignorant about the past or in the vogue, the criminal liability of the targeted CBMA prospect company.

For centuries, right from the decision of *Fogg V. Blair* (133, U.S. 534, 538, 1890), the Contract Law and the Tort Law made it clear that no one should be held liable for acts, he has not committed or contracts he has not voluntarily entered into. There cannot be any compensation from a third innocent party. Successors are non-liable for acts not committed either in law or in fact. Thus, the previously established principle of successor non-liability environmental culpability coupled with the concept of perpetuality of an impersonal organisation was called for the application of the principle of successor liability to the CBMA aspects of the corporation across the world. When the US companies move to new territories like China or Vietnam or Bangladesh, the legal team of the parent companies must be aware and sensitive to potential FCPA violations and even human rights–related liabilities.

FCPA guidelines also clearly make the acquiring company care about the risk that the acquired company does not involve in fraudulent activities like paying bribes to foreign country officials. Legal due diligence related to the FCPA can begin with some basic inquiries by the acquiring company that do not require information from the target. Such inquiries include among others the following:

a   Whether the target company operates in a country with a history or culture of bribery and corruption,
b   Whether the target company operates in an industry where bribery or corruption is more likely to happen, for example, in the industry in which participants bid for government contracts and
c   Whether there are any publicly reported cases of bribery by the target company or any one of its competitors.

Legal due diligence is simultaneously a formal generic term in general and a specific clear term contextually. In the case of CBMAs, legal due diligence should embody the expert scrutiny of financial, sales, profit, loss, liability, asset, returnables, audits and, liability pending suits in courts of both jurisdictions, third-party assessments and automatic government regulator–generated data/reports. The legal due diligence specifically calls for specialised auditor trials as a specific percentage of randomised transactions in areas that may even remotely smell potential foreign bribery– or kickbacks–related corrupt practices.

Corporate liability, corporate law and accountability report mention that the above steps can protect a company from an anticipated foreign corrupt practice act liability related to cross-border mergers and acquisition activity. They continue to write that if a target company is reluctant to provide this information, the company may infer that there could be an issue related to corrupt practices at the target company. The report further advises that a company engaged in international mergers and acquisition activity with the target company under the scrutiny of the FCPA should not move forward without conducting due legal diligence.

CBMA and Legal Due Diligence in Antitrust/Competition Matters

Competition and antitrust matters are an important part of legal due diligence during cross-border merger activity. The antitrust laws present the same risks as the FCPA in connection with CBMAs in the case of the USA. The antitrust regulations have international applications and they also scrutinise successor liability.

> USA Antitrust Laws do not apply only to the US actors. Instead, their scope is defined by the prescribed conducts effect on the US commerce in the United States, an increasingly low threshold in the global economy, and one that may be less a parent in and merger and acquisition deal than the defined territorial boundaries of operations of a target or primary place of business.[63]
>
> In December 2011 the Department of Justice (DOJ) executed a non-prosecution agreement with Wells Fargo Bank as the successor to the previous Bank in connection with an investigation of bid-rigging and other fraudulent conduct by Wachovia Bank and its employees before its merger with Wells Fargo.[64]
>
> The instant case has been well illustrated across electronic and print media.[65]

Due diligence in the antitrust arena needs necessary care to cover the history or culture of collusion or the anti-competitive behaviour that the target operates in a concentrated industry with few actors and significant barriers to market entry and whether there are any publicly reported cases of collusion or other anti-competitive by the target entity or any one of its direct

46 *Meaning of Mergers and Acquisitions*

competitors. The following five tests are of considerable importance in the case of the due diligence of the antitrust arena:

A   Antitrust complaints program including manuals and policies, administration and the details of administrators.
B   List of competitors to review the list for potential antitrust risks.
C   List of trade associations or advocacy groups consultant's advisors and joint venture details.
D   List of the board of directors, executives and owners of the target company. Legal due diligence by visiting the sites of companies to test whether any pending antitrust investigation is there against the target company in the offing.

The two most important Antitrust Laws and Regulations in the case of the USA are:

1   Hart-Scott-Rodino Act, also called the HSR Act, 1976
2   The Sherman Act, 1890

The HSR Act prohibits parties involved in a deal from transferring beneficial ownership or control before the expiration of statutory-imposed waiting. The US government is to assess the anti-competitive effects if any, of merger or acquisition either domestic or cross-border, and if the two merging companies are competitors, in which case united pre-merger conduct may be a constitutive violation of the Sherman Act which prohibits agreements in restraint of trade, price-fixing bid-rigging, and market allocation.[66]

The Corporate Law and Accountability Report (CLAR) of 2015 advises that one should never share commercial transaction counter-party information without first consulting and such information is twisted—for example, for valuation purposes, create a wall between the due diligence team and the commercial team, either through hiring external advisors or by limiting organisation communication.[67]

The report concludes that legal due diligence is a critical component of any international cross-border mergers and acquisition deals. The US anti-bribery and anti-trust laws present particularly important considerations because of their extraterritorial application and the post-closing spectre of successor liability for companies engaged in CBMA deals. A meaningful due diligence protocol should include enquiry and must be designed to assess the risks posed by the target entities under these legal regimes.[68]

The Sarbanes–Oxley Act, 2002

Following the registration of the securities in the United States, the registrant, its directors and its officers become subject to the ongoing reporting and disclosure obligations, established by the Exchange Act. The registrant, its directors and its officers will also be liable for the mis-statements and omissions in reports filed with SEC. Besides, following the registration of its securities in the United States, the registrant, its directors and its officers will become subject to the ongoing corporate governance, certification and other requirements set out in the Sarbanes–Oxley Act of 2002.

"Other specific laws of the United States include the Foreign Investment and National Security Act of 2007 and the Exon-Florio amendment to the all-powerful Trade and Competitiveness Act of 1988. CFIUS, the Committee on Foreign Investment in the United States of America, was given the broad authority to investigate and recommend a Presidential Veto on transactions that threaten the national security or public tranquillity in the United States or on issues involving the critical infrastructure in the United States or the critical technology assets in the United States. The most sensitive corporations involved in the domain of national security include defence, aerospace, utilities, transportation, computer and electronics manufacturing, scientific and technical services, information technology and telecommunications, increasing focus on data privacy, prevention of economic espionage and protection of intellectual property rights, with potential military applications.

The governmental review is triggered and permission may be prohibited in the following areas:

1   Maritime vessels engaged in domestic trade or coastal shipping,
2   Broadcasting,
3   Federal mining leases,
4   Banks are bank holding companies,
5   Primary dealers in the US government securities,
6   Air careers with us domestic routes and
7   Nuclear energy facilities.

By following the above-described arenas, one can surely argue that while the United States of America approves a liberalised regime in cross-border mergers and acquisitions, at the same time, the USA does not allow any compromise or dilution in matters of security or dominant position which may ultimately lead to the foreign control of the domestic affairs. As early as July 2014, the Government of the United States imposed sectoral sanctions that limit certain sectors of the Russian economy from gaining access to the capital and debt markets of the USA, as well as to the US technology and expertise in the energy sector. In the year 2017, the US Congress approved sanctions against Russia which were found to target persons and entities that undermine the cybersecurity of the United States of America. The US Congress prohibits any interaction or transaction with Russian defence and intelligence agencies, and also any propensity or potential to invest in Russia's export pipelines. Until April 19, 2018, such sanctions have not been implemented even though they are on the anvil."[69]

48 *Meaning of Mergers and Acquisitions*

The country-specific pattern is common in countries and similar is the case in the USA. Public utilities, insurance, gaming, banking, media, transportation and mining are some of them. Section 14 (e)[70] of the Exchange Act prohibits material mis-statements and omissions and fraudulent, deceptive or manipulative acts or practices in connection with any activity related to cross-border mergers and acquisitions. Section 11[71] of the Securities Act reprimands any fraudulent behaviour. "The Dodd-Frank Wall Street Reform and Consumer Protection Act also called Dodd-Frank Act,"[72] among others, includes in itself,

> number of provisions that clarify the enforcement authority of Security Exchange Commission (SEC) with respect to the violations of security laws, including, clarifying that liability including person's liability, both, joint and several, for violations of Exchange Act, providing the Security Exchange Commission (SEC) with authority to improve monetary penalties in administrative cease- and -desist proceedings against any person, and modifying the extraterritorial reach of the SEC to on force and the anti-fraud provisions of the federal Security Laws so long as there exists significant conduct in the US or effect on the US security market or some other combination.[73]

The Dodd–Frank Act

> The Trump administration tried to amend the Dodd-Frank Act and got its version passed by the US House of Representatives in the year 2017 but the US Senate has not given its support and hence the original Dodd-Frank Act remains in effect.[74]

The promotion of competitiveness has been an essential feature of the CBMA. The antitrust law, in essence, aims at the prevention of monopolistic tendencies. The main purpose is to avoid status quo its tendencies to stay put in the comfort zone, while competition is knocking at the door. Competition promotion is a win-win strategy for all stockholders since competition allows every company to remain alert towards outside trends and to adequately stress calibrate course correction to stay afloat and relevant. The Hart–Scott–Rodino Act (1976) mandates the issue of notices in connection with voting security. The HSR mandates cover assets over unequivocal thresholds to prevent monopolistic disposition.

Non-compliance with the HSR rules invites penalties to the tune of US $40 every day. Law is both intention and implementation. The HSR Act fulfils the above dual criteria in being the unique law in the world, both as a policy and its implementation. It adds the tertiary dimension too, namely inspiration and the fourth dimension of inclusiveness.

"In the United States, especially in the state of Delaware, there is a short form merger provision which makes a company taking over another company if that company has more than 90% of the shares with it. The conduct of investment banking advisors in mergers and acquisition transactions, in situations where a typical advisor may be having links with both the target and the acquiring company, which, in other words, can be called a conflict of interest, and yet continues with such process of advising without any disclosure to the client, is also considered to be part of the Judicial Review and the Delaware Supreme Court.

In a recent verdict, the Supreme Court of Delaware upheld the finding of the Court of Chancery that is sell-side financial advisor aided and conspired with the target board's violation of fiduciary duties, among other things, failing to disclose conflict arising from the financial advisor's attempt to be part of the buyer's financial group."[75] [76]

"There is no necessity in the United States that both the parties to the CBMA consulting the employees of the acquired company concerning the potential of the merger in terms of their pension treasury are stakeholders pay or even the very concept of the merger, there are certain States whose local rules permit or require the board of directors of the acquired company to consider the interest of the employees of the acquired company while approving a merger or recommending offer.[77]

Form F-4 of the Securities Act of 1933 of the USA makes any company mandatorily fill it to disclose all essential facts about the securities being offered and about the company itself. Through this form, the SEC fulfils its main objective of being transparent and accessible to all investors. If the Securities Act of 1933 is "Truth in Securities," the SEC itself conducts a foreign audit through form F-4. Clearance of any proxy material by the SEC before it is sent through the mail to shareholders is mandatory due to the regulations of the SEC.

The Federal Trade Commission of the Department of Justice in the USA makes passing the following tests it mandatory for determining the requirement under HSR filling. They are (i) the Commerce test (ii) the US $ 50 million size of Transaction Test and (iii) the excess US $ 50 million to 200 million size of Person Test. These tests are applicable to domestic and CBMAs within and outside the USA, respectively.

National Security in USA and CBMAs

The Foreign Investment and National Security Act of 2007 and the Exon–Florio amendment to the omnibus Trade and Competitiveness Act of 1988 permit the President of the United States or any one of his nominees to investigate and intervene in stopping transactions, such as tender offer services, which could result in the foreign control of persons engaged in US commerce, if such control threatens to impair the national security of the United States of America. The critical infrastructure and critical technology assets are deemed to be very important ingredients of national security. Any attempt at foreign control in the above two areas not only compromises the national security in the short run but will derail the sovereignty of the United States of America. CFIUS is the authorised agency to investigate any prospective foreign acquire in terms of the dealings that such acquisition of a company where the products, technology or funds from an acquired US business might be transferred to the sanctioned country as a result of the acquisition. A review of a transaction is commenced either by voluntary notice sent by the acquiring company or by any agency notice if the US government has reason to believe that the acquisition may harm the US national security.

The preliminary investigation and review need to be completed within a time of 30 days. The CFIUS agency may be granted a time of another 45 days if any further investigation is needed. The matter is then referred to the President of the United States who has 15 days to determine the recommendation of the organisation, whether the transaction poses risk to the US national security. If the notice is not given by the above-said organisation, this may result in the unwinding of the entire transaction by the Government of the United States.

CIFUS and the CBMA

Post 26/11 and the 2001 national security incident, CFIUS has been increasingly conducting rigorous investigations in many cross-border transactions to ensure a full-fledged fool-proof, unmistaken, integrated and impregnable security system for the United States of America. This investigating agency received many complaints from the stakeholders within the United States of America regarding Chinese investors' activity, and hence transactions in the information and communication sectors, as well as transactions involving Chinese investors in any sector, whatsoever have received more than optimum attention from this investigative agency. This organisation makes and compels both the target and the acquiree, especially in the CBMA activity, to openly confess their entire intentions and secure a certificate from them that they will not cause or pose any national security threat and such confessions are very minutely scrutinised by the experts in this organisation. "Prospective buyers and sellers of sensitive businesses should be aware of the options available to allocate risk, including mitigation covenants, pre emptied divestitures, and reverse termination fees."[78]

The House of Representatives and the Senate of the USA in the year 2017 introduced a legislation by a bipartisan group of legislators that could significantly expand the jurisdiction, filing requirements and timelines of CFIUS. This legislation is famously known as the Foreign Investment Risk Review Modernisation Act of 2017 and is vital in protecting from the threats that evolve from vested interests . The main aim and vision of this act is the maintenance of American leadership in certain critical technology industries inimical to American national security and its critical infrastructure. FIRRMA is yet to be passed. However, when passed, there would be many additional types of transactions that would be brought under the umbrella of the organisation, CFIUS. Observers always lay their faith in the acuteness and the power of investigation in the instauration of CIFUS in ensuring security for the industries in the USA and in maintaining the leadership of the USA in the areas of new technologies and infrastructure.

In the case of the CBMA, if the target company is a public limited company, it is beneficial to the acquiring company because the acquiring company can have access to all the reports filed by the target company with the SEC. Quarterly reports are vital to observe and measure the progress of any company. Companies are now habituated to the quarterly briefing and offer next quarter "guidance." The ability of any company to meet or surpass its previous guidance is measured four times a year and a consolidated yearly report is thus made without the scope of any confusion. The SEC of the USA compels all companies to file with SEC the above reports. SEC makes the vital information of all the above reports widely accessible to investing public democratically. "All reports, registrations, statements, and proxy statements are all available on the website of Security Exchange Commission."[79]

Clayton and the HSR Acts and Amendments

The principal agents of mergers and acquisitions in the cross-border arena in the United States of America are first the Federal Trade Commission (FTC) and second the Department of Justice (DOJ).

> They both have common action and they control the transactions especially during premature reporting obligations. The notification must be submitted to both the agencies and both of them may conduct a preliminary review. Under an inter-agency clearance agreement, is there (FTC) or (DOJ) will be opening a formal investigation into any particular merger as per the need.[80]

The main legal provision is mentioned vide the section of the Clayton Act. It is codified under caption ISUSC sec.18. Sec. 7 of the Clayton Act is to mandate the institutions to watch for violations of fair competition environment and to punish any attempts of monopoly in any sphere or sector. The Domestic Law provisions in relation to domestic mergers and acquisitions apply in totem to the CBMA cases in the USA. There is no special preventive law in antitrust or prevention of monopoly in the USA. Monopoly prevention and competition promotion are similar concerns in both domestic mergers and CBMAs. The HSR Act mandates pre-merger notifications with a certain period of waiting for a certain type of transaction.

> In other words, the domestic law-related competition regulations apply to the CBMA also in the case of the United States. The sectoral regulator in the case of sectors like banking, communications, transportation, and utilities functions independently within their allocated sectorial specialty under the overall guidance of the Federal Trade Commission (FTC) and Department of Justice (DOJ). Public interest is the predominant underlying ideology in all the above activities. In the United States even acquiring a minority sold holding amounts to merger and it is required to follow the guidelines of Federal Trade Commission and Department of Justice this is as per the provisions of the HSR notification.[81]

52 Meaning of Mergers and Acquisitions

Joint ventures are also subject to the rules and regulations mentioned in the FTC and DOJ. In this special case of foreign mergers and acquisitions, if either of them has substantial assets in the land of the United States of America, the following exemptions are allowed by the HSR amendment.

1 Acquisition of cash,
2 Acquisition of goods,
3 Acquisition of reality in the ordinary course of business,
4 Acquisition of bonds,
5 Acquisition of motor gauges,
6 Acquisition of similar instruments like modernisation bonds,
7 Transfer to or from a federal agency, state and political subdivision,
8 Certain acquisitions by or from foreign governments within their jurisdiction,
9 Acquisitions solely for investment, define to mean the interest of no more than 10% in an issue or and interpreted to mean essentially held passively,
10 Certain enumerated classification subject to the approval of supervision sectoral regulator,
11 Acquisitions in connection with stock splits and prorated evidence,
12 Set and acquisitions by institutional investors such as banks and broker-dealers in the ordinary course of business,
13 Acquisitions of convertible voting securities,
14 Certain acquisitions by creditors upon foreclosure or default or in a Bonafide workout and
15 Acquisition by gift or intestate succession.

Specified time limits and time frames for security clearances and scrutiny of the merger by the major authorities are there, and hence, there is no delay in the process in the USA which is not the case in many emerging markets, especially when compared to the Indian situation.

> Normally every stage is completed within two weeks and at the maximum, it can extend up to 45 days that too upon the request of either of the parties. Normally the notifications are made within two weeks and roughly 95% of the transactions receive clearance within 30 days of filing.[82]

There is a provision for super time clearance in the case of time-sensitive sympathy or because of the present serious competitive complexity. Common initiatives include providing early informal notification to the agency staff and different notifications beyond the typical filing date to the agency staff to conduct preliminary analysis without the time pressure withdrawing a field notification and refilling it to double the initial waiting time to the staff of the agency and voluntarily providing competitive information going beyond the bare-bones HSR notification requirements. Cutting across the time here is judgemental and discretionary and depends on the skill of the lawyers.

Normally, a fee of US $45,000–280,000 depending on the size of the transaction is required to be paid to the court. All US government rules and regulations are available on the following websites of the Department of Justice.

1   www.ftc.gov and
2   www.justice.gov.

Impressionable mercantile information is a product of the CBMA process. The US institutes protect their commercial security except under the following three specific contexts.

1   It will be disclosed in an administrative or judicial proceeding,
2   It may be disclosed to the US Congress and
3   It may be disclosed through a notice of the grant of elimination of the HSR waiting period.

It needs to be published in the federal register, on the FTC websites and the FTC Twitter feed. The HSR process in the United States is not an approval process but only a clearance process. If the FTC or the Department of Justice does not have any objection within the statutory waiting, then the parties may proceed with the operation of the law for CBMAs. On the other hand, if the FTC and the DOJ grant early termination of the statutory waiting enabling the parties to proceed at the time of the grant, then most of the transaction process can proceed without any obstruction/objection from any agency. The US legal provisions in remedial standards to different processes are not discriminatory and all nations are equally treated with fairness and transparency. In other words, it means that most of the rules are common to domestic mergers and acquisitions as well as CBMAs.

Many proposals are pending before the US Congress to make the CBMA process more simplified. One such law pending approval before the US Congress is the Standard Merger and Acquisition Reviews Through Equal Rules (SMARTER) Act.

It is interesting to note that the Chinese anti-competition framework came very late, which was in the year 2008. It is called the anti-monopoly law.

> The basic framework for the US antitrust law as it relates to Cross Border mergers begin with the Sherman Act in 1890. The Sherman Act prohibits all combination, in restraint of trade or commerce this several States or with Foreign Nations.[83]
>
> The Clayton Act and the Federal Trade Commission Act of the years 1914 are the empowered authorities for merger enforcement. The HSR

amendment through the Improvements Act was brought in the year 1976. The Anti Trust division is part of the executive branch of the Federal Trade Commission. Horizontal merger guidelines are under review and the process continues.[84]

The Committee of Foreign Investment in the United States (CFIUS) has been specially constituted to take care of the emerging challenges to the national security of the United States of America. The beginning of the above body dates back to the year 1975 through an executive order of President Carter.[85]

Initially, there was the Defence Production Act (DPA) of 1950 and there was an amendment to it later through the Exon–Florio Act. The US government's framework was given to the above body in the year 1988. Treasury regulations, Congress amendments and executive orders give potency to the law. The Foreign Investment and National Security Act of 2007 gave maximum power to the Committee of Foreign Investment in the United States (CFIUS). CFIUS draws its members from 16 various departments which include, department of state, defence, justice, energy, homeland security sector and the US trade representative.

"The intelligence community is represented by the Director of the National Intelligence as a non-voting ex officio member."[86] Kevin Grand Valley of the *New York Times* wrote on March 5, 2018, that the Treasury Secretary of the United States, Stephen Munchin, who heads the CFIUS, is likely to decide on the hostile takeover bid of Qualcomm by its Singaporean rival Broadcom. This committee investigates the measures that could result in the control of American business by a foreign individual or a company, judging whether the deals could threaten the national interest. According to the *New York Times*, the committee is to decide whether the deal for Qualcomm, whose semiconductors will be used in the next-generation ultrafast wireless networks known as 5G, would pose a risk to national security. It appears to be the first time the committee has to sign on a deal before it has finalised a signal that CFIUS may play a more prominent role in the Trump administration's America's first policymaking. The committee is led by the US Treasury Secretary always. Normally, such deal decisions are not publicly disclosed nor do they even acknowledge that a party to a merger has submitted a deal to review. It has also the authority to intervene and review pending or completed transactions, without being asked by any of the companies, if the members of the committee think that the deal could raise national security concerns. The committee reports are normally sent to the President, who suspends or prohibits the deal. Cristiano, head of global mergers and acquisitions at JP Morgan Chase, feels that CFIUS is the number one weapon in the Trump administration's protectionist arsenal and the ultimate regulatory bazooka. President Reagan in the 1980s compelled Fairchild to cancel the deal with Fujitsu, a Japanese company. *The New York Times* further mentions that China is a frequent element in the CFIUS reviews.

Specific Examples

The investigative journalist of the *New York Times* further mentions an example of the Money Gram and ANT Financial deal. ANT Financial is a Chinese company, while Money Gram is a Dallas-based money transfer finance company. The deal collapsed in January 2018. The deal was for US $1,200 million. The coup came despite a charm offensive by Jack Ma, the Chinese tycoon who controls the financial markets and who had visited president-elect Donald Trump at the Trump Tower and announced his pleasure to create one million American jobs.

The second example is the Canyon Bridge Capital (CBC) and Lattice. CBC is a well-known capital equity firm (CE). CBC desired to acquire a lattice chip-making firm based in Portland, Organ. As a CE, CBC received investable funds from a conglomerate which included a venture capital fund (VCF) company. It is partly owned by a Chinese government–backed front-line company. Lattice objected and preferred the right to appeal to the president, offering to resolve national security concerns. The then President of the USA, Mr Donald Trump, firmly blocked the deal in September 2017.

The Broadcom–Qualcomm's deal does not involve China-based companies. However, the concern is that it could undermine the ability of the United States to compete with China in the race for telecommunication supremacy. The members of the CFIUS desired that Broadcom would take a private equity style approach if it is successful in acquiring Qualcomm. Ipso-Facto, this CBMA would have redirected the focus from long-term research development investment to a mere short-term game. While the United States has remained a standard-bearer in mobile technology, the committee of foreign investment in United States noted that China would likely compete robustly to fill any void left by the USA. The CFIUS rightly observed that by preventing the hostile takeover by the Chinese front-line companies, the USA retained its predominant position in the strategic technology area.

Senator John Cornyn (Texas) of the Republican Party and Senator Dianne Feinstein (California) of the Democratic Party introduced a bill that could compel companies with foreign ties to the list of those reviewed each year by the CFIUS and provide more funding to deal with the same. In the House of Representatives, a similar bill was introduced by Robert Pittenger, a Republican from North Carolina. The CFIUS would be emboldened to bring into its jurisdiction issues related to joint ventures, sales of minority stake real estate deals for property near military bases and other sensitive facilities. Mr Cronyn said,

By exploiting gaps in the existing CFIUS review process, potential adversaries such as China have been effectively degrading our countries military technology by acquiring and otherwise investing in US companies. The reaction of the Chinese was on the predictable line in that the Chinese commerce ministry stated in the year 2017 September, that country should not push protectionism through security reviews.[87]

Traditionally, many of the developing countries which are also called emerging countries have issues with relations to the regulation of the economy and with relations to restricted competition and many of them are found to be closer to foreign entry because of the fear of colonialism.[88]

Comparison between the USA and India

The Indian tax law is a continuation of the past, a curious innovation in the present and an extrapolation of benchmark practices of others in the future.

> In a challenging economy, making every rupee count is part of the corporate DNA. At most companies, planning plays an important role in achieving goal one -namely drawing increasing attention is the issue of economic nexus. The legal concept of nexus determines whether a business has enough of a presence in a country to become subject to its taxes, the extent of physical presence in a country that triggers a company's tax liability in that country. The economic nexus means that the tax nexus exists whenever a business has delivered or derived revenue or income from a customer in a country, the business has no property, employees, or other significant physical presence in the territory. Globally, tax in corporations is based on the concept of economic nexus is gaining significance.[89]

Taxation from the sources as well as from the residence basis has become a custom in the twentieth century, especially when companies are expanding their businesses across international borders. This feature of double taxation was not a welcome step for many developing countries, and therefore, the League of Nations, as well as its successor the United Nations and the Organisation of Economic Cooperation and Development (OECD), are responsible for nearly 2,500 bilateral income tax treaties which make any country to avoid double taxation. Pure residence taxation is not feasible for the following reasons. First, countries will never part with their right to collect tax from foreigners doing business within their territory. Second, residence-based taxation will evaporate revenues for the least.

A section of commentators from academics of developing countries favour pure source taxation as a viable option.

> The major problem with this option is that it enables investors especially transnational corporations to play countries against each other to obtain the lowest base tax rate - the system of tax savings arbitration. Competition already exists for active business income. The semiconductor chip manufacturer, Intel, e.g. legally avoids paying tax on any one of its income outside the US by obtaining tax holidays from the various countries where it located its facilities.[90]

Controlled foreign corporation regimes are there in the United States and the OECD countries also introduced the same to combat tax avoidance devices.

Such regimes enable the residence country to compare the parking of the foreign income in a subsidiary company or other entity formed in a low tax haven by taxing its income directly as part of the income of its parent or owners in the ultimate country of the residence.[91]

Tax havens harm international trade and many studies confirmed how diversionary parking of invertible surplus profits evades tax in the name of avoidance of tax. OECD, the Organisation of Economic Development and Co-operation took an international initiative called Domain International Initiative (DII) for global tax avoidance, a right step against vicious tax operations. DII strengthens residence and source taxation.

An effective means to bring this about would be to impose withholding taxes at source on payments to non-cooperative countries. The OECD has also tried to combat preferential tax regimes, defined as those aiming at having to attract mobile capital with no genuine business activity.[92]

The I.T. Act of India, 1961 has relevant provisions under sec. 2(31) which taxes the total income of a person. Here person includes company and vide sec. 2(23A). The company also signifies a company of foreign origin. Section 6(4) of the Act lays down that a company unless it is an Indian company or unless it is controlled or managed entirely from India, cannot be said to be resident in India. A foreign company, which is not wholly controlled or managed in India is, therefore, a non-resident so far as residential status under the Act is concerned.[93]

The total income of non-resident Indians or non-resident persons whose tax returns are assessed includes the incomes, accruing or origins from India or deemed to arise from the Indian nation. It also infers any income accepted or deemed to be accepted by or in the name of the company of foreign origin. This elementary analysis makes it clear that under the IT Act, so far as foreign companies are concerned, the taxable unit is a foreign company and not its branch or PE in India, even though the taxability of such foreign companies is confined to (i) income which accumulates or flows in India or is deemed to accumulate or flow in India and (ii) income which is accepted or deemed accepted by in the name of the company of foreign origin.

In the case of CBMAs, contracts are signed and executed at places of non-residents of either the owners of the business or their subsidiaries as a normal way of practice and it creates more often than not many legal complications. There is no special provision in the Indian Income Tax Act, 1961, (IT Act, 1961), for the taxation of the permanent establishment of multinational/foreign companies. There are specifically mentioned categories of income that are accrued to a foreign company and such income is taxable as per the provisions of the Indian I.T. Act, 1961. According to informed observers, it is ironic that while the Indian IT Act deals with the scope of income deemed to accrue or arise in India, at great length and visualising

58 *Meaning of Mergers and Acquisitions*

possibly all sorts of deeming fictions, there is not much elaboration about the scope of income which accrues or arises in India in the hands of a tax entity which has a fiscal domicile abroad. The doctrine of taxing based on economic nexus was accepted by the Supreme Court of India.

> In a case, Supreme Court held that under Section 5 read with section 9 of the Income Tax Act,1961 the income accruing or arising in India, an income which accrues arises to the foreign enterprises in India can only be such portion of the income accruing a diverging to such foreign enterprises is attributed to its business carried out in India.[94]

Taxable income accruing out of off-share supply of equipment or service-connected thereto by a foreign company is termed territorial nexus. Since the equipment was supplied during the course of a turnkey project on Indian soil by a foreign company from a foreign nation, the income accrued thus is not taxable. Justice S.B. Sinha observed that the contract was executed in India and it happened entirely into a contract on Indian soil. However, since such a contract was to be complemented abroad, the income that accrues to the contractor from such an extension abroad would be taxable in India.

Historically, capital knows no boundaries or geographical limitations. The institutions that belong to the financial sector are supervised, regulated and maintained by independent regulators in most cases, and, in some cases, like the United Kingdom and Japan by a single regulator. In India, it is SEBI.

International Law

More than 250 research studies were carefully studied, reviewed, consolidated and integrated and the following valuable findings were made. The research reports studied covered International Law regarding cross-border mergers, international business, strategic management finance and economics. From the above studies, the following vital observations emerge:

The seven most vital interconnected paired criteria emerged:

i   Environments dealing with a market of finance and macroeconomic factors.
ii Environments regulation authorities and institutional interplay.
iii Environment dealing with political manoeuvring and dishonest fraudulent extortionist.
iv Environment with taxation policy and tax collection systems.
v   Environment dealing with guidelines regarding valuations and sanders of accounting.
vi Environment dealing with different cutlers.
vii Environment dealing with different time/terrain zones different geographical features.

It is naturally inferred from the above 250 studies that areas of rule of law and with the presence of institutions, holding contractual enforcement and equality and optimally functioning judiciary attracted more CBMAs within that region.

If other factors remain the same, a company from a developed country will prefer to take over a company from a developing country through the CBMA route, despite the socio-political-cultural and economic-political democratic differences, if and only if, the diligence confirms better market size, opportunity, earning cheap labour, cheap raw materials, natural parts and weak enforcement of human rights, labour laws, pollution laws and manageable political leadership. In other words, the East India Company still exists, in search of colonies through CBMAs.

CBMA and BRICS (Brazil, Russia, India, China and South Africa)

The ninth BRICS (Brazil, Russia, India, China and South Africa) meeting of the heads of States/Governments was held at Xiamen, China and India's Prime Minister (PM) asserted the emergence of India into the privileged group of the most transparent and efficient globally respected economies of the world. "PM Modi said that the BRICS Business Council played a vital role in giving practical shape to the vision of the bloc's partnership."[95] "The partnerships you have forged and the networks you have created are energizing the economic growth stories in each BRICS country,"[96] he said, "while praising the council for entering into a memorandum of understanding with the New Development Bank (NDB), the multilateral development bank established by the BRICS member states."[97]

Honourable Prime Minister Modi also voiced his appreciation that the BRICS Business Council has matching priorities of trade and investment facilitation, promoting skills development, infrastructure development, small and medium enterprises (SME) development, e-commerce and digital economy.

The Indian PM further assorted that all-around support would be extended to the rating agency of BRICS in the fields of energy, new industries and digitalisation. The PM stressed upon the common intention of advancement of greater scope for commerce and co-operation in investment environment promotion.

Economic diplomacy at the summit level is taken seriously both by bureaucrats and by businessmen as the following meeting by the heads of the state and the government clearly shows.

"The council's meeting was attended by host Chinese President Xi Jinping, Russian President Vladimir Putin, Brazilian President Michel Temer, and South African President Jacob Zuma."[98] Bilateral and multilateral trade decisions to the tune of billions of dollars were facilitated during the above meeting.

CBMA and International Trade

The USA has constantly occupied the largest share as the following figures indicate, followed by the United Kingdom. While the USA represented the highest value of transactions to the level of about US $271.721 billion and then shortly tumbled to US $123.934 billion. In 2001, this may be attributed to the crisis in the USA which is often termed as the 9/11 crisis. The United Kingdom surpassed the USA between 2004 and 2007 again the reasons being the financial instability in the USA. The United Kingdom is not that severely affected when compared to the other countries in the subprime crisis or other currency crises in the markets. One can safely conclude that, as per the research report, the subprime crisis that happened in the year 2007 and 2008 is a banking crisis and a financial crisis that resulted in an opportunity that was available for Brazil, Russia, India and China and that the maximum advantage was reaped by China and India. It was not for nothing that one should mention here that China also had the Beijing Olympics in the year 2008 which was coincident with the world subprime crisis and China was in a double benefit arena in the year 2008 while India was too because of its political stability and for a large part, being scam free till the year 2008 (Figure 1.13).

36.50 million Indians filed income tax returns in the financial year 2016–2017. Only 0.55 million of them paid income tax of more than Rs 0.5 million. In other words, 1.5% of people paid 57% of income tax and the remaining 98.5% of people paid 33% of the income tax. Indian population is 1300 million and the adult population would be 1,100 million. The unaccounted money is untaxed money and stashed away money. A level playing field demands equality in taxation.

When one plots a trend line for the CBMAs and purchases, represented in the number of deals for the United States of America, the United Kingdom,

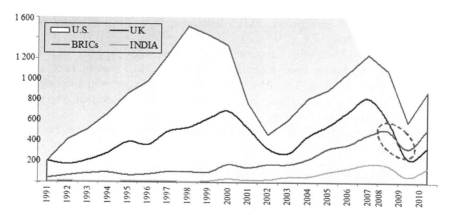

Figure 1.13 Number of Cross-border M&A by Region/Economy of the Purchaser, 1991–2010.

Source: BRICS summit press release.

the BRIC group and India, as it is represented in the figure above, one finds that US firms likely report the highest number of teams followed by the United Kingdom since 1991. Several Indian firms have initiated to internationalise their products and services since the year 2000 and changes are noticed remarkably during 2006, 2007 and 2008. We can also make similar observations for the BRIC group as we have already mentioned earlier that the subprime crisis in the year 2008 and the banking crisis that happened in the year 2008 abroad were a big opportunity for the BRIC countries in general and India and China in particular. The BRIC group has marked improvements in both US and UK since 2008 as we can see in the figure mention above.

The Chinese and the Indian multinational corporations acquired resources and skills to lead the world economy in terms of parental foreign affiliations and also in the number of outbound deals. That is to affirm that the Indian and Chinese main multinational corporations acquiring and establishing mergers and acquisitions abroad. One must mention here that this is pre-Company Act, 2013 and outbound deals were not recognised for the domestic companies. This was the case for Indian multinational corporations and not for Indian domestic companies. This change has been very relevantly brought out by making a new act and making Sec. 234 of Company Act 2013 in April 2017 and thus paving the way for Indian domestic companies also to acquire assets abroad (Figure 1.14).

Since 1991, the United States of America contributed the highest value to the world economy except in the years 1999, 2000 and 2007 wherein the United Kingdom outperformed in the market. From the graph shown here, it is clear that multinational corporations in the United States invest more amount of equity in cross-country deals which means they acquire firms by transferring equity capital. However, US bank lending norms and investment

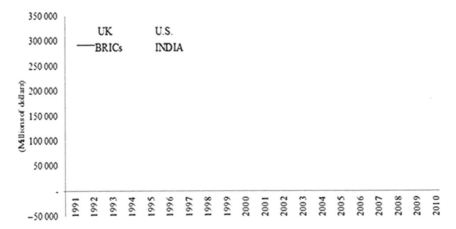

Figure 1.14 Values of Cross-border M&A by Region/Economy of Purchase, 1991–2010.
Source: BRICS summit press release.

guidelines are more flexible, easier and even motivate firms to participate in international mergers and acquisition negotiations. This is in contrast to the BRIC group MNCs which invested significantly in outbound deals in 1999.

The actual growth commenced from the year 2004 for the gap of time lag gap of five years as the result started reaching in the year 2006. As such, BRIC outperformed the United Kingdom but it declined in the year 2007 and surpassed both the USA and the United Kingdom from 2008 onwards. From the figures above one can safely conclude that India alone overtakes the United Kingdom in the years 2009 and 2010 significantly." However, most of the deal amount was contributed by the Chinese firms except in the year 2007 because Chinese MNCs were engaged to overcome their competitive disadvantage."[99] In the year 2007, Indian firms invested US $2900 million. This was a phenomenal growth, representing 333% compared to the previous year. One would notice that the BRIC group has predominantly started pushing international investment since 2003 whereas India from the year 2005. Thus, there is a gap of two years. However, India overcame the difficulties and is witnessing an improvement.

Major examples of Indian acquisitions abroad include Tata Steels' acquisition of Corus for US $12,200 million. Hindalco's acquisition of Novelis for US $6000 million and Suzlon Energy's purchase of 33.85% of the equity in RE Power for US $1700 million.

Indices and Ratios

One proxy variable that shows the effectiveness of the country in terms of its reformed policies in acquiring assets abroad and thus having a robust economy is the figure of how many Parent Corporations (PC) that country has and how many Foreign Affiliates (FA) that country has.

According to the figures in the year 2010, we have in the world economy around 1,03,353 Parent Companies and 8,86,143 Foreign Affiliates. Henceforth, they are referred to as PCs and FAs. Thus, for every PC, if there are 8.5 FAs available in various countries, then the ratio of FA to PC is equivalent to 8.5. Developed economies represent the highest number of PCs which is around 70% compared to 30% of the developing economies.

In the case of FAs, however, developing economies represent 58% and the remaining is shared by the developed countries. BRIC groups to PC percentage of the world economy shows that the BRIC group owns around 20% of world PCs and 50% of world FAs. Asia's share of PCs is around 44% and in the case of FAs, it is 55%. China itself alone contributes to 11.6% of PCs of the world and 49% of the FAs of the world.

Many informed watchers of India, for instance, Mr Changyong Ree (Mr C. Ree) of the International Monetary Fund (IMF), whose work experience is in the field of multilateral lending surveillance in the Asia-Pacific region, state that after decades of liberalisation and adequate experience of economic references, the key to the success of India lies in implementation.

China is much ahead of many countries put together in Asia and also among the BRIC countries. For instance, India has only 1% of PCs and 0.23% of FAs, Brazil has 0.2% of PCs and 0.5% of FAs and Russia has 0.11% of PCs and 0.24% of FAs. However, China has got 11.6% of PCs and 49% of FAs. All put together, one can say that China is almost 11 times bigger than India and 55 times bigger than Brazil and almost 100 times bigger than Russia in terms of PCs and also in terms of FAs. Thus, BRIC countries' contribution, summarised as (11.61 + 1 + 0. 2410), is less than 14% as of and has been already figured. However, BRICS when clubbed with other Asian countries, the figure comes to around 24%.

The Director of the IMF Asia-Pacific region also added that

> India's growth rate is higher than China's growth rate. Many countries are looking at India, whether India can be an growth leader than China in recent decades. India has already many good plans. There is much, but not as much progress.[100]

Foreign investors are uncomfortable with this scenario. The IMF too expected the return of the National Democratic Alliance (NDA) Government post-2019 parliamentary poll but was expecting that structural reforms of the government would continue and was apprehensive that electoral compulsions may derail the structural reforms. A structurally reformed India can make a positive impact in the global financial world at a time when the western economies were suffering from financial crises. It is for the Chinese dragon's growth engine that kept the world's financial furnaces on. India's elephantine run can come to the rescue of these financial furnaces, when the Chinese dragon is dragged down due to recessionary pressures. India needs to open up from domestic inward looking attitude to exploiting emerging global opportunities. The awakened Indian elephant can be a global asset. Mr C. Ree continues to observe,

> Several important reforms have been tried and implemented and that India is a good example of having compared with other Asian countries and global experiences. Running out of cash and GST implementation has some problems here and there but one should look at the bigger picture .GST implementation can help India's development and India can become more integrated. Double-digit growth is a good ambition but when it is pushed with stimulus policy it could damage the economy. Despite the recent scandal in the Indian banking sector, the Indian banking sector is not facing any financial crisis. Indian banks especially the state-owned banks, need to address the non-performing asset issue and the balance sheet. So that's why we believe that the Modi government's effort to recapitalize state-owned banks is a very important issue because without having a very strong balance sheet, their lending ability will be limited. Then it would be very difficult to support a 7% growth rate.[101]

64 *Meaning of Mergers and Acquisitions*

Loans are essential for a growing economy and healthy bank profits are essential for the same. Healthy balance sheets of the banks are possible when banks overcome from Non-Portable Assets (NPAs) syndrome. Recapitalisation and the 2021 FY budget initiative of BAD BANK are great initiatives.

Chinese FAs are dominating the universe through their PCs that represent nearly 50% while India's share is still not more than 2% in both cases. This shows how lagging Indian companies are in comparison to China when compared to the PC and FA figures in the world.

China is a neighbouring country and China attained independence two years later than India, in 1949. However, China has gone very well ahead of India, and China will become the number one economy in the world followed by the USA, and the 3rd or 4th position may likely come to India.

The BRIC Group has varying unequal shares in terms of overall contribution. The share of India is at the least figure of a mere 05.38 %. A decade-old research report of the year 2011, by researchers Santangelo and Meyer, indicated that emerging countries within this group have a unique contribution. China is the only country owning a maximum number of PCs and FAs in each segment such as the world economy, developing economies, Asia and the BRIC group. The PC and FA share of both the US and UK combined is significantly lower than that of China but higher than those of India, Brazil and Russia.

Chinese PCs represent the highest number of FAs in the world, which is around 434,248 out of 800,000. China owns 12,000 PCs and their FAs are at 434,248, which is around 36 times. China will be the leading economy, followed by the US and UK economies and if the trend continues, it must have been the reality. Indian companies, if one goes by this reasoning can find out that India lags due to the following reasons: first, the main causes are the rules and regulations and laws relating to foreign operations. Second, there are complicated processes of acquisitions and collaboration. Third, the environment of cross-border mergers is heavily regulated even after the implementation of the new economic policy in the year 1991 onwards when compared to China, Brazil and Russia.

Brazil and Russia have the highest number of FAs, with 18 times more PCs compared to India. Indian FAs are only 1.89 times of their PCs. Indian companies own less than 1% of PCs and Indian FAs are less than 2% of the whole world. Therefore, Indian policymakers should make an important study and adopt deregulation relating to international operations and transactions. Then, Indian MNCs would get the opportunity to understand reality. Indian-owned MNCs in the world become a virtual cycle by creating more foreign exchange, more employment opportunities to skilled Indians, more remittance from abroad and hence more foreign exchange. More foreign exchange means more surplus investible capital which in turn means more Indian MNCs that create more employment opportunities. On the other hand, if India remains a mere consumer, a mere market, a mere supplier of basic raw materials, a mere banana republic, India, far from being a proud example of a decolonised giant, becomes a written symbol of the colonial cesspool. The choice is between a competent producer and a complaint consumer.

One can safely say here that FAs help PCs to access the global market, technical workforce, technology, culture and ideas, etc. The global economic crisis depressed the Chinese march in terms of CBMAs. There was another opportunity given to the rest of the BRIC group apart from China, namely Brazil, India and Russia among the 25 countries that contributed more than 1% to the world economy through CBMA sales and 22 countries accounted for CBMA purchase. The USA is the leading country which has contributed the highest number of deals for sales as a percentage of the world economy at 17%, followed by the United Kingdom at 10%, Germany at 7% and Canada at 5% each. Similarly, for the ranks of purchase, the BRIC group contributes to sales and purchases. Brazil sales is at 1.6% and purchases is at 3.4%, Russia sales is at 1.63% and purchases is at 1.66% and India sales is at 1.43% and purchases is at 1.49%. In the case of China, sales is 4.3% and purchases is 2.46%, respectively. The Indian share increased from 1% in 1998 to 2.45% in the year 2009 and fell a little by 2.12% in the year 2010. In terms of the value of transactions, the share increased to 1.5% to 2.42% between the two years 2008 and 2009 and fell to 1.6% in the year 2010. India's share represents more than 1% in six years for the number of deals and three years for value in the last two decades.

CBMA Emerging Economies, India and BRICS:

1 Globalisation means different things to different countries but common things among them are access to foreign markets, tariff reduction, complaints with the international systems, membership of many international organisations and having a level playing field to be both a seller as well as a buyer in emerging international-level opportunities across the globe without any restriction. However, the fruits of globalisation are not evenly available to many countries in the world,
2 The international processes of Indian and Brazilian firms are normally endowed with economic motives while those of Russian and Chinese firms receive substantial political support from their governments' investor board as part of the policy.
3 A link exists between the economic activity and global trade and also between global trade and firm performance. This is also under the theory of business cycles in economics the theory of international trade in the theory of internalisation process in international business and the review or resource-based view theory in strategic management.
4 In analysing India's position in terms of CBMA in a comparative framework, especially concerning the other three emerging countries, namely Brazil, China and Russia, one has to follow the available data from World Bank, World Development Indicators and Euro Monitor database. In addition, one has to get the data from old investment reports

66 *Meaning of Mergers and Acquisitions*

and spreadsheets of the United Nations Conference on Trade and Development (UNCTAD) in 2011 and subsequent years. In particular, India's cross-border mergers and acquisition cases can also be viewed from Thomson Reuters' quarterly reports and KPMG, Price Water Coopers (PWC) and Bloomberg's book on mergers and acquisitions.

5 It was found that India's GDP rate dramatically improved on a year-to-year basis for the last three decades because of the new economic policy reforms, deregulation and abolition of the licence raj system. The growth rate of India in the year 1991, that is the pre-liberalisation year, was nearly 2.1% and it has become 10.3% in the year 1997.

6 The GDP rate of Russia was negative right from 1991 to 1997 except for one year and in the case of Brazil from 1991 to 2012.

7 Many researchers in India like Reddy, Nangia and Agarwal in the year 2013, Tan in the year 2003 for China and other countries of Asia inform that the Asian financial crisis in bit 1997 had elevated worries in the Asia regional financial markets and the crash of information technology bubbles in the year 2000 as well. Because of this, there were many opportunities for acquisitions for the developed economies or developed companies in the developed economies towards the Asian countries and the same opportunities were realised,

8 As has been correctly pointed out in the finance report of 2010 and subsequently researched by Mishra and Sharma in the year 2011, the Indian economy saw stability in the changing process from a closed inefficient system to too much robust open and efficient system since the start of the economic reforms of the year 1991,

9 It has been correctly pointed out by global researchers like Michael Read and others that the licence permit raj which also was coincident with the endured lowest rate of the growth was given up in the 1990s and replaced by a direct Foreign Investment Promotion Policy (FIPP) and also by opening up many sectors to competition as well as investment from abroad. This has caused a breakthrough and shakes- up in the traditional status quoist economy of India which was suffering from inefficiency, incompetence and a slower rate of growth missing opportunities globally coupled with poverty, unemployment, inflation and political rivalry to the era of efficiency ,robust new open economic policy. This was made possible by systematic reform in the financial regulatory framework by amending many laws as well as bringing new legislation to facilitate this new paradigm shift.

10 "Researchers also found out the main benefit of liberalization is a decline in the cost of capital for local firms violet increases the efficiency with which investment funds are located,"[102] and

11 The ability of financial resources at a lower cost will invite not only the domestic capital but the foreign capital also either through increased investment in the domestic front and also increased Foreign Direct Investment and ultimately through possible CBMA. This has been proved correct in the case of India because of major reforms that

happened from the years 1992 to 1997 which include a reduction in reserve requirements and interested reform and also referred to remove barriers to market entry. As a result, economic reforms brought productivity gains at the micro-level but also presented a major restructuring of the international competitiveness of most industries.

It is not out of place to mention that many large industrial giants left the non-core business and went in search of foreign takeovers in an outbound manner but the law was the impleading effect and hence there was an amendment in many respects of law first with RBI and then SEBI and ultimately the entire company act was reformed and the new company act came in the name of Company Act 2013.[103]

CBMA in Emerging Economies and Developed Economies

LDC and EM in the CBMA Environment

The COVID-19 pandemic strengthened India's position among emerging economies in comparison to developed economies. India is one of the leading emerging economies. The USA is the most developed economy. To answer the question of the ease of doing business, the relative strength of each nation within-group is vital.

Antonie Van Agtmael, the International Bank for Reconstruction and Development (IBRD) economist, coined the word Less Developed Country (LDC) for the first time. It was the market of the countries other than those of the USA, Japan, the UK, which were commonly termed as LDCs during the 1970–1980 decade.

Alternative terms include "emerging economies," "emerging markets," and "emerging countries." Political researcher Ian Bremer categorises the following condition as a precondition before a region is termed Emerging Market (EM). The political aspects are not driven under the carpet under the pressure of economic aspects and both politics and economics are optimally interactive and are inter operatively influencing each other. EMs are found in all continents, in Eastern Europe, in South Asia, in the Middle East, in the Russian Federation, in the South East Asia and Africa. While researchers including George Haley, Vladimir Kvint, Hernando de Soto, Usha Haley and several others from Harvard Business School and Dale School of Management felt that activity in such countries like India and China as emerging markets are little understood.

> The emerging market country is a society transitioning from a dictatorship to a free-market-oriented economy, increasing economic freedom, gradual integration with the global marketplace and with other members of the global emerging market, and expanding middle class, standards of living, stability intolerance, an increase in cooperation with multilateral institutions.[104]

Another featured EMs is the predominance of power finance capital in shaping the choices of Nations Governments and local cities. The much articulated socialistic slogans of labour class and working-class rights are paid relatively lesser attention.

The crux of the economic performance of a nation depends on its policy administration and implementation than on policymaking, and therefore countries like India must restructure and redefine the public administration aspects. The issues include

First, identifying the problem,

Second, setting up of economics and business research organisations with infrastructure resources, Thirdly, looking closely into rural sectors to promote more economic and financial savings,

Fourth, designing a comprehensive policy that motivates the younger generation to become business entrepreneurs and suitable incubation training in the Universities Fifthly, fraud can be prevented by establishing a fraud search committee, and finally, actions speak louder than words. Indian case clearly shows that there is a cost for the deal. India should remove the multiplicity of regulations, governing product market distortions in the market for land, and widespread government controls. The crucial nature of the economic performance of any country depends not on its intention but its implementation. Policy administration and plan implementation rather than policy-making are important for any country and the same is true in the case of India too and hence India requires a lot of restructuring and re-engineering of their public administration tools in terms of the administrative setup. India has established in terms of tax administration rule administration plan administration for promoting not only mergers and acquisitions but also for all other aspects and when India can do it, then only to be able to attract FDI through CBMAs or encourage its domestic investors to acquire assets abroad. The entire process involves the following initiatives.

1. Providing Administrative Training in the areas of tax administration ,tax rules making consultancy areas with other affecting/affected systems and research areas to make the Indian rules on par with the rest of the countries so that the countries advantages as a destination for CBMAs in terms of inbound logistics will be in favour of the country and also constantly keeping a watch on the global marketing agencies who are constantly observing India's efforts and initiatives.
2. Setting up of economics and business research organisations with infrastructure and resources so that the best talent that is available abroad and India will be there working seamlessly without any trouble and any infrastructural bottlenecks and with synergy and energy.
3. Looking closely into the rural sector has to promote economic and financial savings so that the same economic and financial savings can be utilised for plugging them back to the economy and hence the unemployment and disguised unemployment in terms of product in

productive employment and unemployment issues are not there and people are generally energetic and happy and are not bothered about their earnings tomorrow.
4 Designing a comprehensive policy that motivates the younger generation to take up a start-up India project and not to be dependent only on government jobs as security. In India, it was observed by an informed researcher that a job in the government at any level is more attractive to even a PhD awardee when compared to opening up a coaching academy to enhance the skills of those less fortunate than him/her.
5 Controlling higher education oriented universities and institutions by establishing fraud search committee so that crony capitalism is not reflected in universities because universities are supposed to be temples of ethics. They are supposed to be promoting ethics , and hence fraud search is long overdue to weed out corrupt elements and vested interests among universities as the faith in the system and the faith in democratic establishments, starts with universities and all those who administer universities, must be men of impeccable character. Policymakers should develop a strategy guideline to view the financing choices in rural villages and developing minimum infrastructure facilities.
6 Backward districts are areas in a rural background and villages offer the greatest catchment area for both investment and for talent, and similarly, if neglected, the same can follow the Maoist dictum of encircling the towns with villages and hence it is suggested that the villages, towns and cities should not be like gated communities but instead should be like the place of worship among forest areas so that, because of them, the forest place becomes "tourist place." One can also say that the forest becomes "for rest place."
7 There should be greater coordination and among all departments rather than the Ministries working in compartments. One should never put a lid on the public power and control it for one's benefit as it damages the social good and public faith.
8 Banking and financial institution products and services must reach every corner of the country that would bring more savings and investments.

Emerging Opportunities and CBMA

The following observations of the McKinsey report are interesting. MD of McKinsey, Domenic Barton feels:

> The consultants observed that India is a well-developed equity market compared to the banking sector but the barrier is that growth prospects get impaired due so redundant regulation by governmental bureaucracy in capital appointment arena. Besides, regulations governing product

markets, Land distortions, Licensing, or Quasi licensing are found to be counterproductive. Suggestions include rationalization taxes and excise duties establishing effective leadership in individual regulator's role by removing restrictions on FDI undertaking widespread privatization and reforming private property and tenancy laws to promote competitive markets.[105]

Many research reports in emerging markets are multipoint research which includes strategy management, legal reform, administrative reform, training, motivation reforms in HR practices, and more than anything else which includes the linkages among rural, urban, agriculture, industry, and, among various facets of the service industry and Government and non-Government organisations. This study is to identify the trust deficits and remove them as soon and as far as possible to make the effort in a multi-disciplinary multi-pronged but uni-directional study proving the country standing globally/internationally so that India with all its positives will be able to realise the scope of harvesting the emerging opportunities abroad. Thus, to conclude, in emerging markets India should be able to utilise emerging opportunities abroad. EMI should lead to EOI. That is, Emerging Market India should lead to Emerging Opportunity Investments.

Comparative CBMA in Various States of the USA

Federalism in government functioning is the bad sock of the constitution of the USA. Hence, regulation of merger and acquisition activity falls within the dual jurisdiction of both the federal government and individual states in which the targeted company is located. The federal government regulates sales and transfers of securities through the SEC. The federal government also controls the competition matters through the antitrust division of the Department of Justice and through the Federal Trade Commission. Any offer of a merger or any tender for such a merger offer must be according to the provisions of the Securities Exchange Act of 1934, as amended. Within any state, the merger is normally completed according to the rules and regulations of that particular state. The Securities Exchange Act takes care of minor aspects like the solicitation of shareholders' votes of the target company and if there is any fraud, it is found out and it becomes a punishable offense.

There are registration requirements of the Securities Act of 1933, as amended, if the person who wants to take or acquire another company bids the offers through securities as consideration. There are, of course, exemptions from the registration requirements under certain specified conditions and equality before law enables anyone to utilise the same without any discrimination or any prohibition from anyone. Every state has its law regarding prevention of hostile takeover initiatives, and every state has in place the rules and regulations for the corporates in the internal affairs of a company to the extent that the fiduciary duties word by the company's board of directors to its shareholders are meticulously followed at, not given ago by in an environment of fraudulent self-interest.

Every state has established courts specialised in corporate affairs codes and the notable among them is Delaware, where the maximum number of largest corporations in the United States is incorporated. These takeover statutes are either control share acquisition statutes or business combination statutes. A shareholder needs to obtain permission from other shareholders before such shareholder votes over the issue of certain percentage ownership controls of the shares of the target company. This is the main crux in the control of the share acquisition statute. Statutory provision under the head "Business Combination" however, specifies prohibitions for a business combination with reference of a target company creating a particular limit,

> for the specific period unless the shareholder has obtained approval from a supermajority that is around 66.66 % of the shares held by the target companies other shareholders or before acquiring such specified ownership threshold target Company Board's Approval. Companies incorporated in any state may opt-out of the protection of the state anti-take-over statutes in their certificate of Incorporation. Delaware has a business combination statute. Delaware is the most important state because of the simple reason that it has the maximum number of corporations incorporated in its jurisdiction.[106]

In the case of a merger, if the company is a foreign investor, in that case, the rules of Security Services under the Exchange Act and the US security concern also hold good. For any outbound takeover or merger or acquisition issue within the United States, if a bidder is offering the securities as consideration in an offer in the United States, then the bidder must register with the SEC unless an exemption from the registration is available.

Upheavals in Global Economy

The global economy witnessed recovery after devastating results due to the worldwide recession in the years 2008 and 2009. This sovereign debt crisis of Europe and several geopolitical animosities across the continents constrained the natural expansionism of the cooperative executive conference. Even though China witnessed domestic rates of growth much above the global average, yet, slowing down of the bass is an indication of turbulence of the global economy. While it is a fact that the domestic growth in the United States exceeds most of the Western European countries, compared to the previous history of the United States, the growth rate still is only modest. With revenue growth constrained by sluggish global recovery, corporations are restructuring aggressively to eke out additional market share. Continued low-interest rates and brilliant stock markets are fuelling a recovery in corporate restructuring activity with more companies and willing to take no for an answer pursuing hostile takeovers.

> Other companies continue to streamline operations to increase product and market focus by divesting or spinning off business not considered germane to their corporate strategy. Restructuring of companies essentially reshapes the business centers to possible mergers and partnerships. Joint Ventures among different companies under one conglomerate and spin-off/demergers of one company into many equity holding company is possible.[107]

CBMA and Cyber Business

Business conducted through the internet connects to globally located customers. This aspect causes a crisis in the cross-border arena as a legal issue. Legality and validity is region-specific and enforceability is a different ball game. Not all laws are universally applicable. The creation of wealth through cyberspace would also in time make use of Offshore Financial Institutions (OFI) to store the wealth. Cyberspace can emerge as a tax haven for tax avoidance s a worst-case tax evasion; for instance, its profits are diverted as cryptocurrency assets and taxation may become difficult. It is not only a threat to national sovereignty, but it also overrides traditional principles of taxation namely the transgression of the traditional notion of political and monetary autonomy.

> Cyberspace wealth generation is a different category and hence existing monitorymonetary/tax control enforcement mechanisms are inadequate. Taxes on wealth from cyberspace require special law and special infrastructure of enforcement adjudication. Taxes on cyberspace would be one method of getting some amount of monetary control.[108]

Conclusion

In this chapter, India's position as an emerging economy in comparison with other emerging economies and the experience of the USA as the leader of developed economies were discussed. Corruption, bribery, fraud and transparency issues significantly affect CBMA functioning. In the next chapter, these issues would be discussed to find out answers to valid issues (Figures 1.15–1.17).

Meaning of Mergers and Acquisitions 73

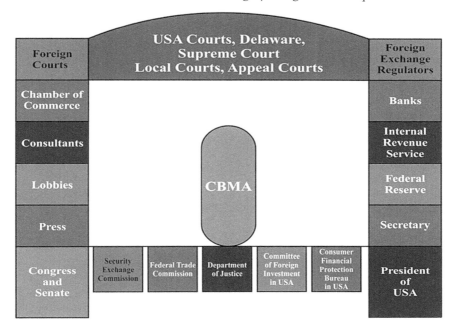

Figure 1.15 USA CBMA Model.
Made by Dr. B. N. Ramesh.

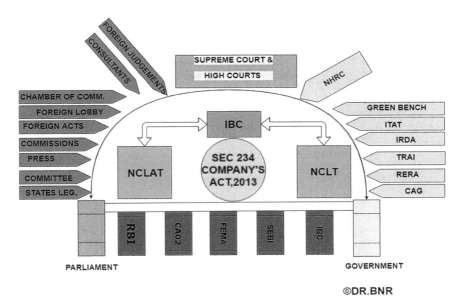

Figure 1.16 Indian CBMA Model.
Made by Dr. B. N. Ramesh.

74 *Meaning of Mergers and Acquisitions*

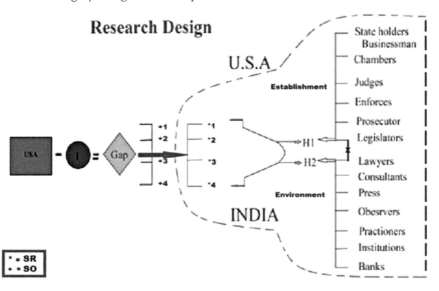

Figure 1.17 Pictorial Design of CBMA in USA & India.
Made by Dr. B. N. Ramesh.

Notes

1 Gubbi, Aulakh, Ray, Sarkar, and Chittoor. Do International Acquisitions by Emerging Economy Firms Create Shareholder Value?, THE CASE OF INDIAN FIRMS JOURNAL OF INTERNATIONAL BUSINESS STUDIES, VOL. 41(3), 397–418, (2010).
2 JAMES PETER HYMERS BARON MACKAY OF CLASHFERN, HALSBURY'S LAWS OF ENGLAND VOL. 72, 1461, 1103, (2008).
3 Company Act, 1956 in comparison to English Company Act, 2006 (as brought by Mr Sampath).
4 Rao-Nicholsona, R., & Ayton, J. Euphoria in Financial Markets, INTERNATIONAL BUSINESS AND FINANCE, VOL. 38, 494–508, (2016).
5 Bekke, T., & Whited, T. Which firms follow the market? An analysis of corporate investment decisions, THE REVIEW OF FINANCIAL STUDIES, VOL. 23(5), 1941–1980, (2010).
6 M&A booster- New Companies Act has it all easy and clean—IN HOUSE COMMUNITY, http://www.Inhousecommunity.com.(Last visited on May 15, 2018).
7 Earnest & Young, L.L.P. "Mergers and Acquisitions in the newer of Companies Act 2013", ASSOCHAM, 14, (February, 2014).
8 OECD New Patterns of industrial globalization: Cross-Border Mergers and Acquisitions and strategic alliances, 14, (2001).
9 KPPB Law firm, Inbound and Outbound Mergers and Acquisitions, https://www.KPPB.law, com/…inbound and outbound Mergers and Acquisitions/, (Last visited on 16.05.2018).
10 Verma, J.C., CORPORATE MERGERS AMALGAMATION AND TAKEOVERS, 77, (2009).
11 Bio-Tech &Genetics, BUSINESS LINE FINANCIAL DAILY, THE HINDU, 3, (Kolkata edn. November 10, 2004).
12 Kaur, G, CORPORATE MERGERS AND ACQUISITIONS, 273, (2005).

13 Bhasin, "Merger and Acquisition: An Overview, ‖ MANUPATRA NEWSLINES, 1, Issue-7, 11, (December, 2006), www.lawjournals.org/download/270/4-1-66-948.pdf, (Last visited on May 10, 2018).
14 Corporate Professionals, "An Overview of The Companies (Amendment) Bill, (July 27, 2017), http://www.companiesact.in/Companies-Act-2013/News-Details/20759/An%20Overview%20of%20The%20Companies%20(Amendment)%20Bill,%202017 (Last visited on May 10, 2018).
15 Sec. 234(1), THE COMPANIES ACT, (2013).
16 Sec. 439(1), THE COMPANIES ACT, (2013).
17 Sec. 439(2), THE COMPANIES ACT, (2013).
18 Sec. 232(8), THE COMPANIES ACT, (2013).
19 ViswanathPilla, Moschip Acquires Three Companies in Semiconductor and IOT Space, LIVEMINT, (September 12, 2016.), http://www.livemint.com/Companies0Rw6QxR2YuZuV60pMRBAoJ/MosChip-acquires-three-companies-in-semiconductor-and-IoT-sp.html, (Last visited on May 16, 2018.)
20 Jianhong, Zhang & He, Xinming & M. Van Gorp, Désirée. Economic Freedom and Cross Border Acquisitions From Emerging Markets Into Developed Economies, THUNDERBIRD INTERNATIONAL BUSINESS REVIEW, VOL. 59, 313–331, (2016).
21 Will Martin, Cross Border M & A Transactions; Using Subsidiaries t185o Simplify Complicated Legal Issues, AMERICAN BAR ASSOCIATION, www.americanbar.org/willmartin/ (Last visited on May 16, 2018).
22 Rawat, D.S., of Associate Chambers accessed from website of Associate Chambers of Commerce on (April 20, 2018).
23 Ibid.
24 Rangachari N., Chennai November 2007, K. R. RAMAMANI MEMORIAL LECTURE, (2007).
25 Ibid 1.
26 Ibid 3.
27 Rangachari N., Chennai November 2007, K. R. RAMAMANI MEMORIAL LECTURE, 18, (2007).
28 Subhash Chandra Jain, "EMERGING ECONOMIES AND THE TRANSFORMATION OF INTERNATIONAL BUSINESS", EDWARD ELGAR, 384, (2006).
29 Forbes, (January 13, 2017). https://www.forbes.com/newsletters/sss/2017/01/13/newrecommendation-january-13-2017/ (Last visited on May 6, 2018).
30 PWC report, (2017).
31 Suman Layek and Baiju Kalesh, ECONOMIC TIMES INTELLIGENCE BUREAU UPDATED, 16–22, (2018).
32 An EY report 2017 on India.
33 ECONOMIC TIMES, 5, (Kolkata edn., March 24, 2018).
34 A. Mehra, Why 2018 May Become A Blockbuster Year for Mergers and Acquisitions, THE ECONOMIC TIMES., weblink-http://economictimes.indiatimes.com/news/company/corporatetrends/why-2018-may-become-a-blockbuster-year-for-mergers-and-acquisitions/... (Last visited on Mar 24, 2018)
35 3 Years of Modi govt.: 6 Economic policies that have made BJP stronger, harder to defeat: BUSINESS TODAY, (May 16, 2017) https://www.businesstoday.in/current/economypolitics/from-demonetisation-to-gst-heres-what-pm-modi-did-on-economic-reforms-in-last-3years-in-office/story/252249.html (Last visited on May 26, 2018).
36 http://www.businesstoday.in/storyprint/252249 (Last visited on June 1, 2018)
37 3 Years of Modi govt.: 6 Economic policies that have made BJP stronger, harder to defeat: BUSINESS TODAY, (May 16, 2017) https://www.businesstoday.in/current/economypolitics/from-demonetisation-to-gst-heres-what-pm-modi-did-on-economic-reforms-in-last-3years-in-office/story/252249.html (Last visited on May 26, 2018).

76 Meaning of Mergers and Acquisitions

38 BUSINESS TODAY, http://www.businesstoday.in/storyprint/252249# (Last visited on June 1, 2018)
39 Ibid
40 PTI, Indian Elephant Ready to Run After Economic Reforms: IMF Official, TIMESOFINDIA., (April 22, 2018), https://economictimes.indiatimes.com/news/economy/indicators/Indianelephant-ready-to-run-after-economic-reformf-imf-official/articleshow/63866286.cms, (Last visited on May 16, 2018).
41 Pretty Li Hui Zhen is a 2017 Chinese television series starring Dilraba ... Written by, Lu Zhirou Yang Qing. Directed by, Zhao Chenyang, https://en.wikipedia.org/wiki/Pretty_Li_Hui_Zhen
42 THE HINDU, 1 (Kolkata edn., June 7, 2017).
43 Sec. 47(vii) of THE INCOME TAX ACT, (1961).
44 Foreign Exchange Management Regulations, (2014).
45 TejasviniShirodkar, Pearl Boga and Karen Issac, Decoding The Big Takeaways of The New Cross-Border Mergers Framework, (June 8, 2018). https://www.vccircle.com/decoding-the-bigtakeaways-of-the-new-cross-border-mergers-framework/ (Last visited on June 9, 2018)
46 Vasconcellos G.M., and Kish R.J., "Journal of Multinational Financial Management", VOL. 8(4), 431–450, (November, 1998).
47 DONALD DEPAMPHILIS, MERGERS, ACQUISITIONS, AND OTHER RESTRUCTURING ACTIVITIES, 32, (2009).
48 ECONOMIC REPORT TO THE PRESIDENT WASHINGTON D.C.US, GOVERNMENT PRINTING OFFICE, (2003).
49 Frank J, Mayer C, Hostile takeovers and the correction of managerial failure, 40/1 JOURNAL FINANCIAL ECONOMIC, 163–181, (1996).
50 Wikipedia CFC (Last visited May 14, 2018).
51 Sec 6651- Sec 7344 Sub F Internal Revenue Code, 26 USA, (2010).
52 Alan J. Tarr, Civil Tax Penalties, US Income Portfolio 634 BLOOMBERG BNA, 16–30, (2012).
53 Sec. 6038, 26 UNITED STATES CODE, INTERNAL REVENUE CODE, (2010).
54 Sec. 7301–7328, 26 UNITED STATES CODE, INTERNAL REVENUE CODE, (2010).
55 Sec. 7201–7217, 26 UNITED STATES CODE, INTERNAL REVENUE CODE, (2010).
56 Sec. 6702, 6673, 26 UNITED STATES CODE, INTERNAL REVENUE CODE, (2010).
57 Sec. 6700, 26 UNITED STATES CODE, INTERNAL REVENUE CODE, (2010).
58 Sec. 6707A, 26 UNITED STATES CODE, INTERNAL REVENUE CODE, (2010).
59 Wachtell, Lipton, Rosen & Katz, Skadden, Arps, Slate, Meagher & Flom LLP ("Skadden"), Cravath, Swaine & Moore LLP, Sullivan & Cromwell LLP
60 Rangachari N., Chennai November, 2007, K. R. RAMAMANI MEMORIAL LECTURE, 3, (2007).
61 Sec 78dd-1, 78dd-2 15 U.S.C. Criminal Division of the U.S. Department of Justice and Enforcement Division of the U.S. Securities and Exchange Commission (SEC) A RESOURCE GUIDE U.S. FCPA, (2012).
62 Sec 78dd-1, 78dd-2 15 U.S.C.; FCPA GUIDANCE, 2, (2012).
63 Hartford Fire Ins. Co. v. California, 509 U.S. 764, 795–96, (1993); 15 U.S.C. 6a.
64 United States v. Wilshire Oil Co. of Texas, 427, Texas Court.
65 www.justice.gov/atr/public/press_releases/2011/278076a.pdf, (2011) (Last visited May 25, 2018).
66 Legal provisons Sherman Act, (1890).

67 Timothy A. Mackey et al., CORPORATE ACCOUNTABILITY REPORT 13 CARE, (2015).
68 Ibid P4.
69 As was evidenced through information in public domain from relevant sources like, in this case, the web site.
70 Sec 14 of FOREIGN EXCHANGE MANAGEMENT ACT, (1999)
71 One of the most effective sections.
72 Dodd Frank Act is yet another legal step with multifarious aims.
73 ICLG www.iclg.com (Last visited on May 4, 2018.)
74 NEW YORK TIMES, https://www.nytimes.com/ (Last visited on May 4, 2018.)
75 Delaware supreme court rulings https://courts.delaware.gov/opinions/list.aspx?ag=supreme% 20 court (Last visited on May 4, 2018).
76 A mandatory requirement under law of USA.
77 Employment rules in many states and not of Delaware in the United States of America.
78 Note by International Comparative Legal Guides as on (April 19, 2018).
79 www.sec.gov (Last visited on May 20, 2018)
80 Rules of FTC & Department of Justice, USA.
81 HSR ACT 1976 is amendment to CLAYTON ACT, (1914).
82 Paragraph 3.9 ICLG on Merger Control In USA.
83 Sec 1 15 United States Code, (1934).
84 Horizontal Merger Guidelines for Public Comment (April 20, 2010) https://www.justice.gov/atr/public-documents/division-update-spring-2011/division-and-federaltrade-commission-issue-revised-horizontal-merger-guidelines (Last visited on May)
85 Foreign investment in United States, 40Fed. Reg 20263 dated May 7, 1975.
86 The Committee on Foreign Investment in the United States (CFIUS) U.S. DEPARTMENT OF THE TREASURY, www.treasury.gov/resoursecenter/international/foreigninvestment/pages/cifusmembers (Last visited on April 20, 2018)
87 NEW YORK TIMES, (March 5, 2018) https://www.nytimes.com/issue/todayspaper/2018/03/05/ todays-new-york-times (Last visited on May 20, 2018)
88 According to Elangu and Patnaik in the year 2011 and according to Modhak and Reyhani in the year 2012, traditionally most emerging markets are highly regulated, with a restricted competition and mainly closer to foreign entry while their regulatory system is more inconsistent and less sophisticated.
89 Ibid.
90 Rangachari N., Chennai November 2007, K. R. RAMAMANI MEMORIAL LECTURE, 5, (2007).
91 Ibid 5.
92 Ibid 6.
93 Sec. 6(4), INCOME TAX ACT, (1961).
94 Hyundai Heavy Industries Company v. Union of India, May 18, 2007. SC.
95 En, Xie. andJie, Liang, Country-Specific Determinants of Cross-Border Mergers and Acquisitions: A Comprehensive Review and Future Research Directions, 52 JOURNAL OF WORLD BUSINESS, 127–183, (February, 2017).
96 Mr. IANS, BRICS Summit 2017: GST India's Biggest Economic Reforms Measure Ever, FIRSTPOST, (September 04, 2017). https://www.firstpost.com/india/brics-summit-2017-gst-indiasbiggest-economic-reform-measure-ever-says-narendra-modi-4007815.html (Last visited on May 6, 2018)
97 Ibid.
98 http://engagedscholarship.csuohio.edu/cgi/viewcontent.cgi?referer=https://www.google.co.in/&httpsredir=1&article=10688&context=bus_facpub (Last visited on May 6, 2018)
99 https://www.business.in/storyprint/252249 (Last visited on May 6, 2018).

100 PTI, Indian Elephant Ready to Run After Economic Reforms: IMF Official, TIMESOFINDIA., (April 22, 2018) https://timesofindia.indiatimes.com/business/india-business/indian-elephant-ready-to-run-aftereconomic-reforms-imf-official/articleshow/63866194.cms, (Last visited on May 16, 2018).
101 PTI, Indian Elephant Ready to Run After Economic Reforms: IMF Official, TIMESOFINDIA., (Apr 22, 2018) https://timesofindia.indiatimes.com/business/india-business/indian-elephant-ready-to-run-aftereconomic-reforms-imf-official/articleshow/63866194.cms, (Last visited on May 16, 2018).
102 Deregulation was seen in the fields of trade and finance and subsequently in technology and infrastructure, (2012).
103 Researcher Ramakrishnan in 2008 feels that the removal of industrial licensing, is a foreign investment, the importance raw materials, capital goods and technology have distinctly in launched the competition in Indian industry.
104 Kvint, Vladimir, THE GLOBAL MARKET: STRATEGIC MANAGEMENT AND ECONOMICS, 234--256, (2009).
105 The developing countries must reduce restrictions and streamline requirements for starting the new businesses and encourage new market entrance as it has been mentioned by many scholars, including Farrell and London, 2006, Farrell and Radel in 2004.
106 ICLG is International Corporate Legal Guides- www.iclg.com (Last visited on April 19, 2018).
107 DONALD DEPAMPHILIS, MERGERS, ACQUISITIONS, AND OTHER RESTRUCTURING ACTIVITIES, 32, (2009).
108 Rangachari, N., Chennai November, 2007, K. R. RAMAMANI MEMORIAL LECTURE, 10, (2007).

2 Cross-Border Mergers and Acquisitions

Statutes, Regulations, Rulings, Legislations and Analysis

Introduction

This chapter outlines various legal provisions, many already in vogue, and some in the offing across various business locations. Many are mandatory, as they originate from regulatory authorities, chiefly from governments—regional, provincial and federal. Some are guidelines of associations of audit and accountancy and others are related to corporates in general and the CBMA in particular.

Culture and the CBMA

The acquirers normally face many challenges because they have to prove the objectives and aims of the acquisition process than the acquired company. The acquired company also may have problems of adjustment to the new culture and the acquired company normally witnesses attrition at the highest level at both the bottom and middle-level management staff. There are political-legal and social-cultural topics related to CBMAs which come up in the integration planning and execution arena. The currently available literature helps in identifying and mitigating cross-border challenges. Secondly, it helps in effectively delivering workflows and is paired with internationally proven aids and technology. It maximises synergies by establishing strong administration and integration tools and lastly, it achieves long-term goals of culture by building action and insights.

Time and timing are of great importance in CBMA. A question often asked is about the date determining the beginning of the period throughout which the creditors of the merging companies are protected. This question was posed by the Director-General of Directorate of Justice and Consumers, Civil Justice Company law of European Commission.

The starting date may be before a cross-border merger takes effect (ex-ante) or after the across-border merger takes effect (ex-post) or in any other way. The starting date of the CBMA process, according to 86% of respondents of a survey, should be the date for determining the protection period while 14% of respondents felt otherwise. Most universities, lawyers and notaries, business federations, chambers of commerce, and other

DOI: 10.4324/9781003396987-2

organizations, trade unions and companies were in favour of harmonisation, whereas replies were divided among public authorities, with slightly more replies in favour.[1]

However, time and resources dedicated to planning and executing the integration are some of the main problems that occur in the CBMAs. The most important reason which was cited by many for the failure of many CBMAs is insufficient time for due diligence. Scott Whitaker and other authors feel that legal, socio-political hurdles too are the most important aspects that affect the process of CBMAs. For instance, in Europe, there are problems with work councils that are similar to unions in the United States, and they require more time and attention to navigate. Christopher G. too feels that the role of the culture is very important in CBMAs because of the following reasons.

Firstly, the importance of culture in the environment, secondly how cultural awareness will improve deal success making a distinction between various kinds of culture that is, global, local, corporate, thirdly paying attention to innovation/being consistently innovative, fourthly how to create cultural awareness in deal teams and fifthly how to integrate cultural elements in the deal strategy.

Without strong leadership, the anxiety caused by the cross-border mergers and acquisition activities can overlap both the acquiring and the target companies and erode productivity and employee engagement leadership. Everyday events can negatively impact momentum and destroy value. Planning and coordination are essential here. During a post-merger integration, the time slot is conditional on the transaction type of industry but difficult areas requiring a good deal of effort for most of any deal include, among others, the establishment of Information Technology infrastructure and integration and employee and customer retention. Whether it is a few small companies or big companies, the challenges are one of the integrations of work culture and deal in size. The industry is secondary and is not the main issue.

CBMAs

Dutton mentions this aspect in his article co-authored with Duncan and informs that,

> the global mindset, and informs that the global mindset, has several distinct components, including multicultural values, basing status on merit rather than nationality, being open to ideas from other cultures, being excited rather than fearful in new cultural settings, and being sensitive to cultural differences without being intimidated by them.[2]

"Here thinking globally means taking the best in other cultures and blending that into a third culture. Yet another advantage of CBMAs is that of geographical and market diversification which is in the interest of the product revolution as well as preparation for strategic growth in the years to com." Harvard Professor "Michael Porter"[3] often maintains that competitive advantage is the new Mantra in the world. CBMAs make competitive advantage a real weapon for the future strategy of survival and growth in an uncertain area of Revolutionary Technologies outstripping the existing ones like the tsunamis. Competitive advantage for any organisation is vital to face the twin challenges relevance and survival, post by its rival organisations. A competitive advantage may include access to natural resources, high-grade ore or low-cost power source labour, graphical location and access to new technology. Michael Porter, the authority on the subject of strategic management, explains competitive advantage in a two-pronged model, the first one being an advantage in connection with the cost of the production process which is the main unique selling proportion (USP) of the company, and the second one is an advantage in connection with differentiation of product/process in comparison to the similar qualities/attributes of the respective product/process of rival competitors. When company "A" offers the same product at a lower cost, because it produces such a product at a lower cost than a rival company "B," it becomes a cost advantage. When a product of company A and B are similarly priced at the hands of the consumer the differentiation advantage of the product of Company A over the product to company B lies in better quality, better attributes, better warranty, better and extra features. The best example is the success of Apple phones; when compared to its rivals, the differentiation of Apple products is encryption.

In general, CBMAs are a quick pathway to enter a new market, permit the acquiring firm to achieve critical mass in a market rapidly, and resulting in more control as compared to other market entry modes. The following five reasons explain the implications for the completion of cross-border positions across the world. Firstly, enhanced market presence; secondly, neutralising entry barriers; thirdly, consideration of launch of new products, brand equity; fourthly, sensing and taking over the emerging market; and lastly meeting the strategic challenges of increased diversification of production services.

Entry and exit strategies are vital components in the CBMA due diligence. The strategic delineation liquidating of the business exit strategy lies primarily in selling the stock the owner to any bidder available and interested as per law and procedure. Under conditions of profitability, selling as an exit strategy results in liquidation and a consequent accrual of huge profits to the owner. Contrarily, the liquidating sales of a loss-making unit will prevent further loss over a while. Market presence is a combination of reform size, competitive challenges and the probabilistic possibility of long-term sustenance in an uncertain market. Enhanced market presence is met through the tools of horizontal, vertical and related acquisitions. Entry is always associated with the current heroes in the market and the policies of the national governments and the taxation policies. Anti-incumbency may be true in the political arena but not in the market.

Philip Kotler, an authority on marketing management, is known for the best quotations in the field of marketing. Marketing is important in surviving and carrying in- carrying on of a business. Philip Kotler, the former S.C. Johnson & Son Distinguished Professor of International marketing at the Kellogg School of Management at Northwestern University, is the father of modern marketing management and a world-acclaimed another of more than 80 books. At 90 years, Professor Philip Kotler is never disappointing in the precision office observations. Most relevant ones for legal due diligence in CBMA are mentioned below:

i   Marketing is the art of crating genuine value to the customer and not deserving the customer to buy what the producer makes.
ii The three mantras of marketing are VSQ—Value, Service and Quality.
iii Heard work by the company is stimulating the product line is vital for all companies.
iv Five years is a long period in business and unless strong efforts are made, there is no automatic renewal in business.
v   Protectionism is the last step before the decimation.
vi The sales department should not be held responsible for the success of a product and the real hero is the Research and Development department.
vii Organisations require more self-managers than bosses.
viii The price of a product should not be decided only by cost.
ix Industries mast knows whether to produce a product or not, by its self.
x   Good quality is infected cheap ultimately cheap goods are cheap.
xi Satisfaction customer is not important. Delightment of customer is important.
xii Future has already happened.
xiii If not treated correctly, present success becomes a future failure.
xiv The creative utility of truth is the main function of marketing.
xv The capacity of a company to deliver its product/process, in a way that cannot be beaten down by a rival is called competitive advantage.
xvi Segmentation and cultivation are vital for marketing growth.
xvii The main ingredients of any marketing effort must be a) actionable b) accessible by search c) measurable d) different.
xviii The by-product from those who search for better opportunities is chaos.

Market uncertainty is a cruel reality in discouraging efforts of the firm in investments for new products and hence CBMAs offer an easier route to launch new products and to take over a potential market or to snatch a potential portion of the market from a possible competitor. In other words, it becomes less risky in search for a possible takeover of a potential ally in a foreign market which will be a win-win situation for both emerging and the merged components of the CBMA activity. Many examples prove the above point. Samsung, the South Korean telecommunications giant of the 21st century, entered the automobile sector in the 20th century. Similarly, Texas Instruments acquired Libit Signals Processing, a high-tech company in Israel. The price of the takeover was US $329 million. This CBMA example is an illustration of the win-win situation among two technical giants, namely the Texas instruments of the United States of America and the Libit Signal Processing of Israel which combined the hardware and the software and this resulted in savings of the avoidable and redundant cost in terms of research and development activity "Wharton School Professor Maurice Schweitzer and Yale University Professor Nathan Novemsky identify the comparison as another critical factor in guiding win-win negotiator satisfaction."

Students of the courses of best business administration institutes know that strategy and finance are the most important elements of the MBA study. The strategy is the most important function of any CEO of the firm because without a strategy the very survival of the firm is at stake. Strategy concerns demand that to save the cost of establishing a new firm in a foreign country of a newly emerging market, it is better to take over an established company of the foreign market in a foreign country. This is the essence of the CBMA. It saves the cost of the management of the local bureaucracy apart from the cost of due diligence and the reinventing of the wheel again and again. By performing due diligence, a perfect strategy can be called is to carry out the merger and acquisition. Tax compliances and local banking rules are always very complicated for any foreign company to master in a short time, as the time of the takeover of the market is very cruel and does not allow any leverage to the foreign firm because of the increased competitive uncertainty.

Strategic concerns of any firm demand increasing diversification to increase the potentiality of survival in the future. Laying all eggs in a single basket has always been bad even in English literature. CBMAs, thus, provide for increased diversification, available for both the merging and the merged firm. An example will illustrate the above point. The largest paper and wood products group company in the United States of America, namely, Weyerhaeuser, took over Macmillan Bloedel of Canada for US $2.45 billion. According to one analyst, "the takeover of one of Canada's most prominent corporate names is the latest in a series of the CBMAs. The North American Forest product group took over a well-known Canadian Corporation." Analysts view this as a prominent event in response to the international wave of consolidation led by the organisation from Scandinavia.

The NDA 2 regime from the year 2019 is expeditious in implementing the reform agenda. India scored a better rank in the Ease of Doing Business Index (EDBI) consistently. The Global rating agencies considered the effective reforms for easing regulations and simplifying the rules, removing redundant obstructionist colonial-era laws, unifying the codes and benchmarking the procedures for conducting business, performing trading activities and starting new businesses (start-up). Since we all work in global environments, CBMAs get maximum mileage of rate of these following reforms. While reflecting on a better EDBI, the following initiatives are some of the mentioned initiatives.

 i Self-certifying mechanism and for inspectorate Raj.
 ii Exemption in taxes.
 iii Legal aid and speedier fast-track patent examination and certification.
 iv Digitising portals dealing with permission and clearance.

CBMAs: Ease of Doing Business

Index making is in essence fair comparison and among many countries and ranks are allotted after impartial scrutiny. The three main criteria are firstly how favourable is the regulatory system of business operations, secondly, how strong contracts are enforced and lastly diligently the property rights are enforced. A high rank is indicative of a better prevalence of rule of law. Business is not conducted in isolation. The EDBI date for the USA was updated in May 2018. In India, restrictions in sectors like defence, civil aviation, pharmaceuticals through Foreign Direct Investment (FDI) were relaxed and the foreign investment promotion board was abolished and is replaced with a simpler approval process.

Ease of Doing Business Index (EDBI)

Rank by the World Bank on EDBI was improved for India from 14 (2015) to 63 (2020). The Prime Minister of India reportedly sought a target of 10 to 15 by the year 2024. Structurally, India implemented 59 regulatory reforms, almost 20% of global reform in the pandemic year of 2020. Junaid Ahmed of the World Bank appreciated the work of the Government of India in business reforms agenda at all levels, like the modern insolvency regime, the reduction of overhead costs in establishing logistics, the improvement in building quality, etc. India is almost the world's fifth rank holder in environment, port handling, and electronic platform. The distance to frontier metric saw India's consistent improvement in the year 2020. Lot of work is visible but critics point out that work relates only to paper, not in practice. While reforms are made on paper most of them are yet to be tangibly translated to the field. Third-party inclusion should not start the empire of power brokers. The G to B (Government of Business) should be done in digital platform with no requirement of meetings of Government officials.

Solvency and Ongoing Concern

The Insolvency and Bankruptcy Code has also been introduced to build investor confidence concerning easier turnarounds and exits. Similar efforts have been made to tackle the non-performing asset (NPAs) issue in the Indian banking sector which ultimately led to public sector banking problems in terms of the recent Punjab National Bank (PNB) and Nirav Modi episode. Insofar as the e-commerce issue is concerned, many global portals started playing important role in the Indian market aiming at greater consolidation. Global conglomerates are actively collaborating and recent sales of Reliance Jio Platform to the Facebook company is an example. Walmart too is on the lookout for collaborators and so is the giant Amazon.

In November 2016, the Prime Minister of India, Shri Narendra Modi, took the initiative of demonetisation. The demonetisation initiative temporally caused an economic downturn in both manufacturing growth and bank lending to industries which also ultimately led to the slowdown in mergers and acquisition activities in certain sectors. However, the future will be not a continuation of the immediate situation in the era of post-demonetisation. In January 2023, the Supreme Court of India ,judicially decided the correctness and legitimacy of demonetisation.

In the case of FY 2017–2018, the Domestic Merger and Acquisition (DMA) date for the 2nd quarter ending with September 2017 informs that DMAs stood at a value of $ 2,142 million; this is 19% of a comparative figure of the previous FY of 2016–2017. Informed analysts attribute this 81% decline to twice the effects of Demonetisation and Goods Services Tax (GST). However, in January–September, M&A activity clocked to $33 billion, recording a promising 22% growth as the year to date (YTD) saw increasing domestic consolidation with deals such as Vodafone-Idea, PropTiger-Housing.com, among others. The published Deal tracker Report (2017–2018) of Assurance Tax advisory firm Grand Thornton for July–September quarter of 2017–2018 maintained that about 118 DMAs transactions worth US $2,142 million were registered as against 139 CBMA transactions with a recorded value of US $11,221 million for the similar period of the FY 2016–2017. Comparatively the CBMA activity underwent a lessening trend in volumes along with values. The decline was measured to 50% less and the financial figure stood at US $5.2 billion for the FY 2017–2018.

With inbuilt efforts to greater transparency and accountability through increased tax collection and investor confidence, it can be hoped that CBMA activity will see a surge in the future. The sectors experiencing the significant activity of CBMAs:

1 Manufacturing,
2 Real estate,
3 Financial services,
4 Information Technology (IT),
5 Oil and gas,
6 Pharmaceuticals,
7 Life sciences, and
8 Healthcare.

IBC (The Insolvency and Bankruptcy Code)

The Insolvency and Bankruptcy Code, 2016 is expected to provide a significant CBMA opportunity for the acquisition of stressed companies undergoing insolvency or the personal bankruptcy regime. It is also expected to make the start-up in terms of CBMAs a reality.

The Insolvency and Bankruptcy Code (IBC) is a new initiative taken by the government of India as part of the second stage of economic liberalisation. The IBC contributed significantly towards the improvement of the rank of India among the Nations in the case of Ease of Doing Business Index (EDGI). The discussions on IBC since its enactment focused on jurisprudence in some of the cases that were referred to and also regarding the case and ordinances that were made by the Parliament and the Central Cabinet. Law is not merely an intention but its implementation. One year performance report has been made on the effectiveness of the Insolvency and Bankruptcy Code (IBC) and some of the findings are as follows. Two standards are the basis of the performance report. The first standard is the economic impact and the second standard is the performance of one of the judicial Institutions under the IBC. Creditors and debtors and institutional players like the banks guarantee insurance employees and many other stakeholders are the supposed clients of IBC. Insofar as the economic impact portion is concerned the identities of those who approached the IBC in greater number are an indication. Insofar as the performance of the judicial institution under IBC is concerned, the National Company Law Tribunal (NCLT) and National Company Law Appellate Tribunal (NCLAT) are very significant.

Since its Inception, NCLT disposed of 830 applications from the period of 2016 till November 30, 2017. Across the time one can see that the number of petitions filed by the creditors is much more than other positions. Initially, many petitions already filed with the present dysfunctional TIFR were transferred and hence the initial positions for the Debtors. There has been criticism in that the more the number of operational creditors approaching the IBC than the financial creditors the more the lobbying taking the position of recovery tool rather than being an effective mechanism for collective action by creditors and forest cheering properties. Among the operational creditors ,vendors and suppliers are using the IBC than other types of operational creditors. The IBC prescribes a timeline of 14 days for the disposal of an insolvency petition by the NCLT. "The Supreme Court in Surendra Trading Company versus JK Jute Mills Company Limited and others stated that certain time lines are merely directory and not mandatory" (Figures 2.1–2.6).[4]

It has been observed that 30 days is being taken even for starting the case. It was also observed that the majority of the dismissals are the settlements and with operational creditors. The Report card concludes that trends have largely remained the same, while these trends provide a glimpse of the first phase of the law, the essence of information is about the entire lifecycle of

Cross-Border Mergers and Acquisitions 87

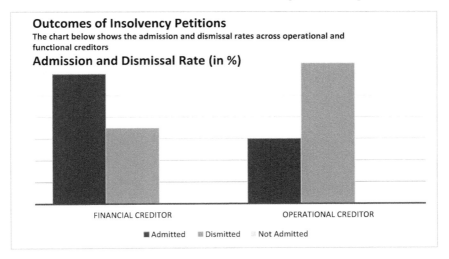

Figure 2.1 Insolvency Petitions Outcome.
Source: FRG Insolvency cases data November 30, 2017.

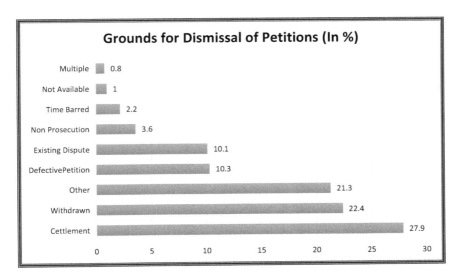

Figure 2.2 Grounds for Dismissal of Petitions.
Source: FRG Insolvency Cases Data Set up to November 30, 2017.

Time Taken For Disposal of Insolvency Petitions

STAGE	NUMBER OF OBSERVATIONS	MEDIAN TIME (IN DAYS)
T0 to T1	69	14
T1 to T2	212	16
T0 to T2	115	34

Figure 2.3 Time of Disposal.
Source: FRG Insolvency cases data November 30, 2017.

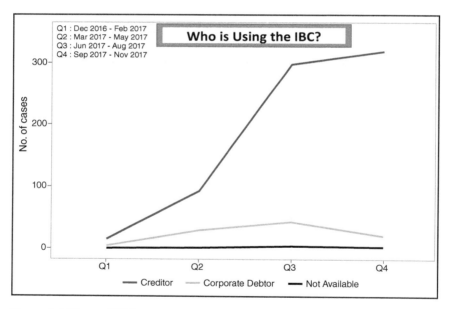

Figure 2.4 Users of IBC.
Source: FRG Insolvency cases data November 30, 2017.

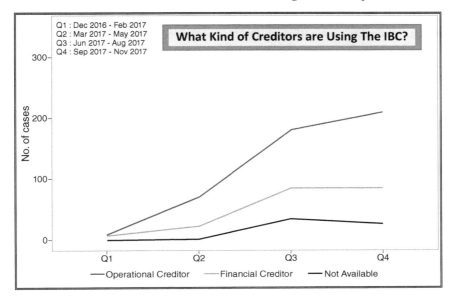

Figure 2.5 Creditors and IBC.
Source: FRG Insolvency cases data set up to November 30, 2017.

Operational Creditors Who Used The IBC	
CREDITORS	**FILINGS**
Vendors	223
Employees	25
Others	26
Unknown	193

Figure 2.6 Insolvency cases.
Source: FRG Insolvency cases data set up to November 30, 2017.

an institution under a holistic analysis of the same. The following graphs illustrate the above-mentioned findings of the reports.

Mr M. S Sahu, former Chairman of Insolvency and Bankruptcy Board of India (IBBI), felt that business enterprises may have to wait for some more time to use the concept of pre-packs. "Time has come to think about pre-pack. It is a little early to implement it here. Systems and practices develop a little more before we take up the step of introducing pre-packs in our insolvency regime."[5]

Former NCLT Chairman, Mr M.M. Kumar, also recently made a similar statement to consider the introduction of Pre-packs in insolvency process resolution in the country. Pre-packaged insolvency, also called pre-Pac, is a procedure where a company agrees to sell all or some of its assets to another before declaring its insolvency. This would be seen as a powerful tool. The NCLT chairman feels that the pre-pack could be a panacea for economies like India. The business line further reports that every pre-pack administration process, in the United Kingdom, envisions making suitable arrangements by a company that is vulnerable to insolvency or has a threat of winding up of selling its assets to a buyer.

The Insolvency and Bankruptcy Code envisages Insolvency Resolution. This necessarily means that the resolution plan must address the root cause of insolvency and then solve the problem undefined solution plan must identify why the corporate debtor has reached the situation and offers a solution. Insolvency Resolution, in its essential ingredient shape, is yet to be implemented to its full potential in India. If the objective of the resolution mechanism is selling, even resolution professional committee of creditors are not required at all as opined by many watchers of the IBC. MCA, the Ministry of Corporate Affairs circulated a draft for changes in IBC and is expected to act by last week of Feb, 2023.

Mr M.M. Kumar felt that if there are good entrepreneurs, a pre-pack is the best solution. "The process can be done in ten days. "The United Kingdom is often cited as the exemplary nation where the pre-pack system functions flawlessly. In England, a smooth transition of management happens under pre-pack. On Friday, the company moves a pre-pack arrangement. On Saturday, the new management takes over. On Monday, it is the same company, same employees and things move on. The Chairman of Punjab-Haryana-Delhi Chamber of Commerce and Industry (PHDCCI) Law and Justice Committee, Mr Lalit Bhashin, felt that introduction of the concept of the pre-pack in India is good. The Regional Vice President, Indore, Mr Aseem Chhabra felt, "It is an efficacious way of selling the business before insolvency petition is admitted. Matured legal environment and with the sound code of conduct of professional practice applicable to intellectual issues or Insolvency Resolution Professionals (IRPs) can be considered."[6]

Corporate Insolvency Resolution Processes (CIRP) numbering 4376 were admitted from the year 2016 and 2653 were resolved. In the year 2021, rupees 60000 crore might be realised for the financial creditors. This was estimated by the Investment Credit Rating Agency (ICRA).

Former IBBI Chairman Mr M.S. Sahoo feels that the Supreme Court of India made the IBC framework as the most effective legal framework with huge case law back up. Within five years, the IBC developed stronger and deeper roots. According to Mr Sahoo, the code has rescued 70% of the distressed assets through Insolvency Resolution Process (IRP) and the remaining 30% through the liquidation process.

IBC and IBBI changed the way business watchers and stakeholders view business failures in India, as published on page 2 of the *Financial Express* of June 21, 2021. The threat of use of the IBC made many defaulters to pay back the loans to the tune of US $14.2 billion equivalent that were almost under the Non-Performing Asset (NPA) category. IBC altered the debtor-creditor dynamics. Under the UK Law, there is a debtor-in-possession model. Similar is the case under Chapter II of Bankruptcy Code (USBC) in the USA. The resemblance of IBC is noteworthy with Chapter II of the USA Code in the case of the Moratorium issue, where a moratorium is automatic and is applicable against the debtor in all legal proceedings.

Under provisions of Chapter 15 of USBC, courts in the USA take note of compromise of US law-governed debt in any proceeding abroad, provided there is fairness, due process and transparency in the said foreign proceeding, on par with provisions of Chapter II of USBC.

Cross-Border Insolvency; India and the USA

The USA follows the UNCITRAL (United Nations Commission on International Trade Law) Model law on Cross-Border Insolvency. IBC too aspires similar provisions. Cross-Border Insolvency Resolution improved the rank of India from 136 to 52 in three years and brought below 50 ranks (47th) in the Global Innovations Index from the rank of 111, by World Bank ranking from the year 2017 to the year 2020.As on October 4, 2022, this figure for India in 2022 is 40, which is a substantial improvement in the COVID era.

Pre-Packs

Pre-packs are via media and golden mean between out-of-the-court and within-court resolution methods. The Insolvency Law Committee, on May 14, 2020, established a Sub-Committee to propose a Pre-Packaged Insolvency Resolution Process (PPRIP) under the IBC. The three fundamental principles therein are:

i   the basic structure of the Code should be retained;
ii there should be no compromise of the rights of any party; and
iii the framework should have adequate checks and balances to prevent any abuse. It identified three features, namely, the creditor in control, moratorium during resolution and binding nature of an approved resolution plan, which could be considered as part of the basic structure of the Code.

The Pre-Pack in the USA

The Ministry of Corporate Affairs, Government of India report analyses the comparative pre-pack position in the USA. According to the report dated January 8, 2021, the following is the essence of Insolvency Resolution through pre-pack in the USA.

The US Bankruptcy Code facilitates three forms of pre-packs, namely, pre-plan sales under section 363, pre-packaged bankruptcy proceedings and pre-arranged bankruptcy proceedings under Chapter 11.

The law does not prescribe either any standards or guidelines that guide judicial evaluations of pre-plan sales or the mode in which a sale should take place. Accordingly, courts have developed their own standards to adjudicate applications and sale typically involves a public auction and a public sale process. Owing to the flexibility in the procedure, the stalking horse method is often used for conducting the sale.[7A]

CBMAs and GST

The Goods and Services Tax Act (GST) came into effect on July 1, 2017, and is anticipated to increase the inter indirect tax regime's revenues in India and simplify the procedures. It reduces the complications of various tax regimes and helps the traders as well as the manufacturers to have an all-India market. It is also a level playing arena in tax resumes throughout the country and it helps an evolving one India one market, the aim of government ultimately. In April 2018, it was announced by the Ministry of Finance (MoF), Government of India (GoI), that total revenue collections under GST cross Rs. 1.03 lakh crores. This is found to be more than 15% above the previous nine months' monthly average collections of Rs 90,000 crores. April collections are for March (one crore in Indian currency means ten million).In January 2023, GST collections touched Rs 1.55 lakh crores.

Late Mr Arun Jaitley, the then Minister of Finance, remarked that the monthly revenue figure crossed Rs. 1 lakh crore, indicative of robustness of Indian economy. The then Finance Minister further expressed his confidence and faith in the efficacy of GST as a timely new reform and initiative. More GST collections mean more investments by government and more loans to start-ups and ultimately more growth rate for economy. All the above indices mean more prosperity for Indian and a better scope of globalised India through a rejuvenated the CBMA. Industrial production has exceeded 7% in the three months to February 2018.

The Finance Ministry also attributed the rise to an economic upswing but struck a note of caution on the numbers, saying some of this could be attributed to arrears from previous months. Increase in GST collections automatically informs to essential effects of the GST as reform. Firstly, when reform is timely, compliance would be voluntary when reform is simple, compliance would be overwhelming.

CBMAs and Real Estate Regulation Act (RERA)

Real Estate Regulation Act (RERA) was recently introduced to reform the Indian real estate sector which is closely linked with CBMAs especially in terms of starting the new project offices and housing for the middle class.

Mr Gautam Chatterjee is the chairperson of Maharashtra RERA. He feels that RERA has brought a lot of professionalism to the real estate industry. Maharashtra saw the maximum registration of housing projects across the country numbering 16000. Even though at the beginning of last year for the first quarter of 90 days, only 1,600 were registered, in the last three days itself when the Act was in a period of closure for registration, nearly 2,000 organisations registered and later on another 2,000 registered with a small fine. Mr Chatterjee informed that till date, RERA in Maharashtra got 2,400 complaints and disposed of 1,200 of them. Mr Chatterjee further feels that when the project is complete and handover able, it becomes a win-win situation for the developer, industry, and cent percent for the buyer. Eight thousand projects registered are running overtime.

Mr Chatterjee comes out with a finding that when a project is incomplete, then only it is getting registered to give a revised date of the proposal for completion. Mr Chatterjee also feels that the non-regulated sector has been brought to regulation and it is a painful process. There would be a bunch of delinquents groups and identifying them will take time. The answer of Mr Chatterjee to the following two questions is relevant here and hence it is quoted verbatim.

Impact of RERA on the Functioning of Real Estate Developers and Other Stakeholders

There will be structural changes but it will not be how some of the media houses have said that only big (builders) will survive and that mergers and acquisitions in the only way ahead. I do not subscribe to that view. I have a feeling this will bring a lot of professionalism to the industry. On the contrary, a smaller player with lesser margins has lesser expenditure and also gets into sectors where there are a huge amount of buyers like affordable housing will survive. Of course, churning will have to take place. This is the most painful period. The initial period of compliance will not be smooth. But after this when we can sustain it, I see a very clean disciplined sector.

CBMAs, RERA Priorities Present, and Future

RERA Maharashtra resolved some complaints. At the higher level, deficiency in completion compels revision of time lines requiring intensive efforts is monitoring. Un-kept promises by builders surely evaporate the trust of buyers on the builders.

Three priorities that I would be pursuing in the second year. There would be serious consequences if, within the revised times, the projects do not get completed. We need to bring that trust. Therefore, we have created a conciliation forum where both developers and consumers can sit together and find a way to solve the problems. The third is to reach out to the interior parts of Maharashtra, bring in greater awareness among both developers and consumers.[7]

There is also a proposal and an effort to simplify the existing archaic industrial and labour laws. There is a proposal to condense 44 existing enactments into four broad categories on

1 Wages,
2 Social security,
3 Safety regulations, and
4 Trade unions.

Amendments to PC Act, 1988 and FDI Rules

Amendments to the Prevention of Corruption Act, 1988 are on the anvil to make India on par with the best practices of the developed countries following the list in the Transparency International (TI). There is also an effort to relax and reform the Foreign Direct Investment (FDI) provisions which may see the light of the day anytime now.

Company Act, 2013 is basic legislation that governs the company structures and amalgamation transactions involving companies in India and abroad. Section 234 deals with the CBMAs. Apart from this, there are relevant provisions in the Limited Liability Act that involve commercial transactions. The Securities and Exchange Board of India (SEBI) regulations are very important in terms of the tax issues as well as in terms of the establishment of the companies. The cross-border activities are also regulated by the Foreign Exchange Management Act, 1999 (FEMA). The department of Industrial Policy and Promotion (DIPP) is meant for the enforcement of compliances by all stakeholders of the rules in connection with Foreign Direct Investment (FDI) policy.

The Competition Act, 2002 needs to be looked into in the case of CBMAs. Income Tax Act, 1961 and other agreements regarding double tax avoidance agreement with foreign countries is an important piece of relevant legislation. The Indian Stamp Act, 1899 which provides for stamp duty on the transfer of the shares issued during CBMAs affects CBMAs. Specific Relief Act and the provision of Contract Act, 1872 in India, and the counterparts of the host country are important during the process of due diligence in connection with CBMAs both in India and abroad. Apart from this, sector-specific laws govern CBMAs activity whose functions include financial transactions. Financial transactions stand regulated by the Reserve

Bank of India (RBI) as the chief banking regulator under the Banking Regulation Act, 1949 and relevant regulations.

The SEBI's Shares and Takeovers Regulations 2011 Code, coupled with a takeover code of capital and disclosure requirements, 2009 and the SEBI's prohibition of Insider Trading Regulations 2015 are important in terms of avoidance of future complications in the CBMAs. Guidelines from SEBI make it mandatory for any company entering into mergers or acquisitions to obtain prior clearance from SEBI before approaching any court or NCLT.

Reserve Bank of India and the Department of Industrial Policy and Promotion regulate the cross-border mergers and acquisition activity. They take the help of many Foreign Exchange Laws. These Laws provide for restrictions and limits on foreign ownership in certain sectors.

Sec. 23A of the Company Act, 2013 is notified to guide the CBMA in India. The notification authority is the Ministry of Corporate Affairs (MCA). The Inbound and Outbound Mergers of Companies in India with foreign companies require following the Foreign Exchange Maintenance Act. Cross Border Mergers Regulation, 2008. M&A transactions that exceed certain assets turnover threshold call for the Competition Commission of India's approval. The Foreign Direct Investment Laws in India are sector-specific. Recently there was a relaxation of Foreign Direct Investment in retail companies, in Insurance as well as in Civil Aviation. The FDI can be up to above 49% in the defence sector and in all other sectors, FDI can be made without any government approval. An automatic route is also available subject to compliance with specific conditions. Pricing returns in terms of reporting norms through FDI and IT services are important in certain sectors. The Reserve Bank of India regulations applies to M&A transactions that involve banking and financial companies. On January 10, 2018, the Government of India permitted foreign Airlines to invest up to 49% in the debt-ridden Air India and eased norms for investment in single-brand retail, construction, and power exchanges. Hailing these measures, the US India Strategic Partnership Forum (USISPF) Chairman John Chambers felt that bold steps are necessary to make effective changes in India that hold vast potential. Such steps as FDI reforms will encourage foreign investors and allow India to realise its dream of becoming one of the world's most powerful economies.

> Mr Anil Talreja, India partner, Deloitte, said that allowing a hundred percent Foreign Direct Investment (FDI) in single-brand retail trade should act as a catalyst for a large number of retailers that have been exploring the Indian market. These investors will likely be relooking at their strategy to refresh their plans for Indian investment.[8]

Legal due diligence is no longer a mere simple act of procedural compliance.

M&A transactions in the telecom sector are followed by the guidelines issued by the department of telecommunications. These guidelines provide for instances where mergers of Telecom licenses cannot be undertaken without the approval of the telecom regulator. It is a key component of any international M&A deal.[9]

There are many ways of mergers and amalgamations which include share acquisition assets or business transfer or demerger. Due diligence is necessary for the buyers because of the following reasons namely

1. The nature and form of transaction,
2. The Identity of the target member,
3. The industry in which the target operates.

Care should also be taken in due diligence in areas of the legality of financial rules, Tax rules, environmental rules, and environmental law. Anti-trust laws and Anti Bribery provisions in the US Laws are two powerful tools in the enforcement of US regulations in the case of CBMAs. The above two tools ensure effective international reach of US regulations and compliance to the doctrine of success liability. Ignorance of domestic law is no excuse. Ignorance of foreign law is no chance event. The Companies in Europe, Japan, Asia or Australia can ill in ignoring the regulation of the USA especially of DOJ, SEC, CFIUS, ERS, and the all-powerful FTC. "U.S regulator's (play's) active role in cross- border enforcement."[10]

The legal due diligence includes:

1. The company structure disputes,
2. Material contracts disputes,
3. Employment issues disputes,
4. Labour disputes,
5. Labour Law regulations disputes,
6. Compliance with environmental laws and regulations disputes,
7. Intellectual properties disputes,
8. Insurance Law disputes,
9. Real state law issues disputes and
10. Disputes regarding financing and security agreements concerning the indebtedness of the company.

The CBMA and Insider Trading

SEBI banned insider trading and laid down the prohibition of insider trading regulations, 1992. According to regulation 2(e), an insider is a person connected or deemed to be connected and who is reasonably expected to have access to any unpublished price-sensitive information in respect of securities like shares and debentures of a company or who has received or has had access to such unpublished information. The directors, the officers of the company, involving professional or business relationships like the chartered accountant and lawyer are connected persons as per regulations 2(c). Any direct or indirect information of a company, substantially affecting the price of the shares of such a company, if published, becomes price-sensitive information.

The price-sensitive information also includes the following:

a "Periodical financial result of the company,
b Intended declaration of dividend,
c Issue or buyback of securities,
d Major expansion plans or execution of new projects,
e Amalgamations, mergers, and takeovers,
f Clearance of entire or considerable past of the company and
g Any significant changes in policies, plan, or operation of the company."[11]

The following observations are a vital part of legal due diligence of transactions deals in share transfer at the time of the CBMA.

Dealing in security is a technically well-defined term. It is any or some of the following activities namely- (a) subscribing (b) selling (c) agreeing to subscribe/sell. Here the person concerned can be either the principal or an agent of the company.

"An insider is prohibited to deal either on his behalf or behalf of any other person in security have a company listed on the stock exchange when in a position of an unpublished price sensitive information."[12] "Another company or an associate of that company also is prohibited from releasing the unpublished prices to sensitive information."[13]

> Any contravention to provisions under regulation 3 and 3A would be called insider trading and is punishable as per SEBI Act 1992 with imprisonment for a term up to 10 years or a fine of rupees 25 crores or both.[14]

"Any person holding more than 5% of shares or voting rights in any listed company shall disclose to the company the number of shares or voting rights held by him."[15] "Listed companies and organizations associated with associated with securities are required to frame a code of internal procedure."[16] "The internal procedure must also adopt a Chinese wall policy which demarcates the area of the organization having access to confidential information as an inside area from other areas organization known as the public area."[17] "The buyers must also consider the shareholding pattern, the minutes of the shareholder meetings, material agreement, agreements regarding arrangements of acquisitions process and acquisition, the details of the capital structure."[18]

"Details of the company's website normally should contain the patent registration information which also must be publicly available in the government websites like www.iPIndia.nic.in. Under SEBI Regulation

2015 of the prohibition of insider trading person specified or known as insiders cannot communicate unpublished price sensitive information regarding the company to outsiders and insider trading is a crime."[19] "An outsider is also similarly barred from requesting for such information by the so-called insiders."[20] All such information needs to be obtained through stock exchanges or consultants and due diligence must be made. The most important law for any lawyer to practice and be aware of full implications is the Substantial Acquisitions of Shares and Takeover Regulations of 2011 of SEBI and the Takeover Code of the same year of SEBI.

The CBMA and Hostile Takeover

"Hostile Takeover is an alien practice. Many Indian corporates did not experience hostile takeover attempts or efforts. The SEBI mandates several disclosures shareholder approvals and procedural requirements and hence hostile takeover is not possible in Indian conditions. Without the co-operation of the board of directors, of the target company and promoters, no foreign company can acquire an Indian company under Indian law. The following are the most important issues."[21]

1. The pricing of convertible instruments that are making so-called poison pill tactics unviable in India.
2. The details of assets, during the takeover/bid process that is making so-called Crown Jewel techniques, are unviable.
3. Another means of protection against the so-called hostile takeover is what is called the brand appeal which the TATA Group normally uses. A brand is not formed in a single day and it takes interactions of various factors and a consensus among all stakeholders to make a brand becoming publicly known. The brand will always have a goodwill value. The logic is that the core value of the well-known brands is concentrated in the brand name and image and therefore weaning that brand from any other deal would significantly lower its component value and negate several post-merger synergies.

The CBMA and Warranties

"Warranties are contractual assurances from the seller to the buyer about the company (or business) and include: who owns the company before the sale; assets of the company (e.g. intellectual property); financial accounts; and whether the company is subject to any litigation."[22]

The number of matters, the warranties covered, varies depending on the negotiating power of the parties and the nature of the shares or assets a party is acquiring. Warranties and indemnities also are provided for sellers in every transaction in the following cases

1. The title of the shares,
2. The incorporation power authority,
3. Capital structure number for legal compliance,
4. Rules of vital regulators,
5. Regulations of Multiple Agencies,
6. Records books and bookkeeping,
7. Profit and loss account, balance sheet, and other financial statements,
8. Formal stations licences,
9. Employment matters including employee benefit plan insurance being paid and labour disputes pending in the courts,
10. Material contacts,
11. Anti-bribery warranties which include foreign buyers typically insist on Foreign Corrupt Practices Act and Warranties,
12. Warranties related to transparency issues,
13. Insurance,
14. Intellectual property,
15. Real estate,
16. Receivables and inventories,
17. Options for charges and underscore liabilities,
18. Related party transactions,
19. A personal loan is given to company Directors from the company accounts, and
20. Environmental law matters.

The CBMA and Industrial Dispute Act and Essential Acts

The Industrial Disputes Act, 1947 (ID Act) provides for the applications in the case of CBMAs. The ID Act 1947 provides that the transferring company must provide a termination notice and retrenchment compensation to the employees unless the transfer is all on a continuity of service basis and the terms are no less favourable than the terms of the general employment In CBMAs normally the employees are transferred within the continuity of service basis on terms less powerful than their terms of employment with the transferring company. In so far as bribery provisions are concerned, the following are the important pieces of consideration.

1. Indian Penal Code 1860,
2. The Prevention of Corruption Act, 1988,
3. The Prevention of Money Laundering Act, 2002,
4. The Right to Information Act, 2005, and
5. The Central Vigilance Commission Act 2003.
6. There are many local acts of states which contain anti-corruption and anti-bribery provisions.

The CBMA, Specific Relief Act, and Corruption

These provisions demand that a public servant be prohibited from accepting gifts for any official acts from any person. There are provisions for penalising the bribe giver as well as a bribe-taker. The recent Aircel-Maxis case in which the son of a former Union Home minister was arrested by the CBI is a case in point.

Corruption and IBC 2016

The Insolvency and the Bankruptcy Code 2016 provides for a multistage process to tackle insolvency. In the first stage, the firm undergoes the Corporate Insolvency Resolution Process (CIRP) which is called CIRP for a period of 180 to 270 days. During these days, the creditors may attempt to resolve insolvency. If in case of the failure of the CIRP then the form goes to the ultimate stage which involves liquidation permanently. An insolvency professional is always appointed in CIRP where the board of directors stands automatically in a stage akin to the condition of suspended animation and Moratorium is also there on the actions against any director of any company. The authority of the National Company Law Tribunal (NCLT) is the final arbitrator and the regional resolver of all disputes.

The CBMA and FDI

> "In India, Cross border merger is majorly regulated under (i) the Companies Act 2013; (ii) SEBI (Substantial Acquisition of Shares and Takeovers) Regulations 2011; (iii) Competition Act 2002; (iv) Insolvency and Bankruptcy Code 2016; (v) Income Tax Act 1961; (vi) The Department of Industrial Policy and Promotion (DIPP); (vii) Transfer of Property Act 1882."[23]
>
> "The two most relevant regulations under FEMA from a merger & amalgamation perspective are Foreign Exchange Management (Transfer or Issue of Security by a Person Resident Outside India) Regulations, 2000 (the FDI Regulations) and Foreign Exchange Management (Transfer or Issue of any Foreign Security) Regulations, 2004 (the ODI Regulations). FRM (C-B-Merger) Regulation of the year 2018 was released by RBI, as an addendum to FEMA, 1999 to 1999 to include enabling provisions for mergers, demergers, amalgamations, and arrangements between Indian companies and foreign companies covering Inbound and Outbound Investments. This is a significant move as there will be a massive surge in the flow of Foreign Direct Investment with the enactment of new laws and tweaking of existing policies."[24]

The following reasons are often cited for a slight dump in terms of the volume of the CBMA in the year 2016.

1 Buoyant domestic market,
2 Unparalleled interest in the technology-driven start-up sector and
3 Large foreign direct investment inflows.

The outbound activity was witnessed in the following sectors:

1 Energy,
2 Natural resources,
3 Cement,
4 Healthcare and
5 Financial sectors.

Inbound the CBMA is found in high-tech areas. The FDI in India jumped 18% and recorded the figure of US $46.4 billion. India is currently the 10th most attractive destination in the world of FDI, while the United States contributed the highest number of FDI.

In 2016, India witnessed 917 private equity and venture capital investment against 1045, in the year 2015. Private equity investments declined for the first time in four years with nearly a thousand transactions contributed to just below US $15 billion. Start-ups contributed to 70% of the transactions in terms of both these values and deal volumes. The market has been driven by both public and private mergers and acquisitions. A public merger and acquisition carry with that act certain additional compliances under the securities laws and therefore transactions can take longer to close in terms of a time frame. In a private transaction substantial information about the public listed target can be accessed easily in the public domain thereby paving the way for better and faster due diligence so that in a private case, the time taken is always less than compared to a public case.

Enough care should be taken for due diligence both in terms of time and in terms of resources. Given that India has several unlisted but good value Enterprises, there is value in their shares. The share of unlisted companies can also be bought and sold. They offer sometimes significant tax benefits compared to transactions to other transactions. Many CBMAs have been successful because of the correct valuation requirements format by the counterparts in India as well as foreigners. This is important due to issues of measures of due diligence and compliance with all the laws that are there in different parts of the world.

Gaps in the CBMA Domestic and International Learning Experience

According to R.B. Warren, courage is not the option against fear, it is doing your most fearful thing. Mergers and acquisitions will become cross-border mergers and acquisitions, following the below-mentioned conditions. Firstly, the merger and acquisition of the two companies that have headquarters in two different countries, Secondly, in a cross-border merger, the assets and operations of the two companies of different countries or groups establish a new altogether totally different and separate legal entity is a challenging task. Thirdly, if the control of the assets, operation conditions are transferred from a local country to a foreign country company and the local company joins the foreign company, then also it is a CBMA. Fourthly, if such deals are treated differently from local acquisitions as they are governed by different sets of Laws in different parts of the country, and also they are culturally different. One example which is reflective of the above-mentioned conditions is that of McDonnel Douglas Company in recent times. In other words, if the country of the acquirer is located in the home country and the country of the target is located in the host country and the headquarters of the newly merged company can be either of them and also if the portfolio investment. The CBMAs can be classified through the nature of the transactions in the following manner that is first, cross-border purchases, and second, cross-border sales.

The CBMAs include the purchase of a foreign company by an Indian firm and purchases will result in outflows. In cross-border sales, purchases of an Indian company by a foreign form will happen and the sales will create an inbound merger. The following are the top ten purchasers and sellers in the geographical locations of countries in the world in the CBMA arena.

1. The United States,
2. The United Kingdom,
3. France,
4. Germany,
5. The Netherlands,
6. Canada,
7. Switzerland,
8. Spain,
9. Australia, and
10. Japan.

Similarly, the seller countries are as follows:

1. The United States,
2. The United Kingdom,
3. Germany,
4. Canada,
5. France,
6. The Netherlands,
7. Australia,
8. Italy,
9. Sweden, and
10. Spain.

In the Asian continent, the top ten among Asia's purchasing countries are Japan, Singapore, China, Malaysia, the United Arab Emirates, Israel, India,

Saudi Arabia, Korea, and Turkey whereas the top seller countries in Asia are Japan, Korea China, Turkey, Singapore, Israel, Indonesia, India, Thailand, and the Philippines.

Purchase and Sales and CBMAs

The USA ranks among the first in the list of high to low corporate tax levying countries of the world. Among the developed nations too, the USA levies the highest corporate tax. In the case of CBMAs, dealing with the USA, a high incidence of corporate tax in the USA is a natural disadvantage. Analysing the statistics of the CBMA, their normal categorisation is in terms of the major purchasers and the major sellers among the countries. The top ten purchaser countries and the top ten seller countries are notified above to understand the role the law plays through the institutions in the listed countries.

CBMAs and Influencing Factors

Business schools and universities in the United Kingdom, Germany, and the USA researched issues like exploring the factors influencing the processes in CBMAs. One eminent research report among the above has the following important findings. That research study provides an empirical examination of the impact of the national cultural distance, organisational attitudinal gaps, systematic attrition reduction, dissemination on the capability of transactions of mediations among the CBMA stakeholders.

The findings indicate that communication has an early influence on the antecedent and concurrent phases of the negotiation process. National cultural distance and organisational cultural differences negatively influence the effectiveness of the concurrent process. National cultural distance moderates the relationship between communication and effectiveness of concurrent face of the negotiation process, as such that the positive effect of communication is lower when the national cultural distance is higher. Effective steps against employee attrition contribute to the consolidation of going past the CBMA entity. The effectiveness of the concurrent phase positively influences the effectiveness of the consequent face which is the CBMA agreement."[25]

Enabling Factors of the CBMA

Accordingly, the following are the main factors leading to the occurrence of the CBMA. The first enabler is the new innovative and creative technology boom that is right now happening in the world almost at the speed of light. The second is the increasing openness of the global capital market because of the increasing globalisation of the trade market, the capital markets, the financial markets and the labour markets. The third reason is the increasing trend of liquidity in the global capital markets and opportunities. As and when they offer among the continents because the information and the communication technologies made the particular countries irrelevant in so far as the global capital markets are concerned. If some countries are moralists, it is basically because of the following or compliance with the rules of international trade. The reason is the lowering of the trade barriers increasingly by different countries due to agreements among themselves, the World Trade Organization (WTO), and also through the bodies like the United Nations Conference on Trade and Development (UNCTAD) as well as through international agreements like the Group of 20 (G-20) or the European Union or the Organization of American States (OAS), etc.

Across the globe, it has been found out that there is an increase in the number of the venture capitalists throughout the world and these venture capitalists have got experts of the investment banks who look for the opportunities across the globe by the constant watch on the stock markets and evaluation of the individual company assets and the takeover cases are very intelligently and diligently scrutinised.

> As companies grow, domestic mergers and acquisitions allow them to access new product Rangers and its market consolidation. CBMAs is a technique used to quickly enter new markets globally. Companies wanting to pursue this strategy will need to consider the upside benefit and downside risk of these ventures when compared to the green field Investments.[26]

The opportunities are not normally left out to the competitors. On equal footing, one can find out the availability of bank loans on easy times throughout the world even though it may lead in some cases to incidents like the bank frauds as it happened in the Punjab National Bank case involving Nirav Modi and Mehul Chosky in the case of India. "Public Sector Banks (PSBs), largely controlled by Government of India are expectedly in the forefront for industrial promotion. Punjab National Bank ranks only second in the size of PSBs, next only to the State Bank of India (SBI). As part of elaborate white collar crime, the management at some level connived with one Nirav Modi, an alleged diamond exporter from India and advanced loans to the tune of US $1.2 billion." This entire fraud came to light when the non-performing assets of PSBs were reviewed. The Central Bureau of Investigation (a parallel to the FBI of the USA) is at present investigating the fraud. Fraudster Nirav Modi was declared as a fugitive criminal and the Government of India hired expensive barristers in London for obtaining court orders from the United Kingdom to get the fugitive expedited to India for facing the trial. All his properties, costly flats were attached under various legal provisions, including among others, SARFAESI ACT, 2002 (Securitisation and Reconstruction of Financial Assets and Enforcement of Security Interest Act, 2002)."Nirav Modi, at best of his Tom Boyish times like all his fellow fraudster gang members, was photographed in elegant dress for and this jewellery advertisement promotion with best-respected actress models like miss Kate Winslet and Madam Priyanka Chopra."[27] The increasing trend has been found out to be of using the stock market quotations as well as the stocks being kept in pledge and similar innovations to finance the purchase. The existence of globally integrated capital markets is a reality. These capital markets provide foreigners with free access to local financial markets and capital markets and the residents also utilise such opportunities to enter the foreign financial big capital markets. Apart from the globally integrated capital markets, we have segmented capital markets also. These segmented capital markets often exhibit similar bond and equity prices in various geographical areas for similar assets in terms of risk and maturity.

According to David Bach, "Capital market integration is the process, by which capital markets are integrated than segmented, convergence of market risk and price."[28] These segmented capital markets, as an opportunity, will arise when investors are not in a position to use capital from one market to another different market due to the capital control mechanisms or a preference for the local market investments in terms of rules and regulations of either the host or the target country.

In a much acclaimed and reviewed article on theoretical foundations of CBMAs and review of current research and recommendations for the future, the authors probed the diversification strategy connected with the CBMA. Cross-Border Mergers and Acquisitions have gained in popularity over the last decade. Diversification strategy of business group utilises opportunities in CBMAs. Research conducted on diversification strategies of business and CBMAs are, however, not consolidated and does not yield any pragmatic overview of the linkages. Gaps in vital areas exist in the research work. Michael Hit and the Vaidyanatu as two vital members of the research group categorised the conclusions and conjectural underpinnings into the following three parts:

1 Entry mode in a foreign market,
2 Cultural inputs from abroad, and
3 Value-modification-addition connection strategy.

International research into the causes insofar as the types of growth strategies adopted by the companies for the CBMA is concerned, found the following interesting dimensions. Firstly, firms started with domestic production, and secondly, firms began or are beginning to export to the foreign markets. Thirdly, there are firms established that are establishing subsidiaries in the overseas market and lastly, there is the case of the firms that are starting or have started to acquire firms in the foreign markets.

The common market strategy, entry strategies according to international research are found to be that in the case of mergers and acquisitions, mergers and acquisitions are quick, accessible but often very expensive, complex, and are beset many cultural issues. However, the green field of start-up ventures offers above-average returns but more often than not the total

investment is at a greater risk. The third option has been alliances and joint ventures but it has its problems which include that the joint ventures allow risk/cost-sharing and access to other resources but many facilitate entry.
However, they must share profits but also create potential competitors.

> International research further affirms that exporting is another strategy but exporting has got the following issues which include that while exporting is cheaper than establishing local operations but still requires local markets/distribution channels. Licensing is yet another issue that has the least profitable and risky entry strategy and a lack of control could jeopardize the brand or trademark in future exports. Cross-border mergers are increasingly important phenomena in the world economy.

A model of oligopoly in general equilibrium draws on the traditions of both industrial organisation and international trade theory. It allows for strategic interaction between companies, a game-theoretical approach to explaining merger activity. The model predicts that international difference in technology generates incentives for bilateral mergers in which low-cost companies located in one country acquire high-cost companies that facilitate more specialisation in the direction of comparative advantage. As a result, Cross-Border Mergers and Acquisitions serve as instruments of comparative advantage.

> Trade patterns are closer to what would prevail in a comparative Recording world. The model further predicts that cross-border mergers and exports are complements rather than substitutes. The model also predicts that cross border merger waves tend to reduce factory demands and so put forward pressure on the returns to productive factors.[29]

Jack Behrman, in the year 1972, categorised the types of foreign investors in the following manner. There are four types of foreign investors. One is resource seekers and the others are market seekers, efficiency seekers, and strategic asset or capability seekers.

Foreign Investors

> Four types of multinational enterprise activity can be broadly identified, which are as follows- natural resource seekers, market seekers, efficiency seekers, and strategic asset or capability seekers. The natural resource seekers are further subdivided into three main types, they are

1. physical resources seekers of one kind or the other,
2. cheap and well-motivated unskilled or semi-skilled labour seekers and
3. seekers of technological capability, and or marketing expertise and organizational skills capability.[30]

Motives for the CBMA

Vanita Tripathi and Ashu Lamba from the Delhi School of Economics (DSE, Delhi University) and the School of Business Studies, Delhi, respectively, categorised motivational factors as the following:

a   Post-merger pay packs,
b   Value creations,
c   Improvement in efficiency,
d   Marketing and trading opportunities,
e   Strategised motives and
f   Synergistic gains.

The following are among the remaining motives for the CBMA activity:

1   Geographical and industrial diversification,
2   Accelerating growth,
3   Industry consolidation,
4   Utilisation of lower raw material and Labour costs,
5   Leveraging intangible assets,
6   Minimising tax liabilities,
7   Avoiding entry barriers and
8   Avoiding fluctuating exchange rates and lastly following customers.

The Benefits of the CBMA

The benefits of the CBMAs are, among others:

1   An extension of markets,
2   The possibility of raising funds abroad,
3   Synergistic benefits,
4   Technology transfer,
5   Tax Planning and benefits,
6   Foreign exchange earnings,
7   Countering pressures and
8   Greenfield investments, international research established the following motives for international expansion.

Challenges and the CBMA

There are many challenges and problems associated with cross-border mergers and acquisitions. Language differences, strains in managerial communication and fluctuations in currencies are some vital challenges associated with CBMAs.

The cultural dimensions of Geert Hofstede are used to analyze the effects of culture on business in Cross Border Mergers and Acquisitions. Individualistic as against collectivist cultures, relationship orientations versus short term relationship orientations, all these have an impact on mergers and acquisitions and one culture group would back down for the other.[31]

1. Legal problems,
2. Accounting issues,
3. Industry consolidation,
4. Utilisation of lower raw material and labour costs,
5. Leveraging intangible assets,
6. Minimising tax liabilities,
7. Avoiding entry barriers and
8. Avoiding fluctuating exchange rates and lastly following customers.

Professor Jere R. Francis and Inder K. Khurana of the University of Missouri at Columbia in their paper wrote that differences in accounting standards across countries can create information costs that inhibit firms from investing in foreign markets. The similarity in accounting principal in pairs of countries promotes better volumes of the CBMA. One matrix of similarity is GAAP (Generally Accepted Accounting Principles). The professors of Columbia University compared the CBMA transactions among 32 countries from years 1998 to 2004 and confirmed the above finding. In the year 2005, the US administration made it mandatory for everyone to follow the IFRS (International Finance Reporting Standards). Post adoptions of IFRS, the CBMA activity underwent increased volumes. It was found that the CBMA in IFRS paired countries was more prominent than paired countries of pre-IFRS regimes of GAAP.

Accountancy issues are other important aspects of CBMAs. Companies often realise that the merging entities do not have equal levels and scales of internal control and options of internal control leading to financial misappropriation. Secondly, accounting standards normally differ from one country to another country and when mergers and acquisition happens, the items in balance sheets have to be adjusted according to the norms prevalent in the acquired country and not in the host country. Thirdly this is difficult for both the companies as assets may either appear to have been overvalued or undervalued in different countries. A classic example is that of Hindustan Lever Limited (HLL) merging with Brooke Bond India Limited (BBIL). In this case, the two companies are to formalise their accounting process as both the companies were following different accounting policies and integral and internal controls. While the HLL used USGAAP, Brooke Bond India Limited prepared accounts under Indian accounting standards.

Synergy—CBMA

Synergy is not a mere arithmetical summation is when different parts are stitched together, they in combination produce a whole part which is more than a mere simple addition of the individual parts. The term "synergy" comes from the Greek word "synergia" and "synergos," meaning working together. Corporate synergy occurs when corporates interact congruently. Marketing synergy essentially means using the existing marketing channels in combination so that the cumulative effect is more than the summation of individual efforts.

Synergy benefits from the amended deal may ultimately derail the whole process. US railroad, Pennsylvania, and New York Central railroad systems were there in the 1968 acquisition process but failed because of the above problem. In the case of technological aspects, such differences make integration difficult and complex. While one country would like to introduce a better technology, the other country may feel that the consumers in their country are still not ready for such technologically advanced products. The best example in this arena is the Columbia Pictures' acquisition by Sony. Columbia Pictures was into movie production, while Sony's competence was in the movie and television business. Secondly, while Sony was innovative and believed in developing and using the latest technology, Columbia was true in this respect and hence each wanted to stick to its core competence and technology does create integration problems for both of them.

Insofar as strategic issues criteria are concerned, the main problem occurs in the case of generating synergies.

> Synergies often occur in issues like the category of the products and services to offer, the accountability for making the above things happen, the addition of cost-saving and the area in which the effort should be made for such cost savings, the HR issues related to the division of the labour and most importantly the strategic price to be paid to the acquired company. The example here is the merger of British Petroleum with Mobil's corporations. The strategic logic of the deal says that the signs on the market forward are required to compete against each other major Oil Companies and the supermarket chain with gas pumps in Europe.[32]

Corporate Governance

"Corporate Governance is the mechanism, processes, and procedure by which corporates are controlled and directed."[33] "There are three types of convergence in Corporate Governance namely, firstly Convergence in Corporate Law (formal convergence), secondly in business practice (functional convergence) and thirdly, in control contracts (convergence by contract)."[34] Corporate Governance is extremely essential for running any company. Valuation of the firm is affected by different Corporate Governance Systems in different countries, Abnormal returns of shares of the acquiring company before the public announcement of the CBMA results in the up-gradation of value for Corporate Governance.

"Rui Albuquerque et al developed and tested the hypothesis that Foreign Direct Investment promotes Corporate Governance pullovers in the host country.

> Using firm-level data on CBMAs and corporate governance in 22 countries, we find that cross-border M&As are associated with subsequent improvements in the governance, valuation, and productivity of the target firm's local rivals. A positive by-product in terms of value creation due to the CBMA accrues when the acquiring Corporation is from a country under the Rule of Law Doctrine with assured shareholder protection and the acquired Corporation is competitive. We conclude that the international market for corporate control promotes the adoption of better corporate governance practices around the world.[35]

The CBMA Culture Governance and Corporate Governance

Fundamental differences in culture are found across countries. Problems arise due to fundamental differences across countries which involve:

1 Corporate governance,
2 Job security,
3 The regulatory and external environment,
4 Customer expectations,
5 Operating styles due to the different backgrounds,
6 The country's culture and values,
7 The tendency to overpay,
8 Failure to integrate, and
9 HR issues.

An example in this category is the one that the employees of the merging entities might have differences in work culture such as employees being accustomed to having access to the top management, flexible work schedule and relaxed dress code. When the two entities merge, the new management may not approve of such practices. This may cause resentment and sinking productivity and result in conflict among the partners.

The acquirer overpays for the target company which results in the anticipated synergies not materialising or getting delayed and the acquirer getting the hurt feeling and depends on the decision to acquire. The best example in this category is Tata's decision to acquire Jaguar and Land Rover. The motives for this idea by the Tatas were to build economies of scale to reach the new European markets and to get global visibility and acquire new brands. As Tata being a substantial Indian brand, Tata wanted to have global acceptance and thus very heavy amount for the two brands was paid. It did not add much value ultimately failing.

Failure happens due to bad interaction, communication and coordination among merging firms. An example in this category is again the case of the merger between Mobile and BP. In this instant case, it was expected to generate market power and cost savings through the consolidation of its refining and marketing operations in Europe. Post-integration issues made them remain rivals.

Employee Attrition and the CBMA

Some employees of merged entities and others are being laid off. The employees normally leave the company:

1   If the attractive opportunity is available elsewhere,
2   If feelings of mistrust exist,
3   If employees' stress and uncertainty are not dealt with,
4   If there are perceived restrictions on the career plan, and
5   If the changes in the organisational culture.

An example, in this case, is the merger of Bridgestone which initiated cost-cutting measures to locate the causes of the losses, and, in that process, huge losses were occurred instead of being saved.

The challenges shouldered by CBMAs deals include the following problems where the target companies face:

Firstly, de-nationalisation of the domestic firms,
Secondly, downsizing of the acquired Enterprises,
Thirdly, employment reduction,
Fourthly, loss of technological assets,
Fifthly, encouraged market concentration, and
Lastly, resistance to handover corporate control from one country to another country.

Comparative Factors, International versus Emerging Countries, and the CBMA

The following factors affect International mergers and acquisitions in the cross-border scenario:

Firstly, foreign exchange rate,
Secondly, interest rates,
Thirdly, stock prices,
Fourthly, GDP growth rates,
Fifthly, inflation rates, and
Lastly, alternative political conditions.

In case of issues about developed versus emerging countries, the developed countries are characterised by:

Firstly, the significant metric of sustainable per capita GDP growth,
Secondly, globally integrated capital markets,
Thirdly, the well-defined legal system,
Fourthly, availability of a transparent financial system,
Fifthly, currency conversion ability, and
Lastly, a stable government.

In the case of emerging countries, they are characterised by a lack of many of the above-mentioned/raised characteristics of developed countries.

Implementation in Developed Countries—CBMA

While implementing cross-border transactions in the developed countries, LLCs are the main instruments.

> Private Limited companies in the USA are of different types. One specific type of private company in the USA is the Limited Liabilities Company (LLC). It is a business structure that combines the pass-through taxation of a partnership or sole proprietorship with the limited liability of a corporation.[36]

The other vehicles include the payment of huge foreign exchange to the target company. This involves following up on both the Foreign Corrupt Practices Act's (FCPA) provisions and the provisions of the domestic law of the target country. The other simplest manner method is the acquisition of the shares from the stock market through Special Purpose Vehicle (SPV) if the domestic country and the foreign country allow the same in terms of the SEC and SEBI regulations if the acquiring country is the United States and the acquired country is in India. The post-merged company realises synergies at a rapid rate. A contradiction may arise because of the decentralised operations being in use with cultural differences in the target company's political-economic social-cultural environment. Mergers strategies include forward triangular Merger, common for the tax base, and reverse triangular merger common for share acquisitions, both involved with involving the shares of the acquired as a form of payment whether it is an inbound or an outbound merger in the case of many developed countries including the United States of America.

Emerging Markets and the CBMA

The presence of a few vital attributes of a Developed Market (DM) and the absence of standards of operation make a market to be categorised as "Emerging Market" (EM). Certain EMs can be DMs in the near future.

Similarly, certain DMs may slip down in their standards and become EMs. "The term Frontier Market is used for developing countries with slower economies than emerging."[37]

In the case of implementing cross-border transactions in emerging countries, the following issues are very important.

1. Aggressive local government regulations,
2. Classification or confiscatory tax policies,
3. Restrictions on cash remittances,
4. Filing of many returns by various tax authorities including the local Municipal and the national authorities,
5. The issue of convertibility of the currency,
6. Appropriation of foreign currency for money laundering activities and other corrupt practice corrupt practices,
7. Expropriation of foreign residents by the local Mafia as well as insurgent groups if any,
8. There is a possibility of breaking of civil war causing tremendous risk management to the life as well as the property of the multinational corporations,
9. Problems of insurance companies working abroad in not having their local offices in the country of the target company,
10. Non - availability of options like special economic zones or export zones, and
11. Credit-default swaps.

India and the People's Republic of China are the largest economies among EMs. The British tabloid *The Economist* treats the team EM as outdated but now the term is in vogue as a substitute. "Emerging Market hedge fund capital reached record new level in the first quarter of the year 2011 to the level of dollars 121 billion."[38] "The four largest emerging developing economies by other nominal and PPP- adjusted GDP are the BRIC countries namely Brazil, Russia, India and China."[39]

Example of the CBMA in Intra-emerging Developing Countries

Some of the above issues are reflected in the following cases of CBMAs concerning India:

1. Tata Steel acquiring Chorus group of England,
2. Hindalco of India acquiring US firm,
3. Basil of the USA is acquired by a petrochemical firm,
4. Algoma Steel Corporation of Canada being acquired by Essar Steel of India,
5. Computer science Corporation India Private Limited purchasing firms abroad for rupees 5350 crores,
6. Wipro acquiring a US-based IT-enabled services provider for rupees 2430 crores,

114 *Cross-Border Mergers and Acquisitions*

7   An Indian company acquiring a German medical equipment producer for rupees 2760 crores, and
8   Sun Pharma acquiring a firm in Israel for rupees 1837 crores.

The main issues that come out of the above discussion are firstly different motives work for the cross-border deals both inbound and outbound. Secondly, the socio political cultural economic environment varies across towns and cities and hence the problems get compounded when mergers and acquisition issues cover continents.

Apart from the above, valuation treatment and tax compliance regimes vary across continents. The compliance of tax regimes is fast enough that they do not leave any time of due diligence to both partners in CBMA. Since most of the time the central government agencies are the real tax collecting authorities in many countries of the world, non-compliance with tax issues becomes criminalised. When tort becomes a criminal act, compliance cost increases.

> "In pre Commerce days, tort and crime were not very different. Criminal law prohibits public wrongs and tort law prohibits private wrongs. According to a procedural analysis by Harvard Law Institute, victim restitution is in the criminal process."[40]

Tort Law prescribes the harm as part of the ingredients of harmful action before the demand of remedy is discussed. Criminal Law does not have such limitations. "The criminal defendant, unlike the tort defendant, must be proven guilty beyond a reasonable doubt, the exclusionary rules sometimes apply, and the double Jeopardy rule precludes the same jurisdiction from pursuing multiple convictions for the same conduct."[41]

Compliance with foreign currency management is a complicated affair because of the inherent issues of convertibility, change of rate exchange daily and a plethora of forms to be filled up by both the assignee and the consignee. To conclude, it is important to remember that ignorance of the law is not only an excuse but fatalistic both in terms of legal issues as well as in terms of survival issues of the firms in the CBMA environment.

The CBMA and Specific Types of Mergers

Apart from horizontal and vertical mergers, there are specific measures like congeneric mergers, conglomerate, cash mergers, triangular mergers that take care of special situations in the environment of CBMAs. For example, a triangular merger is often resorted to for regulatory and tax reasons. If the real acquiree happens to be a subsidiary or substantial acquiree and mergers with the acquired target, such an arrangement is called a tripartite agreement. A triangular merger may be forward or reverse. Acquisition of shares and transferability of the same are important dimensions in CBMAs. With the introduction of the Companies Act, 2013, although the shares of a public company are freely transferable, share transfer restrictions for even public companies have been granted statutory sanction. While acquiring shares of a private company, it is therefore advisable for the acquirer to ensure that the non-ceiling shareholders waive any rights they may have under the articles of association.

Fraud and the CBMA

Insider Trading

According to the Securities and Exchange Board of India (SEBI) Act, 1992 read with SEBI Prohibition of Insider Trading (PIT) regulations 1992, many problems came up in the case of cross-border mergers. The rules stand amended in the year 2015. In the previous era, the crime of insider trading was dealt with only fines to the tune of rupees 10 lakhs to 25 lakhs or three times the profit of the person from the insider trading. The newly amended rules make the punishment stringent because the new rules are very expensive in their outreach and scope. PIT regulations also called the prohibition of insider trading regulations define insider trading as communicating Unpublished Price Sensitive Information (UPSI) and any person from procuring UPSI from an Insider, and an insider from trading in securities when in possession of the unpublished price sensitive information. Thus, PIT regulations prohibit insider trading from both origin and destination. Under the above regulations, an insider is one who is the connected person and who is in a position of having access to UPSI.

According to the SEBI guidelines, a connected person is directly or indirectly in touch with the company, firstly, utilising frequent communication with the offices of the company and secondly, by being in contractual fiduciary employment or relationship and thirdly, by holding any position of professional or business relationship importance.

Regulation 2(n) of the PIT prohibits access to UPSI to immediate relatives, a holding, associate, or a subsidiary company. UPSI means any information relating to company audit security, directly or indirectly, that is not generally available, and which upon becoming available is likely to materially affect the price of the securities. It includes, firstly, financial results; secondly, dividend; thirdly, change in capital structure; fourthly, mergers; fifthly, demergers; sixthly, acquisitions; seventhly, listings; eighthly, disposals; and lastly expansion of business plans and other such transactions.

The PIT regulations have enhanced the role of a compliance officer in that concerning monitoring and regulating trading by employees and connected persons, in particular monitoring and approving of the trading plans, his decisions are of vital importance. To prevent the misuse of confidential information, the organisation shall adopt a Chinese wall policy that segregates routine areas of the organisation with confidential areas of information from sales, marketing, investment advice or strategic planning which the headquarters of the UN communicates with various subsidiaries departments. The PIT regulations further emphasise strict measures for monitoring even the Chinese wall procedures.

Provision of Section 195 of Companies Act, 2013

Section 195 of Companies Act, 2013 prohibits all persons including any director or key managerial personnel of a company from engaging in insider trading. This section does not distinguish between a listed and an unlisted company or even between a private and a public company whereas SEBI insider regulations apply only to the listed public companies. This is an area of further research that will be addressed subsequently in this thesis.

Competition Law and the CBMA

The Competition Act of 2002 was meant to be a replacement of the Monopolies and Restricted Trade Practices Act, 1969 (MRTP Act). By Competition Act, 2002, the competition is viewed in a different environment. It covers anti-competitive agreements according to Section 3, abuse of dominance according to Section 4 and a combination of different possibilities through Sections 5,6, 20, 29, 30 and 31. Competition Commission of India Regulations 2011 is called combination regulations. They govern how the Competition Commission of India will regulate combinations causing or likely causing an Appreciable Adverse Effect on the Competition (AAEC).

Provisions and Implementation of the Stamp Duty Act (1899)

The Stamp Duty Act (SDA) provides for registration and payment of Duty to the competent authority on an ad valorem pro-rata basis. The judgement on Hindustan Lever Limited clarified various contentions of the transacting parties in connection with the stamp duty aspects. The following are the legal requirements:

1   Transfer inter Vivos,
2   Stamp duty to be levied on conveyance deed/instrument, and
3   Stamp duty rate to be prescribed in the schedule of the Stamp Act.

Judicial Review

Judicial pronouncements both the pre-NCLT era and the emergence of case law in terms of the judgments of the Supreme Court of India are wide and varied. Stamp duty laws in various states are different depending on the policy of promotion of industrial investment in such states. Industrial promotion inside the state is normally the responsibility of the state governments. For instance, in Punjab, there is no amendment in the stamp act and there is no high court ruling as of today. In the Delhi, NCR stamp duty is levied at 3% on the consideration based on the judgment of the Delhi High

Court in the matter of *Delhi Towers Limited versus the State of Delhi NCT*. In Haryana, stamp duty is levied on the order of the high court and the NCLT order at the rate of 5% on the fair value of immovable property located in Haryana as per the notification. The driving momentum behind any CBMA is the aspiration for acquiring additional value through the activity of CBMA. Failure to realise such a value is more damaging to the reputation of the acquiring company.; The reason here is that the acquiring company takes the initiative in the normal course of action.

Time consumed during the process of conducting of due diligence and pre-acquisition completion of integration process may not make the aspirations of the cross-border and acquisition process to be realised if such time is not according to the initial plan and shoots up beyond the management capability of both the acquiring and the acquired company.

Time is also an opportunity, and, if time is lost due to mismanagement and bad planning, such a loss will result in making further problems coming up rather than solving them. In the context of the cross-border mergers and acquisitions, it needs to be remembered that since cross-border mergers and acquisitions work in the global environment, the entire process of integration and consolidation must take into account the various changes in the law systems and the taxation systems of both the host and the foreign country of CBMA process. There are disconnections between the due diligence and execution of the integration team and the target process. The gap described above normally results in (Figures 2.7 and 2.8)

a   Non-coordination,
b   Non-availability of subject matter experts.

Innovation and the CBMA

"Change is inevitable. The only area where changelessness is witnessed changes itself. Innovation is creativity in action. The concept of innovation management juxtaposes innovation activities with the change of management."[42] Bringing external expertise in the Innovation Management Office (IMO) is strategically proved as the best-benchmarked practice to begin within any competent the CBMA process. In-house talent in terms of both skill and competency may be available but more often than not, lack of experience is the CFF in such in-house available talent. Substituting the external proven expertise with an immature in-house skill as a cost-savings measure can be a fatal step in the wrong direction. Learning and continuous training in (a) process basics, (b) tools, (c) templates, and (d) strategies is a must in any competent the CBMA process. From the stage of the pre-merger study of the matrix to the stage of post-merger consolidation and integration, the role of competent integration export of multifaceted talent in law, management, psychology, and culture of both the host and the foreign country is a must for any competent the CBMA process. The integration expert is expected to have proven expertise in the following subjects:

118   *Cross-Border Mergers and Acquisitions*

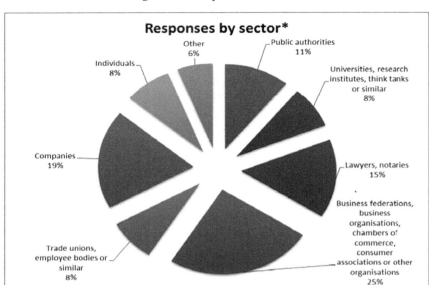

*On the basis of 149 responses, which provided the information about the sector (out of the total number of 151 replies).

Figure 2.7 Sectoral Response.
Source: Survey Report from London.

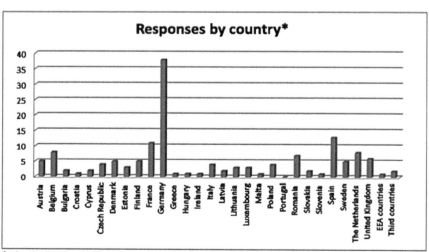

* On the basis of 149 responses, which provided the information about the country of origin (out of the total number of 151 replies).

Figure 2.8 Country Response.
Source: Survey Report from London.

1   Human resources and human rights,
2   Information Technology and Information and Communication Technology,
3   Labour Trade Union and land law, and
4   Law of compensation, damage and negotiation instruments.

Integration and the CBMA

The process of combining two organisations involves assets, people, resources, tasks, and supporting information technology and such a process is called Integration. "Integration planning is one of the most challenging areas to address pre-closure during CBMA."[43]

The integration team must be available right from the beginning till the end with adequate planning and expertise in crisis management at every process both routine automatic and critical phases of the CBMA. The quantum of the teams required for coordination depends on (a) the complexity of the process of cross-border, (b) time availability and (c) the quality of operational details involved in the process.

Normally twelve to sixteen teams of experts are required for the fulfilment of the process. The more the number of coordination teams, the more will be the need for seamless connectivity among all of them so that the sharing of process and modification details in all the stages remain continuous and consistent with the objectives of the process of CBMAs. As has been mentioned in Chapter 1, the year 2015 was a record year of global CBMA activity with a figure of US $4.75 trillion, which does not take into account several unreported CBMAs of micro- and medium-sized industries in Software Architecture and Software Development. Global statistics available from competent agencies point out that US $183 billion worth of CBMAs activity was witnessed in the USA alone in the year 2014 with 331 major acquisitions. US $166 trillion was spent in the cross-border mergers and acquisitions in the USA in the year 2014 out of the above mentioned USA $183.7 billion.

Technology and the CBMA

> "Accessing technology has become one of the important motivations for CBMA. The resistance of the host country, the capacity to absorb the target technical are the main issues."[44]

Technology is the driving force behind the CBMA. The Critical Success Factor (CSF) in the success of any CBMA is found out to be (a) connection, (b) communication and (c) cost reduction. It is further found out that the current wave of mergers and acquisitions across borders is more witnessed both in terms of quality and quantity in start-up Industries across previously untouched areas of the continents of Africa, Asia and the Middle East. Apart from covering virgin areas the current way of CBMAs across continents also covers (a) consumer electronics, (b) the tourism industry and c) the hospitality industry. However, the world over, the areas of North America and Europe continue to exercise this proportional influence on the activities of intercontinental CBMAs. The oil-rich Middle East does not lag behind North America and Europe in terms of acquiring companies in the sectors of oil marketing in the major oil-consuming areas of North America and Europe. Cash richness is the common ingredient among the above-mentioned regions of investment experience. The example of Dubai emerging as the most influential real estate investor and developer across the world including in the hospitality industry of the highest bracket is case in point. New York City of the United States of America is a case in point.

Research and the CBMA

Research is constituted of creative and systematic work undertaken to increase the stock of knowledge to devise new applications. The year 2018 witnessed the big-ticket investment in the intercontinental cross-border mergers and acquisitions and the small and middle-level Cross Border Mergers and Acquisitions are also taking up in the newly emerging areas of Nanotechnology and energy-saving research and development-oriented equipment."[45] It is found out in this research that there is always a cyclical movement in the CBMA activity across the continents and such a pattern involves a delineated and marked cycle of moments from big to the middle to small activity and again followed up by middle to big activities. The transactional cycle goes on taking in its stride the various changing environmental legal and cultural inputs across the globe.

Increasing the activity of the CBMA draws attention to the question of the sharing of assets. Assets mean money and hands sharing of money means regulatory requirement fulfilment of institutions like the Department of Justice (DOJ) of the United States of America if it is the United States of America and requirements of SEBI, DRI, ED, RBI, and CA 2013 if it is the case of India. The efforts of this research found out that there are indeed gaps between performance records of Law enforcement in the case of the USA and India. The maximum impact of this gap is on the inordinate delay that takes place in India for contract enforcement, to (b) access to justice and (c) the timely intervention of the approved agencies in case of prevention of fraud and corruption based on rent-seeking activities of power brokers under the section of the government machinery. It takes a few days to render justice to redress the grievance of a matter in the USA whereas it takes years for such redress of grievance in an equally democratic country like India. This proves another point in this study and through this study, it is unambiguously affirmed that similar political systems believing in similar sociopolitical beliefs do not necessarily mean similar access to government functioning and similar capabilities of institutional trustworthiness in addressing crisis-ridden problems of economic activity across the continents. An effort for synergy is a Critical Success Factor in the process of the CBMA.

Delayed justice does not infer denial of justice. It brings the by-product of evaporation of legitimacy of the justice system. Vacuum so created is occupied by non-state actors like Mafiosi. Non-state activity means non-just action and NON-JUSTICE is the result. The USA is an exemplary country and the way implements were launched on Mr Donald Trump is an example of the doctrine of Rule of Law in the USA.

The Effect of Synergy

The effect of synergy is seen maximum in the following aspects of logistics:

1 Time,
2 Language,
3 Addressing cultural differences,
4 Due diligence process and
5 Tackling the insecurity feelings among the workforce.

Intercontinental cross-border merger position is not as is as simple as the famous saying of Julius Caesar, "I came I saw and I conquered." The major process of complexity and enormous diversity in the fields of law, psychology, ecology and geography is involved in buying a company that is 800 miles away in comparison to buying a company 8000 miles away in a different continent altogether.

Employment laws in France, Germany and the Netherlands are different from the employment laws of the United States of America and Canada. There are minute differences and major differences in both the spirit and the letter of the law even among different states of the United States of America, leave alone the differences among the United States of America and Canada. Cultural expectation regarding work ethic is different from (a) city to city, (b) country to country and (c) continent to continent.

Culture and CBMAs

Culture is felt through:

a Leadership,
b Marketing,
c Consumerist habits and
d Labour Law.

Indian wedding normally takes a week or so time, whereas a western wedding may take a few hours. While the happy occasion of the wedding is no comparison for the serious business of cross-border mergers, it is important to mention that the delay is sometimes built in many activities and a go-slow attitude is seen as the signature of the human race and the culture of the region. Tolerance to irregularities and gloss over corrupt behaviour is reflective of misgovernance in any country.

The CBMA and Corruption

A manual for the prevention of corruption and Foreign Corrupt Practices Act(FCPA) of the United States by the Attorney General's office is meant to be followed by all practitioners, both a domestic entrepreneur and those who pursue intercontinental and intercontinental CBMA. The manual seeks to cover (a) bribery, (b) corruption, (c) export loss, (d) currency risk and e) prevention of fraud in dispute resolution. Institutions of rule of law are reflected in making available provisions like the jury to make immediate access to justice and also to establish the principle of equality before the law for all the persons within its control. The Federal Bureau of Investigation conducted a raid on April 8, 2018, on the premises of the private advocate of the president of the United States of America. This is an example of the prevalence of the rule of law in that great country. Justice is this service that carries the signature of the state. Speedier and concrete justice means effective and just ways of transactions may vary across the USA but in the matters of cross-border practice as well as economic and industrial issues concerned, the regulatory code of the office of Attorney General or any other matters involving complaints to various law enforcing authority, the United States has been an exemplary country with access to very quick justice in the matters related to economic affairs across and among people of different regions and continents. While economic opportunities entice many a practitioner of private equity investment promotion and evincing interest among entrepreneurs in the CBMA activity, the following factors afflict the continent of Africa and some of the trouble-prone areas of Asia and Latin America:

1 Political instability,
2 Terrorism,
3 Insurgency,
4 Unpredictability,
5 Absence of judicial structure,
6 The insecurity of life and property,
7 Non-enforcement of instruments of negotiation,
8 Low reputation,
9 Low-end devices on human development and transparency,
10 Intonation in warfare among different resident groups, and
11 Threatening envelope of civil war.

The often recited case study explaining the significance of the above points is the infamous bombing in France or the Harrods publishing house bombing case. Hence it can be concluded that corruption and mal governance often reduce the reputation of the institution of the state which is reflected both in the private and public sectors of any country.

Lawyers and the CBMA

The Service of "Law" means the prevalence of Justice and enforcement of contract without bias. Justice is the facility, accessible TRUTH, to prevail, in case of doubt and uncertainty, adjudication must ensure the prevalence of Raw. Lawyers are not managers responsible for deal-making through the CBMA. However, drafting and deal stitching after through mastery of legal provision of both countries in case the CBMA must preceed in action before a deal is executed. Legal due diligence is the most essential ingredient in any successful conclusion of the CBMA effort.

Lawyers play a very significant role in the CBMA. Under their professional knowledge and training, lawyers become veteran transaction experts. Transaction and negotiation of details are the important dimensions of an ongoing process of due diligence and integration in complex CBMAs. In Europe, Los Angeles, Latin America, Asia, Malaysia, or for that matter in any part of the world, unfortunately, lawyers are not transactional experts even though they are expected to be one. The USA, however, has been endowed with lawyers having transactional expertise. The lawyers often go to the dinner parties of other experts to increase the interaction among all of them so that they contribute to the process of due diligence to prevent the cropping up of any complicated issue in the future course of action. In contrast, the lawyers of China or Vietnam or for that matter Bangladesh often end up as persons who take the notes and later interpret and email their considered advice. Africa while offering great opportunities is also a mixture of many factors of diversity. There are issues of purchasing contracts and there are also issues of governmental intervention and frequent change of governmental authorities and hence the rules in many African countries. Coupled with the above there is the problem of availability of skilled manpower with work ethic attitude. Tribal and primordial loyalty often dominates the secular attraction towards a professional career. The USA has an experience of their workforce assuming a cultural similarity in the places of work in a different continent and getting shocked when a 180-degree opposite cultural dissimilarity is witnessed in a 360-degree dimension. It has been empirically proved that while it takes three years in the USA for a dispute resolution it may take 7 x 3 years, which means 21 years minimum in Africa.

Reasons for Failure of the CBMA

"Research suggests that intercultural distance is one of the major indicators of why international mergers and acquisitions fail."[46]

It is found out through this study that the following are the reasons for the failure of many attempts of the CBMA

1   Lack of adequate research in the era of pre-planning,
2   Lack of adequate time preparation and
3   Absence of prioritisation.

Notes

1. European Commission Directorate General Justice and Consumers, Summary of Responses to The Public Consultation on Cross Border Mergers and Divisions, EUROPEAN COMMISSION (October, 2015) http://ec.europa.eu/internal_market/consultations/2014/cross-border-mergersdivisions/docs/summary-of-responses_en.pdf (Last visited on May 8, 2018).
2. Jane E. Dutton & Robert B. Duncan, The Influence of The Strategic Planning Process on Strategic Change, 8 STRATEGIC MANAGEMENT JOURNAL, 103–116 (March/April, 1987).
3. PORTER MAICHAEL E, COMPETITIVE ADVANTAGE (1985).
4. M/S. Surendra Trading Company v. M/S. JuggilalKamlapat Jute Mills Company Limited and Others, CAJ 8400, 2017 SC.
5. THE HINDU, BUSINESS LINE ,05 (Kolkata Edn, April 27, 2018).
6. THE HINDU, BUSINESS LINE ,06 (Kolkata Edn, April 27, 2018)
7. GautamChatterjee, First 2–3 years of RERA transition period will be really painful: Maha RERA chief, LIVE MINT, (April 24, 2018) https://www.livemint.com/Companies/PUD9i7o 0gansu6U1gOlK8J/First-twothree-years-of-RERA-transition-period-will-be-real.html (Last visited on May 10, 2018).
8. FDI Relaxation to help attract Foreign Investors, THE ECONOMIC TIMES, https://economictimes.indiatimes.com/news/economy/policy/fdi-relaxation-to-help-attractforeign-investers-usispf-articleshow-62458377.cms (Last visited on May 25, 2018).
9. Timothy A. Mackey, ET AL, Legal Due Diligence in International M&A, https://webstorage.paulhastings.com/Documents/PDFs/legal-due-diligence-in-international-m-a.pdf (Last visited on May 23, 2018).
10. Ibid.
11. Reg 2(ha), SEBI (1991).
12. Reg 3A, SEBI ACT (1991).
13. Sec 24, SEBI ACT (1991).
14. Reg 13, SEBI ACT (1991).
15. THE HINDU, BUSINESS LINE, 06 (Kolkata Edn, April 27, 2018).
16. Ibid.
17. Reg. 2(e), SEBI ACT, (1991).
18. Ibid.
19. Reg. 12 (cha), SEBI ACT, (1991) defines price sensitive information.
20. Reg. 3, 3[A], Insider Trading is prohibited, Insider trading.
21. Difference between warranty indemnity Mergers and Acquisitions, LEGALVISION, (May 23, 2017), https://legalvision.com.au/difference-between-warranty-indemnity-ma-transaction/ (Last visited on May 22, 2018).
22. ShruthiShenoy&Ifla A, India: Cross Border Mergers – Key Regulatory Aspects to Consider, NOVOJURIS LEGAL, (April 25, 2018). http://www.mondaq.com/india/x/695282/M+A+ Private+equity/Cross+Border+Mergers+Key+Regulatoyr+Aspects+To+Consider, (Last visited on May 10, 2018).
23. ShruthiShenoy, Ifla A., India: Cross Border Mergers – Key Regulatory Aspects to Consider, NOVOJURIS LEGAL, (April 25, 2018) http://www.mondaq.com/india/x/695282/M+A+ Private+equity/Cross+Border+Mergers+Key+Regulatoyr+Aspects+To+Consider, (Last visited on May 10, 2018).
24. Team EY, Buying & Selling: Cross-Border Mergers and Acquisitions and the U.S. Corporate Income Tax [2015 REPORT], BUSINESS ROUNDTABLE (March10,2015),https://www.businessroundtable.org/resources/buying-and-selling-cross-border-mergers-andacquisitions-and-us-corporate-income-tax. (Last visited on May 26, 2018).
25. Faisal Ahammad ET AL., Exploring the factors influencing the negotiation process in crossborder M&A, RESEARCHGATE, https://www.researchgate.net/

26. Nirav Modi Scam at Punjab National Bank, BUSINESS STANDARD (March 2016), www.business-standard.com/tiopic/nirav-modi-scam-at-pnb (Last visited on June 6, 2018).
27. Capital Market Integration, BRITANICA, https://www.britanica.com/topic/capital-marketintegration-1916836. (Last visited on June 6, 2018).
28. Cross Border Mergers and Acquisitions, AMAZONAWS, (March 16, 2004) https://s3.amazonaws.com/academia.edu.documents/4624662/crossborderma_jim_pdf?Awsaccesskeyid=Akiaiwowyyg (Last visited on May 6, 2018)
29. JACK BEHRMAN, MULTINATIONAL ENTERPRISES AND THE GLOBAL ECONOMY.
30. Vanita Tripathi, Ashu Lamba, What drives cross-border mergers and acquisitions?: A study of Indian multinational enterprises, EMERALD GROUP PUBLISHING LIMITED, (2015) http://www.emeraldinsight.com/doi/abs/10.1108/JSMA-05-2015-0040?journalCode=jsma (Last visited on May 6, 2018).
31. Legal Issues to Consider in a Mergers and Acquisition Transaction, ZAGRANS, http://zagrans.com/legal-issues-to-consider-in-a-mergers-and-acquicition-transaction/ (Last visited on May 7, 2018)
32. Starks, Laura T. And Wei Kelsey D, Cross Border Mergers and Differences in Corporate Governance, 13 INTERNATIONAL REVIEW OF FINANCE, 265–297, (2013).
33. SHAILER GREGORY, AN INTRODUCTION TO CORPORATE GOVERNANCE IN AUSTRALIA, PEARSON EDUCATION AUSTRALIA, SYDNEY, (2004).
34. Stefano, Rosi. & Paolo. Volpin, The Governance Motive in Cross Border Mergers and Acquisitions. London Education, 05–22, (2013).
35. Rui Albuquerque ET AL, International Corporate Governance Spillovers: Evidence from Cross-Border Mergers and Acquisitions, INTERNATIONAL MONETARY FUND, (November 12, 2013) https://www.imf.org/en/Publications/WP/Issues/2016/12/31/International-CorporateGovernance-Spillovers-Evidence-from-Cross-Border-Mergers-and-41049 (Last visited on May 9, 2018).
36. Schwindt Kari, Limited Liability Companies: Issues in Member Liability. 44 UCLA Law Review, 1541, (2017).
37. MSCI will downgrade Argentina to frontier market - MarketWatchMarketWatch-Russia Faces Specter of Index Demotion, MARKETWATCH, (February 09, 2018), https://www.marketwatch.com/story/msci-downgrade-argentina-frontier-market-new-york (Last visited on May 9, 2018).
38. BRICS Is Passe, Time Now for 3g:Citi, PRESS TRUST OF INDIA, (January 20, 2013),http://www.business-standard.com/article/economy-policy/brics-is-passe-time-now-for-3g-citi111022300246_1.html (Last visited on May 8, 2018).
39. The Long View: How adventurous are emerging markets? FINANCIAL MARKET, https://www.ft.com/content/be77e600-605f-11db-a716-0000779e2340 (Last visited on May 8, 2018).
40. David J. Seipp, The Distinction Between Crime and Tort in the Early Common Law, 76 B.U.L. REV, 59, (1996).
41. William J. Stuntz, Substance, Process, and the Civil-Criminal7J, CONTEMP. LEGAL, 19–24, (1996).
42. Kelly, P. Krangburg M. et al., Technological Innovation: A Critical Review of Current Knowledge, 11–46, (1978)
43. Mergers and Acquisitions Transaction Survey Results, Modalnionds http://modalnionds.com/modality/ma-transaction-survey-results/ (Last visited on May 9, 2018)
44. Cross Border Mergers and Acquisitions, Ieeexplore, (Jun 1, 2014), http://ieeeplore.ieee.org/document/6414271/ (Last visited on May 9, 2018)

45 OECD (2015) Frascati Manual 2015: Guidelines for Collecting and Reporting Data on Research and Experimental Development, the Measurement of Scientific, Technological and Innovation Activities, OECD Publishing, Paris, 12–17, (2015).
46 Managing Culture in Cross Border Mergers, Communicaid, (June 21, 2016) http://www.communicaid.com/cross-cultural-training/blog/managing-culture-in-cross-bordermeg (Last visited on March 9, 2018).

3 CBMA, Competition Law, Antitrust and Demerger

Introduction

Chapter 2 mentioned the relevant laws, rules, regulations in connection with CBMA. In this chapter, the specific laws, namely Competition, Antitrust and De-merger aspects, would be dealt with in finding out answers to research objectives.

Competition, Antitrust and the CBMA

Fair play and trust are the most important elements of both policymaking and in the enforcement of any law. Regulations are part of the legal process to draw a fine line between over-regulation and under-regulation. The enthusiasm for liberalisation through waiving the limitations or removing obstructions on commercial transactions for ensuring necessary compliance with the law is an act of fine and delicate balance in any legitimate activity of the organisation or the government.

"The never-ending discussions and debates surrounding voluntary mandatory notifications, the efficacy of the Effects Test, and the pre-review and post-review schools of thought have been the major contributors to the west puzzle of merger regulation."[1] Most Competition Laws do not prohibit anticompetitive conduct that affects foreign target markets as long as there is no spill-over effect in the home market.

The apparent contradiction between competitive markets and consumer welfare through regulations in Cross-Border Mergers and Acquisitions aspect did not go uncriticised from both economics and legal scholars globally. Many observers commented in negative terms about the utility/relevance of the Sherman Act, 1980.

Pre-liberalised and pre-1990 Indian economy, situated in the command control licence permit system from within and a socialistic figment of imagination from without never had in it an ingredient of the Sherman Act of the United States to control the syndicates and also to promote the competition. The MRTPC Act, 1969 (Monopolies and Restrictive Trade Practices (MRTPC) Act) was a feeble attempt that unfortunately left much to be desired and which was known for its loopholes and its provisions for the

DOI: 10.4324/9781003396987-3

rent-seeking economy. Law reform has become essential when economic reform has become reality post-1990. The Competition Act, 2002 has been enacted to provide a competition law regime that meets and suits the demands of the changed economic scenario in India. There were two models before India at the time of liberalisation in 1991, namely the United States of America Model and the European Model.

The CBMA and Antitrust Laws

In the last part of the 19th century, namely in the year 1890, antitrust law was first introduced in the business environment of the USA. The purpose of the antitrust law introduced, therefore, was to control the concentration of power of capital and industry among a certain few industrial powerhouses. Justice not merely in political life was thought to be extended to economic life. To survive its political projection and equality not merely among political actors but among business houses also need to be felt as a complimentary gesture was realised very early in the 19th and 20th centuries. The purpose was again to enhance competition through core values of freedom, distributive justice and pluralism which underscore the purpose of the antitrust legislation in the United States. Small businesses and individual entrepreneurs were protected from the jaws of the large and powerful capitalistic Leviathan of an emerging world economy in the United States of America. "However, after almost 100 years, in 1980, economic efficiency began to emerge as the goal of antitrust policy, without regard to the inability of small struggling competitors to match the operating efficiency of the large competitor."[2] "The Sherman Act, 1890 provides for the restraint or monopolization of commerce with foreign nations. The Clayton Act, 1914 clarifies that commerce with similar inclusiveness although its substantial provisions limit their foreign applications."[3] "Certain provisions of Clayton Act apply only to scales for consumption or resale within the United States."[4]

"Other problems of the Clayton Act, 1914 are similarly limiting and they are concerned with the mergers whose anticompetitive effects may be felt within a section of a country."[5] Competition is vital for allocative efficiency of resources from the economy. Competition means fairness and a level playing field with equality of opportunity being the philosophical bedrock. Antitrust efforts of the legal framework in the USA, hence, are more concerned about competition. Consumer welfare is ensured by more competition than more profit for monopolists.

The antitrust enforcement agencies in the United States do not view mergers and acquisitions as part of competitive regimes even though the same is a practice in the rest of the world. The countries in Asia and South America that follow socialistic regimes tend to view a big company as a monopoly company and hence do not trust the efficiency of multinational corporations and instead protect the local non-qualitative or low quality in poor industries at the cost of inefficiency and non-production of the consumer interest. They blame capitalism everywhere.

The CBMA and US Antitrust Experience

The Clayton Act, 1914 was passed by the 63rd Congress of the USA. This Act was the contribution of 9-time members of the House of Representatives from Alabama and a latter-day federal Judge Henry Clayton. When the Sherman Act, 1890 was not able to curb the monopolies and predatory pricing to large corporations and trusts who were driving out local small-time businesses of the market through syndicates and industrial coups through acquisitions and mergers, Ohio's Representative Robert Crosser warned that industrial slavery would soon bother the US.

A) if monopolies are allowed uncontrolled growth.

The Clayton Act, 1914 became a very powerful law in strengthening the newly formed structure called FTC, the Federal Trade Commission. The Clayton Act banned price discrimination methods and put strict curbs on mergers that discourage competition. It also permitted strikes and boycotts. It allowed forming of labour unions under federal law. The Clayton Act became law on October 15, 1914, after assent by President Woodrow Wilson.

Section 7 of the Clayton Act, 1914 proscribes the actuation of shares or mergers in order to lessen competition or in order to form a monopoly.

> Apart from the Clayton Act, the Sherman Act states that every contract, combination, or conspiracy that restrains trade, or commerce among the States, or with the foundations, is illegal and that every person who monopolizes, is guilty of a felony. The Sherman Act, 1890 is the one that concerns the CBMAs more than the Clayton Act, 1914."[6]

The US law is effectively controlling and monitoring the regulation of cross-border mergers as merging is the creation of the US Courts."[7] "The so-called best has come out the judicial review under the Sherman Act, 1819 in the case of United States vs Aluminium company of America."[8] It was during the presidency of Franklin Delano Roosevelt that the Department of Justice (DOJ) charged Aluminium Company of America with illegal monopolisation and demanded that the company be dissolved.

Alan Greenspan, the former Federal Reserve Chairman, feels, "it was not a quasi-monopoly and hence should not have been subjected to the antitrust action."[9] Greenspan believes that the vision of the Aluminium Company of America as a threat to competition is erroneous, as the company is being condemned for being too successful, and too good a competitor, whatever damage the antitrust law may have done to the economy of the United States,

> whatever distortions of the structure of the capital of the nation they may have created, these are less disastrous than the fact that the effective purpose, the hidden intact, and the actual practice of the antitrust laws in the United States have led to the condemnation of reproductive and efficient members of the society because they are productive and efficient.[10]

The court must balance the legitimate interest of the state of the United States and the interest of the foreign nations also while maintaining a balance of foreign relations to determine whether the antitrust effects of substantial enough to grant jurisdiction and application of the US Antitrust Law and if they are not substantial enough, then fair play and justice must follow.

> The US Supreme Court has not determined whether a reasonableness test applies to the effects test. In Hartford fire Institutions company versus California, the court held that the committee was the only required when there is a true conflict between foreign and domestic law.[11]
>
> The above judgment is interpreted in that if a US Court could withhold its exercise of jurisdiction based on the doctrine of the committee, the only relevant inquiry is whether a foreign defendant was compelled by foreign law to violate the US law exist or not.[12]
>
> In CBMA, the committee would rarely be the grounds for foreign Acts not to fall under the jurisdiction of the US Courts, unless government-owned entities were participants. The US Courts very rarely ban or intervene in case of large-scale cross-border mergers.

"The concept of the positive committee allows the US government to request the sovereign where the corporations are domiciled to intervene."[13] "Much of the merger enforcement activity in the US today is composed of premerger approvals and notification requirements." "Congress enacted the Hart-Scott-Rodino (HSR) or Antitrust Improvement Act of 1976 by subjecting mergers, affecting the US, to be reviewed by either the Department of Justice (DOJ)or the Federal Trade Commission (FTC) before completing a Merger."[14]

The power and responsibility of review of those occurrences like Mergers Crossing specific the thresholds are entrusted to antitrust agencies. This new review mechanism was the creation of the Hart-Scott-Rodino Improvement Act, 1976. This Act is briefly known as the HSR Act.

> If, after 30 days waiting period, the relevant agency still has doubts about the competitive effects of the notified transaction, the agency will issue a request for additional information and documentary materials also known as a second request opening an in-depth review into the transaction. In the year 2016 and 2015 both the FTC and DOJ recorded the increase in the number of the second request.[15]

As per the legal provisions of the HSR Act, 1978, the DOJ looked seriously into its enforcement activity against Duke Energy Corporation in connection with the acquisition of the Osprey Energy Centers in January 2017. The course of the enforcement is that during the mandatory waiting period, under provisions of HSR, this was the acquisition of securities resulting in ownership advantage. Duke ultimately agreed to pay the US$ 600,000 to resolve the complaint with DOJ.

HSR provisions were repeatedly violated by individual companies and none were spared from paying penalties. In the year 2017, the DOJ combined with the FTC and took joint action against defaulters. Penalties to the tune of US$ 720,000 were paid, for instance, in one case where a man and his wife violated provisions of HSR in purchasing shares of Colfax Corporation and Danaher Corporation in the years 2008 and 2011.

> Behavioural remedies have attracted attention more broadly. In December 2017, US Senator Elizabeth Warren delivered her speech at the Open Markets Institute (OMI) calling for more aggressive antitrust enforcement and commenting on the work of the Department of Justice (DOJ) in filing a suit against AT and T and Time Warner.[16]

Senator Warren noted specifically that in order "to revive competition in our economy particularly images in already concentrated industries, the Law should be viewed with the same critical eye that is needed for mergers between direct competitors."[17]

"Senator Warren's remarks called out Technology companies especially, warning that there is no exception in antitrust laws for big Technology."[18]

> One of the most successful litigations undertook by DOJ in 2017 has been the merger of the health insurance industry and energy solutions acquisition. The health insurance and information technology industry, Anthem and Cigna were going for a US$ 54 billion mergers and the Court found that in two of the alleged five markets where the government alleged harm, in the sale of health insurance and purchase of healthcare services by commercial health Insurers.[19]

Case Study

On May 21, 2017 Cigna and Anthem were making efforts to merge and could not do so after Anthem company broke out due to the Court's order. Anthem/Cigna may be the more instructive case because it serves to remind parties that it is difficult to prove in litigation that anti-competitive effort may be overcome by efficiencies.

> Agencies generally recognized that even measures of the head-to-head competitive can lead to efficiencies that result in lower prices, quality improvements, and innovation. Indeed, transactions are cleared based on such efficiencies. In litigation, parties are much less successful in pursuing courts of these efficiencies. In The Anthem case, parties argued that the combination would generate the US $ 2.4 billion in merger-specific efficiencies on an annual basis and that the merger would result in reduced provider costs that would make Healthcare more affordable for customers.[20]

"The district court disagreed declining to credit the claimed efficiencies and Anthem applied this issue to the DC circuit."[21] "The majority opinion of the three-judge panel sided with the Department of Justice and the states, running but not resolving the availability of an efficiencies defence in the context of an illegal merger,"[22] and "holding that even with such defence, it failed to reboot the case of the government."[23]

> The appellate court agreed with the lower courts holding that, among other things, the efficiencies were not merger specific, were vague and not verifiable, and would not be passed through to the consumers at the rate climate by the parties.[24]

The year 2017 witnessed the Department of Justice being proactively punishing deviant conduct and initiating criminal investigation through ways and means outside of its leniency program. The DOJ prosecuted three executives and one corporate defendant in the year 2017 for alleged collusion in the supply of packaged seafood.

> In March 2017, the DOJ secured a 15-month prison sentence for an executive charged with concealing information and directing subordinates also to do the same and making false and misleading statements during a DOJ civil investigation of a joint venture between two New York tour bus companies. The DOJ collected approximately US $ 107.8 million corporate fines in the FY 2017.[25]
>
> More than 20 individuals received jail terms and order to pay substantial fines. The Department of Justice has taken multiple policy directives over the last 3 years detailing its intent to increase enforcement against individuals involved in criminal antitrust conduct.[26]

The most prominent sectors that underwent the wrath of prosecutions covered (a) automotive parts, (b) electrolytic capacitors, (c) ocean shipping containers, (d) ocean shipping roll on roll off, (e) packaged seafood, (f) e-commerce, (g) generic pharmaceuticals, (h) real estate foreclosure auctions, (i) financial services, (j) heir locators, (k) public school buses, (l) obstruction of justice and (m) diversion of federal funds.

Antitrust Matters and Global Enforcement Guidelines

The first guidelines for issues were available in the year 1995, and new guidelines were issued in the year 2017 which discuss the efforts of the Department of Justice in coordination with foreign countries for effectively conducting a criminal investigation in cartelisation matters. The main point is the non-hesitation of the Department of Justice in prosecuting any foreign authority or official indulging in questionable practices and in extending mutual legal assistance through numerous Mutual Legal Assistance Treaties (MLAT).

The USA has signed MLATs with more than 60 countries, including India. The purpose of guidelines is to facilitate the removal of confusion, duplicacy, redundancy and possible connivance among the designated authorities of DOJ and the foreign designated authorities for the purpose of MLATs. Cooperation becomes not merely a legal requirement but expedient conjoint action in the interest of enforcement of law. The DOJ, in turn, seeks to coordinate with foreign authorities to avoid overlapping or inconsistent requests and decrease the burden placed on such co-operators wherever possible, per the guidelines.

Issuing Red Corner notices has been in vogue for the prevention of international crimes involving narcotics and terrorism-related arms trafficking. Interpol guidelines now stand expanded to cover the financial market criminals, fraudsters and tax evaders. The DOJ uses these new guidelines against money launderers, fraudsters and fugitives. New guidelines empower member signatories to detain any noted person immediately at the sea at any ports or border checking points. Moreover, building on the DOJ's extradition successes in the past decade, the guidelines make clear that the DOJ will seek extradition of fugitive defendants from foreign jurisdictions to the US, if necessary.

The updated guidelines highlight the expansive approach the agencies take to commerce outside of the US and the reach of US antitrust laws. The modified advisory empowers DOJ to control the ingress and egress of any antitrust matter-related commercial matter. DOJ operates the FTAIA (Foreign Trade Antitrust Improvements Act, 1982) and any indirect effect, even in the future to the USA. The commercial interest is monitored. The coloured imports of a difficult category of fixed priced foreign products do not escape the legal eyes uncles FTAIA, 1982. The acute angle of antitrust law becomes expansionary to cover within ambits on the prices of products that were not in US market directly, but sold under a different agreement even by non-litigants. Direct or indirect, straight or remote, if there is a potentiality of adverse impact on US interests, the DOJ swings into enforcement.

Earlier in this chapter, it was mentioned about the conflict of law in a foreign country. In the United States of America, the US authority is the Department of Justice and the Federal Trade Commission (FTC).

> In the year 2017, the US Supreme Court requested views on the case of Vitamin C in which section 1 of the Sherman Act, 1890 is the main contention. The section 1 violation case was registered against the Chinese manufacturers for analyst conspiracy in price-fixing and output which can be termed as Syndicate activity Organisation in case of Vitamin C.[27]

"In September 2017, the important decision regarding US and foreign laws, US Court of appeals for the second circuit vacated the US $ 150 million jury verdict against the two Chinese Manufacturers."[28]

134 CBMA, *Competition Law, Antitrust and Demerger*

The panel recognized the Chinese government's official statement that Chinese law compelled the conduct at issue. Finding the true conflict between American and foreign law, Court dismissed the case under the doctrine of internal comity and recognize that this dispute would be better resolved by the executive branch.[29]

US Supreme Courts of Appeals for Third Circuit affirmed the essence of fairness in anti trusts matters in the *Valspar Corporation vs Du Pont*.

The crux of the *Valspar vs Du Pont* case has been on the oligopolistic market in which a small number of firms dominate the market. The court held that the proof of parallel price increases and limited circumstantial evidence does not provide sufficient evidence to establish the act of price-fixing allegations. The court further held that parallel price increases for example of conscious parallelism theory that parties in an oligopolistic market will raise prices in response to rival price increases if it is believed that doing so will maximise industry profits. Parallelism indicates an authoritative verdict. Parallelism does not specify and conspiracy of actual meetings of minds to mutualise the benefit through upward revision of prices.

> In the instant case, the plaintiff fails to show evidence of an agreement to raise prices amounting to a conspiracy. Valspar's decision is noteworthy because it raises the bar for a plain text to establish an antitrust or price-fixing claim in an oligopolistic market send direct evidence of an unlawful agreement.[30]

Antitrust Litigation in the United States

"Arbitration before approach" has been the essence of the verdict of the US Court of Appeals for the second circuit.

> This case follows after a long history of litigation reflecting a tension between upholding contractual arbitration clauses and the ability of parties to seek damages via civil class actions. This decision was also referred to in the case of an American Express company versus an Italian colour restaurant. In the instant case, the Supreme Court opened that the attrition provision could not be overturned even if arbitration would cost potential plaintiffs more than they could recover in damages. In a significant judgment at the end of 2016 in a case of Foreign Trade and Trade Trust Improvements Act of 1982, Judge James Donato of the US district court the district of California issued a critical decision interpreting the current state of FTAIA. The Judge decided and made the following observations; damages are on purely foreign transactions that are transactions to bill to and ship to customers located outside the United States where the plaintiffs are claiming that foreign capacitor manufacturers implemented Global pricing increases.[31]

"Courts continue to explore the boundaries of immunity defences to Antitrust claims, including circumstances in which parties are immune because they are petitioning the government (Noerr-Pennington doctrine), filed rate and other regulatory doctrines, and sports-related antitrust immunity."[32] "The Noerr-Pennington doctrine shields parties from Antitrust claims when they petition the government to take a position."[33] "The mere existence of a lawsuit does not retroactively immunize prior anticompetitive conduct."[34] "In essence, the mere fact that the defendants brought protected patent litigation against Amphastar does not immunize them from liability for the full the total damage through acts in anti-competitive frame."[35]

Samsung appealed annulling the counterclaims in antitrust matters, quoting the Noerr-Pennington doctrine. In dealing with *Polaris Innovations vs Kingston Technology Co Inc.*, the US District Court for California Central District, the appeal was not upheld.

Frivolous, Bad Faith and Sham Commercial Litigation and CBMA

In an important case that is *Industrial Motors Incorporation vs SNF Incorporation*, the Federal Circuit Court affirmed the definition of antitrust claims because of bad faith litigation against its competitors to gain a monopoly and found that the Industrial Motors failed to show that the SNF engaged in objectives of the best justification or that the SNF engaged in a pattern of sham litigation. It is clear from the above discussion that frivolous litigation and bad faith litigation or sham litigation are to be discouraged by the law and the courts.

> Reverse payment occurs in patent litigation where the plaintiff manufacturer of a brand name drugs agrees to compensate one or more manufacturers of a defendant generic drugs in exchange for a promise of delayed genetic entry in the market. The Supreme Court held that such agreements can be unlawful if the compensation was large and unjustified and results in harm to competition.[36]
>
> In another illustrative case of actors and their antitrust litigation, there was a demonstration that in pay for delay cases bleeding causes with sufficient factual allegations can make or break plaintiff survival of a motion to dismiss for file one's claim.[37]

The USA, Europe, China and India witness drugs and pharmaceutical industries as a major case in CBMAs. "USA has a system of risk evaluation and mitigation strategy which needs to be approved by the FDA."[38]

The US Food and Drug Administration ensures that the voice of citizens is taken seriously in preventing the power of drug companies from impacting the interests of ordinary citizens. This study found that such a provision is not available in India and hence this study suggests such a provision in India.

In the year 2017, the Federal Trade Commission (FTC) filed a first of its kind lawsuit about 46 public filings including 24 citizen positions in recent years concerning a single product."[39] The state actors in the USA enjoy sovereign immunity protection for patents challenged in the Patent Trial and Appeal Board (PTAB).

Competition Policy and CBMA in India

Competition Act was passed in the year 2002 in India and the Competition Commission of India (CCI) came into existence immediately thereafter "Recognising the expertise of the CCI in dealing with broad competition issues in various sectors of the economy and the expertise of different sector regulators in matters of details such as the setting of tariffs and the operating conditions, the legislature has wisely included Sections 21 and 21A in the Competition Act 2002 (the Act). One of the targets of CA 2002 India is to earmark clear in his dictions a many all regulators. CCI (Competition Commission of India) was hence created.

Competition Commission of India, Recent Developments

In a virtual conference on December 5, 2020, the chairman of CCI, Ashok Kumar Gupta, indicated an industry-friendly Competition Commission of India. In essence, it means that the Commission, in its functioning, understands the COVID-19 pandemic is the new normal and adjusts itself in its response to the litigation. The chairman asserted that the competition watchdog may in the coming days assimilate factors like the decision-making process to encourage the parties to cease anti-competitive behaviour and bring about the much-needed market correction faster. Observers point out the recent change in the accommodative behaviour of the CCI. The CCI waved penalties for anti-competitive behaviour and issued cease-and-desist orders. The accommodative response of the CCI, in turn, was available after the Railways and the Industrial and automotive bearings company extended cooperation in the inquiry and investigation. A section of the legal fraternity views this as a confusing signal and expressed fear of engaging in anti-competitive practices becoming encouraged rather than curbed by such a so-called accommodative response. They maintain that cooperation from the party concerned cannot and should not be a get-out-of-the-jail free card entirely, although it can be a factor to minimise the penalty implication. The CCI should take a measured approach and apply cooperation as a factor for penalty waiver on a case-to-case basis. One should never miss the overall objective of competition law namely non-compromise on the quality and level playing field. A significant other section of the legal fraternity, however, feels that the accommodative stance of the CCI is only to revive growth and mitigate the COVID-19 pandemic impact. There cannot be any contradiction in the functioning of the Commission due to the industry-friendly posture of the commission especially due to the COVID-19 pandemic crisis. The accommodative stance would remain as long as necessary and till the time parties cooperating investigate and follow the cease and desist orders.

Coordination among Various Regulators

Table 3.1 Regulators Relationship

Sector-specific Regulator	Competition Authority
Tells businesses "what to do" and "how to price products"	Tells businesses "what not to do"
Focuses upon specific sectors of the economy	Focuses upon the entire economy and functioning of the market
Ex ante—addresses behavioural issues before problem arises	Ex post (except merger review)
Focus upon orderly development of a sector that would presumably trickle down in a sector ensuring consumer welfare	Focus upon consumer welfare and unfair transfer of wealth from consumers to firms with market power
Sectoral regulators are usually more appropriate for access and price issues such as changing the structure of the market, reducing barriers to entry and opening up the market to effective competition	Competition legislation is usually more appropriate for affecting conduct and maintaining competition

Source: Website of competition commission of India
http://www.manupatrafast.com/articles/Articlesearch.aspx?sub=Competition%20/%20
Antitrust

The following are critical tasks that the CCI performs

1 Destroy all obstruction, found opposed to competition.
2 Encourage competition.
3 Consumer protection should never be given up.
4 Protect free trade and freedom of trade.

Competition Act, Competition Commission, Mergers, Amalgamation Enforcement, Suggestions

The Competition Act, 2002 was appreciated as one the best by global bodies. Organization of Economic Corporation and Development (OECD) is one of them. "It generates, the Commission runs the risk of penalizing competitive behaviour, which would stifle the competitiveness of India's vibrant economy."[40] "The inquiry produced a report demonstrating that over 85% of industrial areas had a high concentration of economic power."[41]

Competition Act, 2002 was to remove the MRTP Act lock, stock and barrel. MRTP Act became obstructionist and was not conducive to the new global wave of liberalised trade and free flow of investment.

When litigation regarding the functioning of CCI reached the doorstep of SCI (Supreme Court of India), the court expressed its initial inconvenience with a retired bureaucrat as the Chairman of CCI, as "ultra vires." The

Government of India through its legal Counsel promised the required amendment. "Sections 5 and 6 regulate combinations, which includes mergers, amalgamations, and Acquisitions."[42] "While Sections 3 and 4 were ratified in 2009 (following the litigation over the composition of the Commission), Section 5 became effective in July 2011."[43]

Recent Experience in CBMA and Ease of Doing Business Index

One of the aims of this study was whether the current legal regimes are facilitative of better indexing in case of ease of doing business.

Multiplication of tribunals became parking lots to loyal bureaucrats, on their retirement as passed-retirement placements. The new government took stay on removing the redundant appellate authorities and tribunals and fused them into a single structure namely, National Companies Law Appellate Tribunal (NCLAT).

In March 2011 the Delhi HC restored the jurisdiction of CCI in patent matters.

> In effect, the decision held that a set of facts can be agitated before a civil court or a sectoral regulator and also give rise to a cause of action that may be adjudicated by the CCI in parallel. Such proceedings would not be mutually exclusive. In September 2017, the Court reiterated this position in Uttarakhand Agricultural Produce Marketing Board &Ors v. CCI and Anr.[44]

"where the Delhi High Court upheld the investigation initiated by the CCI even though the factual dispute had been agitated before the Hon'ble Uttarakhand High Court in a writ proceeding."[45]

"The Supreme Court rendered its first substantive judgment on merits under the Competition Act relating to a cartel matter. In CCI v. Coordination Committee of Artists and Technicians of West Bengal Film and Television and Ors."[46] "The Eastern India Motion Pictures Association (EIMPA) and the Committee of Artists and Technicians of West Bengal Film and Television Investors (Coordination Committee) had threatened to boycott channels that intended to telecast the Bengali dubbed version of the serial *Mahabharat* as they believed that such dubbing of Hindi programs in regional languages will obstruct the growth of regional talents and local artists would be unemployed. Given the threats, one of these channels decided to stop the telecast of the dubbed version of the serial giving rise to a complaint before the CCI. COMPAT the competition appellate tribune annulled the CCI verdict, under the concept of the relevance of operational areas cartelisation could not have arisen. The Supreme Court sided with the CCI. The SCI upheld the correction of CCI's verdict citing that the main effects of different acts matter in deciding the relevance of a market. Relevant markets are vital in competition assessment. The SCI pronounced its second vital Verdict in Excel Corp. Care Vs CCI. The SCI turned down the fine levied by CCI (the US$ 48.5 equivalent 318 Crores Indian Rupees). CCI's levy was based on total turnover. SCI differed and maintained that only that turnover from that particular segment must be taken into account why levying fine/penalty. In the year 2017, the matter of cartelisation in the case of tenders floated by Rail India for brushless DC fans was decided by CCI.

"A line of INR 591.01 Crores (the equivalent of US$ 8.10 million) was imposed on the Public Sector Unit, Coal India by CCI for the following reasons.

1   Abusing dominance in the market in non-cocking coal supply,
2   Decreasing in equal, capricious fuel supply clauses,
3   Putting the power producer and sponge iron manufacturers into avoidable difficulty."[47]

CCI views the pharmaceutical sector with importance. Apart from levying fines, as it has done in several cases over the last few years on distributors "associations for imposing restrictive terms on the appointment of new dealers/retailers."[48] "The CCI also ordered its first abuse of dominance investigation against Roche for allegedly blocking the entry of Biocon and Mylan's "generic in Biocon & Mylan v. Roche."[49]

> As a matter of further liberalization, the limits for applicability of Section 5 and Section 6 of Competition Act, 2002 were upwardly revised to INR 350 crores (the US $ 54 million) or turnover INR 1000 crores (the US $ 154.5 million). Now all cases below these thresholds need to be referred to CCI. The notification finally brings India in line with the international practice that looks at only the portion, division, or business being acquired while assessing whether thresholds have been breached.[50]

Time limits earlier were found to be within 30 days of the trigger event. On 29th June 2017, this time limit was removed.

Public Sector banks were united and consolidated, sec 5 and 6 of CA, 2002 were exempted for Bank reunification. "A similar exemption was also granted to combinations involving government companies in the oil and gas sector."[51] "Reports also suggest that combinations involving stressed assets will also be exempted from CCI's jurisdiction to assist and facilitate quick resolution of companies under the Insolvency and Bankruptcy Code."[52]

> The global consolidation in the agro-chemicals sector saw the CCI clearing two transactions with remedies, while the third entered phase II. Valued at USD 130 billion, the global merger between Dow and DuPont turned out to be a complex transaction in the agrochemical sector because of the large number of overlaps in their products and

services portfolios. After considering the divesture commitments made by the parties to the European Commission, the CCI found two India-specific relevant markets where the merger triggered concerns in India and required additional divestments.[53]

"The telecom sector in India also saw significant consolidation that was perhaps overdue, triggered by the entry of Reliance Jio. Bharti Airtel undertook several acquisitions within the sector, namely, the acquisition of Telenor,"[54] "the consumer mobile business of Tata Teleservices,"[55] and a certain spectrum from Aircel and Dish net as well as Videocon."[56] "Amalgamation of the telecommunications businesses of Vodafone and Idea Cellular was also a significant deal also received a swift approval despite the parties'" significant market shares."[57]

Dish TV merged with Videocon to become direct-to-home (DTH). This merger was approved by CCI, such as Essilor's US$ 54 billion mergers with Luxottica, which has been sent to Phase II by the EC and is also still pending clearance by the FTC, and AT&T's US$ 108 billion acquisition of Time Warner, which has been challenged by the USDOJ in court. The merger between GE and Baker Hughes relating to oilfield services and products and HP's acquisition of Samsung's printer business were also cleared with relative ease, save for requiring that HP limit the term of the non-compete clause to three years, reiterating what has now become an age-old requirement of the Commissions."[58]

Even though SCI decreed that real relevant turnover should be considered in levying fines, some issues remained with CCI and appellate tribunal.

Gaps, Tribunals, Scope for Correction

The credibility of tribunals was raised in connection with their functionary jurisdiction since the so-called tribunals lacked all qualities of a traditional court. The result of such absence of attributes is the less credible importance given to the views of tribunals. They never carried the authority of the judicial verdict. "The tribunal in question does not have to be subject to the standards of courts vested with judicial powers. This attempt of the executive to distance tribunals from judicial scrutiny became evident since India achieved independence."[59]

> The word "tribunal" in Article 136 has to be construed liberally and not in any narrow sense and an Industrial Tribunal since it discharges functions of a judicial nature following the Law that comes within the ambit of the article and from its determination and application for special leave is competent.[60]

"Discharge of Judicial functions is the basic duty of any Court or tribunal,"[61] i.e. "the discharge of duties exercisable by a judge or by justice in courts, which makes the nature of a tribunal's function crucial."[62] "To understand what distinguishes a court from a tribunal in India, it would suffice to state that tribunals are exclusively constituted to carry out certain judicial functions in addition to certain administrative /regularity/inquisitorial functions, in a manner not necessarily in part material with traditional courts". Inexperience in Judicial procedures is a definite lacunae observed on the part of many members of the tribunal.

> A court, in the strict sense, is necessarily a tribunal that is a part of the ordinary hierarchy of courts, however, not all tribunals are akin to courts for instance, where no judicial functions are vested in them, or the nature of judicial functions vested in them are only supplementary to the main regulatory/administrative functions, then in such a case, they would not be akin to courts.[63]

"In Sampath Kumar, it has held that to be 'effective' substitutes to High Courts, appointments to the tribunals should be made by the Government in consultation with the Chief Justice."[64] "The Raghavan Committee recommended the enactment of the Competition Act, 2002It provided for the establishment of the Competition Commission of India (CCI) to prevent practices having adverse effects on competition, to promote that sustain competition markets to protect the interest of consumers, and to ensure freedom of trade carried on by other participants in the Indian market, and for matters connected therewith."[65]

"In Sampath Kumar, it was suggested that appointments to the tribunals that were vested with powers akin to courts, should be made by the government in consultation with the Chief Justice."[66]

The Concept of Demergers in India and the USA

Demergers mean that sum of the value of individuals parts is more than the value of the whole. It is the reverse of the CBMA. It is otherwise called split-up. Demerger could be a vital plan to escape from losses due to impending or probable bad publicity or legal action etc. A successful consumer segment being part of the whole business mix can always be split out as a separate entity to maximise its effectiveness in the market.

There are many reasons and benefits of demergers. The most important among them is to make a profit for all the shareholders and the obvious safeguarding of the interesting organisation and also at another obvious objective is remaining competitive in the area of specialisation. Researchers in the year 2011 gave the following eleven generic reasons prompting companies to opt-out for demerger as a strategy.[67]

1   Safeguard against cash loss risks or non-profitability,
2   Separation of management of divisions,
3   Defence against the hostile takeover,

4 Enhancing responsibility and accountability,
5 Decluttering management processes,
6 Focus on core competencies and activities,
7 Counter takeover threats and opportunities creation,
8 Reduction and restriction of government intervention,
9 Introduction of specific business activities,
10 Segregation of family business, and
11 Countering of diseconomies of large scale.

Demerger is a company restructuring process involving the splitting of the whole into parts to make them operate on their own and sometimes to be sold or to be liquidated as separate entities. Apart from the above-mentioned reasons of de-merger, sometimes demerger of a company from a big conglomerate of Companies of various brands may happen to prevent and acquisition how to raise capital by selling of components that are no longer part of the businesses core product line or to create separate legal entities to handle different operations. Globally, one of the most effective demerging processes is its execution that happens through a spin-off. The spin-off essentially signifies the mother corporation getting an equity stake in the child company which is equal to the loss of equity in the original company. There can be a variation called partial demerger also which signifies and retains the meaning of only a partial stake in the demerged company is allowed.

The following are examples of demergers globally. In 2001, British Telecom conducted a de-merger of its mobile phone operations to boost the performance of its stock. British Telecom was struggling then under high debt levels from the wireless venture. In the USA, Cadbury Schweppes was allowed the de-merging of Dr. Pepper Snapple Group in the year 2008. Australian Airline Qantas split its International and Domestic operations via demerger in the year 2014 so that each unit is run separately. De-merger symbolises a company splitting itself into two or more parts. One is to manage its infrastructure receipts and another is to manage the delivery of energy to consumers. De-mergers were very popular in the year 2014, namely in solar power projects.

Demergers in financial markets work as a corporate restructuring process. In India, financial markets like some investment houses, indulge in demergers, in apportioning the wealth among family heirs or when region-wise, product-wise segmentation.

Separate accounting standards, namely accounting standard 14 and accounting for de-merger of international financial reporting standards 3 of business combination, are used in case of de-mergers. The principle of efficient market hypothesis, as established by the work of Lament and Thaler (2001), lies firstly that it is hard to earn excess returns with price correction reflecting fundamental values. Mergers and demergers are expressed through the following equations:

$$[X+Y] \gg [X]+[Y] \text{ in case of the CBMA.}$$
$$\left.\begin{array}{l}[X-Y] \gg [X] \\ [X-Y] \gg [Y] \\ [X-Y] \gg \{[X],[Y]\}\end{array}\right\} \text{Demerger}$$

When Corporation [Y] demergers from corporation [X + Y], the remaining corporation is better off and the demerged corporation too is better off.

The demergers of reliance are the best example in India.

According to Lamont and Thaler (2001), "Two key principals of the different market hypothesis are that first, it is not easy to earn excess returns and second, it is not easy to earn an excess return and the price correct reflecting fundamental values."[68] "According to Hite and Owers in case of mergers thematic is often expressed as 2 + 2 is equal to 5 whereas per spin-offs it is 4 minus 2 is equal to 3."[69]

Legislative Initiatives in India and Jurisdiction of Ministry of Corporate Affairs

Ministry for Corporate Affairs, Government of India

The Ministry of Corporate Affairs is a newly created ministry in place of the previous Department of Company affairs and Law. It is bifurcated from the Ministry of Commerce.

> This Ministry is primarily concerned with the administration of the Companies Act, 2013, the Companies Act 1956, the Limited Liability Partnership Act, 2008, and other allied Acts and rules and regulations framed there-under mainly for regulating the functioning of the corporate sector following the law. [70]

It is responsible mainly for the regulation of Indian enterprises in the Industrial and Services sector.

The Ministry administers the following Acts:

- The Companies Act, 2013
- The Companies Act, 1956
- The Companies Act, 2002
- The Monopolies and Restrictive Trade Practices Act, 1969
- The Chartered Accountants Act, 1949 [As amended by the Chartered Accountants (Amendment) Act, 2006]
- The Company Secretaries Act, 1980 [As amended by The Company Secretaries (Amendment) Act, 2006]
- Cost and Works Accountants Act, 1959 [As Amended By The Cost And Works Accountants (Amendment) Act, 2006]

- Companies (Donation to National) Fund Act 1951
- The Indian Partnership Act, 1932
- Societies Registration Act, 1860
- The Companies Amendment Act, 2006
- The Limited Liability Partnership Act, 2008

"The Companies Act, 2013 come into effect from August 2013. It aims to regulate fraud by corporations and is intended to avoid the accounting scandals such as the Satyam scandal which have plagued India."[71] The Companies Act, 1956 was the outdated relic of licence permit raj of a pseudo-socialist regime which encouraged inspector raj and nepotistic administration.

Figure 3.1 is indicative of the challenges or threats to a nascent CBMA law. The crying baby is representative of the same.

The Ministry is also responsible for administering the Competition Act, 2002 to prevent practices hurting competition, to promote and sustain competition in markets, to protect the interests of consumers through the commission set up under the Act.

MCA is mandated, as the top coordinating agency, to coordinates, supervise, guide the functioning of the following professional bodies.

i   Institute of Charter Accounts of India, ICAI,
ii Institute of Company Secretaries of India, ICSI, and
iii Institute of Cost Accounts of India, ICAI.

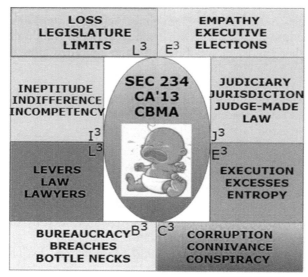

Figure 3.1 Threats to CBMA.

All the above three professional bodies are statutorily created by the Acts of Parliament of India.

The MCA administers the provision of:
i The Partnership Act, 1932,
ii The Companies Donation to National Funds Act, 1951 and
iii The Societies Registration Act, 1980.

The MCA, vide a notification on April 13, 2017, published clear guide liens for in-bound/outbound mergers and acquisitions. The MCA clarifies that cross borders mean the amalgamations (arrangement) among Indian Companies and foreign companies. After two weeks from the above notification of the MCA, RBI issued draft guidelines for application in the case of CBMAs.

This RBI notification dated April 27, 2017, nullified all gaps between the above debuts. This draft ultimately became law on March 20, 2018, vide FEMA 2018 (CROSS BORDERS).

The following are the main important changes for the inbound Cross Border mergers.

1 A limited liability partnership is a body corporate found and incorporated under this act and is a legal entity separate from that of its partners,
2 A limited liability partnership shall help perpetual succession, and
3 Any changes in the partners of a limited liability partnership shall not fracture the existence, rights, or liabilities of the limited liability partnership. The conditions include that any person found to be suffering the bellow mentioned attributes would not be allowed to be a partner under Limited Liability Partnership (LLP).

  a He is of unsound mind by the court of a competent new direction and the finding is in force,
  b He is an undercharged insolvent; or
  c He is obliged to be adjudicated as insolvent and his leave application is pending.

Inbound Mergers

1 "In the case of an inbound merger, where the foreign company is an overseas joint venture or a wholly-owned subsidiary of an Indian company, such foreign company should comply with the foreign exchange management transfer or issue of any foreign security regulations 2004 which are also called ODI regulations."[72]
2 "The joint ventures are wholly-owned subsidiary should assess all applications in the ODI regulation applicable to winding up."[73]
3 An inbound merger between a subsidiary of a Joint Venture Company and another Company through acquisition, needs to follow adhere to financial management conditions and commitments.

4 A two-year time period is the maximum timeline for making the promised foreign funds through loans to be useful to the resultant Indian Company, as an inbound merger.
5 Foreign funds under the loan are to follow separate guidelines and the FEMA, 1999 manual of end-user limitations.
6 A six-month timeline was extended to 2 years under FEMA, 1999 to sell assets; if any
7 Indian Companies under Inbound merger conditions many rules need to company with in connection with the acquisition in a foreign country, some prominent rules are stipulated in FEMA, 1999 and Transfer of immovable Property outside India regulation, 2015.
8 The sale proceeds of the sale of overseas assets are now expressly permitted to be used within two years. No liability abroad is permissible for an Indian Company whose origin is through inbound merger/acquisition method.

Out Bound Mergers

The most important implications for the outbound marriages are as follows

1 A foreign company shall not acquire liability in Rupees payable to Indian lenders and a no-objection certificate to this effect must be obtained from the Indian lenders.
2 The above restriction will need to be further analysed to understand its impact on regular rupee borrowings by the Indian entities from the Indian lenders, since such borrowings may not comply with the FEMA, 1999.
3 As in the case of the inbound merger, the outbound mergers also, the timeline was, also increased from 180 days to 2 years for the rate of sanction the scheme.
4 The resultant foreign company is now permitted to open a special non-resident rupee account in terms of FEMA, 1999 Deposit Regulations, 2016 for two years to facilitate any transactions according to the outbound merger.
5 In general, it can be said that the merger regulations both for inbound and outbound are positive since they provide a non-ambiguous and business-friendly regulatory framework for CBMAs.

Mr Manoj, the partner and Head of Insolvency Resolution Services at Corporate Professionals, feels that a Multinational Corporation interested in the Consolidation Corporation of business can utilise these new provisions. The amended provisions facilitate corporate planning for all Companies Indian, MNC or others.

Companies Compromises and Agreement or Amalgamation Rules, 2016

"The valuations of the Indian company and the foreign company shall be done following rule 25 A of the Companies Compromises and Agreement or Amalgamation (CCAA) Rules 2016."[74] RBI facilitates CBMAs interns of impact on timeless in connection with transactions complying with the RBI directives by mentioning that such transactions are deemed to have prior approval. Observers feel,

> The rules will allow the Indian companies to merge their foreign business with their domestic companies while foreign companies will no longer be required to maintain an Indian company after the merger and instead hold it up into a single entity.[75]
>
> In a positive cascading effect many observers often feel that since there is already an amendment and an impact through the Insolvency and Bankruptcy Code, this passing off facilitating cross border mergers initiative will encourage foreign bidders to consider buying Indian assets.[76]

The Insolvency Bankruptcy Code (IBC) is finally in full swing and it is online with the initiatives taken in the Companies Act 2013, in the RBI notification, in the changes that were brought in the FEMA, 1999 and through SEBI.

According to the guidelines issued by the Reserve Bank of India, the assets can be held by the Indian company outside India. Anything which is not permitted to be acquired is to be disposed of within a timeline of two years from the National Company Law Tribunal (NCLT) sanctioned date.

The Reserve Bank of India has notified that any office in India of the foreign company shall be deemed to be a branch office of the foreign company. Hiten Kotak of PWC India, an expert on mergers and acquisitions and tax issues, welcomes the new changes brought and comments that while, "Liberalization measures concerning cross border mergers is a welcome move in the investment and business world, these measures require expensive parallel amendments to several other laws and regulations in India to establish a comprehensive framework." He furthers maintains that the images are included within the definition of compromises and agreements. It is a welcome measure but this section permitting outbound mergers specifically discusses mergers and does not use the term compromise agreement. It leads to an element of doubt whether outbound demergers would be permitted. He further maintains that current tax laws provide for income tax exemption in the hands of the transferor company and its shareholders, subject to the condition that the post-merger company shall be an Indian Company, after following all mandatory conditions.

However, in the absence of a similar exemption for outbound mergers, the word means that all outbound mergers would be taxable in the hands of the Indian transfer company. "It is a welcome measure to simplify the procedures but there is a risk in establishing a permanent establishment of the foreign company in India."[77]

India normally takes guidance from the United Kingdom and also the United States with whom we share historical and ideological friendship. The recent case law in European Union is clear in that the court of appeal in reviewing the relevant cases looked at the purpose behind the underlying directive, namely the facilitation of cross border mergers in pursuit of the respect of the principle of freedom of the European Union. In other words, the principle of freedom of establishment is held to be the main plank of cross-border mergers.[78]

The procedure to settle the double taxation disputes amicably in a structured manner is called MAP, the mutual agreement procedure. It is a double taxation resolution provided under the double taxation avoidance agreement. It is a special procedure outside the domestic tax code. It is one of the forms of Alternate Dispute Resolution (ADR) and encourages the resolution of differences and disputes through the method of negotiations. There is a model of MAP in the Organization of Economic Cooperation and Development (OECD) countries and the most important among the articles is article 25 of the MAP agreement. This is in line with the rules and regulations adopted for a similar purpose by the United Nations Organisation. Double tax avoidance agreement is in vogue with following countries namely:

1. Australia, 2. Austria, 3. Bangladesh, 4. Belgium, 5. Brazil, 6. Bulgaria, 7. China, 8. Slovakia, 9. Denmark, 10. Egypt, 11. Finland, 12. Germany, 13. Greece, 14. France, 15. Indonesia, 16. Israel, 17. Italy, 18. Japan, 19. Kenya, 20. Korea, 21. New Zealand, 22. Norway, 23. Philippines, 24. Poland, 25. Romania, 26. Singapore, 27. Sri Lanka, 28. Sweden, 29. Switzerland, 30. Tanzania, 31. Thailand, 32. Turkey, 33. The United Arab Emirates, 34. The United Kingdom, 35. The United States of America, 36. Russia, 37. Vietnam and 38. Zambia.

Bilateral Agreements and CBMA

Since India has a bilateral agreement with Finland for the avoidance of double taxation, India agreed to resolve the tax disputes with Nokia India and Nokia Finland through the setup of a MAP. In other words, the mutual agreement procedure enables both India and Finland to negotiate through a mutually agreeable Framework so that the tax dispute between Indian tax authorities and Nokia which is a Finland company can be resolved amicably.

As on April 20, 2018, an outstanding tax due to the tune of INR 1600 crore is under the consideration of the MAP framework. Soon after the change of the government in the year 2014 the new government pledge to put in place a taxpayer-friendly regime and take steps to reduce litigation. Initially, Nokia India had been issued a demand notice for INR 2500 crore in the year 2013 which underwent modification and rectification and came down to the figure of INR 1600 crores. INR 10000 crore tax was raised on Nokia Corporation for the same transaction on the ground that it had a permanent establishment in the country. This move adversely impacted the image of India abroad and subsequently, it was dropped.

The MAP framework enables closing all pending proceedings related to a text matter and globally it is perceived that the MAP is emerging as a preferred mode for settling cross-border disputes. The tax issue pending along with Vodafone and other tax cases have been identified with the aggressive stance of the tax department.

Nokia's Case

Nokia's case is an interesting issue of cross-border taxation. The Indian tax authorities issued a tax notice of INR 2500 crore Nokia for violating withholding tax norms since 2006 while making royalty payments to its parent company in Finland. Nokia disputed the claim saying that the software taken from the parent was embedded in the phone and is an inherent part of its hardware. The company filed a plea in the Delhi High Court on August 15, 2013 on the demand that included interest and penalty.

> Finland initiated MAP proceedings in the year 2013. The company sought to initiate arbitration under bilateral investment promotion and protection agreement in the year 2014. Discussions on the MAP framework started in 2014 onwards and the deal was sealed for the past two-three months leading to a tax payment of INR 1600 crore in March 2018.[79]

This is an interesting case in which the Alternative Dispute Resolution (ADR) process and bilateral agreements are given respect and the vexatious tax problem has been successfully resolved. The National Company Law Tribunal (NCLT) deemed the second round of bids for Essar Steel invalid and directed the committee of creditors to consume to consider the first set of officers from offers from Numetal and Arcelor Mittal, ruling that banks would have to decide on the eligibility of bidders rather than the resolution professional.

> This ruling is also a positive step in the right direction as now the law is taking its course with full speed and the light of all the reforms that are being taken to make the cross border merger Regime on par with the world. In another development, Parag milk foods would be acquiring the French Food Giant Danone's Indian manufacturing facility for a sum of rupees 30 crores.[80]

"FMCG giant Procter and Gamble has made a mandatory open offer to acquire firm's consumer Healthcare business globally."[81]

Even though not directly related to Cross Border Mergers and Acquisitions, one needs to mention here the case of Alok industries which has gone bankrupt and the efficacy in implementation of the bankruptcy code making it possible to be taken over by efficient companies and they are solving the unemployment issue as well as the non-performing assets issue of the banks and lending organizations. This is yet another milestone in India that the bankruptcy code has taken its foothold strongly and everyone is complying with this strong law. When the strong law is implemented strongly by the competent authorities then the country will be known for its enforcement of contract ability and thus the ease of doing business index will improve. 81 companies have already gone into liquidation under the Insolvency and Bankruptcy Code. More than 100 other companies are facing the insolvency process or on the verge of liquidation according to the corporate professionals, as admitted by Mr. Manoj Kumar, expert corporate professional in mergers and acquisitions and insolvency proceedings.

IBC is the correct solution to many pending problems.

It is hence clear that firstly RBI, secondly Competition Act, 2002, thirdly SEBI, fourthly Foreign Exchange Management Act (FEMA), and lastly Insolvency and Bankruptcy Code (IBC) are the most important legal provisions in making the provisions of section 234 of Companies Act 2013 and the circulars of the Ministry of Corporate Affairs (MCA) which gave official recognition to CBMAs by defining and legalising them.

Stamp Duty and CBMA

Stamp Duty Act and Its Implications on CBMA

Stamp Duty Act originated in the year 1899. The stamp is the iconic acceptance of the state and duty is paid for a transaction or for the legality of a document so as to ascribe the right of acceptance as a piece of evidence in any future litigation.

The division of responsibilities of functions between the Union and States according to Constitution of India is via three lists: namely (a) Union list, (b) State list, (c) Concurrent list. This division is provided in the 7th Schedule of the Constitution of India.

"The levy and collection of the stamp duty on M&A, thus, extended to CBMA, is the subject matter of the States in India by the legislative entry 63 in the State List and Entry 44 in the concurrent list in the 7th Schedule of the Constitution."[82]

Stamp Duty Law in India-Legislative Provisions

Stamp duties are levied on commercial instruments and levies vary across states as per individual law.

Maharashtra Stamp Act, 1958

Conveyance is defined in the Maharashtra Stamp Duty Act, 1950 as follows. Maharashtra is an important industrial state. "Conveyance includes,

i a conveyance on sale,
ii every instrument,
iii every decree or final order,
iv Under the old Companies Act, 1956, High Courts were the responsible organisations for accepting proposals for the CBMA. In the case of Banks, it is the R.B.I. whose decisions were final.

Accordingly, activities under Sections 394 of Companies Act, 1956 and Section 44A of Banking Regulation Act, 1949 are relevant sections or any estate or interest in any property is transferred to or vested in, any other person, inter vivos, and which is not otherwise provided for by Schedule 1."

Karnataka Stamp Act

Share certificates are leviable stamp duties in Karnataka ad valorem Rs 1/- per certificate. As per the Depositories Act, the investors have been granted the option of holding shares and other securities in a physical or DEMAT form. All rights concerning the shares held in the depositary lie with the investor who is the ultimate beneficial owner, the Depositary acts as a registered owner only. When transacting through a Depositary, the investor will not be required to pay stamp duty on the transfer of shares.

Controversy

A) Whether stamp duty is payable on an order of a High Court sanctioning a Scheme of Amalgamation/merger under section 394 of the Companies Act, 1956?

Many states have amended the definition of conveyance in their respective stamp laws to include an order of amalgamation or reconstruction under Section 394 of the Companies Act, 1956. Also, these states have accordingly amended the Schedules to their respective stamp law. However, the Main Act is still unamended and there are a few states which have not amended the definition of conveyance.

Li Taka Pharmaceuticals vs State of Maharashtra (1997)

An amendment was made to Maharashtra Stamp Act, 1993 to the word "Conveyance." A case was filed in the Bombay High Court challenging the aid amendment. The court held that an order under Section 394 is founded upon a compromise between the two companies and since the order transfers the assets and liabilities, it is an instrument. The verdict of Bombay High Court was a questioner in the Supreme Court of India.

Hindustan Lever vs State of Maharashtra (2004)

The verdict by SC clarified that HC-sanctioned scheme is an instrument and the state can impose levy on such an instrument order of amalgamation passed by the Court. The Supreme Court further held that:

A   The foundation or the basis for passing an order of amalgamation is an agreement between two or more companies.
B   Under the Scheme of amalgamation, the whole or any part of the undertaking, properties, or liability of any company concerned in the scheme is to be transferred to the other company.
C   The scheme of amalgamation has its genesis in an agreement between the prescribed majority of shareholders and creditors of the transferor company with the prescribed majority of shareholders and creditors of the transferee company.
D   The intended transfer is a voluntary act of the contracting parties. The transfer has all the trappings of a sale. Court's verdict legitimised the transfer. Companies, numbering fifteen (15) of red estate sector decided to merge with Delhi Towers Ltd.

Delhi Towers Ltd vs GNCT of Delhi (2009)

Companies numbering fifteen (15) in the real estate sector decided to merge with Delhi Tower Ltd. These transferor companies were stated to be hundred percent subsidiaries of Delhi Towers Limited, the transferee company. Delhi High Court sanctioned the said scheme of the merger on March 19, 2003. The Authority did not accept the scheme because of non-payment stamp duty.

Delhi Towers Ltd vs GNCT of Delhi (2009)

"The Delhi High Court held that an approved scheme of amalgamation amounts to a transfer inter-vivos between two companies who were juristic persons in existence at the time of Given verdict the legitimate sanction accrues to the transferee the three benefits namely

(a)   Right (b) Title and (c) Interest.

The transfer takes place in the present and is not postponed to any later date and is covered under the definition of conveyance under subsection 10 of section 2 of the Stamp Act."[83]

SC held in the case of *Chief Controlling Revenue Authority vs Costal Gujarat Power Ltd.* that levy of Stamp Duty should be only on instruments and not on a transaction. Without the actual transfer of property, the valuation of shares Fran are the company to another is an instrument and hence Stamp Duty can be levied.

Specific Relief Act, 1963: The Amendment Bill, 2017 Implications on Business Transactions and CBMA

Specific Relief Act, 1963

When a Civil of Contractual rights of a person is violated the provisions of the Specific Relief Act, 1963 are attracted. "It replaced an earlier Act of 1877. The following kinds of remedies may be granted by a court under the provisions of the Specific Relief Act"[84]

i Recovery of possession of the property-
ii Specific performance of contracts.
iii Rectification of instruments.
iv Rescission of contracts.
v Cancellation of Instruments.
vi Declaratory decrees.
vii Injunction.

The Implications of the Amendments to the Specific Relief Act, 1963 (SRA, 1963)

> On December 15, 2017, the Union Cabinet approved the recommended changes to the Specific Relief Act, 1963 (Act) after 54 years, intending to facilitate simple and easy enforcement of contracts. The Act deals with the fulfillment of a contractual obligation and provides for specific performance of a contract where the amount of monetary relief is undeterminable or inadequate.[85]

Ease of doing Business Index is affected by contract enforcement, time-cost overruns and quick settlements in the affair and transparent environment of any disputes. Amendments to S.R.A., 1963 were needed for a better score on Ease of Doing Business.

The Proposed Changes

The Expert Committee (Committee) constituted by the Government submitted the changes for due consideration to the Ministry of Law of Justice, according to which, the Lok Sabha passed the Specific Relief (Amendment) Bill, 2018 (Amendment Bill). The following are the vital elements and implications in the process of amendment.

General Rule, Specific Performance and Changes

In the earlier scenario, the Act was bound by the principle that the relief was to be given after giving due consideration to the ascertainability of compensation and damages in monetary terms. Thus, the general rule was that the party was entitled to specific performance only if the amount of compensation was not adequate relief.[86]

Thus, in practical terms, this released the defaulting party from the performance of the unperformed part of the contract, and the party not in default was left to bear the repercussions of the unperformed contract. According to the Committee, exceptions have to be well defined.

Discretion Given to Courts and Committees

"The previous Act provided the wide authority of discretion to Courts. This includes the discretion exercised for specific performance of contracts,"[87] "grant of relief, or costs"[88] and "injunctions."[89] Discretion is against the rule of Clarity for relief. There is a need to exercise such discretion following the same specified standard for the harmonisation of the manner of exercise of such discretionary powers by all Courts. Delay is caused by discretions. The proposed Amendment Bill removes discretion and lays penalties for breeches. The foreign companies will find it easier now to invest in India. Litigation must be minimum and exceptional—Vide Section 14A of the Amendment Bill, outside experts can be appointed for helping to win a legal suit.

Rights of Third Parties

The rights of third parties in the enforcement of contracts are specifically dealt with through an amendment. The amendment to SRA is similar to the amendment to the Indian Contract Act, 1872. The consideration is the crux of the matter and consideration can move from not only promises but from a third person as well the promise need not move from the promise but can move from any other person as well. Indian courts have been frequently faced with situations where a contract is intended for the benefit of a third party, but they have still been reluctant to enforce the contract at the instance of such third parties. In the name of (a) agency (b) statute (c) trust (d) assignment, relief was given in certain cases in India. Section 20 of SRA was to be amended to provide relief to the third parties. Section 20 of the Amendment Bill now propounds that in case of breach of contract due to non-performance of promise by any of the parties, it would be open the proposed draft section 20 Amendment, the third promises can get relief in case of breach of promised/ performance by any of the parties.

Separate Class for Public Contracts

The injunction is intended as interim measures to examine any legal issue, both substantial and procedural. The injunction is for the prevention of miscarriage of justice. However, chronic injunctions cause delays, denying justice and derailing progress. Sec. 20A of the Schedule of Amendment Bill aims to prevent the Courts from jumping to Injunction at the slightest pretext. Infrastructure projects, as part of public contracts, are essential for developing other sectors of the economy. Interruption to infrastructure is tantamount to destroying growth prospects of the economy.

For instance, in the contract for the construction of a 500-kilometre highway wherein 400 kilometres were duly completed, and subsequently, the contractor becomes bankrupt, various implications arise under the old Act. When a contractor becomes bankrupt after 400 kilometres, till bankruptcy is resolved, the 400 kilometres become useless. This author witnessed such a road in the Gaya district of Bihar, when he went as a Special Police observer for Indian Parliament Elections in April 2019. It becomes a criminal and colossal waste of national resources, specific performance, hence, becomes cogently vital.

Performance is no more exception and delinquent postponement or discretionary delay has been the order of the day. Cost overruns thus became the direct outcome of time overrun due to vested interest-driven frivolous litigation. Performance is the preferred course under the amended section of 20, 20A and sec. 41 (H.A). Third parties can non join to complete projects with compliance guide lines accompanying such eventualities. Delays by the conniving engineer-politician-contractor-mafia nexus are no longer possible under the new regime. If due to genuine reasons, a contractor becomes unable to complete a project, remedies are possible now for the completion of the pending projects. Pending is no longer "ending" the projects, be it a power line, a railway track, a gas pipe line, a communication cable of a waterway bridge.

Implications

Business, and not government job, is the main theme of the new government from the year 2019 in India. "Start up and Make in India," "Make for the World" are the new slogans. The Ease of Doing Business Index is not a mage metric. It is an indicator of trust by foreign companies for CBMA. Any new business started will create jobs and contributes spurt in Growth Domestic Product (GDP). A few years ago, the Ease of Doing Business Index was 164th for India and New India improved itself to a respectful position of 63rd among the major countries of the world. Anti-Indian propagandists still quote licence permit raj and tarnish the image of India by asserting that it takes 1445 days to start a small Company in India.

Effects of the Specific Relief (Amendment) Bill, 2017 on the Law of Remedies for Breach of Contract

Indian Contract Act, 1872 is the mother of the industrialisation of India. The first war of Independence in India, in 1857, completed the British Crown to pass many laws starting with the IPC in 1861 and the Police Act, 1861 and the first globalised business tool was the Indian Contract Act, 1872. Contract enforcement is the essentials ingredient of trustworthiness and ease of doing business, safely and profitably section 10 of the Specific Relief Act, 1963 empowers the judiciary with discretionary power to adjudicate disputes arising from (i) impossibility of ascertainment of damage due to non-performance of contract and (ii) merger monetary compensation un matching with the enormity of actual damage due to breach of contractual obligations. Immovable property transfer related breaches of contractual obligations can never be adequately redeemed by monitory measures. Thus, "the Act in its present form gives discretionary power to the courts to award specific performance only in exceptional cases, with monetary compensation being the norm."[90]

Movable property transfers–related approaches are redeemable by cash compensation.

The Amendment bill became Act of Parliament on March 15, 2018. The new Act has many provisions, which align in spirit with international practices.

Law and courts of Canada, Australia, New Zealand, the other Commonwealth countries like India, questioned the relief granted in case of immovable property issues. The Canadian Supreme Court case of 1996 (2 SCR 415,1996 Canada) *Semel Hago vs. Parama Devan* is vital in specific relief matters. The dispute was due to a breach of contract in a land sale. Before this momentous decision land was treated as unsustainable and any damages or compensation is inadequate. Now, post-*Semel Hago*, the plaintiff needs to obtain evidence and prove the uniqueness of the property. In India too, *Semel Hago* made an impact and now the ball is in the Court to decide the "Uniqueness" of property and the need for specific performance and the Courts now have to deal with special status attached to immovable properties including real estate.

The amendment to sec. 10 of S.P. Act, 1963 implies that enforcement of the contract shall be subject to ingredients of sec. 11(2), 14,16 of S.P. Act, 1963. Sec 11 (2) provides that a contract entered into by a trustee above the powers of such trustee cannot be specifically enforced.

Sec. 16 provides for denial of the right of specific relief to the person/ party who caused the brach abomination.

Similar denial is applicable to parties failing to prove before Court that the breach was due to prevention or waiver of such performance by the disputant party.

Section 14 discusses three specific cases of non-specific performance. First, is the case of the Court's inability in supervising the performance of non-stoppable performance, second, is the case where the skilled self of one party is contingent on the performance and

third is the case of determinable nature of performance. The Amendment Bill asks for the impossibility of performance if the suffered party prefers substitute performance, which is the specific performance by third party o agents of the third party. Substituted performance, it may be noted, is the third kind of remedy for breach of contract contemplated by the Bill. Remedy of substituted party debars the appeal for specific performance.

Monitory compensation debars the appeal for Adequacy of specific performance under Sec. 14 (1) (a). The Amendment Bills seeks to remove this provision, implying thereby that Courts no longer are burdened to adjudicate the adequacy of monitory Compensation as a remedy. Post Amendment, vide conditions under section 11 (2), 14 or 16, being fulfilled, no case of specific performance exists. Otherwise only, the Courts can order for specific performance of the contract.

This brings us to a comparison between the Indian positions (post amendment) with that of the Canadian position. Power of the course in arriving at the quantities of compensation or relief, in case of violations of contractual obligations or breaches. Now specific performance is the norm, except in cases covered by the above-mentioned sections (Sec. 11(2), 14 & 16).

Canadian law post-*Semel Hago* and Indian law question the separate provisions of remedies for immovable and movable properties and the so-called uniqueness of such properties. The Amended sec. 10 of the Specific Relief Act, 1963 offers different remedies for different categories of contractual obligations.

It is submitted that in the economic realities of today, creating a distinction in the remedy for breach of contract on the 'uniqueness' of property in question seems illogical. The uniqueness of property as an attribute is no longer relevant in the 21st-century business environment. Uniqueness can never be universally objective. In fact, it is extremely subjective. Law herein as uniqueness cannot be universal and objective. The law, therefore, needs to be more objective.

The special economic zone has plots of several unequal sizes in several unequal numbers. Every plot is a plot, similar, being a plot to any other plot except that it has a size and a number. Uniqueness can thus not be attributable to any single plot among summary otherwise similar plots.

The remedy is not always Rupee (Indian Currency). Monetary compensation, if left to discretion will lead to corruption unethicality and is consistency. The amended Specific Relief Act, 1963 is a great forward step for Ease of Doing Business in India.

Limited Liability Act, 2008 and Its Implications on CBMA

The United Kingdom, on whose legal model many Commonwealth countries fabricated their systems, has the U.K. Partnership Act, 1890. The partners are jointly and severally liable for all Acts/Omissions. The Limited Liability Act, 2008 of India is different and its provisions encourage CBMAs start-up, Make in India initiative, for the following reasons:

1   Few or entire Partners have limited liabilities.
2   By virtue of limitedness of liability, such LLP, exhibits attributes of partnership and corporations.
3   LLPs enable independence and protection to any partner from misdeed of any other partner.
4   Some of the partners and LLPs are similar to shareholders of a company.
5   However, unlike shareholders of corporations, partners in LLPs can run their LLPs directly.
6   The corporations are run by the CEO, by the Managing Director, Board of Directors, employees, etc.
7   Tax liability is different from LLP from that of a corporation.
8   The main safety net for LLP is that all are limited in liabilities whereas in the case of limited partnerships, in some countries, liability is unlimited to one chosen partner while others are exempted from unlimited liability. In all such countries, LLP is now a preferred option in which partners manage their company with limited liability. As a result, in these countries, the LLP is more suited for businesses in which all investors wish to take an active role in management.[91]

LLP Act in India

LLP is a corporate business vehicle that enables professional expertise and entrepreneurial initiative to combine and operate in a flexible, innovative and efficient manner, as a hybrid of company and partnership. It has dual advantages of:

i   limited liability,
ii Operational flexibility is internal management and external growth. LLP is a partnership-oriented legally accepted equity with limited liability.

- Separate Legal Entity- Continue its existence irrespective of changes in partners,
- LLP itself can enter into contracts and hold properties,
- Partner's Liability limited to the agreed contribution,
- Professional and Non-professional (Businessmen), both can set up LLP.

On January 9, 2009, the LLP Act, 2008 was gazetted. A few sections become operable from March 31, 2009.

"Rules of the Act were published in the Official Gazette on 1 April 2009 and amended in 2017."[92] "The first LLP was incorporated on 2 April 2009."[93]

Official routes of the LLP Act were published on 01.04.2009 and the same rules were amended in the year 2017. The LLP Act became operational on 02.04.2009. LLP is entirely contrasted to LP Acts since LLP does not burden the partners with unlimited liability. The following are the benefits of LLP.

Benefits

Firstly, as per provisions of the Companies Act, 2013 the LLP can bring funds and adapt to the norms of the Law.
Secondly, dividend distributions tax cannot be levied on LLP, as against any corporation. Thirdly, professionals like Chartered Accounts, Advocates, Engineers and Doctors also can start as LLPs.

Federal provisions in the USA empower every with different laws for LLPs. The 1990s saw the inauguration of the LLP season. In 1992 two states in the USA allowed LLPs and now more than forty states have LLPs. These provisions are in addition to Uniform Partnership Act, 1996.

The LLP has compliance circumstances in the US, as the US is the origin of its evolution. Texas witnessed the collapse of real estate prices in the 1980s along with gas prices. A chain reaction ensued, resulting in the collapse of banks, housing loan companies and construction sector-related industries. Banks started chasing the chartered accountants and partners in law farms who recommended the loans for recovery of their dues. LLP came into vogue to protect the professional from personal liability due to professional transactions or work.

Architects, Lawyers, Investment Bankers, Finance professionals, Company Secretaries, Cost Accountants, Chartered Accountants were the initial beneficiaries of LLP in the USA. In some U.S. states, namely California, New York, Oregon, and Nevada, LLPs can only be formed for such professional uses. [94]

Formation of an LLP typically requires filing certificates with the county and state offices. Revised Uniform Partnership Act (RUPA), 1997 emerged in the USA as a model state. Many states adopted and customised the RUPA, 1997 towards their specific requirements.

RUPA, 1997 provides LLP into a limited liability, akin to similar provisions in the case of the corporations. The partnership is almost like a company, a distinct personality, separate from its shareholders or owners, in case of liability. An obligation arising out of the partnership is the responsibility of the partnership to solve, redeem and mitigate. The persons in a partnership are nowadays liable for such mitigation arising out of tort, contract violation, etc. No partner is either directly or indirectly, straight or circuitously can be held liable towards the obligation of the partnership firm.

Two prominent states, namely Tennessee and West Virginia, while extending non-liability protection in case of negligence, did not offer similar protection can case of international ports or contract violation claims.

160   CBMA, Competition Law, Antitrust and Demerger

The above-mentioned states made altercations to section 306 of RUPA, 1997 in the Act, so now only truncated liability protection is provided.

Corporations suffer from double taxation issues such suffering is exempted to partnership farms and limited liability companies (LLCs). In a similar vein, the profits of LLP are apportioned for purposes of tax strategies among the partners. In certain US States, there exist a combination of LP and LL.P. The combined entity is termed limited liability limited partnership (LLLP).

Some consequences of limited liability

The main purpose of LLP is to offer a viable alternative to traditional corporations or companies. Limited liability can enable opportunities for new business growth that was formerly accessible only to those who had access to large amounts of capital or other resources.

Negative efforts cannot be ruled out in LLPs. Negative factors arise due to the firm, space, history and nature of partnerships. For some large accountancy firms in the United Kingdom, reorganising as LLPs and LLCs has relieved them of owing the duty of care to individuals and clients who are adversely affected by audit failures.

Accountancy firm partners share the profits, but don't have to suffer the consequences of negligence by the firm or fellow partners. Accountancy firm LLPs apportion the revenue and do not suffer ill effects arising out of negligible from fellow partners. There are instances where not contended with limited success due to lobbying with political parties. Some big accountancy farms hired the entire government to protect their interest through limited liability.

PricewaterhouseCoopers and Ernst &Young hired the legislature of Jersey to enact an LLP Bill, which they had drafted. "They awarded themselves protection from lawsuits, with little public accountability. Accounting is central to all calculations about institutionalized abuses, tax, and responsibility avoidance."[95]

> Chief Justice Myron Steele of Delaware Supreme Court in the USA opined that common law standards are not applicable to LLPs, since the standards of financial principles of corporations are different in both cases. Instead, he argued that courts should use contractual analysis of the partnership agreement when assessing cases of improper corporate governance.[96]

"This directly led to the elimination of the independent fiduciary duty of good faith in Delaware corporate law in 2006."[97]

CBMA and CAG

The Comptroller and Auditor General of India played a significant role in the previous decade with the exposure of million-rupee scams like the Commonwealth Games scams, 3G spectrum licensing schemes, the coal

CBMA, Competition Law, Antitrust and Demerger   161

licensing scams, and the helicopter deal scams. The previous occupant Mr Rajeev Maharshi has called for statutory amendments at setting up some engagement photo girls between the competition Commission of India (CCI) and sectoral regulators to address the overlap issues.

> The former CAG, Shri. Rajeev Maharshi, IAS(Retired) worked in coordination among many sectoral regulators like CCJ, SEBI, RBI, and ED. Overlapping jurisdiction and duplicate activities are not healthy either for regulators or even for the Indian Economy. This general truth is echoed by the then C.A.G, Sr. R. Maharshi.[98]

Till now, the discussion was about specific legislation in India and the USA on competition, antitrust, and de-merger, legislative initiatives and establishment of the Ministry of Corporate Affairs aspects. In Chapter 4, Indian experience in CBMA and initiatives like IBC (Insolvency and Bankruptcy Code) and new solutions would be discussed.

Corruption Transparency Issues in Cross-Border Mergers and Acquisitions, the USA and India

India's position as an emerging economy in comparison with other emerging economies and the experience of the USA as the leader of developed economies were discussed. Corruption, bribery, fraud, and transparency are issues that significantly affect CBMA functioning.

The USA happens to be the main contributor to CBMAs both in terms of value and in terms of the number of transactions. The USA can be taken as a benchmark in the fight against corruption in the CBMAs arena. Lex Mundi World Ready, under the chapter "Best Practices in Preventing Fraud and Corruption in Global Business," mentions three main reasons for the problem of corruption in the world.

1. Fast-moving competition,
2. Pressure on growth and financial performance,
3. Rigors of expansion into new markets worldwide and
4. A multiplicity of regulations and regulatory authorities and thus creating an environment of confusion.

Developed and developing countries are equally witnessing sharing of information among the regulators more frequently and it has been seen that many regulators are seriously enforcing accountability and ethics in business conduct.

Corruption

> Corruption and fraud are defined fairly consistently by many organisations. Corruption is technically defined as the abuse of entrusted power for private gain. Corruption, in essence, is a planned systematic effort

of abuse of public trust and power in order profiteer personally by those who hold such public power. It can include a variety of conducts in both the private and public sectors. One can categorise corruption into a) public corruption and b) private sector bribery. Public corruption covers one-sided abuses by officials in government through the acts of self-aggrandizement amassing wealth and nepotism, as well as misuses connecting private and public rules and actions through acts of bribery, extracting, influence peddling, and fraud. Corruption often facilitates criminal activities such as drug trafficking, money laundering, and prostitution, and it is not restricted to these activities.[99]

Private sector bribery is an example of corruption by private sector units and refers to corrupt practices within and between Enterprises.... Such as when an employee accepts the advantage granted to him by a person from outside of a company, without informing the corporate bodies is persons.[100]

In business organisations, favours are sought, and sought-after favours are paid for. There can be a further differentiation in the aspect of corruption which is as follows.

1   Against the rule of corruption, and
2   According to the rule of corruption.

If the bribe giver seeks a favour against the rule and his entitlement then he is covered by the first category. The second category is witnessed in areas for speedy payment of pending dues and for which the bribe giver is legally entitled. One can call this no obstruction tax, while one can call the first category has no objection tax or abdication tax.

Organization for Economic Cooperation and Development (OECD) in the year 2007 defined "active corruption or active bribery as paying or promising to pay a bribe and passive bribery as an offense committed by the person receiving the bribe."[101]

When one person internationally misrepresents material facts to another person with appropriate Knowledge of falsity and with an intention to induce the other person to act in a self-injurious manner, resulting in damage, then that person is said to be indulging in fraud.

FCPA in the USA

The Foreign Corrupt Practices Act (FCPA) has existed for more than 40 years in the United States. It has been the main plank against foreign corruption. The FCPA prohibits companies within the United States and individuals from driving the non-US officials including employees of government instrumentalities to obtain or retain business gain an improper business advantage. "The FCPA also imposes affirmative books and records, internal control requirements on entities that qualify as issuers as under USA securities laws and on individuals who act on their behalf."[102] the Year 2010 witnessed 744 actions firm combined effort of Department of Justice. (DOJ). FCPA SEC.

Example of Major Cases

Siemens Germany paid the US$ 800 million as a fine to the US authorities in 2008 to settle anti-corruption charges. In the year 2011, under the Dodd-Frank Wall Street Reform and Consumer Protection Act, whistle blowers who alerted the Department of Justice and the Securities and Exchange Commission about Foreign Corrupt Practices Act violations can now collect between 10 and 30% of any government recovery above the US$ 1million.

The whistle blower report in the year 2013 shows that the number of FCPA-related tips increased almost 30% from 115 in 2012 to 149 in 2013 and is likely to provide the basis for additional enforcement activity in the future. It is interesting to note that industry-wide FCPA applications move from one category to another, because, multi-defendant enforcement actions are becoming a norm.

"The multi defendant enforcement actions phenomena is caused by the seamless flow of information of probable wrong doing by seemingly unconnected other players in the same industrial sector."[103] According to records available with DOJ, the following industries witnessed much of the wrongdoing when compared to others in the CBMAs:

1. Oil and gas, 2. Healthcare, 3. Pharmaceuticals, 4. Consumer products, 5. Extractive industries, 6. Medical devices, 7. Telecommunications, 8. Transportation, and 9. Defence.

Eighty per cent of the largest of the ten United States Foreign Corrupt Practices Act (FCPA) enforcement actions against the entities involved non-US companies in the CBMA arena. The US enforcers extradited and criminally prosecuted multiple non-US citizens in recent years based on FCPA charges.

Enforcement in the USA

US enforcers have sent an unmistakable signal that the companies and individuals who conduct business internationally and have any jurisdictional nexus to the US must ensure that they comply with the FCPA. In November 2012, a resource guide was released by the Department of Justice and Securities and Exchange Commission which contains detailed information about the Act and its provisions. It is in the interest of every prospective participant in the CBMAs with the USA to go through this resource guide and to familiarise themselves with the general enforcement practices are the Department of Justice and the Securities and Exchange Commission.

The difference between the USA and the United Kingdom is that while the United Kingdom has a Bribery Act of 2011 with many similarities including extraterritorial application, the key differences among others include that the Bribery Act of the United Kingdom is purely commercial. In the UK's Bribery Act of 2011, there is strict Criminal liability for corporates offenses. Corporate offenses cannot the failure to prevent Bribery, despite having bribery preventive Standard Operating Procedure.

> The United Nations Convention against corruption is one of the most important of the international anti-corruption conventions which was adopted in the United Nations General Assembly in 2003 and was enacted in the year 2005 and now there are 170 countries that are parties to it.[104]

All the 34 member nations of OECD are signatories to the convention on combating bribery of foreign officials. Other important conventions are the criminal law convention on corruption, the union convention on preventing and combating, the inter-American convention against corruption adopted by the Organization of American States (OAS).

A simple act of throwing a party may appear to be an innocent act in one country but may be interpreted as an ethical question and an act of corruption in other countries. It is therefore imperative on the part of all executives of companies involving in CBMAs to understand the fine print in the law of all the nations in which their activities are spreading. Otherwise, there is a danger of the employees and executives getting arrested and prosecuted by the law of the foreign land.

Transparency International (TI), founded in Germany, comes out every year with the Corruption Perception Index (CPI) and Bribe Payers Index. Between 1999 and 2010 the World Bank publicly sanctioned more than 400 companies and individuals for fraud and corruption and debarred consultants and contractors that it found to have connivance in corrupting while executing Global projects of I.B.R.D (International Bank for Reconstruction and Development).

Companies in their interest need to have articulated corporate standards. The Code of Ethics is as important as the business plan because Ethics do not change by time and space. The following practices by corporates across the world can be beneficial to all the corporates who are partners in cross-border merger activity.

1 Compliance to basic rules, standards, and behaviours expected regardless of geography or circumstance,
2 Fundamental values and principles of the company,
3 The position of the company on issues of driving, corruption, and facilitation payments,
4 Rules of the company on competition and entry trust and how they affect commercial operations and transactions,

5   Policies and procedures for business entertainment and gifts,
6   Policies and procedures for political and other donations or grants, and
7   Policies and procedures for conflicts of interest.

Control Framework and Structures

"Effective program to prevent wrongdoing is through an effective control framework. The following are the three important components of such a framework.

1   Clear written designation of authority and accountability for various issues,
2   Clear lines of reporting, and well-documented mechanisms for review and approval of proposal conduct, and
3   Effective accounting and financial reporting procedures that adequately reflect the company's transactions, dealings, and asset disposition."[105]

Structures are important in complex businesses to have timely information to be responded to. The following three components are of vital importance to the structures.

1   An internal whistleblowing policy that provides anonymity and protects the whistleblower,
2   The hotline, ethics line, or helpline provides employees with a safe way to raise questions and concerns and have them investigated, and
3   Special Audit and investigation teams are closely supported by the legal and finance organisations as necessary.

Compliance Programmes

Compliance programmes certificate should guide by the legal and compliance functions. Global compliances should recognise that responsibility for complaints must be with business functions. Right from the top till the bottom all specialised departments must be part of the same effort which among others includes the following.

1   The Chief Executive Officer (CEO), the Chief Financial Officer (CFO), and the Chief Operating Officer (COO).
2   Board of directors,
3   Legal functionaries' team,
4   Internal audit team,
5   Compliance function,
6   The risk management team,
7   Accounting, financial controls, and treasury,
8   Human resources,

9 Corporate Secretary,
10 Text team,
11 Corporate Communications and government relations teams, and
12 Corporate strategy and development,

Scope of Improvement

Eminent lawyers from expert law firms like Lex Mundi suggest preventive measures to effective communication which include among others the following.

1 Communications and overall messages about complaints are clear and concise and to be understood by the audience for whom they are meant examples need to be used and situations to be explained to demystify the Complaints and encourage an open dialogue,
2 Multiple channels to distribute the message must be used which must include print and electronic, presentations by and conversations with, teleconferences and multimedia,
3 Repetition of the same message in various ways and keep it interesting legal jargon needs to be avoided and one must make sure that qualification is communicated to the audience and the reason for such classification is also be communicated should be made known,
4 The topic of complaints communication needs to be adapted to the local Markets and the cultures and are the examples and situations used needs to be practical and realistic in the Local setting the local language on the local lingua franca should be used within the local culture to have the maximum effect of communication,
5 Multiple methods to distribute the messages, true business leaders, middle managers, in-house lawyers, outside lawyers, operation employees must be used,
6 Education training programs must be taken up to prevent fraud and corruption and such measures will be tailor-made with the approach to the business, value system, and the local culture,
7 A flexible, multifaceted approach with the equal opportunity being accessible to all product and to reinforce the rules and regulations need to be made available,
8 8 External and internal resource combinations must be used for education and education must be a continuous exercise,
9 Webinars, online issues, specific and targeted training, email blast and individual certifications, and top-down complaints reviews need to be used as new tools of communication both within and without, and
10 Care should be taken in training all those involved especially engaging the third party because third-party transparency also is the responsibility of the main concern. No company can work all activities through its employees and it needs to be decentralised through subcontractors. Sub-contractors engaged by well-reputed Contractors can be ill-reputed

and eventually, all contractors became ill-reputed. "Therefore, it is essential to train the employees of the company at the cutting edge so that they will identify the correct elements among the third parties and expose them before the damage is being done."[106]

Vicarious Liability/Responsibility and CBMA

FCPA of the USA, in order to curb corruption abroad, holds the principal responsible for corruption by third parties, abroad or within the USA. The purpose is the implementation of the wisdom of age-old Aristotle so creates ethics vice anywhere make vice everywhere. "Third parties include individuals are companies in almost any type of relationship with the principal including an agent, representative, consultant, distributor joint venture partner, contractor, broker, finder, or a professional service provider."[107]

The criminal liability of the principal is through wilful negligence also if not actual connivance. Informed lawyers call this as Head in the Sand approach. The Foreign Corrupt Practices Act expects pre-engagement due diligence on a prospect to the third party by every principle and to eliminate or adequately mitigate any red flags that may arise. The principals are expected to maintain oversight of the activities of a third party and to respond to any red flags that are presented during the performance or doing a termination of the relationship. It must be understood that even after the termination of the relationship and setting up the account, the responsibility of the principal in releasing the third party cannot be evaporated. Vicarious responsibility will be that of the principal for all times and climes. There is a compendium of manuals available pointing out the best standard operating procedures to deal with third-party engagements in preventing corruption.

Anti-corruption due Diligence and Critical Examples

Anti-corruption due diligence is of great importance in CBMAs because of the simple reason that the target company might have been involved in anti-corruption litigation which may not be known to the acquirer and post-integration, the acquirer also will be suffering from the litigation and prosecution. This syndrome is termed correctly as successor liability for anti-corruption violations. Some examples will illustrate this issue.

1 Halliburton 2008: Halliburton is an oil company in Texas, USA. "It was charged for violation of books and records in Angola operation and was fined US $ 29.2 million."[108]
2 e-LAND/LATIN NODE 2009,
3 RAE systems 2010.
    RAE -systems entered into joint ventures in China with two Chinese companies through a foreign holding company. Both joint ventures engaged in business dealings with Chinese government agencies. It was

discovered later that one of the Chinese companies had previously engaged in improper payments to Chinese officials. RAE ultimately agreed to pay a fine of US$ 3 million and disgorgement in addition to adopting stringent internal controls, and appropriate measures.
4 Pfizer in the year 2012 agreed with the Securities and Exchange Commission for Foreign Corrupt Practices Act violations attributed to corrupt payments made in China, Indonesia and Pakistan.

The FCPA mandates the companies to follow GAAP standards in accountancy. The FCPA violations are severe and the penalties imposed are extreme.

1 Fine of the US$ 2 million to 25 million for each book and records and internal controls violation and felony convictions.
2 Felony convictions for individuals may be 20 years of imprisonment and 5 years of imprisonment for each bribery violation.

Apart from inescapable imprisonment, there may be fines on individuals and loss of reputation and goodwill in the market and thus the ignorance or the risk becomes fatalistic. Therefore, the expansive reach of the FCPA coupled with the aggressive enforcement of the US government compels every partner of Cross-Border Merger Activity to take notice of the same.

In the year 2012, the FCPA resource guide was issued. Among others, the resource guide has a special chapter on mergers and acquisitions. The major points are that

> it places a significant emphasis on the importance of due diligence. Companies should conduct due diligence before acquisition to the greatest extent possible, and if effective diligence is not possible before the acquisition, it should be done as quickly as possible after the acquisition to try to protect the successor company. Nevertheless, the guide indicates that enforcement action may still be brought against the producer company even if it exists now only in its new form as a subsidiary of the acquirer. Although acquiring a company that was not previously subjected to the FCPA does not make the FCPA apply to the target retroactively, the acquiring company should make sure to implement effective complaint controls and training to ensure that there is no unlawful activity following the acquisition.[109]

Effectiveness of FCPA Implementation

Under the aegis of FCPA, it is impossible to escape the prosecution of any wrongdoing. Hence, to avoid the penalties of wrongdoing, it is better to adopt the anti-corruption programmes and make them part of the corporate culture for due diligence. Monitoring of employee behaviour is vital so that no employee will become prey to any possible corrupt practices. In case such knowledge is available with the organisation, it shall immediately share with the Regulatory Agencies and thus making a friendly relationship with the regulatory authorities to make the reputation of the company irrefutable. Cobus de Swardt, Managing Director, Transparency International, so eloquently articulated the efficacy of anti-corruption measures in the following words.

> By taking a strong stance on promoting transparency and fighting corruption, companies not only mitigate reputational risk, but they also live up to their responsibility as corporate citizens and can take an active part in the emerging solutions to some of the greatest issues facing the world today.[110]

Critical Examples of Anti-corruption Prosecution in CBMA

Recently a company named Alere which is a public company that manufactures and sells diagnostic test equipment has resolved the Securities and Exchange Commission that it was stated its revenue and bribed government officials in Columbia and India. Alere agreed to pay US$ 3.3mn in disgorgement interest about US$ 95,000 and a penalty of US$ 9.2 million. One is not sure whether there is any parallel investigation by such enforcement agencies in India. The FCPA of the USA mentions in volume number 6 and number 17 dated September 6, 2017, that there are 101 names to corruption. They were referring to an article by name '10 tips for performing effective anti-corruption investigations in India' dated May 24, 2017. In this article, they mention the following names, which are mangoes, cheese, bonbons, boost, courtesy payment, motivation amount. Risk needs to be mitigated regarding corruption when one acquires companies in a high-risk jurisdiction. Despite the uncertainty, dealmakers avoid the fallout from global factors. In reality, despite cautions by the FCPA of the USA or by the CBI in India, private equity operators and profit-chasing tycoons, looking for ROI (Return on Investment), treat, if so allowed by the Regulators, Corruption as Cost of Operation.

Cadbury India Ltd. expanded in India and its controller in the USA, Mondelez International Incorporation, settled the corruption allegations by paying a fine to the SEC of the USA. US-based Cadbury, which acquired UK-based Cadbury in 2010, agreed to pay a civil penalty of US$ 13 million to settle the allegations concerning payments made to a third-party agent returned by Cadbury India. "The deal is notable for its elimination of acceptable levels of Pre-acquisition diligence and the fact that only civil penalties for incurred with no mention of disgorgement. This is as per the FCPA report."[111]

"The US enforcement authorities announced three FCPA resolutions arising at least in part from conduct occurring in India."[112]

1. "The Embraer maid a resolution with Security Exchange Commission and the Department of Justice, in part, because of the company's payment of US $ 5.1 million to an agent, to illicitly secure the sale of 3

aircraft to Indian Air Force."[113] "A former Air Chief Marshal has been arrested in India country in connection with Augusta Westland case and his name is S.P Tyagi."[114]

2 AB in Bev resolution arose out of payments made by an Indian affiliate company to the third-party sales promoters who, in turn, have made improper payments to the Indian government officials, to increase brewery hours,

3 Cadbury/Mondelez resolved its FCPA matter with the Securities and Exchange Commission, which was based on the company allegedly paying the US$ 100,000 for anything to assist in securing permits and approvals for its factory expansion in India.

The FCPA Anti-Corruption report brings out that it has to make an end India specific consideration because of the peculiar nature of corruption that exists in India.

> While the basic approach to internal investigations remains the same across jurisdictions, we have found it useful to modify our investigation strategy to tackle and to take into account India specific considerations, and have compiled the following 10 tips for conducting those investigations.[115]

1 Amidst the political noise and euphemistic allegations, the main issue is likely to be hidden and hence the investigators shall never miss the real issue.

2 Scoping in the initial stages of the complaint and the complainant is important and this activity needs to be carefully piloted through the services of enable Indian local Counsel.

3 Under Indian law, there is no attorney-client privilege for in-house lawyers. This is not the case with the experiences of the United States with other developed countries. If the privilege is important, it is better to retain outside counsel to lead the investigation.

4 It is important to consider the local Counsel of India since India is a vast country with 22 official languages. While a skilled Counsel at the Metropolitan cities is an asset, the local language knowing local Counsel sometimes is necessary.

5 Protecting the identities of the reporter is essential because there were cases wherein whistle blowers or complainants were brutally murdered. It is prudent to take extra steps to avoid sharing the Identity of the reporter with other employees of the Indian subsidiary. Even for companies with robust anti-retaliation policies, whistle blower retribution is unfortunately common in India and can aggravate an already emotionally and legally precarious situation.

6 Law enforcement action needs to be prepared for, during the investigation pro cess itself. Law enforcement in the United States and India

work on two different paradigms. The law enforcement objective in India is focused on securing the conviction of individual wrongdoers. Bribery investigations can move quickly resulting in press and media coverage. Such events obviously can change the fundamental calculus of Investigation, including the issue of self-disclosure in the United States. Therefore, there is a need to have a contingency plan in the place readily.

7   One must be careful about the possibility of all the conversations either video or audio recorded in India. Smartphones are very innovatively used in India.
8   One should have a careful observation regarding cash management by the investigated organisation. When conducting internal investigations in India, one should pay special attention to any cash expenditure, whether or not it is related to the transaction in question. Cash is often not as critical to the operation of the business as Indian managers are claiming. Cash expenditures can often signal potential bribery.
9   The third-party intermediary expenditures must be carefully examined. Improper payments in India are very often made through agents, consultants, and other intermediaries.
10 One must keep a watch for Red Flag terms, some of which are given below.

a. Brokerage charges or fees, b. Consultancy charges, c. Covering charge, d. Management fees, e. Documentation charges, f. Managing expenses, g. Out of pocket expenses, h. Protection fees, i. Special expenses, j. Expenses for obtaining the licence, k. Expenses for liaising, l. Expenses for clearances, m. Expenses for getting no-objection certificate, n. Expenses for obtaining approvals, and o. Expenses for any other grammatically awkward or vague reference on invoices like for example motivation amount.[116]

To conclude, it is worthwhile to mention here that the highest-ranking Air force officer was arrested after the investigations in the United States were made public and that too due to investigations by the FCPA. Upholding of the value of truth demands that India is nowhere near the ethical standards and the investigation capabilities of organisations like the FCPA. The Serious Fraud Investigation Office of India is no match, nor the Central Bureau of Investigation has any capability or matching skills of organisations like the SEC, FCPA and the Department of Justice of the United States of America. The empirical evidence to support the above claim is that there is no document available of a parallel nature of India in the USA. A lot more remains to be done in India to catch up to the global standards and the global organisations. It is suggested here that since the work is already being done in an open environment by American organisations, nothing should prevent the bureaucrats of India to learn lessons from their counterparts in the USA.

It is hence proposed that the establishment of the Central Bureau of Financial Security to cover cyber/bank/money laundering/foreign corrupt practices in India to work under the supervision of Chief Justice, Supreme Court of India.

Transparency and Evaluation of Indian CBMAs

Another proof of India, not being till recently in the pink of the colour of reforms on par with the global standards and that a recent beginning is being made, can be felt from the recent article in *The Economist* dated April 19, 2018, the following are the highlights of the write up in *The Economist*.

> The nature of India is capitalism is changing. For decades personal connections have provided a well-trodden path to success in India's business. State-owned banks provided cheap financing for organizations whose success often rested on winning official approvals. If a venture is lost, the taxpayer frequently ended up being left to shoulder losses. There are plenty of gifted business people in India but cronyism, not competition has been the shortest route which is prevalent even after the partial dismantling of the license Raj nearly three decades ago in the year 1991. A large number of industrialists are always uncomfortable with a constant fear of losing their wealth. The fate of 12 troubled large concerns is due to be settled within weeks and another 28 cases are said to be resolved by September 2018. Between them, these organizations account for about 40% of loans that banks themselves think are unlikely to be repaired. For enforcing a bankruptcy system that is usually scripted by those with the connection, the Government of the present time deserves much credit. Yet the job is far from being done.[117]
>
> Industries such as mining, power generation, telecom, and infrastructure require large chunks of capital and lots of interactions with the government. Here, unfortunately, the core competence was not in the industry but in the manipulation and the management of the connections to arrive at a favourable decent by paying money through channels of corruption and sharing the luggage with the political bureaucratic nexus. Many tycoons count on ministers to put in a word with a recalcitrant banker. Every banker's would frequently extend repayments only to preserve their jobs. Overburdened courts were unequal to the task of enforcing contracts.[118]

Bankruptcy and Insolvency happened among banks largely due to bureaucratic Politician bankers and fraudulent industrialist nexus.

> The core competency of many of them was not in running businesses but in forging contacts through contracts and exploiting their connections by awarding lucrative contracts to firms controlled by the family members to make reap huge windfall profits.[119]

The Economist further maintains that

> this system is under three-pronged assault. The first is the reformed bankruptcy code that makes the seizure of business easier. New setup of dedicated insolvency professionals, is help banks seize assets and sell them to fresh owners. To focus the minds of both bankers and borrowers, if no deal can be cut within nine months, the organization is shut down and its equipment is sold for scrap.[120]

Since the nonperforming assets have ballooned to the tune of nearly Rs 720,000 crore, the authorities, now tired of recurring bailouts, are forcing them to recognise which units are unlikely to be repaired, and to initiate insolvency proceedings in double-quick time. Thirdly most tycoons have lost influence in Delhi, as politicians from the Prime Minister down realize the toxicity of being seen to be in "cahoots with bollygarches."[121]

"The Economist mentions that ensuring permanent change requires deeper reforms. If wholesale ministerial corruption is reportedly much reduced, there is still little clarity on how political parties are financed."[122] Less government and more governance is the new mantra of the BJP Government. A certain brand of tycoons has arrived because getting things done requires sharp elbows and sharper business practices. Magnates

who are politically connected will still have an edge if knowing how to dodge a price cap imposed on the ministerial win, for example, is a sure guide to success than knowing how to run a factory. On the implementation front, this corrupt practice is still going on,"[123] according to The Economist.

> Reforming these state-owned banks is the most important task of all. Their balance sheets are where you find 70% of loans and nearly 100% of the problems. Ensuring banks make commercial lonely realistically be achieved by privatizing at least some of them. The salary structure of CEO compensation also needs to be on par with the best Global practices to ensure full dedicated importance for state-owned banks.[124]

A decent systematic financial ecology is the most effective antidote against venomous crony capitalism. Sadly, this kind of Reform still seems to be anathema.

" The Prime Minister has made his thought on tackling the tycoons. But if he is to entrance revolution in Indian capitalism, he must do more."[125]

Conclusion

Corruption kills and absolute corruption kills absolutely. Transparency is a tool for the Rule of Law. CBMA has to be ethical anywhere and everywhere. Issues related to corruption, bribery and fraud in a comparative environment brought out the lacunae in India. In the next chapter, a few remedial initiatives by the Indian Government would be discussed.

Notes

1 Florian Becker, "The Case of Export Cartel Exemptions: Between Competition and Protectionism", JOURNAL OF LAW AND ECONOMICS, 3(1), 97–126 (1999).
2 Shakar A. Singham Symposium Article „Shaping Competition policy in the Americas Scope for Transatlantic Cooperation", 24 BROOK JOURNAL OF INTERNATIONAL LAW, 363385, 368, (1998).
3 Sec. 83, CLAYTON ACT, (1914).
4 Sec. 82(a), CLAYTON ACT, (1914).
5 Sec. 87, CLAYTON ACT, (1914).
6 Sec.1–2, 15 USC SHERMAN ANTITRUST ACT, (1994).
7 Goetz, Charles J., Fred S. McChesney, Antitrust Law: Interpretation and Implementation, DANVERS LEXISNEXIS, (2002).
8 148F.2d 416, 444(2d Cir, 1945).
9 Alan Greenspan, THE AGE OF TURBULENCE, NEW YORK: PENGUIN PRESS, (2007).
10 Ayan Rand, CAPITALISM: THE UNKNOWN IDEAL,NEW YORK: NEW AMERICAN LIBRARY, (1967).
11 Ayan Rand, CAPITALISM: THE UNKNOWN IDEAL, NEW YORK: NEW AMERICAN LIBRARY, (1967).
12 In the famous case Timberlane Lumber Company versus Bank of America the supreme court, the court in United States which is the Ninth circuit Court that the US jurisdiction would be granted only if the intended effect on US commerce was substantial magnitude, or whether extraterritorial jurisdiction should be granted as a matter of international committee.
13 Ayan Rand, CAPITALISM: THE UNKNOWN IDEAL, NEW YORK: NEW AMERICAN LIBRARY, (1967).
14 Sec.18(a), 15 UNITED STATES CODE,
15 Fiscal year 2016 covers October 1, 2015 through September 30, 2016. Fed. Trade Comm'n & Dep't of Justice.
16 Elizabeth Warren, Three Ways to Make the American Economy for All, Remarks at the Launch Event for the Open Markets Institute, MONOPOLIESAMERICAN-ECONOMY, (December 6, 2017) https://www.theguardian.com/commentisfree/2017/dec/06/elizabeth-warren-monopolies-american-economy, (Last visited on May 19, 2018)
17 Elizabeth Warren, Three Ways to Make the American Economy for All, Remarks at the Launch Event for the Open Markets Institute, MONOPOLIESAMERICAN-ECONOMY, (December 6, 2017) https://www.theguardian.com/commentisfree/2017/dec/06/elizabeth-warren-monopolies-american-economy, (Last visited on May 19, 2018).
18 Elizabeth Warren, Three Ways to Make the American Economy for All, Remarks at the Launch Event for the Open Markets Institute, MONOPOLIESAMERICAN-ECONOMY, (December 6, 2017) https://www.theguardian.com/commentisfree/2017/dec/06/elizabeth-warren-monopolies-american-economy, (Last visited on May 19, 2018).
19 United States vs Anthem, Inc., 236F. Supp.3d 171 (D.D.C. 2017).
20 United State vs Anthem, Inc.et al., No -16-cv-01493-ABJ (D.D.C.2017).
21 United State vs Anthem, Inc.,236F Supp3d at 231–53; United State vs Anthem, Inc.et al., 855F.3d 345 9 D.C. Cir.2017.
22 United State vs Anthem, Inc.et al., 855F.3d at 355–59.
23 United State vs Anthem, Inc.et al., 855F.3d at 353–55.
24 United State vs Anthem, Inc.et al., 855F.3d at 355, 356–359.
25 The DOJ has historically published total annual criminal fine statistics. As of the publication of this Report, those official statistics were not yet available for

fiscal year 2017. See Leah Nylen, Cartel Fines Dropped to Lowest in Decade in Fiscal 2017, MLex (October 6, 2017).
26 For example, in early 2016, the DOJ's Deputy Assistant Attorney General in charge of the criminal enforcement program at the Antitrust Division, Brent Snyder, who became Acting AAG in early 2017, stated that the DOJ would "do even better" to identify potentially culpable individuals early in the investigation to minimize the risk of prosecutions against individuals being time-barred. See Brent Snyder, U.S. Dep't of Justice, Remarks at the Yale Global Antitrust Enforcement Conference: Individual Accountability for Antitrust Crimes (February 19, 2016). In testimony before the Senate Judiciary Committee, former Deputy Associate Attorney General William Baer echoed this message, stressing that the DOJ will hold "senior executives accountable for criminal antitrust misconduct" and will seek jail sentences. See Oversight of the Enforcement of the Antitrust Laws, Hearing Before the Subcommittees on Antitrust, Competition, & Consumer Rights of the S. Comm. on the Judiciary. 114th Cong. (2016) (statement of Bill Baer, U.S. Dep't of Justice). In October 2017, the DOJ's Deputy Assistant Attorney General in charge of international affairs, Roger Alford, stated that "[a] key component of [DOJ's] criminal program, and of rule of law generally, is individual accountability.... [W]e at the Antitrust Division have a long history of holding individuals accountable for antitrust crimes, and we have consistently touted prison time for individuals as the single most effective deterrent to criminal collusion." Roger Alford, U.S. Dep't of Justice, Remarks at International Conference on the Rule of Law and Anti-Corruption Challenges (October 3, 2017).
27 Animal Sci Prods., Inc Vs Heibei Welcome Pharma. Co. Ltd, No. 16–1220 (US).
28 In re Vitamin C antitrust litig., 837 F.3d 175 (2d Cir. 2016)
29 Valspar Corporation versus I Du Pont De Nemours & Co. 873 F. 3d 185 (3d Cir. 2017)
30 WILSON SONSINI GOODRICH & ROSATI PROFESSIONAL CORPORATION, WSGRANTITRUST YEAR IN REVIEW, 25, (2017)
31 In re Capacitors Antitrust Litigation, No. 14-03264 (N.D. Cal. sept. 30,2016) (Dkt. No. 1302.
32 WILSON SONSINI GOODRICH & ROSATI PROFESSIONAL CORPORATION, WSGR ANTITRUSTYEAR IN REVIEW, 27, (2017).
33 WILSON SONSINI GOODRICH & ROSATI PROFESSIONAL CORPORATION, WSGR ANTITRUSTYEAR IN REVIEW, 27, (2017).
34 Amphastar Pharms. Inc. vs. Momenta Pharms., Inc., 850 F.3d 52, 57 (1st Cir. 2017)
35 Amphastar Pharms. Inc. vs. Momenta Pharms., Inc., 850 F.3d 52, 57 (1st Cir. 2017)
36 FTC. Vs. Actavis, 570 U.S., 136, (2013).
37 In re Suboxone (Buprenorphine Hydrochloride & Naloxone. Antitrust Litigation., No. 13-MD2445, 2017 WL 4910673 (E.D. Pa. Oct. 30, 2017 AT *11)
38 In re Suboxone (Buprenorphine Hydrochloride & Naloxone) Antitrust Litigation., No. 13-MD2445, 2017 WL 4910673 (E.D. Pa. October 30, 2017).
39 https://www.ftc.gov/system/files/documents/cases/170216viropharma_unre dacted_sealed_complaint.pdf
40 Dorothy Shapiro, A Competition Act by India, for India: The first Three Years of Enforcement: Under the New Competition Act, p-62.
41 Report of the Monopolies Inquiry Commission, (1965).
42 Acquisition is defined as "acquiring or agreeing to acquire, (i) shares, voting rights, or assets of an enterprise or (ii) control over management or control over the assets of an enterprise." See §2(a) of the Competition Act. The

definition of combination includes "acquiring of control by a person over an enterprise." Thus, a merger can be a combination between two existing companies but also the absorption of one company by another.

43 A draft of the merger regulations was issued in February 2011, but were revised and finalized in May 2011
44 Uttrakhand Agricultural Produce Marketing Board & Ors v. Competition Commission of India & Anr, W.P. (C) 10411/2016, (September 22, 2017).
45 Abdullah Hussain, Modhulika Bose, Indian Competition Law Year in Review Highlights of 2017, MONDAQ (January 22, 2018) http://www.mondaq.com/india/x/666164/Antitrust+
46 Co-Ordination Committee of Artists and Technicians of W.B. Film and Television and Ors v. Competition Commission of India. Civil Appeal No. 6691 of 2014, (March 10, 2017).
47 Vidharbha Industries Association and oths. v. MSEB Holding Company Ltd. and others, Case No. 8 of 2014, (April 21, 2017) and Case Nos. 05, 07, 37, & 44/2013 (April 21, 1027).
48 Case No. 8 of 2014, (April 21, 2017) and Case Nos. 05, 07, 37, & 44/2013 decision dated (April 21, 1027).
49 Case 54 of 2015, (October 31, 2017); Case No. c-175/09/dgir/27/28-MRTP, (March 02, 2017)
50 Abdullah Hussain, Modhulika Bose, Indian Competition Law Year in Review Highlights of 2017, MONDAQ (January 22, 2018) http://www.mondaq.com/india/x/666164/Antitrust+Competition/Indian+Competition+Law+Year+In+Review+Highlights+Of+2017 (Last visited on May 15, 2018).
51 Ministry of Corporate Affairs, Notification dated (November 22.2017).
52 Abdullah Hussain, ModhulikaBose, Indian Competition Law Year in Review Highlights of 2017, MONDAQ (January 22, 2018) http://www.mondaq.com/india/x/666164/Antitrust+Competition/Indian+Competition+Law+Year+In+Review+Highlights+Of+2017 (Last visited on May 15, 2018).
53 Notice under Section 6 (2) of the Competition Act, 2002 given by Piramal Enterprises Ltd. Combination Registration No. C-2016/05/400 (June 8, 2017).
54 Notice under Section 6 (2) of the Competition Act, 2002 given by BhartiAirtel Limited and Telenor (India) Communications Private Limited,Combination Registration No. C-2017/03/494 (May 30, 2017).
55 Notice under Section 6 (2) of the Competition Act, 2002 given by BhartiAirtelLimited Combination Registration No. C-2017/10/531 (November 16, 2017).
56 Combination Registration No. C-2017/05/509, decision dated 21.06.2017 and Combination Registration No.C-2017/05/510, (June 21, 2017).
57 Combination Registration No. C-2017/04/502, decision dated (October 03, 2017).
58 Combination Registration No. C-2016/11/456, decision dated (February 13, 2017).
59 Bharat Bank Ltd., Delhi v. Employees of the Bharat Bank Ltd., AIR 1950 SC 188 (The Supreme Court first dealt with such an attempt, which was in relation to the tribunals constituted under the Industrial Disputes Act, (1947).
60 Bharat Bank Ltd., Delhi v. Employees of the Bharat Bank Ltd., Delhi, AIR 1950 SC 188, 58 (per Mahajan J.).
61 Associated Cements Companies v. P.N. Sharma, AIR 1965 SC 1595, 9
62 Royal Aquarium and Summer and Winter Garden Society Ltd. v. Parkinson, [1892] 1QB431(per lopas L.I).
63 In India there are many such tribunals vested with regulatory functions, for instance, the Airports Authority of India, Telecom Regulatory Authority of India. Principally, those are not involved in adjudicatory functions. Instead, there are involved in regulating a market or an Industry. Nonetheless in the

CBMA, Competition Law, Antitrust and Demerger   177

process of such regulation, they may also undertake, in certain circumstances, functions which require them to act in a judicial manner.
64 S.P. Sampath Kumar v. Union of India, (1987) 1 SCC 124, 21.
65 The Competition Act, 2002, statement of objects and reasons.
66 S.P. Sampath Kumar v. Union of India, (1987) 1 SCC 124.
67 Sofat, Rajini & Hiro, Preeti. STRATEGIC FINANCIAL MANAGEMENT, (2011).
68 Lamont and Thaler, (2001) http://www.nber.org/papers/w8302 (Last visited on May 25, 2018).
69 HITES AND OWERS DEMERGERS, (2001).
70 http://www.mca.gov.in/MinistryV2/about_mca.html, (Last visited on May 25, 2018).
71 Jen Swanson "India Seeks to Overhaul a Corporate World Rife with Fraud" THE NEW YORK TIMES (August 15, 2013). https://ipfs.io/ipfs/QmXoypizj W3WknFiJnKLwHCnL72vedxjQk DDP1mXWo6uco/wiki/Ministry_of_Corporate_Affairs.html, (Last visited on May 26, 2018).
72 RBI Gazette Notification (April 27, 2017).
73 Ibid
74 Chitravanshi, Ruchika, Company Act Amalgamations, ECONOMIC TIMES, 13, (Kolkata edn., March 28, 2018).
75 RBI, Gazette Notification, (April, 2017).
76 FINANCIAL TIMES, 3 (Kolkata edn., April, 2018)
77 L. Street india.com/ experts/ c o l accessed www.wikipedia.com (Last visited on January 3, 2018).
78 Davis Polk and Wardwell LLP, https://www.davispolk.com/news/list (Last visited on March 7, 2018).
79 THE ECONOMIC TIMES 1,12 (Kolkata edn., April 20, 2018).
80 THE ECONOMIC TIMES 5 (Kolkata edn., April 20, 2018).
81 THE ECONOMIC TIMES 10 (Kolkata edn., April 20, 2018).
82 S. Buch, Stamp Duty Implications of Mergers and Acquisitions https://www.wirc icai.org/material/Stamp-Duty-Implications-of-Mergers-and-Acquisitions-SRB.pdf (Last visited on May 25, 2018) A. Bansal, Stamp Duty Implications on Mergers and Amalgamations https://www.linkedin.com/pulse/stamp-duty-implications-mergers-amalgamations-abhishekbansal, (Last visited on February 3, 2018).
83 https://en.wikipedia.org/wiki/Specific_Relief_Act_1963, (Last visited on Feb 4, 2018)
84 G. Shah, Implications of the Amendments to the Specific Relief Act, 1963, (April 11, 2018) https://indiacorplaw.in/2018/04/implications-amendments-specific-relief-act-1963.html (Last visited on February 4, 2018).
85 Sec 10 of the SR Act
86 Abdul Haq vs. Mahommad Khan, AIR 1924 Pat 81.
87 Sec 21 of the SR Act.
88 Sec 37 of the SR Act.
89 Chinnaya Rau v. Ramaya, (1882) I.L.R. 4 Mad. 137.
90 R. Indapurkar, Effects specific relief amendment bill 2017 law remedies breach contracthttps://indiacorplaw.in/2018/04/effects-specific-relief-amendment-bill-2017-law-remediesbreach-contract.html (Last visited on May 5, 2018).
91 https://en.wikipedia.org/wiki/Limited_liability_partnership#Some_conse quences_oflimited_liabililty & "Limited Liability Partnership" (PDF). (Last visited on May 10, 2018).
92 "Limited Liability Partnership (Amendment) Rules, 2017" (pdf). www.mca. gov.in. 2017. Archived (Last visited on September 30, 2017).
93 "MCA Services". www.mca.gov.in. Ministry Of Corporate Affairs, (Last visited on May 5, 2018).

94 Thomas E. Rutledge and Elizabeth G. Hester, Practical Guide to Limited Liability Partnerships, section 8, 5 State Limited Liability Company & Partnership Laws (Aspen 2008) http://www.lawyersclubindia.com/articles/Limited-Liability-Partnership-Act-2008-A-long-wayforward-2771.asp, (Last visited on May 5, 2018).
95 Jim Cousins; Austin Mitchell; PremSikka (2004). "Race to the Bottom: The Case of the Accountancy Firms" (pdf). Association for Accountancy & Business Affairs, 2, 3 https://www.researchgate.net/publication/242214259_RACE_TO_THE_BOTTOM_THE_CASE_OF_THE_ACCOUNTANCY_FIRMS, (Last visited on May 6, 2018).
96 Steele, Myron "Judicial Scrutiny of Fiduciary Duties in Delaware Limited Partnerships and Limited Liability Companies" (PDF). Delaware Journal of Corporate Law, (2007).
97 Stone v. Ritter, 911 A.2d 362 (Del. 2006) (en banc) (holding that no independent fiduciary duty of good faith exists in Delaware corporate law).
98 THE HINDU BUSINESS LINE 6 (Kolkata edn., May 23, 2018).
99 The US aid Centre for democracy and governance, Handbook on fighting corruption, (February13, 1999) https://1997-2001.state.gov/global/narcotics_law/global_forum/F700ocr.pdf, (Last visited on May 21, 2018).
100 WaitheraJunghae, Controversial South Korean anti-corruption law faces further revisions, GLOBAL INVESTIGATIONS REVIEW, (July 13, 2016), https://iccwbo.org/news-publications/policies-reports/icc-principles-on-combating-corruption/. (International Chamber of Commerce), (Last visited on May20, 2018).
101 Organisation for Economic Cooperation and Development, OECD, Bribery in Public Procurement: Methods Actors and Countermeasure, (2007).
102 FCPA Guidelines, 2012. https://www.justice.gov/criminal-fraud/fcpa-guidance, (Last visited on May 22, 2018).
103 Patrick Stokes, Statement to The Press (2014). https://www.wileyrein.com/newsroom-articles3052.html, (Last visited on April 20, 2018).
104 United Nations Convention against Corruption, UNODC, http://www.unodc.org./unodc/treties/CAC/signatories, (Last visited on April 20, 2018).
105 website of Lux Mundi as on 20 April 2018. http://www.luxmundi.co.za/, (Last visited on April 20, 2018).
106 Halliburton Paying $29.2 Million to Settle FCPA Violations, U.S. SECURITIES & EXCHANGE COMMISSION, (July 27, 2017) https://www.sec.gov/news/pressreleases/2017133, (Last visited on May 20, 2108).
107 Blog of a Low, Lucinda of Steptoe and Johnson LLP, the Lex Mundi member for USA from the District of Columbia
108 https://www.sec.gov/news/pressreleases/2017-133.
109 The FCPA Guide, The United States, DEPARTMENT OF JUSTIC, (November 2012), https://www.justice.gov/criminal-fraud/fcpa-guidance, (Last visited on May 19, 2018)
110 Transparency International, https://www.transparency.org (Last visited on 20 April 2018).
111 Anti Corruption Report, Vol. 6(2), (February 1, 2017) www.anticorruption.com (Last visited on April 20, 2018).
112 David W Simon and SherbirPanag mention 10 tips for performing effective anti-corruption investigations in India. The authors maintain that doing business in India continues to present a complex challenge for US companies.
113 Richard L. Cassin, Embraer pays $205 million to settle FCPA charges, THE FCPA BLOG, https://fcpablog.com/2016/10/24/, (October 24, 2016).

114 Devesh K. Pandey, Former Air Force chief Tyagi arrested by CBI in Agusta Westland case, THE HINDU (May 19, 2018) https://www.google.co.in/anp/www.thehindu.com/nuws/national/former-air-forcechief-tyagi-arrested-by-cbiin-augustawestland-case/article16784671.ccc/amp, (Last visited on May 19, 2018).
115 FCPA report, 1 (May 14, 2017). https://www.transparency.org (Last visited on May 20, 2018)
116 FCPA Anti-Corruption Report on India). https://www.transparency.org (Last visited on May 20, 2018)
117 THE ECONOMIST, 3–5, (April 19, 2018).
118 Ibid.
119 Ibid.
120 Ibid.
121 Ibid.
122 Ibid.
123 Ibid.
124 Ibid.
125 Ibid.

4 New Legal Initiatives by India in CBMA Environment

Introduction

Corruption kills and absolute corruption kills absolutely. Transparency is a tool for rule of Law. CBMA has to be ethical anywhere and everywhere. Issues related to corruption, bribery, fraud in a comparative environment brought out lacunae in India. In this chapter, a few remedial initiatives by the Indian Government would be discussed. One of the initiatives taken by the new government after taking over in the year 2014 is the proviso of the Foreign Account Tax Compliance Act (FATCA). FATCA enables the automatic exchange of financial information among institutions of the countries namely the United States of America and India. The financial institutions operating in India have to provide necessary information to the tax authorities of India which then will be transmitted to their counterparts in the USA. Many agencies work in the USA and an agreement was reached out among the many inter-governmental, inter-ministerial groups to implement effectively the FATCA on August 31, 2015. From the periods July 1, 2014 till August 31, 2015, the US Government directed the financial organisation to go for self-certification. Due diligence activity was expected in the case of accounts of all individuals and farms. In case of failure to give self-certification the account may stand frozen by May 1, 2017. Similarly, for the National Pension Scheme (NPS) account holders as of July 1, 2014 who are maintaining their accounts with National Security Depository Limited which is the Central Record Keeping Agency (CRKA) for the National Pension Scheme self-certification under EATCA and the same applies for mutual fund holders also. It is clear from the above that money laundering needs to be prevented even through official channels so that ill-gotten wealth/money or untaxed money may not be able to be hidden in the days to come.

Money Laundering and CBMA

In the area of CBMAs, this reform was much needed to plug all the loopholes of money laundering in the name of CBMAs. To bring India on par with the best practices in the developed countries, there is a need to make a new body akin to Consumer Financial Protection Bureau (CFPB) on par

DOI: 10.4324/9781003396987-4

with a similarly named institution in the United States. The CFPB which is the second regulator after the Comptroller of the Currency (COC), imposed a fine of US$ 500 million as part of the US$ 1 billion on Wells Fargo over mortgage and auto loans and other aspects of financial miss-propriety. It is to be noted that Wells Fargo and the company have agreed to pay the US$ 1 billion to settle with the US regulators who said it abused customers in its auto and mortgage business and the bank and informed regulators on April 20, 2018. This is one of the most aggressive steps taken by the present administration to punish a major bank for Bottom of Form following its rules and regulations. In a well-publicised move, Wells Fargo opened millions of sham retail accounts that some customers did not want. India also requires having a similar institution like the office of the Comptroller of the Currency of the United States. In the present case of Wells Fargo, a press release from office of the Comptroller of the Currency mentions number of factors, including those related to the banks.

It is vital to develop and implement an effective Enterprise Risk Management Program (ERMP) to detect and prevent unsafe or unsound practices, scope and the duration of such desirable practices. The CFPB looks after the interest of the consumers and in the instant case, the CFPB ordered Wells Fargo Bank to refund all the customers. Harvard Law School Professor, Elizabeth Warren was the first to propose the institutionalisation of the body under CPFB. "It was in the year 2010 that the Congress passed Dodd-Frank Wall Street Consumer Protection Act to take care of the recession and the financial crisis in the United States."[1] America for Financial Reforms (AFR) is a potential body of 250 expert members across professional of law, Banking, Economics, Financial and protection of consumers. The AFR activity supported the proposal of CPFB. It was Professor Elizabeth Warren, as Senator from Boston who prosecuted the CEO of Wells Fargo Bank and was chiefly responsible for the recovery of US$ 1 billion as fine. One can see her on the YouTube channel prosecuting and cross-examining this Chief Executive Officer of Wells Fargo bank. The efficiency of CFPB can be reflected by the fact that for the past seven years more than 7,30,000 complaints were handled as per law.

There was a move to further empower the CFPB by renaming it as Financial Product Safety Commission (FPSC) after including units' umbrella safety, soundness improvement of the consumers, real estate aspects and investor aspects. India lacks these kinds of robust bodies. Merely aiming high of contractual enforcement without adequate bodies like the CFPB or FPSC is a pipe dream.

Amendments to clauses of the Insolvency and Bankruptcy Code (IBC) are required according to some experts to make it on par with global standards to facilitate better CBMAs. Former Company Law Board Chairman, Advocate S. Bala Subramanian feels that section 29a clause and subclause need changes because there is a strict ban on relatives and connected parties from bidding for the assets due to the blanket ban on the defaulting promoters. According to Mr Bala Subramanian, IBC is a very good actor and is on the right path for the revival of enterprises. Senior legal advisor A.K. Mayilsamy said that the only concern is the section 29a clause. Many genuine promoters would have defaulted due to the market conditions. "They would have undergone issues sufferings at the beginning and the following years in building an enterprise, particularly in an infrastructure company, and hence they should at least be heard or given a chance."[2] Buddhi senior legal advisors contended that the promoter should be also involved in the assessment process because they will be able to pinpoint out the gaps. The Committee of Creditors (COC), which mostly comprises of bankers, outsiders, and resolution professionals, typically has no significant exposure to the Industry. Hence this professional should at least consult the promoters during the judges' resolution process. Eliminating the promoters from the process is not correct.

The Business Line also published the views of Mr K. K. Balu, former Vice Chairman of the Company Law Board (CLB) who felt that the major objective of the Insolvency and Bankruptcy Code is to maximise the value of assets and promote entrepreneurship. The objective is not to squeeze the entrepreneurs. Referring to the Binani case where an unsuccessful bidder made an attractive open offer outside the IBC process, Bala Subramanian noted that when a third person offers a better deal, there should not be any objection. "I am of the view that there could be an auction system instead of a bidding system" was the final opinion of Mr S Balasubramanian.[3] The above opinions of these legal eagles, however, are not well-founded by evidence. There is a vested interest in the above argument in that in the first place, the managers were responsible for the mismanagement of the company which went to the insolvency stage and to be given again another chance to further continue the process of mismanagement, thus to loot the limited public resources, destroy the public sector banks and make the 125 crore Indians victimised for their vested interest. One can empathise with the so-called professional interest of the retired Chairman and Vice Chairman of the dysfunctional CLB as the loyalties are not towards the Constitution of India but to their ex-masters. Perhaps there is a betrayal to the cause that the Prime Minister of India is apparently trying his level best to clean up the tables to make India on par with the best practices of the world. The need of the hour in the light of the above discussion is that section 29 must be further strengthened so that the defaulters are not be allowed to have any backdoor entry to again control their enterprise which wilfully are the causes of the bankruptcy and insolvency in the first place.

SFIO and the CBMA

In the ongoing investigation of Punjab National Bank (PNB) fraud being handled by the Serious Fraud Investigation Office (SFIO) of the Ministry of Finance, officials of PNB including the Managing Director and CEO Sunil Mehta appeared before the anti-fraud agency in Mumbai after being summoned for recording statements in connection with the Rs. 12,636 crore fraud at the bank. The bank officials of the private banks Axis and ICICI were also summoned by the SFIO. It is expected that the SFIO is likely to call all those who were involved in frauds of the 31 public sector banks in connection with the Nirav Modi, Mehul Choski fraud case. "CBI, so far arrested 12 persons including former and current officials of the Punjab National Bank and companies related to Nirav Modi and Mehul Choksi."[4] In June 2017, SFIO floated a tender for the selection of a managed service provider to develop an Early Warning System (EWS).

The purpose of EWS is to help in the early detection of corporate frauds and safeguard gullible investors from fly-by-night operators. The necessity of the EWS was found out in the year 2009 after the Satyam fraud was first investigated. The SFIO was also given a green signal to proceed ahead with the Kingfisher investigation and to bring the fugitive Vijay Mallya to India. Earlier, the SFIO also investigated the fraud case of Reebok the Sports Company in a complaint filed by the sports giant Adidas.

According to Kunal Gupta, "the battle against financial fraud and malpractices has a significantly intense fight over the recent year." Globally, establishing structure regulatory framework and compliance standards to combat fraud in commercial transactions. A manifestation of such heightened awareness and regulatory action in India is evident under the provisions about the SFIO introduced under the Companies Act, 2013 and the rules thereunder.

The New Companies Act, 2013 made certain provisions to prevent financial frauds and to avoid consequent arrests. Any arrest of a CEO of any company will dent the confidence of investors about conditions of environment promotions or preventing the Rule of Law in India. "SFIO is a Central Government organization being a multidisciplinary expert from diverse areas. The company rules of 2017 were recently notified after April 2017 empowers the SFIO to arrest any person who is believed to be guilty of fraud."[5]

> It defines fraud as any act to include an act, omission, concealment of any fact or abuse of position by any person with the intent to deceive, to gain undue advantage from or injure the interests of, the company, or it'share holders,s creditors, or any other person whether or not there is any wrongful gain or wrongful loss.[6]

Provision of the Company Act (Amendment) 2017 uses the term "person" which implies that the charges can be made for investigation against directors, officers, employees, or any other person about the affairs of the company. Hence, auditors, advisors, consultants, experts, and independent or non-executive directors, and any other key managerial personnel can also be held liable for fraud for acts or omissions which occurred within their knowledge. According to the provisions given, the previous directors who have put up the papers can also be called for the investigation and can also be charge-sheeted if found guilty for the offenses committed during the tenure. According to the Indian Penal Code, fraud is a cognizable, non-bailable, non-compoundable offense.

It is suggested for implementations the following remedies. These remedies arose after interactions with many company executives in Kolkata, Delhi and Mumbai, by the author.

1. Prevention is better than cure. Fraud management is not a separate risk. It is part of the overall risk management of the company. The basic bottom line is that where even there is scope for fraud, there will be a fraud.
2. Timely inclusion of toolkit and mechanism for detection and early warning system through internal policies adequately for detection investigation of the fraud and forensic auditing is extremely important.
3. Having observed similar measures in developed countries like the USA, it is important to introduce a proper code of conduct, anti-corruption policy, stringent accounting policy, Bottom of Form rewarding of the whistle-blower policy, intelligence on the computer vendor observation policy and competitor contact policy is extremely essential.
4. Proper human resource policies through the organising of mandatory workshops seminars and briefing sessions to make the employees aware of the risk and the challenges of the various possibility of frauds is another important step in the right direction.
5. Accountability enforcement is of great importance in making committees for specific fraud management and identification and a close watch on the activities of vulnerable company executives who are in important positions of decision-making.
6. Companies must go for the internal mechanism through proper reporting investigating evaluating and also timely response through remedial actions.
7. "Establishing of concrete reporting protocols requiring specific monitoring transactions through the stipulated monetary threshold is of great relevance."[7]

The Importance of Credit in the CBMA

Creditors are important for any ongoing business organisation and if the creditors are not given a fair deal in running of the organisations, problems would arise in every stage of the ongoing concern. When creditors are granted greater stakeholdership, they would be motivated to participate proactively in the rescue operation than indulging in the negative activity of separate litigations for enforcement Because of the old style of insolvency resolution systems in India, Ease of Doing Business in India rank has been hovering around 137 out of 189 countries till the year 2015. The World Bank, every year, calculates resolving insolvency indicators as part of the Ease of Doing Business Index. The proposed changes in the Insolvency and Bankruptcy Code are expected to improve the resolving insolvency indicator and hence improve the position of India in this regard. Dr T.K. Viswanathan, in his report on the Banking Law Reforms Committee (BLRC), felt that the changes suggested would bring in a new era of a powerful corporate Insolvency Framework in India and that since corporate failures always have ripple and trickling effect on the entire economy, correct intervening measures of the insolvency process resolution of the unviable and insolvent companies promptly is important for the overall health of the entire economy.

BLRC in its report submitted to the Finance Minister of India made a striking observation in that an ideal insolvency regime needs to strike the right balance between the interest of the main players by a fair and transparent apartment of risk among the players. The BLRC report adds that "given the multiplicity of loss and adjudicatory forums governing insolvency matters in India, the BLRC thinks that developing an insolvency code and its operationalization will require more time."[8]

The committee further observed that liquidation should not be seen as a measure of last resort for unviable businesses that have become insolvent and be acted upon to minimise losses for the parties, there is a case for reforming the corporate insolvency regime in India through a combination of substantial and institutional changes.

Dr T.K. Viswanathan acknowledges in the report submitted to the Finance Minister of India that "India is one of the youngest Republic in the world, the high concentration of the most dynamic entrepreneurs."

As the game changes and growth drivers are crippled by an environment that takes some of the longest times and highest cost by the world standards to resolve any problems that arise may in course of the tune. "India has least contribution of credit in its economy, when compared the size of Indian economy. This is a troublesome state to begin, for the young emerging economy with the entrepreneur real dynamism of India."[9]

Dr T.K. Viswanathan continues by saying that the Limited Liability Company (LLC) is a contract between equity and debt. "As long as debt obligations are met, we have complete control, and that is in how the business is run. When default takes place, post to transfer to the creditors; the owners have no say."[10]

It is felt that not always the creditors are the banks and many a time many ordinary citizens believe in the robustness of the economy when they buy the corporate bonds and therefore become the lenders or the creditors to the company. The importance of the Insolvency and Bankruptcy Code is essential to protect the interests of these creditors who also happened to be bondholders and whose number is huge in an emerging economy like India. Unfortunately for the past 70 years, the Indian corporate scene witnessed the lowest rates of debt payment. Statistics and financial audit reports mention that the recovery rate is a mere 20% of the value of the debt on Net Price Value (NPV) on a future basis. In the case of CBMA, insolvency problems may arise not only in the case of large corporations but also in limited liability companies, individuals, sole proprietorships, and limited liability partnerships. An implementable bankruptcy and insolvency code is hence

186 *New Legal Initiatives by India in CBMA Environment*

and therefore essential in the CBMA arena to take care of all the above-mentioned various variations.

The IBC is an essential appendage to IFC, namely the Indian Financial Code which was handled by Justice Srikrishna in the Financial Sector Legislative Reforms Commission (FSLRC). Removal of the three contradictions in the legislation is one of the mandates of the IBC. The committee suggested the formation of a body of the creditors to have the first right to decide the course of action on the insolvency process. According to the provisions of the Company Act 2013, the following organisations can apply to the National Company Law Tribunal for the declaration of the sickness of a company.

a The company,
b Any secured creditor,
c The central government,
d The Reserve Bank of India,
e The state government,
f The public financial institution,
g State-level institution,
h Scheduled bank.

This study developed an equation connecting the above initiatives.

$$IPC + IFC + IBC = IEC$$

where

IPC is the Indian Penal Code,
IFC is the Indian Financial Code,
IBC is the Insolvency and Bankruptcy Code and
IEC is the Indian Excellence Code

SARFAESI and the CBMA

"Under the SARFAESI Act 2002, debt enforcement rights are available for secured creditors only."[11] (SARFAESI Act is Securitisation and Reconstruction of Financial Assets and Enforcement of Security Interest Act)The IBC proposes that irrespective of the nature of the creditor whether financial or operational, the creditor should be able to initiate the Insolvency Resolution Process, IRP under the proposed code.

Operational creditors include employees and workmen whose wages are to be paid by the company. Therefore, the proposal will empower the workmen also to initiate Insolvency Resolution Process (IRP). CBMA regime demands a level playing field between India and the rest of the world and hence it is expected that nobody strips the assets of a company in insolvency facing the company or steal away understand manner the raw materials or the inventories of the company to cause wrongful loss to the creditors and wrongful gain to the promoters. On June 25, 2018, IBBI came out with a rule that no IRP can leave during the process except on the health ground.

Delay in resolution is a deal of destruction. This truth holds good much application in the arena of the IBC concerning CBMA. The stipulated period, also called a calm period can keep the company alive with full clarification and accountability to make it still an ongoing concern. Governance coupled with mature leadership is a sure shot of complications in the IBC arena of the CBMA aspect. The more the gap, the more will be the complication, and the more the loss of time, the more will be the loss of whatever little value that is left. The twin issues of insolvency and bankruptcy in the domestic arena are a challenge before the committee. This is an important first milestone for India. The next frontier lies in addressing cross-border issues. This includes Indian financial firms having claims upon defaulting firms which are global, or global financial firms having claims upon Indian defaulting firms. Some important elements of internationalisation—foreign holders of corporate bonds issued in India, or borrowing abroad by an Indian firm—are dealt with by the present report. The report of the committee left some vital issues not addressed. Examples of these problems include thousands of Indian firms that have become multinationals and Indian financial investors that lend to overseas persons. "The committee mentions its intention to take up pending issues in near future."[12]

The CBMA and Banking Reforms

Banks as institutions play a very important role in any economy especially in an emerging economy for two following reasons. Firstly, banks attract idle savings in the economy and channelise them for investment purposes. Secondly, banks work as an interface between consumers and producers on the one hand and between the government and the industrialist on the other. The laws that govern the banking system in India include (a) Banking Regulation Act (BR) 1949, (b) Banking Companies Acquisition Transfer of Undertakings Act 1970 and 1980, (c) the State Bank of India Act 1955, (d) the Reserve Bank of India (RBI) Act 1934.

The above Acts are expected to work in conjunction with the Companies Act 2013, the Securities Contract Act (SCA) 1956, the SEBI Act 1992, the Industrial Development and Regulation Act 1951 (IDRA), the Securitisation and Reconstruction of Financial Assets and the Enforcement of Security Interest Act (SRFAESI) 2002 also. "Banking is the central pillar of the economy. The major part of the banking sector in India is government-owned, there are also private minority shareholders in some of these banks."[13]

Law regarding banking amalgamations and banking transactions is therefore important in any general research on the effectiveness and success or otherwise of CBMA in emerging economies. "Banks are encouraged to gain global reach and better synergy through bank mergers and also allow larger banks to acquire these stressed Assets of weaker banks."[14]

In the domestic arena, some of the biggest mergers in the banking sector include the merger of IDBI with its subsidiary IDBI bank in the year 2004, the Centurion Bank and Bank of Punjab in the year 2005 and Centurion Bank of Punjab and HDFC Bank in the year 2006.[15]

Company Act, 2013, does not have jurisdiction on banking mergers as banking mergers are controlled by the Banking Regulation Act 1949. The BR Act governs and regulates all the procedures related to the banking company; however, the registration of banking companies is governed under the Companies Act, 2013. Empowered by the legal provisions of the Banking Regulating Act, (B.R. Act) the RBI, mergers weak banks with strong banks. The Companies Act, 2013, is subordinate to the BR Act. In that, if there ever is any contradiction between any provision of Companies Act, 2013 with any provision BR Act, then the Banking Regulating Act prevails over and above the Companies Act, 2013. The following case law is important in this connection. "The Court asserted in the Judgement of the case between liquidator of the bank Presidency Industry Bank Limited Vs. Com. Income Tax that transferred assets and liabilities are effective from the date of amalgamation."[16] The interaction between the BR Act and the Companies Act becomes very important in the following case.

> There exists a restriction under the BR Act, that any compromise or arrangement under Section 230 of the Companies Act, 2013, that between the banking company and its creditors or any class of them or between such company and its members or any class of them or arrangement unless the compromise or arrangement or modification, as the case may be, is certified by the RBI in writing as not being incapable of being worked and as not being detrimental to the interest of the depositors of such banking company, could be sanctioned by the High Court only if such a scheme is certified, in writing, by the RBI as to such scheme being capable of being worked out and as not being detrimental to the interest of the depositors of such banking company.[17]

The CBMA and Banking Sector Reforms

Successful running of a nonbanking financial company is a challenge in facing many risks that are inbuilt in the business environment and which are sometimes complicated by the rules and regulations of the country. The disaster witnessed by India due to the non-performing assets of many public sector banks as well as the collapse of the companies like IL&FS and DHFL is vast. The overall regulator, namely RBI, is now making efforts for the conversion of certain sized non-banking financial companies (NBFC) into banks. Suggestions from the internal working group set up for the above purposes include reviewing the ownership structure in the financial sector and the relaxation of the existing ownership norms for conversion of NBFCs into banks. To prevent canalisation and to promote competition, dilution of ownership has to be balanced with adequate inbuilt facilities for the proper functioning of the newly emerging banks.

A significant incentive has been created that the banks currently under non-operative folding financial company structure can exit from the structure if they do not have other group entities in their fold. Industrial houses can be allowed to set up banks without violating the competition rules as well as the ethics in business transactions. The regulations here should be framed so that the management should be professional and transparent and they should not be any darkness, especially from the family-owned business houses. There are problems within the banking structure and the recent examples of the failure of Laxmi Vilas Bank are startling enough to create an environment of care and caution before taking any decision as far-reaching as the conversion of the NBFCs to banks.

RBI Reforms and the CBMA

For proper functioning of the CBMAs, India's tools should have a level playing field with other global banking systems. The digitalisation of banking systems is extremely essential to have a level playing field at every stage of the efforts of the CBMA. The Reserve Bank of India rightly prevented HDFC Bank recently from going ahead with sourcing new credit card customers before addressing digital business generating activities and the gaps in the Digital Infrastructure. Value transactions through UPI saw an almost 90% increase while amount transactions through Bharat Bill pay saw an increase of around 90%. A recent report by Accenture estimates the shift of Castro Cards and Digital Payments from US$ 270.7 million to US$ 856.6 billion between the years 2023 and 2030.

It is in the interest of both public sector banks like the SBI and also the private sector banks like HDFC, ICICI and many other NBFCs that they adhere to the following initiatives.

1 To invest more time and money in upgrading the Information Technology Systems.
2 To obtain the latest state-of-the-art technology in order to meet both the volume and the value expectations of the customers.
3 To make the system is robust enough that they are hassle-free and threat-free as well as hijack-free and hacker-free for the proposed Digital Payment Security Control Directions, 2020 of the Reserve Bank of India should be implemented immediately.
4 Ensure stronger controls in terms of security for channels like Internet, Mobile Banking, Card Payments, and other Inter-Banking Transactions.
5 RBI will do very well through the National Institute of Banking to conduct an audit of the existing IT structures of all institutions in the finance industry and to be equally strict with all to make the digital payment on par with the global standards instead of confining at the piecemeal action against HDFC Bank here and an ICICI Bank there.

Tax Havens and the CBMA

A senior researcher at the Political Economy Research Institute at the University of Massachusetts Amherst USA, Ms. J Ghosh recently brought out a research paper that argued for taking steps against tax havens which are creating the annual loss of billions of dollars to both developed and developing countries. She mentions that the lost revenue in terms of tax can cover the salaries of 1.1 5,000,000 nurses in the USA and 4.2 million nurses in India. Different tax rates and bilateral tax treaties exist that enable multinationals to shift profit to advanced countries like Ireland, the Netherlands, the Channel Island, and the United Kingdom, and some other US states. The need of the hour is to have a comprehensive public register of beneficial owners of companies' trusts and foundations in order to make tax evasion a very difficult process. Public Services International, and Global Alliance for Tax Justice in a report, called the state of tax Justice 2020, mentioned how the world loses to corporate and private tax abuses. Secrecy in these tax havens made a very bad habit profitable. Bringing transparency to choose profit and private fortunes held offshore should not be left to investigative journalists or whistle blowers or watchdogs but should be declared by and to all the global organisations and government bodies during the COVID-19 pandemic crisis; this differential in the fortunes of a very few at the cost of a great many needs immediate attention.

Banking Sector and the CBMA

Ms Neeti Shiksha, an associate professor with the Indian Institute of Corporate Affairs, Government of India, argues for a fresh look at the regulation of the banking sector and feels that the industry, in India, may be allowed to have their banks. She refers to the examples of Bandhan Bank and Kotak Mahindra Bank, as private sector banks, working well with an adequate return on investment as well as healthy profit and loss book with the least non-productive assets. A blanket ban on the initiative of the industry to start a bank because of its probable misuse and diversion of funds and ultimately committing a fraud, compelling the Government to come to the rescue as it happened with many cooperative banks and recently with the Laxmi Vilas Bank and the Yes Bank, is not proper in her view.

Banking and New Initiatives

No licence can come without any conditions. A banking licence is no exception. The internal working group of the RBI in its recommendations mentioned about opening up of banks by the industries. The last two licences granted were to IDFC First Bank and Bandhan Bank. In 2015, RBI discussed differentiated bank licences which allow banks to operate in specific subsectors of banking verticals. Small finance banks and payments banks are examples of this category. Small finance banks are working now and a level number of players were given licences for payments banks out of which only six are working. They are the Kabbalah Vodafone idea payments bank filed for liquidation in 2019 citing that the business model was unviable. RBI conducted an internal analysis of payments bank failure and found that the limited operational space available to the small payment banks and the large initial cost involved in setting up payments banks prevents them from breaking even. The important lesson is that the deposit restriction is in no way a solution for credit growth. Most of the Western nations and neighbouring China have got a ratio of 150% for credit to GDP, whereas India has a poor credit to GDP ratio of 56%.

"The Custodian market has the potentiality of Rs. 45,000 crores per deposit."[18] There are 19 custodians in India but the bulk of the assets are controlled by if multinational corporations India does not allow specialised custodian banks. The assets under custody increased by a massive 36 times between the years 2002 and 2020. There is a discriminatory US Securities and Exchange Commission Rule 17 EF-5. This rule forbids Indian non-bank custodians to be appointed as custodians where American investment foreign portfolio investors do not want to appoint Indian public sector banks as custodians because of lack of faith in them. With the high Non Performing Assets (NPA) of the Indian public sector undertaking banks, the custodian banks have a lower risk profile with NPAs of less than 0.02%. As the custodian banks do not loan long-term FPI, mutual funds insurance companies prefer custodian banks for their requirements. Custodian banks can have a new scope in India to bring on par with the level playing field available in the USA. The Financial Express mentions that 90% of the custodian market of the FPI is covered by overseas custodians. This also affects the intraday funding needs of FPIs and lessens the freedom while raising the costs of transactions for Indian Markets. It prevents diversification of FDI is base beyond US investors as they do not find a private-sector Indian custodian banking service provider. RBI needs to consider custodian bank licensing the assets under custody of the Indian custody market as of May 2020 stands at Rs. 97 lakh crore which is still 2% of the world GDP and has the potential to double over the next few years. There is an opinion suggesting consideration by the RBI to examine the opening up of assets under custody banks in India to realise the potential scope.

According to SHRI ALOK KUMAR MISHRA, Professor of Economics and Finance at the University of Hyderabad, India's banking reforms need stronger regulation and immediately need to modify the existing law and to strictly enforce to remove the gaps in Indian banking which adversely impact the functioning vis-à-vis global banking system. The banking laws in India failed to prevent scams and failure is in banking, namely PNB, PMC, IEL, and FS, Yes Bank, Dewan Housing and Laxmi Vilas Bank. The continuous recurrence of the above-mentioned scams calls for objective assessment of the following aspects.

1 Law
2 Competition
3 Institution
4 Regulation
5 Enforcement
6 Constant review
7 Research
8 Speedy calibration
9 Coordination with stakeholders.

The Internal Working Group (IWG) of the RBI referred to the US Federal Reserve Act section 23A and 23B that regulate connected lending. The Banking Regulation Act 1949 of India has a weak section through section 6 and section 60 which are no match to section 23A and 23B of the US Federal Reserve. Because of this lacuna, the Infrastructure Leasing and Funding Society (ILFS) could create hundreds of subsidiaries and the Reserve Bank of India has no clue about it. When the PMC bank organised over many years of its information technology and income tax link fraud, the RBI did not have any information. Prevention is the only way available to cure bank frauds because of its size, and its impact on the concept of the rule of law in the country. Leaving the scope for corruption and allow the corruption to happen and later on making noises through new institutions like the Insolvency and Bankruptcy Code or the National Company Law Tribunal or the Directorate of Revenue Intelligence tantamount to failure in anticipation and prevention.

The major European economies namely, the United Kingdom, Germany, and France allow corporate entities to own banks and the banks to own corporate entities. To date, the USA and Japan have maintained a policy that separates banking and commerce. The main purpose in Japan and the USA is the prevention of fraudulent manipulation of credit and also to enforce failed competition coupled with ensuring the deposit insurance and the taxpayers with enough security from greater risks that arise in commercial activity. The other purpose of the separation of commerce and industry in the US and Japan is to prevent the additional burden on the regulatory agencies. This classical view of separation of commerce and industry through different channels of banking becomes redundant with the advent of fast-changing financial technology products, 'chain technology, machine learning, artificial intelligence, big data analytics. Apart from these above, there are many applications related to fifth-generation analytical tools which many multinational corporations use in conducting their business operations. The banking institutions that lag in this race will either disappear or will be under perennial losses. Mr Keith Noreika, former Comptroller of the Currency, USA, in a lecture in the year 2017, argued for a re-examination of this classic suppressed banking and commerce in the USA and advised that it is not the best thing to put all your eggs in one basket. Classical separation of banking and commerce, while being in place in the USA, did not prevent the USA to go for Gramm-Leach -Bliley Financial

Modernisation Act, 1999. The GLB FM ACT allows new financial holding companies with an enhanced scope beyond traditional bank holding companies. Now the financial holding companies can engage not only in financial services but also in securities trading, underwriting, insurance, traditional commercial banking activities as a single holding company entity.

Reputations are not made in one day but they can be destroyed in a minute. In a country like India, when a big public sector undertaking bank or a private bank fails, it is not a mere isolated incident of business failure. It creates a tectonic impact on the faith of ordinary people who use banks as a safeguard for their hard-earned money. The concept of gender accounts made banking not merely an economic empowerment tool but banks emerged as places of real development at the grass-root level in India (JAN DHAN ACCOUNTS). Well-functioning banking is required so that people can save their money through banks instead of investing in gold or land. The parallel economy that operates in the prices of gold and the land is regressive and rent-seeking. Parallel economies always make the poor poorer and the rich, richer. The RBI needs to strengthen the state bank of India. "Micro-foundations cannot be ignored by macro logic." [19]

Stamp Act and the CBMA

The combined application of the Stamp Act, the previous Companies Act of 1956, and the Reserve Bank of India Act, Section 44a and the Banking Regulation Act 1949 in respect of amalgamation and reconstruction of Banking companies is a field in the two following cases: "Hindustan Lever and another versus the state of Maharashtra and another and Chhatrapati Sambhaji Maharaj Sahakari Patsanstha Maryadit versus Assistant Registrar of Cooperative Societies Satara and another."[20]

"In Hindustan Lever & Anr vs State Of Maharashtra & Anr,"[21]

> the Bench of the High Court upheld the validity of Section 2(g)(iv) of the Stamp Act which included every order made by the High Court under Section 394 of the Companies Act, 1956 in respect of amalgamation or reconstruction of companies; and every order made by the Reserve Bank of India under Section 44A of the Banking Regulation Act, 1949 in respect of amalgamation or reconstruction of Banking companies by which property, whether movable or immovable, or any estate or interest in any property is transferred to, or vested in, any other person, Inter Vivos is valid. A similar view was provided under Chhatrapati Sambhaji Maharaj Sahakari Patsanstha Maryadit v. Assistant Registrar of Co-operative Societies, Satara, and Another.[22]

When a merger takes place between an NBFC and a banking company, the rules are also clear in the bare act as well as the Companies Act. The specific sections include Section 230, section 231, and section 232 of the Companies Act 2013 read with section 44a of the RBI. However, the approval needs to be made by a Tribunal or High Court in this concern. In the case of a scheme of amalgamation of Industrial Enterprises and Financial Limited with IndusInd Bank Limited, the transfer was between an NBFC and another banking company, and the court held that "where one of the companies is not a banking company, still prior permission of The Reserve Bank of India is necessary for the amalgamation."[23]

> when one bank amalgamates with another bank, the latter would be entitled to continue this suit and requires to transferee company to resort to Section 45-1 (4) of the Banking Regulation Act 1949 and apply under section 543 erstwhile Companies Act 1956.[24]

"Apart from the BR Act, the Council of the Institute of Chartered Accountants of India(CICAI) issued guidelines for amalgamation termed as accounting standard 14 in the name of accounting for amalgamations."[25]

Latest Developments

In May 2018, Tata Steel announced its takeover of Bhushan Steel under the instructions of NCLT within the framework of the IBC. Rightly described as a historic breakthrough in resolving the legacy issues of the banks, this resolution of an insolvent company called Bhushan Steel is a trendsetter. Several other companies were also referred to the Reserve Bank of India and the RBI referred significant ones to the National Company Law Tribunal for resolution. Over 800 cases have been admitted, and over 3200 cases have been rejected for the past two years under the IBC. More than 200 cases ended up in the winding up of the companies according to the new Company Law 2013.

The Indian Express states, "The Government conceded that it is uncharted territory here, and that implementing the law was a learning experience and that the government would continue to make changes to it."[26] The law of IPC impacted positive behavioural change among promoters and company management. Coupled with Nirav Modi's PNB scam and the PSUs tightening lending norms, corporates and promoters are under pressure now to ensure payments. The Bottom of Form cash flow of the companies is the key influencing factor and the promoters are compelled to bring their capital in what is known as more skin in the game and thus their commitment business without a corrupt Extend support is being hammered upon as on today.

> Many of the glitches, in not because of the law, but because of the capacity constraints in developing quality resolution professionals, getting very more ventures, is driving institutional change and the behaviour of lenders. Recent experience shows that the bankers agree to forego a part of their dues or setting for a haircut continue to have reason to fear action by investigating agencies, soften oversight committee notwithstanding.[27]

The informed commentators on resolution processes feel that in the coming financial years, the law of IBC will be more effective. But in the medium term, this could well test banks and the government with new challenges. While promoters raise funds to reduce their debt burden through bonds or external commercial borrowing, the IBC made lenders deal effectively the resolution processed proactively.

> But as policymakers welcome this shift away from banks, they will have to reckon with the challenge of good borrowers migrating to that market or other forms of borrowing. The vacuum created by public banks that now control 70% of assets in India, will be reflected in the expansion of Non-Banking Finance Companies (NBFC) and their lending portfolios.[28]
>
> Revival of investment is the real challenge before the Government of INDIA, as on today. It is a formidable task in this environment, with banks weighed down by debt, a tax regime that many businessmen view as being unfriendly and unstable, and an atmosphere of perceived promoter bashing. The worry also is that banks and industry are weighed down at a time of strong global growth; the contrast is with 2004–2008 when India was able to capitalize on such growth. Few will disagree with what the new law seeks to achieve namely creative destruction but the pain could last longer than expected.[29]

The Hindu writes,

> "Good news has finally started to roll out of the refurbished bankrupt courts. Tata Steel acquired a 73% stake in the bankrupt company Bhushan Steel for about rupees 35000 crores last week (15/05/2018), resolving a bankruptcy case under the new IBC. Bhushan Steel was one among the 12 major accounts to refer to the National Company Law Tribunal (NCLT) at the best of The Reserve Bank of India (RBI) in 2017 to ease out the burden of bad loans on banks. Bhushan Steel has outstanding liabilities of over rupees 56000 crores to the banks. This resolution is an encouraging sign for the banks because they typically manage to recover only about 25% of their money from defaulters. in April 2014 and September 2017, the bad loan public sector banks were as low as 11% with nonperforming assets worth 2.41 lakh crores were written off from the books. The Finance Ministry now expects banks to recover more than rupees 1 lakh crore from the resolution of the other cases referred by the RBI to the NCLT. If the banks indeed can cover funds of the scale, it reduces the burden on taxpayers, otherwise, they have to foot the bill for any recapitalization of banks. The IBC, as admitted remains a work in progress. This is a welcome piece of legislation to the extent substance a plethora of lost that confused creditors; state it now offers a more streamlined way to deal with troubled assets."[30]

To its credit, the government has been willing to hear our suggestions. It would do well to implement the recommendations of the insolvency law committee which, among others, things have watched for relaxing better eligibility criteria. This requires a robust market for stressed assets that is free from all kind of entry barriers.[31]

The intention of the law is better known through its implementation. The Enforcement Directorate (ED) of the Government of India on 21/5/2018 attached assets worth rupees 171 crores in the Punjab National Bank (PNB) case against the fugitive diamond merchant, Nirav Modi. The Hindu maintains that the present value of all the property attached so far amounts to rupees 7800 crores. The attachment includes 106 bank accounts, 11 modern cars, shopping complexes, 135 acres of land, 15 Demat accounts, and 21 immovable properties.[32]

The CBI submitted the chargesheet in the Nirav Modi PNB scam which says that the PNB employees abused their positions and fraudulently and dishonestly issued a large number of letters of understanding (LOU) without any sanctioned limit and without obtaining a hundred percent cash margin. Financial fraud was committed connivingly by the fugitives Nirav Modi and others like Vipul Ambani of Firestar International and Hemant Bhatt.

CBI's chargesheet mentioned that

> Gokulnath Shetty, now retired Deputy General Manager of the PNB issued 150 LOUs used with due dates from January 25, 2018, to April 20, 2018, on behalf of the three companies based on which the firms obtained buyers credit from overseas branches of Allahabad Bank, Axis Bank and Bank of India The accused persons did not bother about the guidelines given by the Reserve Bank of India on August 3rd, 2016 about cybersecurity controls, advising banks to get their SWIFT infrastructure audited and ensure strict vigilance on SWIFT transactions.[33]

Security Exchange Board of India (SEBI) attempted, in 2017, to make the disclosure norms for default of loans taken from banks are financial institutions stricter but due to the opposition, the efforts of the SEBI could not succeed. On 21/05/2018 SEBI made it mandatory for all the companies to disclose the possible fault on debt securities or even if the possible delay of default in the payment of interest on the principal amount to the banks. SEBI has proposed amending the listing obligations and disclosure requirements regulation 2015 with which all listed companies have to comply with the above instruction.

These directions will make every company compulsorily to disclose within 24 hours any default or any expected default or delay in the payment of interest on dividend on debt instruments such as NCRPs (Non-Convertible Redeemable Performance Shares) or NCDS (Non-Convertible Debt Securities).

> There a view that circular of SEBI in 2017 wanted default disclosure went beyond the securities market. The proposed changes are to tighten the regulations for disclosure by amending the Yellow or regulations, which listed company has to comply with.[34]

Material deviations in the use of the process of proceeds are a serious issue and need to be intimated more frequently than the instant provision. SEBI has sought to address two key issues about the listed companies that have their debt securities listed. "First, to strengthen the norms of disclosure while freely disclosing on relevant information. Secondly, also rationalize the disclosure norms to mitigate the unwanted hardships faced by the issuers."[35]

> Less than thirty percent higher cost for financial creditors, as a deal allows the financial creditors to recover profits, better than liquidation value Public sector banks will get a much-needed breather from this deal with rupees 35000 crore reduction in the non-performing assets (NPA) and Rs. 7000 crore in the process to shore up their bottom lines.[36]

The expectation of the repetition of the same enthusiasm in the case of other industries in other sectors is at the least unrealistic at the most fraudulent. In industries such as infrastructure, power, commercial building road construction, and other nonferrous industries repetition of the above experience would not be possible. The abovementioned areas are suffering because of overcapacity and lack of due diligence and evaporation of the demand for the goods that they produce. There are not many takers for the distressed assets through the bidding process.

> CLSA, (Credit Lyonnais Securities Asia) feels that higher casts in non-steel assets may touch alarming levels at 75–80% and such a scenario is very troublesome for public sector banks, who already in a parlous state. This puts the center in a quandary because rupees 2.1 lakh crore capital recapitalization largesse it can ill afford to spend for the taxpayer money on shoring up the public sector banks perpetual short capital adequacy ratio.[37]

The important lessons from the above episode are as follows:

a   "(a) IBC Bands promoters from bidding, which is correct and legal. Flexibility, however, too is the need on hour. The code then can take a more liberal view on connected persons bidding for assets.
b   In the Essar Steel and Bhushan Power cases bidders submitted their offers after the expiry of the initial deadlines leading to legal tangles.
c   Close repeating to a competitive open auction system may not just obviate the need for multiple rounds of the building, ensure vs competition about Builders, therefore maximizing gain for lenders."[38]

198 New Legal Initiatives by India in CBMA Environment

Essar Steel's debt resolution under the IBC crossed the initial 270-day deadline on April 29, 2018, and was extended up to May 28, 2018. There has been another extension till July 23, 2018, by the NCLAT as was announced on May 22, 2018. The NCLAT was hearing the petition filed by both Russian Banks promoted Consortium Numerical Mauritius and Arcelor Mittal who are the only contenders for the stressed Essar Steel asset which has already seen two rounds of bidding. In a case, Rewant Ruia had issued guarantees to banks for loans taken by the group companies. Although Numetal has removed Rewant Ruia as a shareholder in the second round of bidding, it has to clear all the dues to become eligible in the first round. Numetal argued that the second round of bids should be opened up as it had bid rupees 37000 crores at removed Rewant Ruia from the consortium.

In the Bhushan Steel case too, the National Company Law Appellate Tribunal (NCLAT) has ordered the resolution professional and the committee of creditors of Bhushan Steel to file the response to a petition filed by Larsen and Toubro by May 28, 2018, while including Tata Steel as a party in the case. L&T's main contention was that the NCLAT judgment refuses to consider this as a financial creditor as an operational creditor so that it can recover part of the 900 crore dues from the Bhushan Steel sale.

> Mr. Neeraj Singhal of the Bhushan Steel also filed a petition claiming that Tata Steel is ineligible to bid is MVC under IBC. "While approving Tata Steel, NCLAT has dismissed the Contentions of Larsen and Toubro and imposed a fine of Rupees 1 lakh on Larsen and Toubro".[39]

A similar controversy was there over the Binani Cement asset sale value and the NCLAT announced that Binani cannot now repay the dues and settle while accepting UltraTech Cement's revised resolution plan in November 2018.

Improvement in Ease of Doing Business Index

GST and IBC completed four years by June/July 2021. Other initiatives by SEBI and RBI also are yielding results. Now most vital of the gaps between India and the USA need to be mentioned. Suggestions relevant to effective implementation of CBMA as per empirical survey made are also given below.

The Ease of Doing Business Index in India has been registering improvement for the past six years. Doing business includes among others, level playing field both in the entry and exit aspects of starting the business. The laws which include the labour laws play a vital role in

(a) Starting a business,
(b) Operating a business and,
(c) Winding up of the business.

Recently the Government of India came out with labour law reforms. *The Financial Express* on October 5, 2020, in its editorial, mentioned the following facts,

> Of the 1536 Acts that govern all economic activity in the country, 30% pertain to just labour; in terms of the compliances and periodic filings, 46–47% pertains to labour, going by the compilation by Avantis Regtech, a Team Lease company that deals with compliances.

The four codes which convert the 44 Central Acts having 1458 sections, 937 compliances and 135 filings in the year reduces the burden by nearly 67%. It is not surprising to mention here that there is a Karnataka law that has 1440 minimum wages while the Central law demands 52 minimum wages. The code on wages also minimises this burden by bringing the number of registers from 20 to 2 and the number of returns from 36 to 1. While the need of the hour is to have a uniform policy throughout the country so that the state law also is on par with the Central law, various state governments need to make amendments to a similar effect.

> Despite appreciable improvement is Ease of Doing Business Index ranking 70% of 1536 Countries Act and State Acts are yet to reformed even been touched; if the business still needs to make 3570 filings in a year-other than labor-it is difficult to see how any credible claim of EODB can be made.

Efforts for Modifications of Law

Law relating to CBMA cover from Contract Act to the Human Rights Act. It is a complicated interaction of both the Indian law and the law of the country from which they acquire or the acquiree is originated. It was found that there is a need for modification of many a law of India to make on par with the global standards.

There is a need to bring in the provisions of the Security Exchange Board of India in the related codes like the takeover code and the prevention of fraud through insider trading on par with the Securities and Exchange Commission's provisions of the United States of America and that of the United Kingdom and many countries of Europe. It may not be possible to have a commonality in the regulatory law insofar as CBMA is concerned among all the leading players of the world.

Reserve Bank of India is the main anchor that controls both domestic and cross-border mergers. The parallel of the Reserve Bank of India in advanced countries like the United States is the Federal Reserve Bank and the Bank of England in the United Kingdom. India being an emerging country in the world and being an originally powerful player in South Asia needs to have flexible laws in the central bank and flexible guidelines to take care of the emerging opportunities and threats both within the neighbourhood and across continents. While it is difficult to pinpoint any change in any section of the law at any point of time because of the non-permanence of any direction of movement of the global economy, preparedness for modification is important to stay at least with the time if not ahead of the time but surely to avoid being behind the time.

Stamp Duty Act is a pre-Independence Act and it also needs sufficient modification to make mergers and acquisition activity a welcome feature and to reduce the cost of such activity. There are 29 provinces in India which compete with one another to attract maximum foreign direct investment or maximum foreign direct investment through CBMA. There is a unique Government of India initiative in terms of making in India and Start-Up India. There is a need for coordinated efforts of the Government of India with various states of India so that there is little confusion and more clarity among both domestic players and the players from abroad insofar as genuine and legal activity of cross-border positions are concerned

Serious Fraud Investigation Office in white-collar offenses is important abroad than within the country for the simple reason that the reputation of the country as a country of contractual enforcement is important to attract both foreign direct investment and initiatives through CBMA. It is here that the investigation of prevention of fraud by the domestic agencies and enforcement agencies to be on par with their counterparts of the United States and the United Kingdom and other developed countries. However, many gaps are identified and the recent examples of bank scams like the Punjab National Bank, and the fugitives going abroad in taking shelter are a case in point. The Government of India recently took initiative and proclaimed an ordinance by making provisions stringent in preventing the fugitives from showing contempt for the Indian law. Secondly, there is a need to prevent fraudulent activity through games like IPL and consortiums of international importance for keeping ill-gotten wealth through corrupt roots and also through hawala channels.

The Benami Transactions Prevention Act is a step in the right direction. Real estate is another avenue for stashing cash. The Real Estate Regulatory Authority Act is also a correct step in the right direction. Telecom and spectrum are fast emerging as super game-changers with enormous scope for windfall profits. The 2G scam is a case in point. With the advent of the Telecom Regulatory Authority of India and the tightening of implementation norms, some positive steps are being taken. However much remains to be done to bring the spectrum and Telecom law on par with the global practices. A recent example of the auction of the spectrum being done in a transparent environment is indicating the use of the positive changes that can be expected shortly.

Protection of patents and copyrights as important intellectual property and investigating the infringement and actively and forcing the rights of inherent intellectual creativity is an essential ingredient of an emerging knowledge economy. The IPR Act is unfair in many areas with Global standards. However, with the new technology emerging daily in many areas of information and communication, pharmaceuticals, chemicals, drugs, and medical diagnosis equipment, software, energy substitutes, nanotechnology, it is imperative to implement patent rights protection in a simplified manner. Intellectual Property Rights (IPR) Act 1970, as far as provisions are concerned, is praiseworthy law, but its implementation needs improvement. The time lag in the disposal of applications in India is four times that of in the United States and other advanced countries. The establishment of institutes of excellence in research and development in emerging fields of science and technology is another imperative of the emerging knowledge economy. The law that is related to this field lags behind their International counterparts in the advanced economies. Not even one Indian university is being shown in the first top 100 universities in the world while our neighbourhood has some institutes of reputation which is a case in point. A small country like Singapore has effective educational institutions when compared to a nation with a 1.31 billion population.

Conclusions

1. It is hereby suggested that there is a need to have a paradigm shift in the meaning of the word CBMA. The stakeholders, post-cross border Merger and acquisition, in any geographical area of India should not be reduced to the level of migrant labour living pitiably in their ancestral place of residence because of the threat of the Agents of Mafiosi, masquerading themselves as the advocates of development.
2. It is hereby suggested that an optimal modification must be made in the uman Rights Act, 1993 so that the rights of workers and managers of both acquired and acquiring companies across the continents are recognised and addressed, instead of leaving them to the vagaries of weather or manipulations of Machiavellian market forces as the chasers of billion-dollar dreams often disrespectfully and contemptuously dismiss their fellow human beings.'
3. It is hereby suggested that TRAI, like SEBI, be authorised to ensure that the rights of the workers or any other stay home stakeholders and the right of the Indian state have a taxing authority or not taken negligently by any big global multinational organisation.
4. It is hereby suggested that there be the modification of the domestic law relating to the protection of women and the girls in the workforce exposing themselves not only to the Indian environment but the environment abroad. Matters become complicated because of the migrant labour especially from the sectors of domestic nurses and domestic helps both within India and without increasingly becoming victims of human trafficking.
5. It is hereby suggested that while it is important to pay maximum attention to minor detail on the shop floor, it is more important to pay maximum attention to the minutest psychological core problems of adjustment with the environment in the case of a fellow human being. This is to prevent the possible infliction of harm either on self or on others for frivolous causes.

6   It is hereby suggested that collective leadership of both acquired and acquiring companies must be actively engaged by both the government's agencies and enforcers of the law, to address the issue of demoralisation among the stakeholders rather than leaving them on their own in an environment of free for all. Disengaged employees are not productive it has been found in this research that they have a lower chance of commitment. Disengaged employees are often involved in issues of indiscipline, misbehaviour, and the spreading of rumours at the workplace.

7   It is hereby suggested that a modification to youth services related law in addressing the core issues of:

   a   Building trust
   b   Foster team spirit
   c   Addressing the issues of motivation.

8   It is hereby suggested that proper accounting of this differential aspect is taken care of in the rules and regulations and the directions given to the labour tribunals and the labour officers of various public and private sector organisations.

9   It is hereby suggested that the modification of the medical establishment rules be made in the workforce arena so that these psychiatric disabilities of the workforce are adequately taken care of on par with the best benchmark global practices available in the Scandinavian countries.

10 It is hereby suggested that it must be made mandatory for the welfare officers in both the target and acquired companies to do an engagement survey beforehand to know the positioning and the ideological comfort of the stakeholders to the challenge of the prospective cross-border merger and acquisition activity affecting their future.

11 It is hereby suggested that making proper modifications in the syllabus of management studies to include the above-mentioned errors and possible solutions arising therefrom. Just by asking the right questions, more transparency is ensured.

12 It is hereby suggested that the situation calls for modification of the law relating to the whistle-blowers' Protection Act in that adequate protection must be given to those who dare to ask questions and more production to those who dare to ask the right questions.

13 It is hereby suggested that an adequate modification to the service and the conduct rules of the government servants as well as the labour law of industrial disputes act and other acts in back the organisations of both the government and industry must be granted enough freedom to recognise the cancerous cells and deal with them properly to protect the body politic of the organisational core competency.

14 It is hereby suggested that the rules and regulations of best HR practices be modified to take initiatives of recognising the proper qualities of leadership and incubate the same to convert them into the real assets of the nation.

At the present moment, security agencies in India are not part of the decision-making authorities in so far as conducting the due diligence regarding CBMA. The developed economies respond optimally to retain their soft power. Future research and further research need to concentrate on this vital issue.

Secondly, little coordination is found among enforcement agencies of the law in India. Future research may take up the methods of action on time on line coordination in a single-window framework.

The potential areas that need a fresh look are as follows:

- SEBI for fast-track CBMA
- NCLT For fast-tracking Of CBMA
- MAP and PRE PACK for fast-moving CBMA (FM-CBMA)

History does not forgive those who forget history. It repeats itself. "Those who wait for the future in the present will become past."—Dr B.N. Ramesh

Notes

1 Eaglesham J, The wall Street Journal (February 9, 2011) http://www.wsj.com/public/page/ archive-2018-2-09.html (Last visited on April 21, 2018).
2 THE BUSINESS LINE, 5, (Kolkata edn., April 21, 2018)
3 The Serious Fraud Investigation Office, (April 4, 2018) www.ndtv.com/topic/sfio (Last visited on May 16, 2018).
4 https://economictimes.indiatimes.com/industry/banking/finance (Last visited on May 20, 2018.
5 Sec. 447, THE COMPANY ACT, (2017).
6 Sec. 447, THE COMPANY ACT, (2017).
7 KunalGupta, orate.cyrilamarchanddlogs.com (Last visited on May 20, 2018).
8 KunalGupta, orate.cyrilamarchanddlogs.com (Last visited on May 20, 2018).
9 Dr T K Viswanathan, The report of the Bankruptcy Law Reforms Committee: Rationale and Design 1, (November, 2015) http://ibbi.gov.in/BLRCReportVol1_04112015.pdf (last visited on May 21, 2018).
10 Dr T K Viswanathan, The report of the Bankruptcy Law Reforms Committee: Rationale and Design 2 (November, 2015) http://ibbi.gov.in/BLRCReportVol1_04112015.pdf (last visited on May 21, 2018).
11 Provisions of the SARFAESI ACT, (2002).
12 Dr T K Viswanathan, The report of the Bankruptcy Law Reforms Committee: Rationale and Design 2 (November, 2015) http://ibbi.gov.in/BLRCReportVol1_04112015.pdf (last visited on May 21, 2018).
13 MONDAQ, Merger Regime Under The Companies Act, (2013). http://www.mondaq.com/india/x/289180/Corporate+Commercial+Law/Merger+Regime+Under+The+Companies+Act+2013 (Last visited on May 22, 2018)
14 Amiya Kumar Bagchi and SubhanilBanerje, "How Strong Are the Arguments for Bank Mergers?", ECONOMIC AND POLITICAL WEEKLY, 40 12 1181--1182, 1187–1189, (March, 2005)
15 Anand Manoj & Singh Jagandeep (2008), "Impact of Merger Announcements on Shareholder's Wealth Evidence from Indian Private Sector Banks", Vikalpa (33 No 1 January – March 2008). http://Papers.Ssrn.Com/Sol3/Papers.Cfm?Abstract_Id=977119&Rec=1&Srcabs= 1635077 (Last visited on May 22, 2018).
16 L.M. Devare, Liquidator of Bank of … v. Commissioner of Income-Tax on 15 September, 1998, 234 ITR 813 Bom.

17. Sec. 44(B) of the BANKING REGULATION ACT 1949.
18. Financial Express, 08.02.2020, page-7
19. Business Line, 10.12.2020, page-4
20. Delhi Cloth And General Mills Co.,... v. Shri RameshwarDyal And Anr on 22 November, 1960, 1961 AIR 689 1961 SCR (2) 590.
21. Delhi Cloth And General Mills Co.,... v. Shri RameshwarDyal And Anr on 22 November, 1960 1961 AIR 689 1961 SCR (2) 590.
22. Electronics Corp.Of India ... v. Union Of India &Ors on February 17, 2011, Writ Petition No. 1883 OF 2011.
23. Scheme of Amalgamation of Indusland Enterprises and Finance Ltd. with IndusInd Bank Ltd., [2004]120CompCas457[Bom].
24. Merchants Bank Ltd. v. M. DharamsambarthaniAmogal, AIR 1966 Mad 26: 78 Mad LW 569.
25. Compendium of Accounting Standards, http://cga.nic.in/writereaddata/Compendiumof AccountingStandards.pdf (Last vissited on May 23, 2018)
26. ShajiVikraman, THE INDIAN EXPRESS, 05, (Kolkata edn. May 22, 2018).
27. ShajiVikraman, THE INDIAN EXPRESS, 05, (Kolkata edn. May 22, 2018).
28. ShajiVikraman, THE INDIAN EXPRESS, 05, (Kolkata edn. May 22, 2018).
29. ShajiVikraman, THE INDIAN EXPRESS, 05, (Kolkata edn. May 22, 2018).
30. THE HINDU, Editorial, 10 (Kolkata edn. May 22, 2018).
31. THE HINDU, Editorial, 10 (Kolkata edn. May 22, 2018).
32. THE HINDU, Editorial, 10 (Kolkata edn. May 22, 2018).
33. THE HINDU, Editorial, 10 (Kolkata edn. May 22, 2018).
34. THE HINDU BUSINESS LINE, 06 (Kolkata edn. May 20, 2018) editorial states that, given that other NCLT cases may face a tougher road, the rules must be tweaked to ensure that the widest possible range of bidders participate.
35. THE HINDU BUSINESS LINE, 06, (Kolkata edn. May 20, 2018).
36. THE HINDU BUSINESS LINE, 06, (Kolkata edn. May 23, 2018).
37. THE HINDU BUSINESS LINE, 06, Para 3 (Kolkata edn. May 23, 2018).
38. THE HINDU BUSINESS LINE, 07, (Kolkata edn. May 23, 2018).
39. https://indiankanoon.org/doc/78288892/

5 COVID and the CBMA

Cross-border mergers and acquisitions across nations are treated as strategic initiatives by expanding and growing corporations. Pandemics throughout the world's history never left the status quo undisturbed. All pandemics, right from the 15th-century plague to the 21st-century COVID-19 pandemic, have never left the world undisturbed either politically or economically. The COVID-19 pandemic similarly caused suppressed business activity in Europe, Asia and most importantly in the USA. The National Bureau of Economic Research, NBER of USA is the most important body and also the most powerful yet unofficial arbitrator of US economic waves in terms of sluggishness or expansion. The NBER does not isolate all identify any recession or depression, yet, all indicators from NBER point out that COVID-19 Pandemic forced recession in the USA.

According to informed sources, depression is less precarious than deflation because depression is of lesser duration. Recessions are always prolonged and extremely harmful as they sabotage wages and vitiate economic activity on a longer timeframe. History's worst depression is remembered during the 1930s for both the difficulties it created for major economies of the world and also for the huge unemployment it created almost at the level of 25%. The vice-chair of the Federal Reserve, USA, Richard Clarida, in an interview with Bloomberg Television in April 2020, maintained that "Central banks' aggressive response to COVID-19 Pandemic can prevent the economy from slipping into outright deflation like the 2007–2009 recession."

The Impact of COVID-19 Pandemic Crisis on Mergers and Acquisitions

Three authors in an article in *Harvard Business Review*, namely Richard Harrow H, David Lipkin and Richard V Smith, maintain that hundreds and thousands of businesses are likely to be closed and millions of Americans would be unemployed coupled with the consumer spending being slashed with the desertion of the supply chains and the plummeting of the oil demand are going to be the normal features due to COVID-19 pandemic. The dot-com crisis in the year 2000 or the depression of the year 2007 and 2009 created different effects on the US economy. However, the COVID-19

DOI: 10.4324/9781003396987-5

pandemic would go beyond the following areas. (A). Financial systems. (B). Valuation of sellers. (C).The buyers' attraction. All the above will be subjected to the newly appearing due diligences which include

1   The convenient deal financing,
2   The amount of attention that the government approved regulators and
3   The due diligence to be rendered by any required third party.

COVID-19 Pandemic and the CBMA Trends

The Centre for Monitoring of the Indian Economy (CMIE) observed that the mergers and acquisition trends in India were found to be lowest in 16 years due to COVID-19 pandemic. Due to the precautionary measures of the COVID-19 protocol, namely social distancing, time travel restrictions, isolation, lockdown, et cetera, sectors like civil aviation, travel, tourism, and hospitality suffered physically. However, new opportunities were seen in the telecom and digital space. Facebook and Google invested in the Jio platforms of Reliance India Ltd. to the tune of US$ 10 billion. Recently, Think and Learn, an education technology platform company, acquired WhiteHat Jr in a US$ 3 million all-cash transaction.

Telemedicine and telemetry consultancy in medical supplies, as well as medical services, is yet another opportunity during the COVID-19 pandemic times. Amazon recently launching Amazon Pharmacy online (from January 2022) and Reliance Industries acquiring a majority stake in Netmeds to convert it into a big online pharmacy sector are the primary steps in this emerging industry. The Wal-Mart-controlled Flipkart started Sastasundar, a 30 % discount online medicine service during the pandemic era. Online gaming and virtual reality gaming happen to be other emerging sectors. Lending payments, wealth management and insurance technology coupled with the mainstream cleantech industry also witnessed keen interest in terms of spurt in investment. The COVID-19 pandemic called for adopting new measures and strategies which among others include concern for liquidity, valuation, regulatory changes, and practical aspects related to lockdown and migration of labour. Pricing mechanisms are part of the due diligence. The COVID-19 pandemic changed the conditions of negotiation. The delay due to the education because of the restrictions of travel and also the consequent exchange-rate changes, as well as the new market reality, are some of the factors which compel retention/holdback of a portion of the purchase price to secure potential indemnity claims due to the uncertainty arising from the pandemic.

The internationally accepted norm has been the acceptance of the net working capital adjustment as the most common purchase price mechanism, the parties to the CBMA may look to negotiate in terms of the new emerging conditions. The FDI policy of the Government of India already allows 18 months from deferring payments with this evening of 25% of the transaction value for the quantum of deferred payments. Providing additional relaxations for the negotiating parties to structure their price adjustment mechanisms is the need of the hour and will attract an institutional foreign investor to look for opportunities for acquisitions in India. The material adverse change which is naturally applicable due to the COVID-19 pandemic situation will certainly prolong the negotiation timeframe. This situation calls for additional areas for warranty protection which among others cover the following areas:

1 Financial performance and accounts,
2 Business continuity and operations
3 Solvency risk
4 Performance or termination of material contracts
5 Employee rationalisation

There is a need for warranty and indemnity insurance to be widely used in India in the CBMA arena. This new awareness also will be working as a level playing field for industries between the USA and India in equalising the country-specific domestic area of operations. The Government of India will do well in examining the possibility of inviting foreign companies with expert eyes in warranty and indemnity insurance to participate in providing warranty and indemnity insurance to Indian companies participating in Cross-Border Mergers and Acquisitions.

The Institution of CIFUS in the USA has been very effective in protecting the interest of sovereignty of the state of the USA. A similar measure is initiated by the Government of India recently when FDI restrictions were imposed on countries that share their land border with India with an intent to curb opportunistic takeovers of Indian companies by persons or entities of such bordering countries. The insurance sector has been opened for 100% in the automatic route while 74% of FDI is allowed in Defence Manufacturing.

Logistics, Transportation, Supply Chain Management and COVID-19 Pandemic

The COVID-19 pandemic offered opportunities in supply chain management. The world witnessed increasing tension in the US-China trade even before the COVID-19 pandemic. The US business house typically performs due diligence in the following three areas.

1 Diversification of the supply chain
2 Quality check on the infrastructure for movement of goods in the new area
3 Availability of reliable business and political environment in the new area.

Machine learning, artificial intelligence, robotics along data analytics are the new varieties of interest both in terms of application and research development during the COVID-19 pandemic times during the COVID-19 pandemic times also, several multinational corporations exhibited an interest in shifting their factories to India. Recently Japan offered incentives to Japanese companies for shifting their manufacturing base from China to India. The following issues need concern and attention from the Government of India to resort to immediate corrective action:

1. Reduction of cost of doing business in India
2. Simplification of the regulations on par with the best benchmarking practices in the world
3. Reduction in tariff costs to international level
4. Localisation of Data protection with no hassles and less bureaucratic control of IPRs
5. Free pursuing of Intellectual Property Rights
6. Provision of tax incentives
7. Single window system of quick response teams

The strength of India in terms of business is well known among the following areas:

1. Auto components
2. Pharma Industry
3. Speciality Chemicals
4. Electronics

Government Regulators

The COVID-19 pandemic moved officials risky and hence negotiations have to be done in remote locations. In other words, it requires new technology and a new order of negotiations. According to the trade statistics of the USA, in March 2020, CBMAs became zero and the domestic merger and acquisition activity in the USA recorded a fall of 50% to the mere US$ 253 billion. The main attention of the CEO of all companies now is shifted to the preservation of the company than expansion. For instance, Xerox company dropped a US$34 billion offer to Hewlett-Packard. Secondly, Softbank terminated US$ 3 billion tenders for a company called We WorkShares. Thirdly, Bed Bath and Beyond company also dropped the case in Delaware. Fourthly, Boeing supplier Excel also called off a US$ 6.4 billion merger proposal.

Scope for Increases in FDI and FPI through CBMA during COVID-19 Pandemic

FDI in India has shown a long-term growth trend even in the post-pandemic period. FDI among private business is driven by factors depending on the host of criteria which, among others, include:

1   Rarity of natural resources,
2   Market size,
3   Infrastructure,
4   General investment climate,
5   Macroeconomic stability,
6   Investment decisions of foreign investors.

The Government of India reviewed the FDI policy and liberalised safety rules to make India an attractive investment destination. FDI is now permitted up 100% under the automatic route in most sectors' activities. Except in real estate or construction of farmhouses, a hundred percent FDI under the automatic route is allowed in construction-development projects, completed projects for operation and management of townships, malls/shopping complexes and business centres, and also real estate broking service. There is a discussion going on for allowing the limited liability partnerships also for the construction development sector. FDI inflow in India increased by 15% despite the COVID-19 pandemic lockdown period. India has been adopting a non-discriminatory policy towards investors which includes the multinational corporations in India despite the COVID-19 pandemic being prevalent, a lot of interest was witnessed in the fields of electronics, information technology, data analytics, renewable energy, medical devices, mobiles, and computing devices. Global Investors and MNCs evinced a keen interest in FDI during the COVID-19 pandemic period. The new draft e-commerce policy of the department for promotion of investment and internal trade should also look into issues like consumer interest protection, export promotion, protection of small and organised traders, and also data protection.

Travel and Tourism

Worldwide, the COVID-19 pandemic made people cautious in their travel. The travel industry which includes railways, airways and automobiles, and the tourism industry which includes event management, hospitalities, and hotels would be the major segments of industries facing the brunt of the COVID-19 Pandemic. Supply chains originating from China and subsidiary industries that depend on such supply chains would also be severely affected. However, the same companies offer distress sale opportunities to any intelligent entrepreneur. The COVID-19 pandemic demands extra due diligence which ipso facto will require more time for negotiations. Third-party consent would also require a longer time because of the inability to meet in a smaller office space.

Regulator Dilemma

Approvals by the regulatory authorities like the antitrust authority would be requiring a lot of time because of the non-availability of officials and the fixed time framework being given an exemption. The current example is by the European regulators. The COVID-19 pandemic makes the buyers taking special care of their interests and hence the buyers are likely to shift the closing and indemnity risk to the sellers. On the other hand, the sellers would like to prevent the buyers from walking away with all benefits.

COVID-19 Pandemic and the Changes in the Structure of Business in the Context of the CBMA

The modes available for digital payment in India during the pre-COVID time include UPI, immediate payment service, Bharat Bill pay, which recorded significant growth except on April 2020 when the lockdown was first imposed. The following graphs show the growth. The reasons for migrating to digital channels include the most essential elements of the COVID-19 pandemic precautions, namely,

1 Social distancing,
2 Pent-up demand,
3 Festival season,
4 Wedding season and

the measures are given by the government to boost the economy. The UPI transactions recorded more than the Rs 200 crore mark in the current period with the amount reregistering at Rs 3.9 lakh crore worth of payments according to the vice-chairman. The consistent steady rise of the UPI is a clear indication that the population is now gradually becoming comfortable with digital transactions. The firm Exchanger estimated that India can record 6660 crore transactions worth US$ 270.7 billion by the year 2023 which may cross to US$ 856.6 billion by the year 2030.

Investment Funds and SEBI

SEBI, the market regulator of India, amended norms about automating investment funds to define relevant professional qualifications. The new requirements include adequate experience with at least one key personnel having at least five years of experience in advising or managing pools of capital or asset or wealth or in the business of buying and selling and dealing with securities. Professional qualification in finance, accountancy, business management, commerce, economics, capital market or banking from a recognised institution is the second essential qualification requirement for the manager who would be responsible for the management of the alternative investment fund. All this is to prevent fraud in the name of investment vehicles. The role of regulator assumes great importance in crisis times, and the COVID-19 pandemic is no exception.

Letters of Intent

The starting point of the CBMA process is the letter of intent. The COVID-19 pandemic in its impact does not spare either the seller or the buyer insofar as the letters of intent are concerned. 'Buyers will feel justified in seeing longer periods of exclusivity than in the recent past ever since the Pandemic and due diligence challenges.' In CBMA, financing is a crucial aspect, and financing is normally done through the private equity route and also through the debt financing arrangements. The COVID-19 pandemic makes it difficult because of the instability in the financial markets and the collapse in the currency trade. Coupled with the negative futures of petroleum products having an impact on the movement of global currencies, the arrangements of funds for the CBMA activity will face many challenges due to the COVID-19 pandemic.

Due to the above-mentioned reasons, the controlling of the initiatives in the CBMA will move towards the buyers as many sellers will be facing the problem of illiquidity, huge inventory of receivables, huge payment crises due to the vendors, and paucity of orders of execution for delivery. When the leverage becomes monolithic towards one partner leaving the other partner as less a partner and more distressed seller, the entire process becomes a hostile takeover and not the CBMA.

Non-Uniform Impact of the COVID-19 Pandemic

The COVID-19 pandemic impacted negatively the following sectors of business:

> Retail, B. Travel, C. Tourism, D. Automobiles, E. Aircraft Manufacturing spare parts and F. Air journey.

The COVID-19 pandemic made the trends to be more favourable towards online retail, co-working spaces, video conferencing facilities, cloud computing, artificial intelligence, robotics, online technical platforms, bioethics, safe food delivery and just-in-time systems of manufacturing.

The MAE/MAC Impact on the CBMA vs. COVID-19 Pandemic

MAE means materially adverse effect and MAC means materially adverse change. These are inbuilt in the CBMA as risk-averse measures for the protection of genuine parties. In essence, 'the buyer is not obliged to close the deal if they release a seller suffering MAE since the signing of the agreement.' The carved-out portions as clauses in the MAE cases are important. In Delaware, any event would constitute MAE if it substantially threatens the overall earnings potential of the target in a durationally significant manner.

The Strategic Outlook of the Global Economy Due to the COVID-19 Pandemic

Researchers Rich Lesser and Martin Reeves, while emphasising the strategies in the post-COVID-19 Pandemic era, recalled their proposal which they made a year ago, as part of the strategic foresight, that the lever of competitive advantage was shifting. This shift is majorly affected by three forces namely-

1   New blockchain emerging technologies.
2   Declining long-term growth rates.
3   Innovation and the need for engineering.

All the artificial intelligence, coupled with a semi-hybrid learning organisation is needed for the new times and the climes. The COVID-19 pandemic with the huge cost of short-term impact in quadrupling contagious rate and social distancing, in turn, is leading to economic disruption. Resilience is not a future acquisition; on the other hand, it is the relevance of yesterday if the industry of today needs to survive. Survival is essential both for the humans from an employer point of view and of the organisation from the employee point of view. The short time goal is the changed situation as of today because if one fails in this short-term goal, the oft-repeated long-term goal of thriving and growth becomes redundant and meaningless.

Resilience and COVID-19 Pandemic

Human resilience is a democratised discipline and concern for others is no longer an altruism but is an essential quality to save oneself. It requires coordination among humans, habitats, boroughs, mayors, ministers, governments, universities, security agencies and medical, rehabilitative workers. Here it is important to mention the five most vital imperatives for leadership practice. The schools of Public Policy and Economic Development as well as the institutions' expertise in crisis management harp upon these five imperatives. They are as follows.

Flattening of the Pandemic Graph

The killer effect of the COVID-19 pandemic lies in its geometric spread of the contagious virus. The slope of the graph of the affected population needs to be brought down by both old benchmarking practices and new customised inventions. The age-old Pandemic practices include the following namely

1. **"Quarantine"** and 2. **"Committed social distancing."** During the time of the crisis-ridden Pandemics, there can be no trade-offs among choices. There is only one option namely "the survival of mankind." There can be no trade-offs between death and the dollar. Decreasing the slope of the curve is essential to save human lives and livelihoods.

Experts from the Global Observatory Institutions like the Harvard Business School feel that COVID-19 pandemic-infused behaviour patterns have a long-term impact on economic recovery. Social distance norms and the mandatory mask-wearing coupled with co-morbidity risk compel new behaviour adoption in individuals as well as groups of individuals. Larry

Summers of USA on April 14, 2020, in a fireside chat with Harvard University faculty, observed,

> You can open up the economy all you want, but when they are hiring refrigerated trucks to deliver dead bodies to transport them to the morgues, not many people are going to go out of their houses.... So blaming the economic collapse on the policy, rather than on the problem, is fallacious in the same way that observing that wherever you see a lot of oncologists, you'll tend to see a lot of people dying of cancer and inferring that that means the oncologists kill people

Lockdown and COVID-19 Pandemic

Immoderate forethought full of measures/actions and the accompanying behaviour is more often than not in all probability is likely to suppress the natural growth of demand and thus dampen economic normalcy/recovery. Empirical studies conducted by researchers informed that one size for all kinds of responses is counter-productive. A full lockdown for a longer period is likely to bring out the heterogenic quality in the behaviour of citizens coupled with the failure of the execution of such lockdown measures to their full scope. The need of the hour is to have a balanced approach which is a golden means between a full lockdown with stringency measures and a partial lockdown with giving due diligence to values of dignity deliberation and social norms

Impact of COVID-19 Pandemic on International Business Law

Accountancy Issues

Accounting-Related Issues

The COVID-19 pandemic caused disruptions across borders, within industries, and across value addition- Product links including services like cost management, logistics and the crucial financial accountancy. Four areas emerge in terms of topmost priority in this aspect. They are, first, the Supply Chain Management (SCM); second, the downsizing of the business cycle process, production schedule inventory management, warehouse hiring; third, employee accountability in terms of managing the accounts of receivables and payables; and fourth, the bank transactions, working capital and liquidity management of funds.

Many cross-border industries and companies, in an environment of flexibility, started adapting themselves to the new challenges in the era of the Pandemic.

Long-term Stability vs. Short-term Crisis

While a typical particular solution is not feasible across industries even in a single country, it is impossible to extend the same logic in an international context, Industries focus their productivity from quarter to quarter, and due to the Pandemic crisis, the focus shifts from the present crisis emergency to the long-term stabilisation and post-COVID-19 pandemic response mechanisms. In the immediate timeframe of any establishment of a major or small-scale industry, the employee safety and the small-scale rescue measures for venders, service providers and also the insurance premium which needs to be paid on a chronological basis and any failure to do so will have a larger impact on the health of the industry or the establishment.

The Response of Major Centres and Industrial Sectors

Many countries including the USA and India already took measures towards rescuing the economies in the current financial year. The European Union introduced a temporary framework through its commission. Stabilisation measures across the international economy need close coordination among the leaders of the industry as well as the governments. Pandemic panic is likely to induce obsessive or excessive protectionism which may seem to be a temporary goal of self-interest but ultimately may dampen and damage the individual country or the industry's credibility in the global environment. The specific measures are the provision of subsistence wages to the employees and specific needs and circumstances in terms of the dividends and are the action of combined pools to see to it that the essential services of the companies and the organisations keep going.

Prevention is Better than Perishing

Anticipation Is Better than Precipitation

A new economic landscape is certain to dictate its own rules and those who fail to anticipate strategy in adapting to the new environment are likely to be the losers in this race for survival. Many industries already started filing bankruptcy both in the USA and in India, and the following discussion highlights the essential relevant points.

International Rules on the CBMA Restructuring

The normal time rules on international cross-border restructuring are very complex and they become more complex during the times of the COVID-19 pandemic. When nations adopt protective measures in a COVID-19 pandemic environment to protect the health of the population, responsible national leadership will not think twice about adopting any stringent protective measures in the next area of economic survival. The restructuring issues among industries across the nations in the CBMA arena will be undergoing a complex dynamic churning out process with both time and cost overruns being the main features. There are experts in the private as well as in the government sectors who keep a watch on the emerging situation, and one such expert office is the CMS[1] which has 70 offices throughout the world paying major attention to the issues of, firstly, stabilisation, secondly, restructuring, and, thirdly, post-crisis challenges and calibrations.

RCEP and the CBMA

The Government of India chose to stay out of the Chinese-sponsored RCEP. There were criticisms that India missed an opportunity of becoming a beneficiary of an emerging big-sized trading bloc contributor to global supply chains. India correctly recognised that the free trade agreements with a communist China are going to de-industrialise India in the long run. The most effective initiatives taken by the Ministry of Finance, Government of India in this concern are as follows:

1. Policy changes for self-reliance.
2. Rising of imported duties on certain items for product protection of the domestic industry.
3. Production-linked incentive scheme with an outlay of over Rs 2 lakh crores covering ten major industrial sectors.
4. Protectionism is bad but realism is good.
5. Make for India and make for the world programs to incentivise the migration of manufacturing jobs from China and other countries to India.
6. Learning from history in terms of, firstly, the Japanese; secondly, the Koreans; and thirdly the Chinese in terms of operationalising "War economics."
7. Adopting lower prices as a market entry strategy and value addition in terms of better quality to sustain the market and to occupy global heights in the market.
8. Financial support to the manufacturing companies by suitable modifications to the structure and function of the banking, borrowing, and browbeating competition.
9. Preventing the fall of the rupee value in the international exchange market.
10. Understanding the strength of the public sector banks and nurturing them by implementing essential reforms.
11. Pragmatic approach of having a well-oiled system for effective Government and business connectivity so that both business and Government will play a mutually reinforcing role in supporting each other for global excellence.
12. The ease of doing business index in India is to link it to the competitive index of the Indian Government and the effectiveness index of Indian Governance.
13. Quality, Reliability and Sustainability are the new iconic concepts to enter, stay and sustain in a global market.
14. Starting a Government promoted Quality Council of India, Accountancy Council of India, Accountability Council of India, fraud prevention Council of India, opportunities realising Council of India.

15 Paving way for green and clean manufacturing hubs along with the special economic zones so that both can function as special carbon footprint economic zones and non-pollution economic zones.
16 Brand name for Indian products, not merely of Indian company products. Here the Government of India needs to play an important role through the coordinated activity of various ministries which include among others,

    a Ministry of Commerce,
    b Ministry of external affairs,
    c Ministry of industrial promotion,
    d Ministry of Finance and
    e Ministry of Law and various departments that work Cyber Security, prevention of serious fraud, promotion of quality, adherence to global standards of excellence, coordination and cooperation with the best institutes of engineering and manufacturing in the world, and Central Bureau of Investigation and Vigilance Commission to prevent any corruption indirectly or directly.

The creation of a fair level playing field in an environment of transparency and accountability with adequate support of fiscal resources, at least on par with the Chinese banks offering to the Chinese Industries is required. Supporting the start-ups and promoting the risk for the newly emerging high-end technology services and products will keep India ahead of its competitors.

The goodwill India generated because of its institutions and democracy among the democratic West and European countries and especially with the largest trade partner namely the United States of America needs to be utilised for the promotion of trade, commerce, industry, and GDP growth. The USA can be an entry point to the rest of North America and South America. Good relations with Germany can bring in the best technology available in manufacturing and also enter the markets of Central Northern and Southern Europe. Relations with Japan can do wonders in reaching out to the markets of forest Asia East Asia and Southeast Asia. India's China competition is not merely a trade competition but is a competition of systems, aspirations of the people, and ideologies. India cannot afford to lose this battle.

COVID-19 Pandemic, the CBMA and Corporate Fraud

More than a hundred countries in the world, in the interest of public health, declared various periods of lockdown for the past few months. While this lockdown cannot last forever, surviving the business contacts and contracts needs the adoption of quintessential and new strategies and measures in reducing the liability risks of the business in the CBMA environment. The COVID-19 pandemic made, among others, CBMA also lose the already existing advantage of known and reliable supply chain management (SCM). The recent conference at an international forum made many countries articulate their fears about the repetition of the COVID-19 pandemic and the suspected attribution of the Wuhan epidemic turning into COVID-19 pandemic has now many takers, led by major partners of the European Union and the USA.

Risks and Threats to the CBMA

The following are the main associated risks for the CBMA business environment in the possible post-lockdown opening up of the global economy. Critical employees of Information Communication Technology (ICT) systems either losing their lives or becoming critically ill because of the pandemic and thus their services being not available.

Mergers and Acquisitions and Distressed Assets

During the financial crisis of the years 2008 and 2009, acquisitions were taking place globally of those companies who have strong balance sheets, which were targeted for quite a long time. During the COVID-19 pandemic, the old tactic of acquiring strategic assets of most of the companies not surviving the economic fallout from the COVID-19 pandemic is going attention. It is estimated that the new deals will be dramatically dealing in a different environment than in the past. The merger and acquisition risks of a distressed company become further stressful due to COVID-19 pandemic.

Protective Measures and Impact of COVID-19 Pandemic

Due diligence and documentation are two important issues in the CBMA apparatus and they assume critical importance during COVID-19 pandemic times. The critical questions that need to be asked are whether the supply chain of the target company is intact, whether the employee attrition rate and the safety of the workforce are being taken care of, whether the spread of the virus is being tackled by the local authorities and lastly whether the demand still for exist the products of the target company. Cybersecurity law is also important. While the deal pricing is normally based on the recent earnings, the process of acquisition must also take care of the COVID-19 pandemic inputs in this process. According to practicing lawyers like Brian Fahrney,[2] while documentation of the merging process is important as in the earlier times, COVID-19 pandemic makes meetings very difficult. The COVID-19 pandemic further brings in the Material Adverse Change (MAC) risk and hence and the merger process will be seriously affected by litigation due to MAE/MAC.

Law Business Strategy, the CBMA and COVID-19 Pandemic Impact

From the starting point of the outbreak of the COVID-19 pandemic in one province of China to date 4,634 death and 83,021 active cases people were affected on June 2, 2020 and the majority of those affected had to face huge inconvenience. As on March 3,2023, total COVID-19 pandemic cases worldwide are 67,56,22,359 and deaths are 68,75,314. Quarantine and stay-at-home orders along with the closure of colleges and factories made the life of many people very inconvenient. While the COVID-19 pandemic is a very severe health hazard, yet, implications for consumer spending and in turn for the business growth and running of many factories and initiations are also at peril. Disruption to supply chains and huge unemployment burden apart from disturbing the energy prices and bottlenecks in transport, hospitality, and aviation sectors caused enormous disruption which in turn also created new effects on Global Merger and acquisition activity by having a direct impact on negotiations and risks associated with uncertainties.

Economy and Cross-Border Mergers and Acquisitions

November 2020 saw an interesting event of the presidential election of the United States. This presidential election saw not only the effect of the COVID-19 pandemic but also in increasing tension in the US-China trade war. The COVID-19 pandemic offers scope for innovation and also the experiences of many multinational organisations that were relying on the manufacturing positions in China are now slowly looking at opportunities in India. Indian companies will do well in grabbing the new opportunity the recent increase in the request for quotation is an even order from the global players who were hitherto sourcing from China is a good indication. The Government of India reduced the corporate tax rate as an incentive during the COVID-19 pandemic from 34% to 17.01% for the new manufacturing companies which are to be incorporated after October 2019. The production linked incentive scheme launched by the Government for 13 sectors involving an outlay of almost Rs 2 lakh crores is also usable by the companies to focus on backward integration and strengthening of their supply chain logistics. Emphasis can be seen in the fields of

1. Pesticide,
2. Pharma,
3. Electronic and white goods manufacturers,
4. Textile companies and
5. Man-made fibre textiles. Indian companies can also look for cross-border mergers and acquisitions during the COVID-19 pandemic especially of those who are having manufacturing facilities in China. The impact of the COVID-19 pandemic on the industry is varied and it has been extremely cordial on small and medium-sized players when compared to the bigger ones. This is a threat and an opportunity at the same time depending upon the ability to utilise an emerging opportunity. Cross-brder mergers and acquisitions between India and the United States can harp upon the transfer of technology whereas Cross-Border Mergers and Acquisitions between India and China can harp upon the creation

of markets and manufacturing facilities. No country can become a global manufacturing hub without its industry taking the required risk. The COVID-19 pandemic is a game-changer, and it will be in India's wisdom to use for the industry.

The COVID-19 **pandemic and the banking industry**: The internal working group of the Reserve Bank of India recently came out with a working paper discussing an idea to allow the industries and non-banking financial companies to own up banks. Indiscriminate lending and poor governance standards resulting in huge non-performing assets and inadequate capital have been the major problems facing the public sector and private sector banking in India. The non-performing assets stood at Rs 10.35 lakh crore. Except for the State Bank of India, none of the other 34 public sector undertaking banks features in the top hundred global banks.

The Indian public expects the banks to work within a system of safety and security of the deposits. Banks cannot be merely custodians of cash. Banks have to be the financial industry. The internal working group of the RBI proposes adequate safeguards as a precondition before making necessary amendments to the banking regulation act 1949. The rigor of the appraisal system and the vigilant oversight of the board have been absent in the public sector banks transactions especially while giving a huge amount of loans to other chronic defaulters. Separation of banking and commerce, as prevalent in the US cannot be transferred lock stock and barrel to India. India with an aspiration of emerging as a US$ 5.0 trillion economy by the year 2025 has to make successful the following three issues.

1   Make in India
2   Make for India.
3   Self-reliant initiatives (ATMANIRBHAR).

The following issues are also important to be kept in mind in this regard. They are

1   Various aspects of risk management
2   Process of appointment of full-time directors
3   Appointment of CEO of the Bank.
4   Fixing the tenure of the Board of Directors.
5   Fixing the tenure of CEO.
6   Designing a safe internal audit and compliance system.
7   Implementing a well-designed system of Governance.

The process of lending and standards of Governance with an increasing utility of artificial intelligence and machine learning is the need of the hour. It is also suggested that the industrial houses can examine the possibility of taking over the public sector banks up to 26% of stakeholdership. Banking reforms are essential for India to incorporate itself and the Global Financial

System. The target of its US$5 trillion economies is possible only when the integration of Indian banking with Global Banking is faultless and boundaryless.

Litigation and Cross-Border Mergers and Acquisitions

Flipkart International and Flipkart Company were represented by senior advocate Shri Harish Salve, who argued in the Supreme Court of India, and the Supreme Court of India was convinced and stayed the probe order which was issued by NCLAT New Delhi against the order of CCI, the Competition Commission of India. The initial order by the CCI was in November 2018 and after two years the stay order was obtained. The main issue here is the competition and market dominance of the e-commerce platform. It was argued by the legal counsel that the decision of the CC I was correct and it was frivolous on the part of NCLAT, to unnecessarily prolong the litigation. Linking income tax issues with the competition issue is a matter of no application of mind, as was argued by the legal counsel for Flipkart.

Due Diligence and Emerging Technology

Virtual data rooms and video conferencing through electronic meetings are emerging as a new tool for conducting due diligence. CBMA buyers need to ensure care and caution for the effective use of the same for business continuity plans and crisis management procedures. Supply chain risk is a reality that makes the players in the CBMA environment to be wary of the costs associated with and utilising alternate sources of supply. Due diligence also demands cognizance of the differentiated impact of the COVID-19 pandemic on various parts of the globe both geographically and functionally in terms of suppliers, vendors, customers. In accountancy, accounts receivable and accounts payable are to be differentiated. The financial services industry as a special case needs special attention in terms of focus on regulatory authorities and the new policies that may crop up in the areas of data privacy and licensing implications that will arise due to the compulsion of remote working and working from home measures and quarantine requirements.

Legal Implications and Labour Law

The legal implications here include the healthcare needs of the employees in the affected countries or the affected plants of the organisation within the same country coupled with the lockdown policies of the local/state/federal governments. Compliance with the ever-increasing health guidelines from the global bodies to the local bodies and the possible impact of total isolation and closure of ports and airports may cause both physical and psychological impact on the highly mobile and the migrant workforce. The places of stay of the migrant workforce themselves may cause the outbreak of the Pandemic. The migrant labourers of Singapore are a case in point. Privacy laws and personal freedom, being very different in different parts of the globe may cause problems for those employees of one country working in another country. Issues of Insolvency and working capital management of many high yield to debt organisations (Y2B) are of great concern. Contract law obligations including exercising force majeure or similar provisions and the compelling obligations under material contracts assume importance during the COVID-19 pandemic crisis. There is a cascading impact of a single failure in the supply chain throughout the length and breadth of the supply chain.

Impact, Short- and Long-Term of COVID-19 Pandemic on the CBMA

The COVID-19 pandemic being a crisis will cause tailspins of the prices and a vexatious purchaser may try to exploit the crisis in demanding the so-called favourable price and thus compelling the seller to be a distressed seller. An exploitative seller can also attempt to take advantage of increasing the price by citing the COVID-19 pandemic crisis, thus creating problems for the buyers. Since the CBMA negotiations are entirely private at the level of the agreement, unless the price negotiations affect the competition law, antitrust law or any other regulatory directives of either Securities and Exchange Commission (SEC) of the USA or the SEBI of India, the goodwill and the long-term relationship between the buyer and the seller assume major importance.

Legal Implications of Failed Negotiations on Price Front

The quarantined humans and the locked-down system are pitted against a flexible system to take care of the risk in this COVID-19 pandemic environment. However, the tendency towards post-closing purchase price adjustment mechanisms may create unwarranted legal tangles creating further time and price overruns, ultimately bringing problems to the CBMA process. The possibility of the litigation being caused by the affected interests of either the seller or buyer, given the fact of the highly transparent nature of the COVID-19 pandemic information being made available on all global platforms is real, because the sellers may resist the deferred post-closing pricing system of the buyers, while the buyers insist on the same.

Revenue and Solvency Issues

The COVID-19 pandemic in its widespread impact may seriously damage the revenue and solvency of businesses at their various stages. Maintaining adequate cash ratios and the ability of buyers in having acquisition financing are likely to be affected. Credit risk of the counterparties in any negotiation should undergo the process of due diligence on the financial viability of the purchasers and examination of the probability of the use of Special Purpose Vehicles (SPV) like the ESCROW arrangements, guarantees with the parent company, and adequate guaranteed termination fee to face the probable failure of the buyer in respecting the payment obligations under acquisition agreements. A careful review of all financing documents and risk agreements including letters of credit are important steps in the right direction. Material Adverse Change (MAC) needs to be taken care of by both the buyer and the seller in the CBMA environment since the COVID-19 pandemic risk is very well publicised and is known to all stakeholders. Buyers in their wisdom must be aware of strong resistance by the sellers to the MAC clause.

Date-line Compliance

The COVID-19 pandemic compelled many regulators to work from home. Inaccessibility to vital documents is a reality and full compliance to agreed-upon dates during the COVID-19 pandemic may be a far-fetched idea. While most of the CBMA agreements mention the drop-dead date or outside date or long stop date, which in turn facilitates the closing of the agreement due to the failure of such a date, COVID-19 pandemic created a changed work environment demand flexibility.

Since the pandemic effect is neither static nor anticipatable, the flexibility of all stakeholders in the interest of the CBMA will be a welcome measure. Interim conducting of the business before the date of takeover also needs to be planned and nothing shall be left to assumptions or goodwill. The COVID-19 pandemic impact is a reality and it may affect the buyer, the seller, and the regulator. Representations and warranties also play an important role in terms of emergency protocols. The contingency planning business continuity process also assumes a critical role in the COVID-19 pandemic environment. Choosing the governing law and mentioning the same in most certain and unambiguous terms is of greater importance during the COVID-19 pandemic times than otherwise. The interpretation of the contractual clauses in different countries is so diversionary that both the seller and the buyer will try to take maximum advantage of the process. It is better if the buyer, the seller and the consultants recognise the fact that no single law is entirely seller-friendly or buyer-friendly in the context of the contractual issues arising from the COVID-19 pandemic.

Legal Position of Merger Law and the Changes in the USA

The Federal Trade Commission (FTC) and the Antitrust Division of the Department of Justice (DOJ) of the USA are the two institutions that control the merger in the USA, both local federal and cross-border. One of these two agencies under an inter-agency clearance agreement will be initiating a formal inquiry and investigation into any proposed particular merger. Many regulators including the Security Exchanges Commission (SEC) also exercise jurisdiction subjected to the overall control of the FTC or the DOJ. The jurisdiction can be exclusive, primary or concurrent. Section 7 of the Clayton Act and also section 1 of the Sherman Act coupled with section 2 of the Sherman Act and section 5 of the FTC Act are all relevant provisions in this connection. For instance, section 5 of the FTC Act prohibits monopoly and unfair methods of competition. Section 7A of the Clayton Act covers the procedural provision in case of a merger review and is commonly known as Hart-Scott-Rodino (HSR) Act Antitrust Improvements Act. In the CBMA, the USA relies on National Security Law and is controlled by the Committee on Foreign Investment in the US (CFIUS). Sectoral regulators in specific industries like banking, communications transport and utilities also function simultaneously. Public Utility Commission, Insurance Commission and many other regulators also have authority over a specialised sector. The public interest is the primary notion of legislative jurisdiction and functional authority.

Regulatory Law in the USA

The word "control" has been clearly defined in the HSR Act for fair play, justice, prevention of monopoly and protection of competitive spirit. The acquisition of even a small non-controlling stake can attract HSR notification. Similar is the case of joint ventures. The three jurisdictional tests, essential for the procedural reach of premerger notification obligations, are the Commerce Test, the Size-of-Transaction Test and the Size-of-Persons Test. The foreign-to-foreign transactions need HSR notification if the target happens to own substantial assets in the United States. The HSR Act is clear in the binding of the transaction waiting period and any act either by the buyer or the seller to exercise control over the target before the transaction being closed is illegal and such violations may incur huge civil penalties and also may invite the wrath of the law in unwinding the entire transaction. To assess the correctness of the merger, the USA adopts "substantially to lessen competition test" following the provision of section 7 of the Clayton Act. Vertical Mergers happen to be of more importance in the United States because of the efficiency considerations. Safe harbour provisions also are impactful on the horizontal merger guidelines.

Competition considerations are the main hallmark of substantive tests in the United States. Issues such as effects on labour wages and industrial policy which are essentially unrelated to competitive matters are not taken cognizance of in the USA insofar as the CBMA is concerned. The HSR process in the United States is essentially an endorsement process and not approval.

Pandemic COVID-19 and Lessons

Stephen Roach of the Project syndicate feels that extraordinary damage was done due to the COVID-19 pandemic-inspired lockdown, and with a new second and a more forensic wave of quantum coronavirus being at hand, there is a possible repetition of the 1918–1920 influenza outbreak. Stephen Roach feels that while COVID-19 vaccine may be effective to the pandemic, it does not provide immunity against the lasting economic damage. He feels, "recent research on the impact of 19 major pandemics dating back to 14th century – each with death counts above a hundred thousand – highlights the long shadow of the economic carnage." Real rates of return on the safe European assets – a measure of the interplay between aggregate supply and demand – were found to be depressed for several decades following these earlier horror flick outbreaks. The confluence of the pandemic cycle and the business cycle – the second wave of the COVID-19 pandemic and a double-dip in the US economy – has left the US policymakers with little choice but to approve of the relief package, this time for US$ 900 billion.

Attempts to Amend the Merger Law in the USA

The proposal for Standard Merger and Acquisition Reviews Through Equal Rules (SMARTER) is pending before the Congress of the USA and the aim of this act is to remove the authority of the FTC in using administrative proceedings to challenge the merger under the Clayton Act. Similarly, the Merger Enforcement Improvement Act also proposes to impose post-settlement data reporting requirements and would adjust merger notifications. The Consolidation Prevention and Competition Promotion Act aims to lower the substantial test of illegality under section 7 and also would like to shift the burden of proof on the government to the private parties in larger transactions and would also like to impose post-settlement reporting requirements and other substantial reforms. The Food and Agribusiness Merger Moratorium and Antitrust Review Act propose to place a moratorium on large agribusiness, food, and beverage manufacturing which includes grocery retail mergers till conferencing legislation is on the table.

Work from Home and Quarantine Care and COVID-19 Pandemic

Work from Home and Quarantine Care are the two strategies adopted by different state administrations as well as the federal administration in the USA. Increasingly adopting digital services and platforms through videoconferences and database management is the order of the day in the COVID-19 pandemic time. Antitrust enforcement needs improvement in general and during the COVID-19 pandemic times and shortly too, the digital platforms and the digital services in the CBMA environment require necessary legal response from the lawmakers. They reject consensus, however, that the dynamic nature of the digital markets and their mergers may not require any more supervision than already in vogue. Senator Elizabeth Warren from Boston, previously a candidate for the Democratic presidential nomination, proposed a law that those companies having more than the US$ 25 billion as revenue and offering a public online marketplace exchange platform connecting third parties should be designated as platform utilities and such companies must be prohibited from acquiring others utilising their platforms. She also proposed that appointing regulators is necessary to enforce the Antitrust Law. Senator Elizabeth Warren mentioned the examples of acquisition of Whole Foods and Zappos and WhatsApp, Instagram by Facebook and Wage, Nest, and Double-Click by Google. The evidence available so far points out that FTC and the DOJ protect innovation by keeping close supervision on the CBMA. The proposed merger between Applied Materials and Tokyo Electron Ltd in the year 2015 was void and null due to the scrutinising functioning of FTC and DOJ.

Global Economic Distress and COVID-19 Pandemic

Merger controls during a time of economic crisis arising out of the COVID-19 pandemic cannot be uniform throughout the world. Pandemic COVID-19 pandemic also created economic distress which can be measured in the last week of May 2020 in the USA with almost a hundred thousand deaths and more than 6 million filings for unemployment subsidy. The economic distress is uneven with its maximum intensity being laid on the following segments: (1) Travel. (2) Tourism and (3) Hospitality industry Politicisation of merger control through mechanisms of protectionism and the lobbying by the local pressure groups across countries like Italy, Spain, Germany and England in Europe and also the USA are chronic. The exploitative predatory deals with any conglomerate or syndicate are unlikely to succeed because of the stringent policies of the government in all the above-mentioned countries. The indirect strategic route of taking over a failing firm by any company, posturing as a weakened competitor defence may not work. The merging parties must be able to prove that despite the COVID-19 pandemic-induced economic slump, potential buyers and their financiers do exist and such potential buyers and financiers are financially viable. Post-COVID-19 pandemic crisis, protectionism is likely to be adopted as a survival strategy by many companies as well as governments whose main focus will be on a quick economic recovery aided by local strong industries, and export promotion may be either unreliable or untrustworthy. While welcoming the foreign direct investment in terms of capital movement within the country, no country worth its name is going to allow the flight of capital especially the foreign currency reserves outside its borders.

Business during COVID Era

When going gets tough, the tough get going. The *Business Line* on November 27, 2020 reported that an analysis of 3827 listed companies shows a strong sequential improvement of 37% in the turnover and up to 470% of net profits mainly because of the resumption of operations post the lockdown of the COVID-19 pandemic. The net profit saw an improvement of 31% from year to year till date. The CRB INDEX by Thomson

Reuters which is an indicator of core commodity prices dropped over 15%. Discounted termed as a major contributor on the saving front in terms of the input costs. There is a 13% reduction in the raw material powder and fuel costs the employee costs also saw a drop of 7% and the employee-related costs draw saw a drop of 2%. The savings were occurring mainly due to work from home, pay cuts, and furloughs, companies are also adopting other schemes to bring down the employee costs. Many companies which include the public sector undertakings like the SAIL, the Steel Authority of India Limited, are also living up to the expectations in being innovative to save the employee costs and thus to reduce the operational costs overall. Approximately 72,000 employees will be able to opt for lower working hours, in return for proportionate foregoing of their salary benefits.

It was also observed that FMCG and telecom companies recorded savings to the tune of around 7 and 3% respectively in advertisement costs. The *Business Line* further reports that while operating profits improved, net profits were not very impressive even though from a 7.5% drop in interest costs. With an emphasis on receivable collections coupled with strict working capital measures, there has been a significant reduction in debt for many companies. Much of the debt reduction came from stress and sector such as infrastructure, metals and mining, oil refineries, and telecom. The rating agency Credit Suisse classified Corporations as stressed companies if they either incurred losses in the last couple of quarters or their interest coverage ratio was lower than 1. Keerthy of the *Business Line* comments that the combination of lower input costs, cost reduction, rationalisation measures and declines in interest and tax outgo help the Indian incorporations managed 39% year-on-year net profit growth for the quarter ending September 2020.

Innovations in Administration

The Law Committee of the Goods and Services Tax Council developed a two-pronged strategy to curb fake invoices. They are respectively, (1) Aadhaar linkage for fresh GST registrations and (2) Business Intelligence Fraud Analytics (BIFA). The criteria here is the no filing of the returns for six months. The Law committee further suggested that a fresh registrant should opt for compulsorily physical verification and personal identification in case of an option for non-Aadhaar authentication. In the absence of adequate financial capability reflecting income tax return, the applicant must submit two recommendation letters from two taxpayers of adequate reliability.

There are conditions even for the non-trustworthy applicants which are more stringent otherwise. The sequential filing of returns and statements is made compulsory from the starting of the new financial year. The system-enabled input tax credit flow includes (1) E-invoice, (2) The auto-populated input tax credit, (3) Auto-failed ITC in return. The purpose of business intelligence and fraud analytics is the design of a tool for the identification of riskier traders based on criteria such as non-filing of returns for the six months. The Law committee further proposed that no income tax credential will be given if 99% taxes parade through ITC.

COVID-19 Pandemic and Govt. of India's Response

The effect of COVID-19 pandemic covered all aspects of governance which include economic and financial management by the Government of India, among others, even the private sector dealing with commerce and economics also had to pay a heavy price in terms of failed commitments, non-delivery of raw materials, breaking of commitments by the vendors, and evaporation of orders from the market. No consultancy expert can offer any solution to this unprecedented global event. On November 2, 2020, the Government of India announced a programme of self-reliance, 3.0 (Atmanirbhar). The salient features of this program are to empower the consumers and to revive the economy by the DBT (Direct Benefit Transfer) scheme. Rs 500 was transferred to 200,000,000 women. The revival of the economy is seen through the figures measured by independent observers which include the stock market indexes. Mr S. Adikesavan, the Chief Executive of one of the top leading public sector banks in India, feels, "from the depths of the lockdown induced contraction, high-frequency indicators point to a lift off. It is reasonable to state that the government's infusion of cash into rural India from the FIRST TWO packages has hit the mark" by transferring 5 KG rice and 1 KG of pulses per person per month to around 800,000,000 beneficiaries under the Prime Minister's special programme for the poor,, the Government has largely ensured adequate food, cash in hand and stimulated rural demand and supported the farmers. In addition, the Government provided guarantees for credit dispersal to all major sectors like MSME, agricultural infrastructure, street vendors, NBFCs, and gave liberal terms of repayment.

> The quick response of the Government of India towards the demands of the industry with a communication channel including the feedback from the operational fronts generate optimism for the continuation and effectiveness of the policy in reviving the Indian economy despite the threats from the Covid-19 Pandemic.

Opportunistic and Predatory Takeovers

Executive Vice-President, European Commission, Margrethe Vestager, in a statement to the Financial Times (FT) appeared to influence the European Union countries to resist Chinese takeovers which include defensive stakes in the European business that are struggling to survive because of the COVID-19 pandemic and hence becoming vulnerable for acquisition. The USA has the formidable, initiation called the Committee on Foreign

Investment in the United States (CFIUS) which works against any Chinese predatory strategy. It is very clear even before the outbreak of the COVID-19 pandemic, CFIUS has been at the forefront in preventing merger control from being used as a tool for geopolitical positioning in the soft power games China and its allies were playing and continue to play.

Effects of Timelines and Antitrust Review Mechanism by the State:

COVID-19 pandemic impacted the following three events: (1) The suspension of proceedings of the merger process. (2) The non-application of proceedings in accelerated form. (3) Strict guidelines from the State Merger Control Authorities like the FTC or DOJ not to file new matters.

The above three measures were caused by the inability of the authority to collect sufficient responses from market participants within the tight framework of the timelines coupled with the problem of the foreign-trained staff who were compulsorily working from remote areas. The courts too became dysfunctional. The FTC–DOJ combine is already keen to emphasise that the scrutiny of anticompetitive transactions will not be relaxed. COVID-19 pandemic may increase the distressing sales in traditional retail, consumer brands, travel which include airline hotels and travel agencies, smaller oil and gas players, automation parts, and small insurers. In the year 1930, the US Supreme Court in the famous case of International Sue recognised the doctrine of a failing firm but such arguments are only accepted in exceptional circumstances. Previous responses due to different crises like for instance the financial crisis in the year 2008 can also work as a guideline in anticipating the responses of the state authorities. Thus, it is unlikely that distressed companies can invoke the failing firm doctrine. The European Commission in the context of the financial crisis of the first decade of the new century submitted the doctrine of the lenient failing firm should be rejected in crisis time. The former Assistant Attorney General, USA, Shapiro in a 2009 speech affirmed that overreaction is not welcome during times of economic downturn as otherwise, such overreaction may ultimately hurt the consumer. The famous statement by Shapiro that recessions are temporary but mergers are forever is a very relevant guideline here.

T-Mobile Sprint Case

Introduction[3]

T-Mobile USA was to be taken over by AT&T on March 20, 2011. On August 31, 2011, the Antitrust Division of the United States Department of Justice formally announced that it would seek to block the takeover, and filed a lawsuit to such effect in federal court.[4&5] The bid was abandoned by AT&T on December 19, 2011.

The Verdict of DOC, the USA

United States v. AT&T, T-Mobile, and Deutsche Telekom is a lawsuit brought by the US Antitrust Division of the Department of Justice (DOJ) seeking to block the merger of AT&T Mobility and T-Mobile USA.

Had the purchase been completed, AT&T would have had a customer base of approximately 130 million users, making AT&T the largest wireless carrier in the United States. Regulators questioned the effects such a deal would have on both competitors and consumers, with critics stating the deal would likely increase prices for customers; interest group Public Knowledge stated the merger would cause "higher prices, fewer choices, [and] less innovation."[6] R. Stpehenson, CEO, AT&T, felt that it was a win-win situation in that a better network quality and increase in savings would ensure for AT&T. The Public Relation Officer of AT&T informed about homework and some sales of assets to get regulator's nod.

Plaintiff states claim that the effect of the proposed merger would substantially lessen competition in the market for retail mobile wireless telecommunication services in violation of section 7 of the Clayton Act, qualified at 15 U.S.C0 Section 18. Defendants countered that the proposed merger would be increasing competition in the market at that plaintiff states have thus failed to state a claim for relief. The Court heard both the parties on January 15, 2020, and made the following interesting observations which are worth quotations insubstantial." Adjudication of antitrust disputes virtually returns the judge into a fortune teller. Deciding on such cases typically calls for a judicial reading of the future. In particular, it asks the court to protect whether the business arrangement or conduct at the issue may substantially lessen competition in a given geographical and product market, thus likely to cause price increase and harm consumers. To aid the courts perform that multifunction demands a massive enterprise, in most cases, the litigation consumes years at costs running into millions of dollars. Skilled attorneys charge huge numbers, costing billions of dollars to retain, to win a legal suit of any enterprise. In turn, the lawyers enlist the services of other professionals—ingenious economists, business executives, academics— all brought into the dispute to render expert opinions regarding the potential pro-competitive or anticompetitive effects of the transaction. Qualification of a specialist can sometimes be intimidating. Those authoritative views of the witnesses stated understand under both in "can leave the layperson wondering whether word so expertly corrupted and credentialed can admit room for error or even doubts. Together, Counsel and experts as documentary and testimonial records for a trial that can occupy the ante storage room capacity. Perhaps most remarkable about antitrust litigation is the blurry product that not infrequently emerges from the huge expenditure and correspondingly exhaustive efforts. Arguments by litigants show the path towards judgement. Justice Robert Jackson once remarked that a century and a half of partisan debate and scholarly speculation yields no net result but only supplies more or less apt quotations from respected sources on each side of any question. (Judgement of the above case is available on the internet.)

Conclusions of Law

The law prohibits a merger if its effect may be substantially to lessen competition in any line of commerce in any part of the country. This point was proved in the following case United States versus Philadelphia National bank 374 U.S. 3 21, 355(1963). This prohibition requires a finding of a reasonable probability of substantial impalement of competition, rather than a mere probability as proved in the case of the United States versus Moraine Banco Corporation incorporation, 418 U.S.602, 6 22 -23-(1974). Courts must get the likelihood of anticompetitive effects in the context of the structure, history, and probable future of the particular markets that the merger will affect. The case law being, the United States versus Gen Dynamics Corporation, 415 U.S. 486, 498–1974.

FTC and COVID-19 Pandemic

The FTC warned in a recent press release that it will not, as a consequence of the current pandemic, loosen in its usual rigorous approach to ferreting out the anti-competitive form and seeking appropriate relief, even in the face of uncertainty. Across the world, governments are aware of the concerns flowing from the COVID-19 pandemic about predatory acquisitions of strategic assets by foreign powers. Spain suspended plans to liberalise the economy and foreign investment plans. Germany also came up with stricter foreign investment rules. Akin to the CFIUS kind of arrangement, Australia through its Foreign Investment Review Board (FIRB) announced that all foreign bids for an indefinite period will be scrutinised. The COVID-19 pandemic impact on mergers and acquisitions in the international arena is likely to remain at least as much as the similar impact of the financial crisis of 2008–2009 even after a decade.

Employee Attrition and Precautions in the CBMA Environment due to COVID-19 Pandemic

The American Law demands that the medical information of the employees be kept confidential clearly and separately from the employee's files when a merger takes place during COVID-19 pandemic time. It is likely that the medical information and the confidentiality attached to it also need to follow the same rules. The remote working permissions given by the employers should enable the employees to take information security compliance obligations and the best practices into confidence and constantly evaluate any changes to the information of the company's security posture. The risks that result from such quarantined work from the home environment in the light of the COVID-19 pandemic are real. Apart from the federal law which generally issues the guidelines, there is a need to follow the state law which may declare certain area-specific rules on the employers concerning the collection of data concerning the Pandemic. The question of border postings and travel restrictions apart from the visa regulations for the hired workers is a reality. During this current COVID-19 pandemic time, the US Citizenship and Immigration Services banned all personal interviews and biometric appointments in the USA. The processing of the Green Card cases from abroad was also banned by the President of the United States and the Department of State also suspended the routine visa services at all US Consulates abroad. There are special compliance implications to all the employers in matters related to work-from-home policies, workplace office closures, work stoppages and also similar effects of the disrupted and distressed business activity.

Post-COVID-19 Pandemic Strategies in the CBMA

No crisis leaves the world in the status quo. The COVID-19 pandemic is no exception, and in fact, it may exacerbate the status quo to such an extent that a new CBMA world order may emerge. Stressed assets of distressed companies may be leveraged about being kept in a coma. Secondly, cash/rich companies may look for opportunities for acquisitions of a win-win combination. Government intervention through amendment of business Law in either discouraging or banning the takeovers by hostile foreign companies is a reality as self-interest is the best interest in international diplomacy, political or economic. CBMA will not be the same post-COVID-19 pandemic. Four factors matter in the post-CBMA effort. They are firstly Due Diligence, secondly Proper Legal Documentation, thirdly Unbiased Realistic Business Evaluation, and fourthly Probable Projection of Post-Merger Business Structure and Supply Chain Management.

Proper Due Diligence

Cash is important and cash flow more than anything else plays the chief priority factor. The contractual obligations during the pre-COVID-19 pandemic time of the acquired entity need to be carefully scrutinised. Cybersecurity and risk assessment coupled with insurance issues and key employee details are important. Employee compensation due to either health or termination by the target company also plays an important role. The pre-COVID-19 pandemic EBITDA (Earnings Before Interest and Taxes Depreciation and Amortisation) estimates too are vital. Lastly, Cross-Functional Effective Assessment Team must realistically estimate the recovery time for graduating into normalcy from the impact of the COVID-19 pandemic in conducting the business for the post-merger entity. The post-merger entity also needs to factor in the new style of work from home and also the virtual meeting systems in place of the physical meeting systems.

Evaluation of Business Worth in the Post-COVID-19 Pandemic

Contractual law provisions need to be paid maximum attention concerning revenue assessment-projections during the post-COVID-19 pandemic. Debt obligations coupled with the specific costs and settlement obligations play an important role in the very survival of the post-merger entity. While the uncertainty of the economic viability and the risk associated with the probabilistic model vulnerability is real, fear cannot replace wisdom. Pre-COVID-19 pandemic benchmarks, hence, need to be replaced by industry/business-specific benchmarks that need to be arrived at by cross-functional teams and constantly looked into for their improvement towards the achievement of better efficiency in a sustainable manner.

Post-COVID-19 Pandemic Regulatory Aspects by Government and Autonomous Agencies

Tax is levied by the Government. The tax compliance is by different sub/units of any industry to different transaction structures needs specific time-bound compliance, failure of which will involve penal sanctions. Frivolous litigation may be assuming the role of a big threat especially so if there is a likelihood of spurious and notorious exploitative claims under the pretext of being victims of the COVID-19 pandemic by the vested interests. Measures like the cashless form of transactions through shares swaps, provision of tax waivers, benefits, concessions and thus reducing tax liability, and ultimately linking the cash payment to an escrow and holdback module are likely to be effective strategies.

Compliance to Legal Provisions and Documentation

Procurement of deals, specific warranties, and claims coupled with representations need to be part of the legal documentation. Secondly, material adverse impact events also need to be factored in to face the possible challengers to the above process in the courts of Law, and an inbuilt flexible timeline must be made at the initial stage itself. Specific information rights till the time the deal is closed can ill afford to be forgotten. Indemnity and risk mitigation also need to be factored in.

IBC, CBMA, COVID-19 Pandemic, India and the USA

Without credit from any bank, no industry can maintain its working capital or manage its top-line and bottom-line concerning its vendors, its customers and also its other stakeholders. The banks can be either from the public sector, owned by the Government, or from the private sector. The Reserve

Bank of India (RBI) controls the activities of the banking and regulates the interbank loan rates as well as Capital Adequacy Ratio (CAR). It also monitors the movement of capital and fixes the quarterly interest rate interest rates which are called the Prime Lending Rates (PLR) against which the inflation and the intra-banking rate and the availability of the capital to both large-scale, small-scale, and medium scale industries are made available. When an organisation fails to pay back its dues to its creditors or lenders, the question of filing for bankruptcy because of it being insolvent is allowed by the Law across the world.

The Insolvency and Bankruptcy Code (IBC), 2016 in India came into existence on August 5, 2016. Its purpose was to renovate the outdated and repair the complex corporate insolvency laws that were existing in India. The IBC 2016 was an important step in the direction of achieving desirable ease of doing business index so that the advantage of India as a favourable destination for the foreign capital is established and it is in the interest of all government and private industries in India. The COVID-19 pandemic complicated the execution of IBC processes, and the Government of India postponed the strict implementation of certain provisions of financial laws during the pandemic tenure.

Insolvency and Bankruptcy Code and Its Effectiveness

Since its inception, especially during the COVID-19 pandemic time, the World Bank customarily analysed around 200 countries in apportioning the ranks on the aspect of ease of doing business every year. The lost examination was done on October 24, 2019, which saw India improving its rank by 14 spots and attaining the rank of 63 on the list. India also earned a place among the 10 best improvers. In terms of resolving insolvency, India improved from 108 in the previous year to 52 in the current year, largely due to the Insolvency and Bankruptcy Code (IBC). Resolving insolvency is a measure of convenience with which one can exit from the business. In any strategy of starting a business sustaining it and expanding it or closing it involves the twin issues of exit and entry barriers. Insolvency and bankruptcy code largely caters to the issues of exiting from the business.

The purpose of IBC 2016 is to empower the companies with effective tools to remain financially viable and without any contradiction, to make the creditors empowered enough to negotiate for the recovery of their legitimate money. IBC, in a way, is thus a win-win situation. The World Bank appreciated the recovery rate for the creditors having a jump from 26.5 cents on the dollar to 71.6 cents on the dollar while reducing the time taken for such recovery from 4.3 years to 1.6 years.

According to the former chairperson of the IBC MrM.S. Sahoo, the World Bank did not mention the remarkable achievements of the IBC which has revived around 200 companies from deep distress, altered the debtor-creditor relationship, made the default are accountable, enabled the businessmen is a respectable exit route before being suckered into deep distress.

Resolving Insolvency

The literature of the World Bank informs us about indicators regarding the issue of resolving insolvency. They are, firstly, the strength of the insolvency framework and, secondly, the recovery rate. The literature further corroborates that the strength of the insolvency framework is a cumulative output of four interrelated aspects, namely:

1   Commencement of proceedings,
2   Assets of the form of the management,
3   Reorganisation Proceedings,
4   Participation of the Creditors.

The insolvency framework enabled the direct liquidation of the Corporate Debtor (CD). An amendment to the IBC in August 2019 clarified that the committee of creditors may decide to liquidate the corporate debtor at any time during the Corporate Insolvency Resolution Process (CIRP). The Supreme Court reiterated in November 2019 that it is further COC to decide as to whether to rehabilitate or liquidate the corporate debtor. With regard to the management of the assets of the form, the IBC encourages operations of the corporate debtor during the corporate insolvency resolution process there was an amendment in December 2019 to the IBC which mandates that any license, permit, registration, quota, concession, clearance given either by the Union Government or State Government or a local authority or regulator or any other competent authority under the law given to the corporate debtor shall not be suspended or terminated on the grounds of insolvency.

Once the resolution plan has been approved by the competent authority it becomes binding on the Central Government and all other similar authorities. The amendment of August 2019 is a step in the right direction in that a resolution plan may provide further restructuring of the corporate debtor through the corporate mergers acquisitions amalgamation and the demergers.

The second aspect is the recovery rate, and as per the World Bank's process, it is a function of time, cost and also the result of the entire proceedings of the insolvency. With the amendment in December 2019, the outcome of the recovery rate by means of releasing the corporate debtor from the liability arising from an offense committed under the erstwhile management prior to the commencement of the corporate insolvency resolution process is a right step in the right direction. The certainty of the process and predictability of the outcomes are two important issues. The binding of the time limit 330 days of the Corporate Insolvency Resolution Process (CIRP) through the amendment of the IBC in August 2019 which includes the time spent on litigation is also a welcome step. There is also an initiative by launching the graduate insolvency program in the headquarters of the IBC process in July 2019 several value-added features have been added to the insolvency process which includes cross-border insolvency, group insolvency, individual insolvency, valuation profession, the market for distressed assets, automation of loan contracts, resolving ability of the companies. There is a lot of scope for improvement in the performance with respect to resolving insolvency in India. The COVID-19 pandemic period also underwent significant adjustments to offer relief to stakeholders.

Banks, Non-Performing Assets, Insolvency and Bankruptcy Code

There has been a relentless increase in the Non-Performing Assets (NPAs) of the banks due to various reasons which among others include loan frauds and corruption apart from the general economic slowdown and the risk-reward issues. NPAs corrode the bank's performance and factually include the health of the banking system in terms of its creditworthiness and operational ability. While wilful default due to fraudulent reasons and the slow-moving law missionary is a probable and possible cause, misgovernance and malgovernance with in the banking processes has been a major factor which has been highlighted by many committees appointed to look into this aspect by various governments in India some of the measures that were taken in the post-1991 liberalisation era include the following:

1 Asset Reconstruction Companies,
2 Corporate Debt Restructuring,
3 Strategic Debt Restructuring,
4 Scheme for Sustainable Structuring of Stressed Assets and
5 Legal Reforms.

Debt Recovery Tribunals (DRTs) were established to speed up the resolution of the NPAs. SARFAESI (Securitisation and Reconstruction of Financial Assets and Enforcement of Security Interest Act 2002) was passed for the prevention of money laundering and also enforcement of the finances of the country. Rearrangement of the NPAs needs a synchronised approach and activity of the Reserve Bank of India, the concerned public sector bank, the regulators like the SEBI, and the Ministry of Corporate Affairs. As per section 6 of the IBC, CIRP was supposed to take care of the corporate defaults in payment and to secure the interests of the financial creditor, operational creditor and the corporate debtor also. In June 2017, the RBI issued an order for the immediate recovery of stressed assets for 12 of the largest defaulters of the RBI. Rs 35,200 crores, which was paid by Tata steel in buying Bhushan steel became the first successful story even though with a loss of around 35%. This author never understood why the term haircut is used here. Haircuts are hygienic and this haircut is an acknowledgment of improper management of the accountability in the first place. The success story, however, is that the gross NPAs of the scheduled commercial banks which stood at Rs 10,36,187 crores on March 31 2018 a declined by Rs 97,996 crores. This reduction of almost a hundred thousand crores of rupees is subtly credited to the efficient and time-bound CIRP.

Even though IBC has been effective, yet some challenges remain. Delay is the main challenge in litigation coupled with the failure of timeline adherence is the second challenge. In the last week of October 2020, the Supreme Court of India transferred to itself many insolvency cases from different high courts. Madam Finance Minister of India Nirmala Sitharaman also issued an ordinance in September 2020 suspending the functioning of section 6 of the IBC because of the peculiar COVID-19 pandemic situation in the country. Kindly see the appendix for this ordinance.

The third challenge remains the implementation of the Sunil Mehta Committee report. This committee classified the net NPAs into three types and requested a differential and differentiated treatment to each sectorial non-performing asset rather than having a similar treatment to all different asset classes.

Timely amendments to IBC overcame the so-called moral dilemma in preventing the fraudulent bidding by the original defaulting promoters. Banks at one point in time were astounded when there was an offer by the defaulters for the creditors to pay back and to withdraw the insolvency proceedings. Recently, a real estate tycoon jailed in Mumbai also made such a proposal. The Government stepped in and amended the IBC to give primacy to the committee of creditors's decisions which also comprises the financial creditors. This amendment was challenged in the court of law. Shri Balachandran, an expert investment banker, wrote,

> with the legal battles continuing ad infinitum, the yet unresolved case has dragged on for more than two years, much beyond the original 270 daytime frame in which charged in the Code, with the judiciary ignoring the time-bound aspect of the process.

The IBBI (Insolvency and Bankruptcy Board of India) supervises the registration and regulation of insolvency professionals and rules out many rules and regulations elaborating on the code for its proper operation and functioning. Of the 2162 cases admitted till June 2019, 445 have exceeded 270 days. A total of 120 cases saw the approval of the resolution plan and 475 cases are under liquidation.

NPA and IBC

The standard performing asset loan loss provision in India is modestly pegged at 0.4%. IDBI being the worst public sector bank has a gross NPA of 29%. The malaise is not due to a single factor of corruption or fraud but due to multiple factors of misgovernance, unchecked for decades of the period of continued negligence. The recent example of an Indian-origin businessman having spent more than £ 500,000,000 on the wedding of his daughter, also becoming insolvent due to insolvency in England is an example. Prevention is certainly better than cure in the case of NPAs. When a single rogue applicant defrauds many banks, the so-called alarm bells surprise many by the malfunction. The audit and the ombudsman are normally external to many commercial banks. However, fraud has been all-pervading irrespective of the ownership of the bank. We have IDBI and also YES Bank simultaneously.

Post commission of the fraud, the investigation by the CBI, SFIO, ED, and the DRI become a routine process and it's rare that the real culprits are punished. NIRAV MODI CASE is the glaring example in this connection. When the promoter has little interest in the company and when the promoter starts the company only to loot it from within, conniving with bankers, having greased his pockets readily drives in, investigative agencies take an enormous time to unearth and by the time the investigation ends in the charge sheet and the trial process starts, it is not uncommon to see the death of the main accused person due to age and sickness. Thus, it is both IPC and the IBC working together that is a need of the hour. The following suggestions are relevant contextually.

There is a need for learning from the past in nonrepeating it. The board of directors needs to be held accountable and the process of due diligence must never be let up. The following persona connected with the entire process needs to be vigilant and be under vigilance.

1. All the stakeholders
2. Independent board members
3. Credit rating agencies
4. Auditors
5. Bank risk managers
6. Activist shareholders
7. Proxy advisory firms
8. Internal audit teams
9. Rating agencies
10. Independent analysts
11. Informed media
12. Social media commentators
13. The regulators of the government
14. The international regulators
15. The economic press Council

Non-Performing Assets

Unpaid loans are called as Non-Performing Assets (NPAs) in the ledger books of the banks and the common parlance. They are treated as bad loans with a maximum impact on the health of the banking sector for the simple reason that when loans become bad, the capital of the bank which it can lend to the needy applicants become reduced in size as a result of which the cascading effect of the shrunken credit will be reflected in the reduction of employment opportunities, the precision of the economy, problems of payments, violations of contract obligations, and reduced tax income to the government. To put it in one word, the fact of the matter is the more the NPA, the less will be the GDP. Additionally, no well-functioning democratic economy can afford a growing burden of NPA, since, such NPA will remain as a venomous NTL, namely Never Terminable Liability. The IBC 2016 coupled with institutional support from The Insolvency and Bankruptcy Board of India (IBBI) and the new Companies Act 2013 were all the right steps to salvage the drooping image of the economy of India. The Insolvency and Bankruptcy Board of India (IBBI) estimates that the cause of the IBC repayment to the tune of US$ 2.142 billion in loans was paid in the last two years. The main advantage has been in the privately owned businesses in that filing in an insolvency petition will make them lose the control and thus the manifestation of obtaining the loan through fraudulent means has become a criminal offense and resorting to such fraudulent mergers was punished and there are many examples in the history of Indian business for the past two years.

IBC vs Insolvency Proceedings in the USA

Chapter 11 of the US Insolvency Code is vital for dealing with Bankruptcy issues. In a similar vein, the insolvency proceedings include company voluntary agreements administration. Schemes or arrangements are utilised respectively in the USA and UK to give relief to a financially distressed debtor. Liquidation of a financial debtor and auction of the same is not the aim of the IBC of India, while it is different both the USA and UK, on par with the provisions of chapter 11 of US Insolvency Procedures and Voluntary Agreement Scheme (VAS) of the UK company Law.

According to an earlier report of 2018 of the World Bank, India is ranked as 108 out of 189 countries in the insolvency resolution. This was a little improvement from the 136th position in the year 2016. The World Bank found that the insolvency proceedings in India used to take 4.3 years on an average time but the new IBC reduced this resolution as it was clear in the statement of Sri M.S. Sahoo, former Chairperson, IBBI. Instead of selling the industry piecemeal, IBC empowers all the initiations to sell the distressed concern as an ongoing company. On par with the global standards, the IBC intends to achieve the maximisation of the asset value for the benefit of the operational creditors and more so of the financial creditors. This is a move from the debtor in possession to the creditor in question model.

IRPs, (Insolvency Resolution Professionals) are to be appointed by IBBI and are expected to play a major role in the resolution process. Financial creditors, more often than not, happen to be public sector banks. Hence, the IBC through the IBBI and National Company Law Tribunal (NCLT), are expected to reduce the Non-Performing Assets (NPAs). The creditor lead model in the IBC code is fundamentally different from the debtor in possession model under Chapter 11 of the US. The creditor lead approach suits India because of its particular conditions of the public sector banks and the government money is involved. In the US, it is the pension funds and the capital market instruments like the Commercial Paper (CP) or the private investors who are the interested parties.

Timelines and IBC

Timeline deadlines are imposed in procedure but unfortunately, the practice is mired in unwarranted litigation.

The Similarity between IBC and USBC

One similarity exists between the IBC and Chapter 11 of the US which is in the moratorium being automatic and its application to all legal proceedings against the debtor. Initial observations about the nature of the moratorium are getting fine-tuned due to the dictums of the court and clear-cut interpretation is emerging. The IBC moratorium does not extend to guarantees given concerning the debt of the debtor undergoing resolution. These moratorium provisions are yet to evolve to clarity to stand the test of procedural fairness such as the issue of notices and due process as one can witness the same under chapter 15 of the US Bankruptcy Code (USBC).

International Opinion about IBC

The international legal opinion about the IBC insofar as solving the problems associated with Cross-Border Insolvency leaves much to be desired. In contrast to the above lacuna, the US Bankruptcy Code-Chapter 15 adopted the UNCITRAL (United Nations Commission on International Trade Law) Model Law on Cross-Border Insolvency. There is in existence a resolution in October 2018 by India to follow the model Law of the United Nations. The international legal expert opinion also points out one important drawback in the Indian proposal namely that while India is likely to allow for the establishment of concurrent proceedings limited in scope to domestically situated assets on par with the international best benchmarking practices. However, the proposal does not cover procedures to tackle issues in enforcing the judgements of the insolvency-related court/tribunal of foreign origin as per the UNCITRAL Model Law on recognition and enforcement of insolvency-related judgements.

Effect of IBC in India

The recent four-year functional experience of the IBC informs that the IBC ended the dysfunctional relationship between corporate debtors and lenders and once for all destroyed the blackmailing tendency of the fraudulent debtors and their conniving bankers. The statement of the Finance Minister of India, Madam Nirmala Sitharaman, in May 2020 as part of the package for the improvement of the economy due to the COVID-19 pandemic is a case in point. The fear of the public sector banks in the probability of facing a probe by the Central Bureau of Investigation (CBI) was addressed by the Finance Minister.

Mr I. Srinivas, former Secretary to the Ministry of Corporate Affairs (MCA), Government of India (GOI), expressed the following comment on India's performance in insolvency, "Indian Government desires speedy progress and is desirous of having the best bankruptcy lawyers in the world." He further observes that the biggest contribution of the present IBC regime is that the lending and borrowing culture in India is changing and thus there is a culture of mediation between the debtors, the lenders and that nearly 4500 cases have been settled by the mediation compared to 66 reported resolutions the Alternate Dispute Resolution (ADR) settlement process. If such a system becomes abundantly acceptable to all, this will certainly reduce the cost of the State and the IBBI and also achieve timely solutions to long-pending insolvency resolution issues. the then Secretary of Ministry of Corporate Affairs, Government of India felt that the Bankruptcy law must have inbuilt tools of transparency, competition and procedural teeth in order to contribute towards a better rating of Ease of Doing Business Index in India.

Shri Girish Chandra Murmu, Comptroller and Auditor General of India, while delivering the keynote address on the lecture on the occasion of the fourth year of the functioning of the IBBI, that is Insolvency and Bankruptcy Board of India (IBBI), felt that the recent amendment of the suspension of the IBC for a period up to December 25 of 2020 is not a setback for the Economy of India nor the insolvency process. The same period was further extended due to pandemic situation. Due to force majeure conditions, suspension of the IBC is important in order to prevent the dragging of the non-viable firms to insolvency due to the COVID-19 Pandemic. The theme of the lecture by the Comptroller and Auditor General(CAG) was with reference to the adaptability in sustaining the reforms due to the COVID-19 pandemic. The CAG felt that when once the COVID problem becomes passed, the two main issues deserving maximum attention will be, firstly, group insolvency and, secondly, cross-border insolvency. It has also been emphasised to the judicial infrastructure needs further strengthening to deal with the emergence of new problems arising out of the peculiar canned COVID-19 Pandemic situation with reference to the insolvency and bankruptcy matter. It is important to maintain the life of the companies and also preserve the livelihood of the persons in distress. According to CAG, the main objective of the IBC's rescuing the life of the form and not to take it away prematurely.

The threshold limit of default for the initiation of the insolvency process in credit from rupees hundred thousand to Rs one crore. In this process, a relief measure is provided to MSME debtors from being pushed to insolvency due to pandemic-related financial distress. The IBC and the IBBI already led to significant behavioural change among the debtors in the creditors like the main purpose is to avoid the default. There is always an encouragement for the debtor to settle the default with the creditors outside the IBC. With the IBC in place, non-retail part of loan is no more an option and the ownership of the firm is no longer guaranteed to a corrupt bureaucratic nexus of the blessing of an unseen Godfather in corridors of power.

The IBC has incentivised the secured and unsecured creditors irrespective of whether they are from a bank or non-bank financial institutions or whether they are financial and operational creditors or whether their financial domestic creditors because of its inherent provisions. IBC helps to reduce the non-performing assets of the public sector Banks of India. While assessing the performance of the IBC and the IBBI, the CAG felt that the code has also created a quality when a competency ecosystem by creating markets for services of insolvency professionals, infact insolvency professional agencies, registered valuers, registered valuers organisations, insolvency professional entities and information utilities. CIRP saw the admission of around 3900 corporate applications mentioning NPAs of the banks. The CAG further added, "Rescuing the lives of forms being the prime objective of the Code, must not be used to take away their lives prematurely."

Insolvency and Bankruptcy Bureau of India, IBBI, has been functioning to help resolve the process of corporate insolvency resolution. Mr M. S. Sahoo, the former Chairman of IBBI, came out with the re-solvency index in order to communicate the resolvability of a company. Resolvability became an important issue after the Global Financial Crisis, 2008. The Resolvability index is aimed at measuring institutional stability to overcome the challenges of creating insolvency. The capability of any institution to implement efficiency strategies for rescue.

Broadly speaking, the resolvability index indicates a cooperative advantage in terms of access to capital. The resolvability index reflects the living vision of the company to remain afloat and to avoid insolvency. It aims at increasing the competition which in the ultimate analysis is a win-win situation for all the players within the industry. The higher the resolution index, the higher is the probability of the company being free from encumbrances. On the other hand, less value of the resolvability index indicates the problem in terms of personal relations among promoters, disputed titles, complicated structures, contingent contracts, and avoidance transactions.

"Initiation of CIRP means transparency, quick disposal and improved probability of amicable resolution. If initiation is a resisted and the process is protracted, for reasons other than the merit, the value diminishes making resolution difficult."[7]

Banker's View on IBC

Darwin is not confined to plants and animals. Even market animals follow Darwin. When there was no IBC, borrowers were the bosses. The former SBI Chairman Mr Rajnish Kumar feels that, before IBC, Bankers had to chase the money offer disposal of money to the borrower. It was not unusual to hear borrowers tell banks, "The loan is your problem. You have to find the solution, not us."

Mr Rajnish Kumar, further feels that IBC has become a remedy to the lenders in bringing discipline to the borrowers. Mr Rajnish Kumar asserted that "he did not witness a single example of turning down of delicious made by the Creditors Committee."[8]

Section 29A of IBC prohibits the conjoint parties from bidding for assets and need modification to avoid the disease. Non-serious bidders also need to be discouraged and stiff penalties need to be imposed if reason cannot rely on fraudulent non-serious bidders. The Supreme Court of India's decisions in the recent resolution process is the right step in the direction of IBC becoming very effective in the future. The National Company Law Tribunal (NCLT) and the National Company Law Appellate Tribunal, in the views of many practicing advocates, have not been of much help in the Insolvency Resolution Process (IRP).

Origin growth and decay are natural to every organism and they are natural to every organisation. Bankruptcy Code is in aid towards maintaining harmony in these three vital steps and like the new water replacing the old water, the Bankruptcy Code empowers the stakeholders to replace old ricketing, dying organisation with a new dynamic organisation to realise the true economic value of a form rather than to keep a coma patient alive in the so-called opium of optimistic /pseudo-optimistic superstition of future health.

Justice Marshall of the USA is renowned for having said, "Law is what the Judge says it is." The NCLT, (National Company Law Tribunal) and NCLAT (National Company Law Appellate Tribunal) are two bodies, with the legal role to implement the IBC resolution process. The Tribunal is not the Constitutional Court. The NCLT in the Binani cement case opined that the result was unfair, saying small creditors should recover value at par with the banks. There were allegations of interference by NCLT in the resolution plan approved by the lenders. There is a danger of the debt being purchased by a cash-rich inquisitive acquirer abroad and using such a strong arm to destabilise the entire IBC resolution process. This compels corrective steps. The recent directive by the Union Government of India through the Reserve Bank of India directive in prohibiting the hostile takeovers by the Chinese companies of Indian companies is a case in point.[9]

The US Bankruptcy Code, 1978

The US Bankruptcy Code was adopted in the year 1978 and through various judgements both of the bankruptcy courts and the appellate jurisdiction, the US Bankruptcy Code is moving towards perfection.

Prof. Edward R. Morrison, Charles Evans Gerber Prof of Law, Columbia Law School and Co-director, Regimen Centre for Business Law and Public Policy, Columbia University, thinks that 42 years of the US Bankruptcy Code made the five following seminal contributions. They are as follows.

1 Speed,
2 Planning and pre-packs,
3 Merger and acquisition strategy,
4 The debt market and
5 The rarity of bankruptcy.

From a period of 42 months, the typical timeframe for a bankruptcy case got reduced to a mere five months. This is almost a 90% reduction in time nearly 50% of the cases today are pre-packaged. The entire company is an ongoing concern being acquired through the Cross-Border Mergers and Acquisition (CBMA)strategy was a rare event when the US bankruptcy code came to the origin. However today 33% of distressed companies are sold as an ongoing concern which is the right step in the correct direction. The specialised investors in the hedge funds emerged due to the US Bankruptcy Code and their business was doubled from US$ 20 billion to US$ 404 billion. Negotiation outside the periphery of the bankruptcy courts has become a norm and now fewer than 15 bankruptcy filings for every hundred business deaths undergo through this process of US Bankruptcy Code. One interesting contribution filed by the US Bankruptcy Code is that when the bankruptcy decision becomes almost predictable, it encourages the parties to reach a decision outside the bankruptcy system and thus the delay is minimised and the appeal process becomes redundant. Prof Morrison maintains that there is a need to have a sustainable balance in a harmonious relationship between tough rules and amenable administration. The flexibility in the execution averts unwarranted extravagance of both assets as well as time, crafty vexatious cherry-picking of vulture culture, incompetent decision making. It also helps to make more credit available to the borrowers and converting the illiquid distressed debt into a more liquid tradable item. Illiquidity is the enemy of growth. Flexibility also helps the bankruptcy process to maximise the firm value and creditor recoveries.

The US Bankruptcy Law has always been perceived to be a debtor-friendly law. However, until the bankruptcy process is not started, the US legal structure governing debt collection is extremely creditor friendly. Even during the COVID-19 pandemic time, the time taken for residential foreclosures is a mere 18 months in the states of Texas and California.

Comparison of Bankruptcy Regulations between India and the USA

Compared to India, the United States has powerful Bankruptcy Laws which include Contract Laws and secured Lending Laws. In India, civil laws are notorious for the delay. In contrast to the American experience, the IBC has to perform the double effect duty insofar as covering the delay caused by similar law matters is concerned. The pre-packs cases in which the resolution plan is made much before the approach to the Bankruptcy Code is an important revolution in the United States.

In the United States, there is another category called the free-fall category which comprises around 40% of the cases and which involves companies and organisations suffering due to working capital problems, vendor disputes, natural calamities, or failed negotiations. In the USA the promoters/shareholders are thought to be having first-hand knowledge about the operational problems for the ongoing concern and hence are given the first right to start the bankruptcy case and also has the luxury of exclusive right to propose a resolution plan during the first few months of the bankruptcy litigation. There is the provision of "cram down" in the United States to overcome the obstructionist strategy of the resolution plan. There is also a similar move by the IBC infrastructure to obstruct the obstructionists in that the holding of 75% limit of financial depth has been reduced to 68% today.

The recent amendments to the IBC which are on par with the best international benchmark practices gave 30 days for potential buyers to submit their bids. There is a need to maintain an optimal balance between credit friendliness and debit friendliness because both have their advantages and disadvantages. Too much credit friendliness may dampen the growth of the economy by disturbing the risk-reward ratio and drop ownership being compiled to be afraid of a future possible probable distress leading to liquidation rather than facing the distress through a manageable debt-equity strategy.

Post-Bankruptcy and Reconstruction

IBC emerged as a solution to the complex resolution processes that resulted from the simultaneous and sometimes contradictory application of multiple legal provisions of both the Central and the State governments. Notable among them were the Sick Industrial Companies Act (SICA), 1985 and Securitisation and Reconstruction of Financial Assets and Enforcement of Security Interest (SARFAESI) Act, 2002 coupled with RDDBFI Act, 1993. The CBMA under Section 234 of the Companies Act, 2013 also deals with the reconstruction of stressed assets of participating companies in the CBMA process. There are three types of stakeholders in the resolution process, namely,

1 Secured Creditors,
2 Unsecured Creditors and
3 Equity Holders.

The legal provisions both in India and in the United States have a varied emphasis on the above three stakeholders. Chapter 11 of the US Bankruptcy Code deals with equity holders. The equity holders are allowed to have the bonuses because they are supposed to be functioning under high risk and management. In India too, there is no evidence to point out that equity holders and the owner-managers ever went empty-handed or to prison as part of a sentence. Insofar as the secured creditors' case is concerned, the secured creditors have a priority over the other creditors. In the United States, the secured pool consists of the outstanding collaterals and the rest goes to the unsecured poll, while in India, the entire process is in favour of the secured creditors only. Insofar as the unsecured creditors are concerned, in the United States, a part of a reorganisation of a distressed organisation caters to the unsecured creditors, who will become the new operators of the resolve company while in India the operational creditor plays a very subdued role when compared to the financial creditor.

Composition of Creditors Committee and the Law

In the US, there is a legal provision of unsecured creditors committee (UCC), which is comprised of several major unsecured creditors. These are chosen by an empowered body of exports from the DOJ of the USA and under the provision of the office of the United States Trustees. In contrast, in India, there is a Committee of Creditors (CoC) that comprises all the creditors. Since most of the time the banks happened to be the major creditors, the banks send their advisers in the form of IRP, the insolvency resolution professional. In the interest of perfection of IBC for making India as an economic supergiant on par with the USA and to improve its positioning in the rankings of ease of doing business index, it is imperative that the IBC also adopts after customising itself to local conditions and of the well-known efficient systems of USA.

Historical Evolution of Bankruptcy Law in the USA and India in the Context of the CBMA

Insolvency and bankruptcy are not the same. Bankruptcy is a due legal process for getting back the unpaid credit given by the creditors to a person or to an organisation and which is also documented in the contract or the agreement itself. Insolvency connotes failure to repay the credits or the loans or the debts that were taken by any individual or a business organisation. Bankruptcy declaration gives leverage to individuals and organisations in terms of procedural protection from any arbitrary physical taking over of the assets without the judicial pronouncement. The common law principles and the doctrinaire of equity and justice cover both insolvency filing and bankruptcy procedures. Bankruptcy is essential as a provision for business organisations to take care of the risks that inbuilt in the business both from the point of the creditor as well as debtor since the creditor would like to get back the due amount in a quick manner and the debtor would like to have the resolution also done quickly. Normally the bankruptcy procedures have a post-facto effect that the person who filed in an insolvency petition cannot be part of the resolution process and is also disqualified until the business of the same name.

The word bankruptcy has Latin origin and it came into vogue when the creditors broke the bench of the merchant who paid failed to pay his loans to the creditors in Italy. BancoRotta, meaning broken bench came to personify the failed businesses and the action that follows is a response. While the new bankruptcy law area in the United States of America or India does not aim to break any industry the literal form, in effect, however, is that the stressed assets of a bankrupt organisation are not going to be status quoist. The Bankruptcy Law in the US started in the year 1800, and after many amendments, the Bankruptcy Code came into the picture in the year 1978. In the year 2005, there was an amendment, in the name of the Bankruptcy Abuse Prevention and Consumer Protection Act, 2005. The US Bankruptcy

Code allows the filing of the petition under the Bankruptcy Code under chapters 7, 9, 11, 12, 13 and 15 for both corporate send individuals. Chapters 11, 12 and 13 deal with a reorganisation of the assets of the debtors. Chapter 11 is essential for the business in a case of sole ownership, or partnership, or corporation. Chapter 15 is relevant for the study of cross-border insolvency which allows for seamless cooperation among different jurisdictions in which include the courts in the USA and the foreign lands.

Insolvency and Bankruptcy Code in India (IBC) is of 2016 origin. It does not aim to make any differences between the rights of international or national creditors nor does it allow any differences among different classes of financial institutions. The IBC came into existence after repealing Presidency Towns Insolvency Act, 1909, Provincial Insolvency Act, 1920. Various important amendments were made in the following five statutes/laws. They are as follows.

1 Indian Partnership Act, 1932,
2 Companies Act, 2013,
3 SARFAESI Act, 2002,
4 Limited Liability Partnership Act, 2008, and
5 Sick Industrial Companies Repeal Act, 2003.

Thus to conclude, both the Bankruptcy Code of US and the IBC of Indian venture to play an important role in the CBMA, through a fast and clear resolution of the insolvency process to reduce time and cost overruns due to unending litigation and also to solve other problems associated with pending insolvency petitions which include wastage of land resources and huge unemployment problem and an opportunity cost for the entire business chain.

Impact of Current Pandemic Wave-II in India

The Pew Research Centre put the figure of 32 million Indians getting out of the middle class due to pandemic in 2020. The labour participation rate fell to 40% in the financial year 2020–2021. The second wave of COVID-19 pandemic in May, 2021 to June, 2021 taught many lessons to India. Initial COVID attack did not leave its imprint completely erased. The health care costs, the oxygen cylinder crisis, the crisis for hospital beds, ventilators remain critical challenges. While India made remarkable progress in start-ups and unicorns, with a combined business value of US$ 240 billion, India's climate basic index is 16.67 and India is ranked seventh in the top ten most affected countries due to climate change in the year 2019. Other challenges include anti-microbial resistances, more pandemics, natural disasters, cyber-attacks, water shortages and geopolitical crises. However, the strengths of India include willingness to reform, change management and visionary planning and implementation.

Notes

1 https://en.m.wikipedia.org/wiki/CMS_(law_firm)
2 https://profiles.superlawyers.com/illinois/chicago/lawyer/brian-j-fahrney/7f741a5a-0474-44aa-8c37-d5d35ed6db7e.html
3 https://en.wikipedia.org/wiki/Attempted_purchase_of_T-Mobile_USA_by_AT%26T#Announcement
4 Schoenberg, Tom; Forden, Sara; Bliss, Jeff (August 31, 2011). "U.S. Files to Block AT&T, T-Mobile Merger". Bloomberg. Retrieved August 31, 2011.
5 Kang, Cecelia; Jia Lynn Yang (December 9, 2011), "How AT&T fumbled its $39 billion bid to acquire T-Mobile", The Washington Post, washingtonpost.com. Retrieved 9 December 2011.
6 Wyatt, Edward (August 21, 2011). "U.S. Moves to Block Merger Between AT&T and T-Mobile". The New York Times. Retrieved September 1, 2011.
7 Business Line, November 30, 2020. P-11.
8 https://www.financierworldwide.com/corporate-bankruptcy-resolution-juxtaposing-the-us-and-india#.XsNcWGgzbIU
9 Economic Times, May 15, 2020.

6 Pandemics, Business Response, Law and the CBMA

Supply Chain Logistics and COVID-19 Pandemic

The Chairperson of Global Talent Track Uma Ganesh feels that business sustainability is affected by the volatility of supplies and changes in demand forecasts. To date, during the pre-COVID-19 pandemic times, dynamic parameters are different, from the previous parameters used for supply chain logistics projection. Lockdown alters the supply chain operational metrics. Blending the external Parameters with internal data for key decisions is impactful on business continuity and innovation.

Descriptive, prescriptive, predictive and cognitive analytics need to be synchronised to solve the problems in minimising the risks and predict future scenarios based on dynamic demand due to COVID-19 pandemic-related operational exigencies. Supply chain analytics acts across functions and disciplines with common factors being the risk assessment, scenario building and identification of the loopholes and black holes which burden on the cost criteria.

Cross-border mergers and acquisitions in retail and FMCG require country-specific solutions. Real-time visibility becomes extremely important to cut down inventory carrying costs and to avoid overstocking and rerouting products from new destinations to newer targets. Technology aided by artificial intelligence and machine learning is a critical factor at this juncture.

Eighty per cent of the Indian logistics market is in the unorganised sector, and 14% of the losses are due to inefficiencies in the supply chain.[1]

Insurance and COVID-19 Pandemic

In a recent conference at the National Institute of Insurance, Pune, it was affirmed that there is a risk at present in three forms, namely: climate risk, cyber risk, and pandemic risk. The insurance sector functioned like a caution rather than an amplifier during the COVID-19 pandemic period in India. This was the opinion of a member of the Insurance Regulatory Development Authority of India. The pandemic exposed the weakness in the health system and there is not only a huge production but there is also no protection for a lot section of the population. The Insurance Regulatory

DOI: 10.4324/9781003396987-6

Development Authority of India came out with three standardised health plans to address the issue of trust deficits in health insurance and make it simpler for policyholders and purchase health insurance without hassles.

Case Study of Start-Up and Acquisition during COVID-19 Pandemic Era in India

WonderLab, a marketing firm, announced the acquisition of WYP (What's Your Problem). WYP is a creativity/advertisement firm. It is a high-impact acquisition. The COVID-19 pandemic, in this fashion, offers an opportunity for strange talent to come together.

Case Study Example of the Law Enforcement in India as the Cause of Ease of Doing Business in India

The Enforcement Directorate, ED, filed a prosecution complaint, a la charge sheet, in case of a crime to be dealt with by the Indian Penal Code (IPC) against E M Breyer SA. After investigating a complaint lodged by the Chief Controller, Research and Development, DRDO (Defence Research and Development Organisation), Government of India, the CBI found proof against an Indian company, Inter Dev Aviation Services Pvt. Ltd., and private individuals. The allegations include that E M Breyer SA engaged middlemen in facilitating the contract with the Government of India. The unity is probed under the provisions of the Prevention of Money Laundering Act India (PMLA).

> It is revealed that M. Brier obtained the contract for the supply of aircraft to the Indian Air Force US $ 4 210,000,000 and paid a commission of US$ 5,7 6,000,000 to a broker by name Khanna, Vipin for swaying the contracts towards E M Breyer SA. The kickbacks were routed by E M Breyer through its subsidiaries to INTEREDEVD aviation, Singapore, in lieu of a Sham agreement.[2]

New Technology Banking Reforms and COVID-19 Pandemic

Application programming interfaces as part of new technology made banking into an open banking facility. Banking systems based on old non-digital methods of operation cannot sustain businesses, increasingly being conducted digitally and regulated by the digital network of the Governments. API (Application Programming Interface) facilitates banks to instantaneously exchange information and arm the bank with service tools towards the customers through qualitative and quantitative enhancement and engagement in a digital framework. With the promised 5G network, soon to be a reality in India, digital banking will no longer remain a luxury. Digitalised banking will contribute exponential growth in the market by democratising access to the banks through its wide and varied financial services equally and equitably. The digitalised open banking system allows the interface of the export outsider who can help the bank as well as its customer to conduct the transactions safely and securely. The COVID-19 Pandemic made Digital banking services boomed and the social distancing norm panties automatic and digital banking. Contactless banking is needed for contactless order and contactless delivery of goods in an increasingly relevant e-commerce supply chain management logistics syndrome. Phillips Kotler once affirmed that the customer is the king. Open banking's ecosystem centres around the customer and the platform of services, as a collaboration between product and technology companies, also make the custom consumer not only the target but the controller of the entire operations.

Banking services are more than mere account keeping of money as the main medium of communication. A personalised and comfortable interface of a digitally savvy bank to its distant customer make the time and distance redundant,, in sharing his feedback with the product manufacturer, in being able to return the product with his comments, in being able to receive the warranty without many hassles and lastly to feel the worth of the money he spent. The banking experience of an ordinary villager in rural India, coupled with his ease of doing cell phone communication makes him high in his Ease of Doing Business Index. The Masters of Business Organisations heard of the Ease of Doing Business index among nations, but the need of the hour is to make every customer enhance the ease of doing fair business index. When there is a match between these two indexes, the growth of India becomes its development.

Data safety and privacy are in a seamless flow. Products and organisations require the critical consent of the consumer, namely the customer of the bank. Coupled with an enforceable consumer production law and armed with the help of the bank's digital framework. Cybersecurity System becomes a critical success factor. A cashless digital economy also becomes an automatic tax evasion-free economy. Banks, financial institutions, and cybersecurity experts must work in close collaboration to run an error-free and breach free-framework. Digital banking in the COVID-19 Pandemic era becomes thus, a crucial link between open banking and smart banking.

Industrial Labour Reforms and Ease of Doing Business Index

Forty-four existing labour laws were amalgamated into four codes under Industrial Relations, Wages, Operational Safety, Health, and Working Conditions, Welfare, and Working Conditions. These reforms were made with the aim of "simplifying procedures provisions and also conducive harmonious environment for doing business."[3] The Industrial Relations Code will Combine Trade Union Act 1926 and the Industrial Employment Standing Orders Act 1946 and the Industrial Disputes Act 1947. The Government recently dropped the plan to bar outsiders from the trade unions while giving effect to the request of established trade unions in the country. Only those persons who are working in an office for profit and who are Central State Ministers are now barred from being members of trade unions.

In a recent article written by Gautam and Rishi, it was mentioned that "businesses in India function in the regulatory universe of 1536 acts that demand 69233 compliances and 6618 filings across the Central and State Governments. Of these, 30% belong to labour's issues in the case of Acts, and 50% in the case of compliances. 97.1% of the compliances are governed by the State Governments."

Legal Innovation

Online Dispute Resolution and Ease of Doing Business

India has nearly 40 million cases pending which includes 62,000 cases at Supreme Court, 51.5 lakh cases at High Courts, and 3.46 crore cases at the lower courts. The COVID-19 Pandemic in the year 2019–2020 facilitated disposal in a virtual mode which resulted in the disposal of around 25 lakh cases. However, the registration of cases also increased by a margin of 3.6% in the Supreme Court, 12.5% at the High Courts.

A 2018 study by Johannes Boehm and Ezra Orefield on production and sourcing decisions and study of manufacturing plants in India concluded that productivity inundation making suffered due to weak enforcement mechanisms and the same study empirically proved that

> reducing the average age of pending cases by a year would, on an average increase aggregate productivity of a state by about 3%. Rs. 1400 per day is the average cost for an individual in attending to any court matter irrespective of any outcome.

A study by Manaswani Rao in 2020 after analysing 6,000,000 cases in 195 districts with a large and statistically significant sample of 13,928 companies showed that sales revenue, wage bills, and profits are negatively associated with the average case of duration for disposal.[4]

Conflict is natural in contract enforcement and resolution is necessary as per law. The routine way of disposal of the cases undoubtedly increased dependency because the structure was designed for a slower economy and fewer transactions. Online dispute resolution henceforth emerges as a viable solution in this context. ODR (Online Dispute Resolution) is based on trust, convenience and expertise. The feedback rating system in e-commerce incentivises reputation building through scaling activity and smooth transactions. "Separating together" is a successful process of dispute resolution for family and debt disputes adapted in the Netherlands. "A software asks the parties a series of lucid questions and then only and is the reply is in a manner such that the parties know their rights and optimum intervals, and are eventually guided towards an amicable agreement."

Professor Richard Susskind, of the United Kingdom, envisages a three-stage mechanism for ODR. They are firstly online evaluation with dispute diagnosis and exploration of options of litigants and secondly online facilitation with automotive negotiation tools aid in a non-adversarial resolution and finally online hearing. In the Indian context, ODR can raise equity, fairness and access in the dispute resolution ecosystem. Electronic local ballots were already conducted in Chhattisgarh, Karnataka, Rajasthan, Gujarat and Kerala are experimenting. Simple mechanisms of WhatsApp audio obligated calls as the first ODR is, therefore, a suitable mechanism which can increase India's rating in the Ease of Doing Business by facilitating a low-cost, remote, technology-augmented, linguistically friendly, amicable and incentivise dispute avoidance, containment and resolution without compromising on the principles of natural justice and rule of law.

Digitalisation and Cross-Border Mergers and Acquisitions

The unified payments interface for the first time made Rs. 4 lakh crore for December 2020 in India. The Reserve Bank of India developed an index called the digital payments index. The RBI announced that the digital payment index grew from 153.47 in March 2019 to 207.84 in March 2020. The digital payment index stood at 377.46 in September ,2022 against 349.30 in March 2022 and 304.06 in September 2021. The pandemic period saw a huge jump in digital payments. The National Payments Corporation of India observed that several banks were live on the UPI platform; in December 2020 the Aadhaar-enabled payment system also saw an increase. The digital payment index comprises five parameters which include the following:

1 Payment and enablers
2 Payment infrastructure
3 Payment infrastructure supply-side
4 Payment performance
5 Consumer Centre City.

The new institutions that came into India, post passing of the Companies Act 2013, in order to make the Cross-Border Mergers and Acquisitions environment and ecosystem workable which can be reflected through a better Index of Ease of Doing Business includes among others CCPA, the Central Consumer Protection Authority. The CCPA focuses on protecting and enforcing consumer rights and regulates matters relating to the violation of the rights of the consumers, unfair trade practices and false or misleading advertising winds that are prejudicial to the interests of the public and consumers. The CCPA recently issued suo moto notices and show cost notices to companies in the sectors which include water purifiers, paints, floor cleaners, operas and disinfectants. The Ministry of Corporate Affairs and the Consumers Affairs Ministry are the two ministries coordinate activities related to the CCPA. The Ministry of Consumer Affairs announced that the show cause notices issued suo moto by the CCPA certainly deter unscrupulous traders from launching misleading advertisements to exploit the sentiments of the consumers with cheap commercial profits. There is joint coordination of CCPA and Insurance Regulatory and Development Authority to ensure that the money is returned to the consumers who reported and won the cases through law. The IBBI adapted itself to the new environment of the COVID-19 Pandemic in striving to provide the flexible regulatory framework within the confines of overall insolvency law.

The IBBI has the following important issues on its agenda:

a   Specific insolvency framework for micro, small and medium enterprises,
b   Feedback,
c   Cross-Border Insolvency,
d   Group Insolvency and
e   Fresh Start-up processes of the Insolvency and Bankruptcy Board of India.

The Finance Ministry, Government of India, sought feedback from key stakeholders in the financial system to rationalise the major acts of law under the Department of Financial Services. Essential human interface compiled with transparency, time-bound delivery and predictability are parts of the objectives of the Department of Financial Services. There is a need to rationalise the compliance burden for the citizens in the business and also making the regulatory framework simple and stakeholder-friendly. The feedback is sought from banks, insurance companies, micro-finance institutions, and also all the large non-banking finance companies. The following Acts are the major Acts administered by the Department of Financial Services, Ministry of Finance, Government of India:[5]

1   The Reserve Bank of India Act, 1934
2   The Banking Regulation Act, 1949
3   The Insurance Regulatory and Develop and Authority of India Act, 1999
4   The Insurance Act, 1938
5   The Credit Information Companies Regulation Act, 2005
6   The National Housing Bank Act, 1987.

India improved its ranking of doing a business as reported by the World Bank for the period from October 7, 2019 to October 16, 2020 among 190 countries.

Fraud Prevention

Whistle blower Protection and Rule of Law as a Tool for EASE OF DOING BUSINESS IN CBMA Environment

Ease of Doing Business is critical in the CBMA environment because of the necessity of a level playing field on both ends of the transaction in the mergers and acquisition, from the point of view of trust and rule of law in both the countries. Whistle blower protection is linked to False Claims Act, USA initially through which a whistle blower can collect an amount up to 30% of the penalty that the company pays off to the successful litigation by the whistle blower against the company in a civil suit. There are specialised advocacy firms in the USA who expertise in whistle blower cases. After the blow to the financial world due to the 2008 financial crisis in the USA, Senators Christopher Dodd and Barney Frank introduced the famous Dodd-Frank Wall Street Reform and Consumer Protection Act. The whistle blower can get a reward of 15–30% of the penalty that the government collects from the company under the above-said law. The Dodd-Frank Act also enables foreign informers to get the reward. Mr Dinesh Thakur, a whistle blower of Ranbaxy Company, being a former employee, got US$ 47,000,000 six years ago.

The Securities and Exchange Commission of the USA for the financial year 2019 received the second largest number of whistleblower information. During this current period, the SEC received 27 tipoffs from India alone which happen to be the 4th largest outside the USA. *The Economic Times* on December 21, 2020 mentions that

> In India, the Whistle blower Protection Act. passed in 2014 is yet to become operational. Indian companies do not have a whistle blower mechanism as yet. Even though, a provision has been made in the Companies Act. 2013, the whistle blower mechanism is yet to be operationalized. SEBI, the Security Exchange Board of India, recently introduced an award system for informants.[6]

The USA has the Sarbanes-Oxley Act whose section 10 protects the whistle blowers from the issuers of public securities. Section 922 of the Dodd-Frank Wall Street Protection Act 2010 commands the Security Exchange Act of 1934 to add section 21F. Section 20 1F incentivises and protects the whistle blowers, through monetary awards and confidentiality assurance coupled with protection from possible repression from the employers. The Attorney General of the United States is empowered to grant a reward for any judicial or administrative action perpetuated due to information from a whistle blower. Similarly, any self-regulatory organisation, any appropriate regulatory authority and any state Attorney General in any criminal case are also empowered to award money for any judicial or administrative help accrued due to the information provided by a whistle blower.

Enhancement of the reward to the whistle blower is at the discretion of the SEC. The following four criteria affect the enhancement:

1   The importance of tip/information,
2   The physical risk and assistance rendered by the whistle blower,
3   The relevant legal angle of the law enforcement agency and
4   Contribution of the whistle blower information towards the internal compliance process.

The negative factors which may diminish the award are as follows.

1   The criminal culpability of the whistle blower,
2   The unpardonable delay of the reporting of the misconduct by the whistle blower,
3   The recorded criminal interference of the whistle blower fits the internal compliance and reporting systems of the enforcement authorities.

The Dodd-Frank Act also makes provisions for the protection of the individual physically and allows the whistle blower to communicate through an appointed lawyer for the purpose of communication. Whistle blowers are also entitled to be reinstated at day pre-whistle blowing level of employment, double back pay with interest, compensation for reasonable attorney fees, litigation costs, and expert witness fees. The Dodd-Frank Act also made amendments in 2015 through which the whistle blower is protected even if he directly reports to the SEC. The US Court of appeals for the 2nd subacute was confirmed on 10 September 2015 in a case of Bergman versus Neo while LLC overturning the Court of the District of Southern New York District Judgement.

In 2011 the US SEC established the office of the whistle blower. An example will illustrate the functioning of the SEC s whistle blower protection office. "In the Matter of Parading Capital Management, Inc. and Candace King Weir (16 June 2014), SEC changed the level playing field through retaliation against the whistle blower's job function, stripping the whistle blower of supervisory responsibilities, and otherwise marginalizing the whistle blower."[7]

On April 1 2015, the SEC of the USA invoked rule 2 1F of Dodd-Frank Act and collected a fine amount of US$ 130,000 from a company that attempted a confidentiality clause former potential whistle blower employee. This instance shows the dedication of the SEC of the USA in both letter and spirit in so far as protection of whistle blowers is concerned. In the international arena, several internationally recognised anti-corruption compliance tools for the private sector advice and for the adoption of protected reporting mechanisms and measures to prevent retaliation are available. They are as follows:

1   Transparency International business principles for countering bribery,
2   Rules of conduct and recommendations to combat extortion and bribery of ICC, the International Chamber of Commerce,
3   The OECD guidelines for multinational Enterprises,
4   Integrity compliance guidelines of the World Bank,
5   WEF (World Economic Forum) principles per countering bribery,
6   The Anti-corruption Ethics and Compliance Handbook for the Business of the World Bank,
7   The UNCAC (United Nations Convention against Corruption) and
8   The US Sentencing Commission guidelines manual

It has been found out that private-sector employees first report internally about any wrongdoing. A recent survey in the US private sector employees found that only 18% report externally. Only 2% of the employees exclusively go outside and never report the wrongdoing to their employer. This means that everyone prefers a mechanism for internal reporting firstly. According to a report from the office of the whistle blower of the SEC of the USA, over 80% first appraise their concerns internally to their supervisors before reporting this to the SEC. To the question how self-reporting companies become aware of foreign bribery in their business operations, 28% reported that they learn from the due diligence in the mergers and acquisitions process.

Ultimate Suggestions

1. Ease of Doing Business Index symbolises productivity, predictability perfection of efforts, rules, and execution respectively in the case of CB MA. SEZ (Special Economic Zone) as a concept is as old as economic liberalisation in India. The SEZ Act 2006 was not implemented properly in India. The critics maintain and assert to prove the above contention by the fact that, as of September 2 018 more than 84% of actual employment in the manufacturing SEZ units is in shortfall.
2. Make in India, Make for India, and Self-reliant India should not remain as mere slogans. Private sector investment needs to be improved as governments cannot alone take the load of employment needs of more than 1.3 billion people. Private gross fixed investment as a percentage of GDP was shortened from 27% in 2011 to 22% in 2018. Critics point out the following issues, for instance, lack of institutional trust, policy uncertainties outcome, bureaucratic controls, political interferences, the politics of vendetta, caste and religion, a continuous cycle of elections, deep penetration of politics instead of policies in every aspect of social life.
3. Baba Kalyani Committee reported on the policy on SEZs. Apart from the committee report, the other issues include the building of consciences for strategic changes, making special economic zones as a buffer to promote ease of doing business in India, incentivising tax breaks only to promote good compliance reports, promoting merit-based incentives to priority industries, single-window clearances, stability in rules and regulations, efficient administrative services, promotion of logistics zones to contribute a significant reduction in lusty costs, port and airport connectivity, the establishment of integrated logistics parks. A report by the Government of India in July 2019 points out that India has only eight free trade warehousing zones in comparison to 91 of Indonesia, 22 of Malaysia and 262 of the USA.
4. Artificial Intelligence (AI) and Machine Learning (ML) are two tools having the potential of changing the human workspace metrics in the world. CB MA between India and the USA involves high-technology fields which include AI and ML, Artificial Intelligence, and Machine Learning. The US company Intel conducted a survey in India on the

topic of the suitability of Machine Learning and also on the topic of Artificial Intelligence and the future of work with more than 309 and employees across 106 Indian occupations and 301 firms respectively. The main finding of the surveys is that AI is one of the leading cutting-edge technologies of the current era to generate value for humanity at scale. Ninety per cent of the respondents indicated that AI is essential and highly relevant to their business. Over 80% said that their workforce will undergo significantly scaling due to implementations. There will be a broad impact on innovation, productivity and worker behaviour. There will be a significant change in the organisational mechanisms underlying such impacts.

COVID-19 Pandemic and Cybersecurity and the CBMA

The COVID-19 pandemic compiled online working and work from home as the new reality. Most online businesses use third parties to develop applications but such third parties may involve leakages in the Cybersecurity protection systems. The script kiddies and organised hacktivists use multiple security weaknesses to disturb the business environment. The importance of cybersecurity need not be over-emphasised in the CBMA environment for the simple reason that the health recorded data of 120 million Indian consumers comprising of discharge date, consultation details, X-ray reports and CT scan reports are available for sale on the darknet web.

Data of multiple companies was breached during the lockdown, and it has been a matter of concern for the law enforcers. The bank account details, bank transaction details and the database of 3.5 million unique email addresses are all available on the dark web according to some informed sources. There is no data protection law currently in India, and the Indian Information Technology Act is not according to the strict cybersecurity protocols as per informed opinion globally. Many companies, henceforth, are compelled to hire CID investigation and cyber law firms to prepare a response and train their auditors and public communicators.

Cybersecurity protocols include preventive measures and a drill to handle as a critical response team in case the hacking already takes place. In the absence of such transparency, the company's reputation may be at stake which is in the cybersecurity threat target, arena. Start-up companies especially in the digital start-up arena always live with the fear of cybersecurity threats not merely because of the basic cybersecurity threat but also because of its follow-up in terms of investors withdrawing their cash and no fresh investor coming up. The reputation of a digital start-up is extremely important for its very survival. Through cybersecurity response teams and protocols in place are important because most businesses are moving from offline to online through increased digitalisation of transactions. Many venture capitalists and private equity investors are found nowadays taking interest in cybersecurity aspects and in having an opinion from cyber experts for carrying out a cyber-risk assessment and cyber forensic report before taking any decision of investment as part of their due diligence the CBMA is no exception to the environment of cybersecurity threat proof.

Cybersecurity, CBMA and DSCI

The COVID-19 pandemic created peculiar situations all over the world calling for cybersecurity framework not only for the start-ups but also for the established industry. Data Security Council of India (DSCI) is a body set up by NASSCOM in India (National Association of Software and Service Companies) for the protection of data to roll out initiatives for cybersecurity and data privacy besides building an ecosystem for the development of start-ups focusing on cybersecurity solutions in India. DSCI along with the Ministry of Electronics and Information Technology, the Government of India, is working together for formulating a perfect data protection law for India. The focus of this joint effort has been on the following areas.

1 Cross border issues,
2 Localisation,
3 Innovation on Data,
4 Analytics industry growth,
5 Promotion of best practices of various global data protection regimes,
6 Promotion of digital economy and
7 Balancing data protection regulations with industry growth and innovation.

The need of the hour is to have a globally benchmarked and well-established capacity-built National Technology Repository for cybersecurity. There are 25 technologically priority-based areas. The most important five areas are as follows:

1 Cyber forensics,
2 Artificial intelligence,
3 Blockchain,
4 Internet of things,
5 Cryptology.

The following are specialised agencies namely,

1 Freelancers,
2 Start-ups,
3 Large services firms,
4 Global in-house centres,
5 Academic laboratories are structurally vital organisations in this regard.

DSCI looks for enabling market access to start-ups in India and abroad for identifying links in connecting the customer and the investor in order to make the flagship make India program successful in terms of cybersecurity. Funds amounting to US$ 35 billion have been earmarked for the cybersecurity task force of the DSCI. Nearly 64,000 work opportunities exist for skilled cybersecurity professionals. Approximately 200,000 employees are working for cybersecurity in India as of January 2021. Digital payments, transactions, and the need for Work From Home (WFH) need more experts and cybersecurity today than in the past. According to the DSCI, "the growing popularity of connected devices, bring your device (BYOD), and Internet of things technologies is projected to increase impact in the endpoint security segment. Regulations on increasing volume of data are driving interest in data security."[8]

The general view is that by the year 2025 the global expenditure on cybersecurity may touch US$116 billion. The COVID-19 pandemic globally increased the potentiality for cyberattacks and apart from a larger number of government agencies in the United States, many Fortune 500 companies were also targeted. The well-known American security firm FIR_E_EYE alerted the intelligence agencies of the USA regarding a fierce attack on the American establishment from cybercriminals. Solar Winds, the company which has its clients, among others, Pentagon and the Department of Homeland Security of the USA, was also hacked. The well-known cybersecurity writer Bruce Schneier compares cyber-attacks with cyber espionage. Cyber-attacks are direct and indirect in profit-making at the cost of the team for the attacker. Cyber spying works both ways for the spy and for the person who hires the spy. The National Security Agency of the USA needs to be aware of these dangers. The lessons for India in this regard are to keep up the visit and be prepared in advance for such cyber-attacks. "While there is nothing like perfect cent per cent security, they realise a cent per cent preparation for a critical response to such acts of breach of security in cyber espionage." The private investigative activism in the USA is commendable and is an inspiration to agencies like the DSCI in India.

National Company Law Tribunal

COVID-19 Pandemic and Resolution for Liquidation

The National Company Law Tribunal (NCLT) approved a record number of resolution plans during the period from January to September of 2020. The following graph shows the details. Seventy-eight resolution plans were approved by the bankruptcy courts in the COVID period of nine months in the year 2020. Managing partner at KS legal & associates, Mr Sonam Chandwani, is of the opinion that given the debt-ridden ecosystem that existed for decades, four years is a very short period to curb the menace from the roots, and hence, cases of a large number of originators were resolved through liquidation. Advocates practicing at the NCLT feel that the Insolvency Bankruptcy Code (IBC) needs to be more flexible than the current code in that the peculiar pandemic situation also may be taken into consideration through a new IBC 2.0.

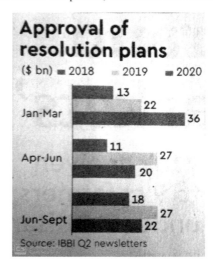

Figure 6.1 Insolvency Bankruptcy Code – India.

Veena Sivaramkrishna, a partner at law firm Shardul Amarchand Mangaldas, among others, feels that pre-packs would continue to be the need of the hour and would need to become a formalised mechanism to meet the demand. The prepacked resolution allows a company to prepare a restructuring plan in cooperation with creditors before initiating insolvency. IBBI chairman Mr M.S. Sahoo submitted a report to the government on the prepacked insolvency framework in October 2019. The United Kingdom has the prepared facility available Rajeev Chandak, partner at Quality India, feels that liquidation value should be calculated closer to the submission of the resolution plan. The process of resolution takes a time beyond 270 days and hence earlier liquidation value is not an appropriate indication at the time. It can be hoped that the Insolvency and Bankruptcy Code in India will be on par with the best benchmarking practices in the world and thus will be contributed towards better Ease of Doing Business Index in India.

NCLT, COVID-19 and New Electronic Initiatives

The NCLT of India decided to implement the e-filing and electronic generation of automating case numbers. E-filing has been mandatory for the past three years. E-court will now cover e-filing, e-security, e-cause listing and case allocation.

Digital India campaign needed the e-filing facility in ensuring government services be available to citizens electronically by improving online infrastructure. It is felt that an automatic case number helps case proceedings and would be useful in tracking the life cycle of the matter is before the NCLT. Digitalisation will always help in lessening the pendency because of better monitoring and coordination among all the stakeholders with an emphasis on disposal and accountability.

Digitalisation through better technology of cloud computing has banking applications also cloud computing by the big cloud providers in the banking sector needs to invest heavily in security and safeguarding the data.

Notes

1 Financial Express, December 7, 2020, P-11.
2 BUSINESS LINE, December 10, 2020, P-2.
3 Financial Express, December 2, 2020, P-2.
4 Financial Express, October 31, 2020, P-6.
5 Business Line, January 1, 2021, P-3.
6 Economic Times E-paper, December 21, 2020.
7 SEC announces award to a whistleblower in a first retaliation case, April 28, 2015, www.sec.gov/news/pressrelease/2015-75.html.
8 Business Line, January 2, 2021, P-3.

7 Fairness in Acts and Activity

Competition Commission of India

More than 130 countries in the world have competition law for the simple reason that without competition the productivity and effective functioning of the markets is impossible. Monopolisers always are exploitative because of their survival instinct. Monopolies cripple the economy, drive up the prices in an anti-competitive manner, lead to anti-competitive mergers and acquisitions, and structure the markets which scuttle the development of new products and encouraging innovation talent and destroy fair play which is the backbone of the concept of Rule of Law. In India, the liberalisation of the economy resulted in a shift from the command control regime to a competitive and productive economy. Liberalisation started with a gap of 15 years in India when compared to China. Deng Ziao Ping's China entered liberalised state- capitalism phase in 1976, and India, under the leadership of Late Mr P. V. Narasimha Rao, the Prime Minister (1991–1996), in the year 1991. In the year 2002, the Competition Act replaced the regressive Monopolised and Restricted Trade Practices Act, 1963. The Competition Act, 2002 empowered the Competition Commission of India (CCI) to regulate the mergers and acquisitions with a forward-looking assessment, and also many state-owned enterprises were brought under the control of the Competition Commission.

In the annual report of the Competition Commission of India, the Commission mentioned that it received 94 notices of the proposed combinations in the year 2018–2019. The provisions regarding the competition aspect of the Competition Commission came into force on June 1, 2011. The Act defines combination to mean the acquisition of one or more enterprises by one or more persons or merger or amalgamation of enterprises, whose value of assets or turnover meets the threshold specified under the Act. The intended merger was not impacting adversely any aspect of the Competition of India Act, in India. The website of CCI (WWW.CCI.GOV.IN) presents the details of notices received and disposed of by the commission till date.

According to Shri Ashok Kumar Gupta, Chairperson, Competition Commission of India, the key to the success of any merger review is to conduct a quick assessment so that the firms are able to consummate their

DOI: 10.4324/9781003396987-7

transactions and save time and costs on account of the necessary approvals. The CCI considers the market dynamics including the level of concentration, degree of countervailing buyer power, the possibility of failing business, and the contribution to the economic development to examine whether the merger is likely to result in any harm to competition. Consumer welfare protection is one of the aims of the Competition Commission of India. Remedies were imposed in 21 cases to prevent likely market distortions resulting from the combinations. In industries like cement, pharmaceuticals, seeds, agrochemicals, automobile components, electoral equipment, entertainment, industrial gas, e-platforms, and mineral processing, the Competition Commission of India intervened. The CCI has been successfully handling various global mergers such as Dow Chemical–DuPont, Lafarge, Bayer, Monsanto, Linde, Praxair. The above cases demanded interaction and coordination among counterparts and in multi-jurisdictional contexts. The Competition Commission of India has been interacting with the platforms of the International Competition Network, Organisation for Economic Cooperation and Development, BRICKS. The challenges posed in the new era include common investments in computing firms and data driven mergers. Notification thresholds are not triggered due to low-cost or low assets or low turnover of target companies in some cases. The following measures have been adopted by the Competition Commission of India. They are:

1. The threshold for notification in India is relatively high thus imposing the notification requirement only on larger transactions. Mergers in public sector banks and oil and natural gas have been exempted by the Government and public interest.
2. The acquisition of smaller enterprises below the monetary threshold is also exempted.
3. Green Channel and a fast-track approval route have been recently introduced from August 15, 2019 which is the first of its kind and trust-based system in the world where notifiable transactions having no overlaps be it horizontal and vertical or complimentary between the parties are deemed approved upon its filing and can be consummated immediately. The main aim is to sustain and promote speedy, transparent, and accountable merger review, and to strike a balance between facilitation and enforcement. The aim is to create a culture of voluntary compliance supporting economic growth. New reforms incorporate insolvency aspects and calling for changes rapidly in domestic consolidations and the entire international environment during the COVID-19 pandemic.
4. As India prepares for post-COVID economic recovery, the stage is set for all enterprises to benefit from the objective, transparent and business-friendly combination review regime of the Competition Commission of India. The following case study symbolises the speed with which the Competition Commission of India approves cross-border mergers and acquisitions. On June 18, 2020, the Competition

Commission of India approved the acquisition of the mineral business of Mezzo by Auto Tech. Auto Tech is a public limited liability company incorporated and registered under the <u>Laws of Finland</u>. Mezzo is a public limited liability company incorporated in the register. The proposed combination involved a partial demerger of mezzo to affect that all minerals business of Mezzo will be acquired by Auto Tech.

5   On July 15, 2020, the CCI approved the acquisition of Cisco company private limited up to 58.92% of the share capital of Healthcare Global Enterprises Ltd. through Security and Exchange Board of India's substantial acquisition of shares and takeovers regulations 2011.

On July 10, 2020, the CCI approved the proposed acquisition of 9.09% of the total issued, subscribed, and paid-up share capital of Escorts Ltd by Kubota Corporation and acquisition of 40% of the total issued subscriber and paid-up capital of Kubota agriculture Machinary India Private limited(KAI) by Escorts. The intended merger was not impacting adversely any aspect of the Competition of India Act, in India.

The CCI approved the same under subsection 1 of section 31 of the Competition Act, 2002.

IBBI Initiatives and Accountability

IBBI initiatives include the promotion of a platform for distressed assets with the following four elements namely:

1   Marketplace for interim Finance,
2   Virtual data room,
3   Invitation of resolution plans,
4   Auction of liquidation assets.

1   Mr M.S. Sahoo, the former chairperson of the Insolvency and Bankruptcy Board of India, asserted that keeping a company resolvable is a win-win for the company, its promoters and directors and creditors. The establishment of IBBI improves the probability of resolution of bankruptcy issues easily. The IBBI intends to work towards promoting resolve ability of the companies. One of the possible CBMA in the auto sector in India was Mahindra and Ford Motor of India and the USA, respectively. The plan was to have a Mahindra Ford model for emerging markets and the distillation of Ford Motor through the Mahindra network in India. However, the COVID-19 pandemic situation compelled the postponement of this plan.

Shobana Subramaniam, of the *Financial Express*, feels that Insolvency Bankruptcy Code should never have been kept in abeyance for so long and if it is not handled well the pre-pack and can deal with it big blow. According to her, IBC is an excellent piece of legislation that has shown a dent on wilfully defaulting promoters and has given hapless bankers a better shot at recovering their money. IBC restored the sanctity of the debt contract which was in full erosion earlier. The industry promoters and the debtors know that they can no longer swindle the banks. The COVID-19 pandemic situation compelled the Government of India to keep in abeyance the IBC for many months. The Government of India's thought includes the possibility of a window for the lenders so that the promoters will be given a chance to revive the business before declaring it insolvent and putting it through the Corporate Insolvency Resolution Process (CIRP). This will result in the business cycles being better operationalised. Due to the severe blow of the COVID-19 pandemic globally on the business cycles and logistics, the start-up promoters do deserve the chance to put their enterprises on track. Medium-sized and small entities that are new to the market need such incubate protection.

It has to be remembered that CIRP cannot be hammered to become a fraudulent repetition of the so-called Corporate Debt Restructuring (CDR). The CDR was the most ill-conceived mechanism of all times and cost the taxpayer thousands of crores of rupees, according to Shobana Subramaniam, she continues that the banks were compelled to take hefty haircuts while the promoters retained their business cess with most of them bringing in very little additional capital or none at all. At one point in time, the CDR cell of the Finance Ministry approved exposures close to four lakh crore rupees for a recast. None of the money came back, however. And banks had to allocate this CDR money as NPA money. In other words, the mistakes done by the banks, politicians and the businessmen had to be borne by the citizens of the country. Empirical statistics prove this point. Between April and October 2013, the number of successful cases was 45, but the number of cases that failed was twice that at 90. Subramaniam finds faults with the banks. She says that the Indian banking system has a penchant for restructuring through CDR.

The banks approached this problem the way ostrich approaches the incoming sand dune. The dune here is created by the incompetency of the debt-ridden industrialists/promoters and a corrupt conniving politician and abdicating conniving bureaucrat. The pre-pack scheme cannot amount to a kicking pack scheme that needs to be adopted here with a lot of due diligence. The promoters must be compelled to bring their capital rather than a capital borrowed from another bank in another country. In the name of a financial re-engineering, no fraudulent tricking should be allowed to make the banks increase their NPA. There is a danger that the NPA if allowed to continue the way it goes as an upward slope figure, NPA becomes the NPL (Non-Performing Liabilities). Despite appeals through NCLAT, the IBC worked well. Shobana Subramaniam still feels that the pre-pack scheme should be reserved for the small borrowers. An airing promoter is to run for fresh capital in order to save his business being liquidated by the IDBI and the NCLT.

The Reserve Bank of India assesses that the Special Mention Accounts (SMA) may arise from the current 7.5% level. The then Economic Affairs

Secretary, Mr Tarun Bajaj, observed recently that the government is exploring all options, including setting up a bad bank to improve the health of the banking sector of the country. Government is duty-bound to recapitalise the banks and hence made budgetary provisions accordingly. Bad banks as an idea may not be good because playing with public money has never been good. The successful functioning of the Insolvency Bankruptcy Code coupled with other measures brought the NPA ratio for banking from 9.1% in March 2019, 28.2% in March 2020, and to further 7.5% in September 2020. The effort needs to be continued.

The Federal Trade Commission of the USA and Its Performance Snapshot for the Year 2019

The Federal Trade Commission (FTC) intends to guard the consumers by preventing unfair trade and business practices through enforcing the law and public communication through publicity, advocacy and education and also strives for the prevention of anti-competitive, deceptive trade practices. The FTC activities do not intend to obstruct or harass legitimate business functioning.

The FTC levied $478 million in redressing their legitimate interests of the consumers through the activity for consumer protection and competition matters. It also ordered litigants like Volkswagen, Greentree, and Adorn to distribute $ 344 million to consumers directly. The FTC saved $ 4.8 billion through its merger and non-merger actions. Competition enforcement is not a voluntary activity. As was required, stronger regulator like the T.E.D, the Technology Enforcement Division, was established by the FTC in the USA to enforce Competition Law in markets of emerging technologies.

An example is illustrative in the articulation of the activity of the FTC in that, the FTC secured a stipulated injunction in the Federal Court compelling Reckitt Benckiser to pay $ 50 million to settle charges that violated the antitrust laws to a deceptive scheme to make profits at the cost of low-priced generic competition. The involved drug is Suboxone. Another example mentioned was the activity of the FTC is that Google and YouTube agreed to pay $170 million to settle the allegations by the FTC and the New York Attorney General that the YouTube video-sharing service illegally collected personal information from children without the consent of their parents in violation of the Children's Online Privacy Protection Act. The effectiveness of the FTC can be measured by the fact that the FTC ranked first on the Employee Engagement Index and the New IQ Index. Apart from the mandatory legal functioning that FTC supposedly performs, the FTC added the following missions and challenges which are mentioned below:

1. Protecting consumers from fraud,
2. Protecting consumers as technology evolves,
3. Protecting the privacy and data security,
4. Stopping deceptive advertising and marketing practices,

5   Protecting consumers in the financial marketplace,
6   Protecting small businesses, seniors, veterans, and service members,
7   Stopping harmful uses of new technology without hindering innovation,
8   Promoting competition in healthcare and pharmaceutical markets,
9   Preventing anti-competitive activity in the energy industry,
10 Maintaining robust competition in retail markets.

Security Exchanges Commission and Mergers Acquisitions Joint Venture Guidelines, an Update in the USA

The following laws are mentioned in the case of the Securities and Exchange Commission activity in the USA.

1   Securities Act of 1933,
2   Securities Exchange Act of 1934,
3   Public Utility Holding Company Act of 1935,
4   Trust Indenture Act of 1939,
5   Investment Company Act of 1940,
6   Investment Advisers Act of 1940,
7   Williams Act of 1968.

FDI and Its Links with Foreign Trade Growth in India

A recently published study by Shiv Shankar Jana, Tarak Nath Sahoo and Krishnadayal Pandey in the *Journal of Economic Structures*, Volume IX, Article Number 30, 2020, concludes the following aspects.

a   Foreign investors are interested more in the domestic market.
b   Foreign investors lay less emphasis on exports from India.
c   The consequence of the above two resultants is the absence of chronic long-term causality towards exports from Foreign Direct Investment.

Banking Sector Reforms and the CBMA

Mismanagement by political bureaucratic nexus on a chronological basis made the Indian Banks, both private and public sector unproductive, and loss-making. The Banking Regulation Act, as a Law, is meant to regulate banking activity so that credit is accessible to all sections of society and the ideals of the Constitution of India are carried out through banking activity. Corporate ownership of the banks was suspected for the obvious reasons of monopoly and wrongdoing ab initio. However, with huge non-performing assets piling up, and creditworthiness being in question, the RBI in its working group recommendations came up with an idea of allowing the corporates and NBFCs with assets of Rs 50,000 crores and above and a good track record of ten years to start banking activity. The Government of India's statistics shows that the credit to the non-financial sector as a percentage of the GDP stands at 56% in India as against 150% and 205% in the USA and China respectively. The MSME sector credit needs are largely unmet by the banking channels and there is an estimated gap of credit at Rs 25 lakh crores.

RBI, in a communiqué in September 2020 redefined the classification so that MSME would be able to get better credit from the banks. Trustworthiness and creditworthiness go together. Empty promises by fraudulent political authorities do not increase the deposit collections of the so-called public sector banks just because they happen to be public sector. The public continues to be taken for a ride with scams in the banking sector, Cooperative banks, scams with public deposit schemes, and some nonbanking financial companies in the name of chit funds caused huge damage to the image of public sector banking. The delay even by the Central investigating agencies like the CBI, in the case of the "Sarada scam" of West Bengal is a case in point. The huge deposit base of Sundaram Finance, which is an NBFC, when compared to the State Bank of India in Tamil Nadu is an illustrious example to establish an empirical truth in the above paragraph.

The Reserve Bank of India has sufficient powers to restrict intragroup exposures and control the lending activities of the corporate bank and prevent the corporate bank to lend only to its group companies. The loss-making public sector banks like the IDBI Bank or the Punjab National Bank or the Syndicate Bank can be taken over by industrial houses like the TATAs and Larsen & Toubro or the Sundaram Finance or the Bajaj Auto Finance Group. As of January 1, 2021, Bajaj Auto Finance's base has reached more than Rs 1 lakh crore capital which shows the trust of the public in the best benchmark practices of how Bajaj Auto Finance is conducting itself. Hence it is suggested here that loss-making public sector undertaking banks can be taken over by well-run private sector experienced NBFCs so that the entire banking sector can function addressing the real credit needy MSME sector which has tremendous employment potential.

Best management efficiency of a proven successful private sector NBFC combining its strengths with a poorly functioning but adequately penetrated public sector banking network is going to be a win-win situation for both of them. If Bajaj Finance agrees, it can take over IDBI Bank or Syndicate Bank, or Punjab National Bank. MSME network needs to be enhanced within the framework of Make India and Make for India and Self Reliant India with the backing up of a professionally managed corporate banking sector. The expertise of the micro-finance organisations and the micro banks in coming up for the MSME can be extended to the public sector banking arena. Agriculture-based start-ups within the framework of the new Farm Laws and Industrial Laws need a protective layer and incubating space that can be given by a well-functioning bank with the experience of the good management credibility coupled with a proven private sector efficient brand.

The previous history of 40% failure rate of 12 banking license granted between the period of 1993–1994 and 2013–2014 coupled with the unwelcome experience in case of the Indian Airlines failure to get a private sector master is indicative of a tough way ahead to convert this design into delivery. The good news is that Indian Airlines was taken over by TATA group. Law also needs an amendment to make entry easier for the willing, risk-taking private sector to enter the public sector banking area. The fact remains that it is not easy to build a cost-efficient reliability base while meeting all the stringent priority sector obligations of the Reserve Bank of India to offer any new entrant from the private sector into the banking area. RBI mandates 40% of the bank's lending be directed towards priority sectors like MSMEs agriculture and weaker sections and many corporate houses rightly so remain worried about such directed credit allocation targets. A bank is not a political party office with a mandate to win the next elections cheaply. If bankers are continued to be pressurised to save their skin in lending to political crime time, non-performing assets will become non-performable liabilities soon.

The recent experience with Laxmi Vilas Bank and the Yes Bank taught us a lesson that RBI must be prepared with willing persons to take over these troubled banks. CBI and RBI must come together along with the intelligence bureau in collecting information and intelligence about probable candidates so that screening and due diligence will become easier when any occasion arises in the future. It is important to remember that in an increasingly competitive post-COVID-19 pandemic environment, it becomes risky to take a chance of failure as a routine event. Banking is not politics and lending is not elections.

Start–ups and New Technologies

The COVID-19 pandemic in the year 2020 created an unprecedented experience, leading to compelled initiatives and extraordinary modifications in the way of doing business in many areas. The compulsion to stay alive of a person is as relevant as for industry and trade. Quick drug development, effective distribution, remote control care and delivery of medicines, efficient supply chain management are the new strategies increasingly adopted everywhere.

The world may witness drones delivering food and medicine not only in remote areas but also in congested areas and quarantined areas. Internet of things led to the Internet of behaviour. Cloud computing-oriented applications and movement measuring telemetry have become the new norm in controlling human behaviour both within the work environment and also outside in crucial areas like marketing so that necessary and mandatory guidelines of competent authorities are maintained without contradicting the business interests of the organisation. The academic environment taught the students to take distance learning and distance examination at a time under remotely monitored and proctored surveillance systems through thorough identity verification and authentication in real time.

The following nine issues assume importance in this connection. They are mentioned below:

1. Start-ups the world over may be speedily merged and may speedily be acquired. Today, Quantum Computing and Artificial Intelligence, Cybersecurity coupled with Quantum Computing as a service are all emerging as the new trends world over. With the Internet of Things and the Internet of behaviour merging, business amalgamations are an immediate afterthought of business ideas globally. The ability to perform better with speed and skill is the new premium in the post-COVID-19 pandemic. The new areas include, firstly, financial forecasting; secondly, weather predictions; thirdly, drug and vaccine development; fourthly, blood protein analysis; and lastly supply chain planning and optimisation.
2. Technologies like Artificial Intelligence and Machine Learning display the possibility of bringing the minds and hands together globally. The processes of conducting the business may radically see a change inspired by the new developments in the new frontiers of the new technologies. The time lapse between an idea and a thing is going to be narrowed down.
3. Quantity computing has the potentiality to become quality compounding. Cloud providers such as, among others, AWS of Amazon, Azure of Microsoft and Google are increasingly becoming AI tool providers for many organisations relying on real-time experiments in their business process, post-COVID-19 pandemic.
4. William Gates of Microsoft is credited with the quotation of thought at the speed of light. Post-COVID-19 pandemic era may see automated machine learning and machine learning operations coming together to make business at the speed of light possible. The machine learning operations enable organisations visibility of their models and can become an efficient tool to reduce and nullifying the redundancy in efforts through artificial intelligence.
5. Cybersecurity may gain prominence and emerge as an employment provider of essence and survival in the post-COVID-19 business of the current year 2023. The COVID-19 pandemic also gave great opportunities to hackers and cybercriminals all over the world. Even the most advanced USA is not spared. Cyber Crime Prevention and Hacking Prevention is essential for businesses even to survive the cause of the competition and the business taking place at the speed of light. Advanced prediction algorithms along with automation intelligence are required to play a decisive role in the times to come for the prevention of breach of security both in Data storage and Data retrieval and interpretation.
6. Data protocol maintenance and management are of extreme importance. Edge computing, the Data posting near the source close to the device at the edge of the network is emerging as a new era of actionable insights from the vast amount of Data. It is probable that the evil memory accelerated real-time, AI would emerge as the essential tool and framework when the 5G becomes a reality.

7   New fund allocation and the new emphasis on research and development in the new technologies is the new normal in the post-COVID-19 pandemic years 2021,2022 and 2023. According to NASSCOM, more than 40% of the start-ups were compelled to stop their operations due to the COVID-19 pandemic in the year 2020. Hence, in the year 2021 mergers and acquisitions of start-ups would be a reality.
8   Poaching of the small by the big is a natural by-product of any crisis. The smaller companies in the niche areas and innovative segments like vaccine development, Cybersecurity, artificial intelligence chips, cloud computing applications, machine learning operations, etc. are likely candidates for taking over and acquisition by the big companies of the world.
9   Coordination and cooperation are no longer ideals but essentials in post-COVID-19 in the year 2023 for the businesses to survive. Businesses have to become efficient workplaces with the power of technology propelled by new ideas implementable at the speed of light. All the activities or Nader Independent of each other nor can be developed in silos. The inter-connectivity and the inter-application go together hand in hand.

Suggestions

1   Effort through empirical ways found out the following suggestions to address the above problems. Law cannot enforce motivation and leadership. Hence appropriate modifications must be made in the labour law to appreciate those who run the extra mile and take the extra Marathon there and to fulfil the objectives of the company. Legal provisions must also be there from the point of the Government to appreciate the spirit and the effort of the best among the workforce as they do in the case of the soldiers protecting the country.

Cross-border means the following issues:

1   Cross function
2   Cross people
3   Cross law
4   Cross-culture
5   Cross polity
6   Cross quality
7   Cross custom
8   Cross system
9   Cross structure.

2   The lawyers must contribute to the process of completion of the CBMA in a Project Evaluation Review Technique and Critical Path Method by using the latest tools of Technology in Microsoft Excel. Another suggestion is the legal recognition accredited to the external support by

standardising the available talent and making them as a body of accredited experts on par with the body of Chartered Accountants or Doctors or Architects.

3. Modification to the Industrial Disputes Act 1947 and annulment of irrelevant are urgently required to bridge the culture apps and in order not to lose the emerging opportunities abroad.

4. Right-sizing and right business models are the most important critical success factors for the Cross Border Mergers and Acquisitions and hence operational freedom must be granted to those experts and consultants who are involved in the integration process.

5. Modifications to the rules and regulations of the trade union law are required so that the workers were encouraged to speak up their minds without fear in a democratic environment as the right to work is now a fundamental right.

6. Modifications to the Law of Intellectual Property Rights and Copyright Act are required to recognise the new developments and technologies that are emerging in terms of planning production planning enterprise Resource Planning and using software models for increasing the productivity of the labour force as well as the new technologies like the 3D printing.

7. The new law needs to be made by the Parliament of India which makes the contributions of the senior management in being ambassadors of clarity and being extraordinary communicators for push up of decisions in integrating this country as the leader of emerging countries in the process of becoming a developed country. At the moment there is no law catering to the needs of the White Collar workers.

8. Information Technology Act is a powerful tool which if modified and customised to the emerging cross-border mergers environment can do wonders. Hence, there is a need to appoint A committee comprising of experts from Banking, Finance, Software, Real Estate, Medicine, Pharmaceuticals, Chemicals, Tourism, Hospitality and other Emerging Fields of cross-border positions to suggest modifications to the Information Technology Act.

9. Change management is extremely essential in CBMAs. Change management occurs at the crucial levels of the psychology of the employee the psychology of the employer and the perception of change among both of them. Robust communication with a clear-cut division of responsibility and Accountability in the following roles of (a) key player, (b) Key audience identification and (c) Key messenger and the key messaging is essential.

10. Right to Information Act 2005 is a game-changer in enforcing the fundamental rights of many Indians across different economic strata. Right to Information Act thus becomes a great tool for the employees to be rightly informed of the right message at the right time instead of, keeping them at a non-ending guessing game. There is a need to modify the existing provisions of The Right to Information Act and making it

apply to the private sector also and making it a tool of justice virtue and information of both right and the right information to make the workers the real stakeholders instead of becoming victims of the profit motive of any CBMA warrior. War and welfare are mutually contradictory. CBMA activity does not need a warrior every year and instead, it demands the bearers of truth. The Right to Information Act mentions more on the information and having the information being the right and less on the concept of right being truth. This study would like to have a paradigm shift in the meaning of the word right here. The stakeholders post CBMA in any geographical area of this country should not be reduced to the level of migrant labour leaving pitiably their ancestral place of residence because of the threat of the Agents of Mafiosi, masquerading themselves as the advocates of development.

11 Coupled with the Right to Information Act, there must be a Right to Communication Act. In a developing economy with optimal opportunities being available abroad in an increasingly globalising world and with a growing youth population in the environment of skill up-gradation, India requires a Right to Accountability Act also. The right to adequate communication addresses the right to be treated well psychologically as it recognises the concept of Audi Alteram Partem. The doctrine of Audi Alteram Partem is the cornerstone of the rights of natural justice which are also otherwise called the basic Human Rights across the globe.

12 Human rights are the other side of the word human resources; HR commonly is both human rights and human resources. Careful examination of this word makes a human being an aggressor and l simultaneously a victim. Industries engulf in the era of scientific management of FW Taylor view the human being as a resource not much different from any machine. FW Taylor was a conceptual contemporary of Max Weber, Scientific management and bureaucracy are two sides of the same coin of industry and government. Cross-Border Mergers and Acquisitions by their very nature destroy the borders in search of an opportunity and profit and hence lay emphasis more on the resource part of the HR than on the right part of the HR.

Hence this study suggests that an optimal modification must be made in the Human Rights Act 1993 so that the rights of workers and managers of both acquired and acquiring companies across the continents are recognised and addressed too, instead of leaving them to the vagaries of weather or manipulations of Machiavellian market forces as the chasers of Billion-dollar dreams who often disrespectfully and contemptuously dismiss their fellow human beings.

13 Commentaries through Facebook, WhatsApp, Instagram and other tools of social media are both assets and liabilities. With the maximum Tele density being recorded on the face of the earth in India, it is important to control calibrate and customise these tools of social media of instant communication across the globe as instruments of expression of

rights in a responsible manner rather than spreading hatred and mayhem against fellow human beings. This study hence suggests that TRAI, like SEBI, may be authorised to ensure that the rights of the workers or any other stay home stakeholders and the right of the Indian state as a taxing authority is not taken negligently by any big global multinational organisation.

14 Insofar as the human resource concept of HR is concerned, there is a need to modify the Sexual Harassment Act in the field because of the increasing participation of women in the workforce. The sexual harassment aspect becomes a critical failure factor because of the multicultural workforce that works cutting across different cultures across the group. Hence there must be the modification of the domestic law relating to the protection of women and the girls in the workforce exposing themselves not only to the Indian environment but the environment abroad. Matters become complicated because of the migrant labour especially from the sectors of domestic nurses and domestic helps both within India and without increasingly becoming victims to Human Trafficking. Human Trafficking law needs to be amended to cover this aspect of the Indian labour force working abroad because of cross-border mergers and acquisitions. The recent incident of 39 people from Punjab, Bengal, Orissa and Telangana being tortured by the terrorists of the Islamic State in Iraq and Syria in the province of the Mosul in Iraq is a case in point. While it is important to pay maximum attention to minor detail on the shop floor, it is more important to pay maximum attention to the psychological core problems of adjustment with the environment in the case of a fellow human being. This is to prevent the possible infliction of harm either on self or on others for frivolous causes.

15 Human rights of the labour force deal with the concept of disengagement in the era of cross-border mergers. People are a valued resource. However, it has been found out that for various reasons beyond their control, 54% of the people are not engaged and 19% of the workforce is actively disengaged while only 4% of the workforce is deeply engaged in becoming the amazing champion of innovation and productivity in complying with the objectives mission vision statements of the organisations for which they work for the remaining 25% are nearly engaged in some form or the other and it is important to increase the number 4% to at least 51% so that organisations have many deeply engaged rather than deeply disengaged workers in their areas of production, management, and service.

16 Due diligence in man management is important in the planning stage of the exporter mergers and acquisitions while the integration of manpower at every level is extremely important in the post-closing phase of CBMAs.

17 Intangible assets are more important than tangible assets for the long-term survival of any organisation in a competitive environment across continents. Satisfied employees are an important part of such intangible

assets. It is natural but when a company is being acquired the long-term employees of such a company start having job insecurity and the discussions to happen in the canteen rooms. In an environment of proven disengagement and un-engagement to the level of approximately 71% of the workforce coupled with the failure of collective leadership of both the acquiring and acquired company, the cumulative effect on the employees' morale is disastrous. The collective leadership of both acquired and acquiring companies needs to be actively engaged by both the government's agencies and enforcers of the Law, to address the issue of demoralisation among the stakeholders rather than leaving them on their own in an environment of free for all. Disengaged employees are not productive it has been found in this research that they have a lower chance of commitment. Disengaged employees are often involved in issues of indiscipline, misbehaviour and the spreading of rumours at the workplace.

18 Most of the workforce in India in the domestic industry as well as in the industry through CBMA belongs to the young generation. Broadly speaking youth across the world are subdivided into generation X and millennials. While the aged persons are called baby boomers the generation X and millennials often have ideological and adjustment issues with their seniors off and on the shop floor. A modification to youth services-related law in addressing the core issues of (a) building trust, (b) Foster Team Spirit c) addressing the issues of motivation is needed.

19 The Industrial Disputes Act 1947 deals with the category of worker not taking care of his age of retirement or age in service. The differentiation among age groups is a reality and it needs to be accounted for in the legal treatment of the workers regarding the generation to which such workers belong. Proper accounting of the differential aspect is taken care of in the rules and regulations and the directions given to the labour tribunals and the labour officers of various public and private sector organisations.

20 Welfare law relating to issues of pension, health, death in harness, golden handshake, loans for treatment, etc. take care of the welfare needs of the employees in the organised sector. Cross Border Mergers and Acquisitions talk only of employees of the organised sector by leaving almost 9 to 10 times the employees in the unorganised sector. Most of the employees of the unorganised sector or other self-employed or work for micro industries. While they are an active workforce in terms of their age and contribution to national productivity, they are faceless in terms of the Welfare law. Hence, insofar as the so welfare benefits are concerned all workforce must be brought under the same umbrella. The Government of India recently announced health for all schemes and insurance policies under Swastya Abhiyan. This program does not differentiate the unorganised labour while there are employment Agencies that measure these unorganised labourers as part of the workforce. All agencies are required to be brought under a single Window system to

tackle the issues of unorganised labour both in the agricultural and in the industrial front based on their Aadhaar card.

21 The law cannot qualitatively control the engagement aspect but it can address the quantification through the welfare measures of the State in terms of the facilities of psychiatric treatment of the affected in preventing psychiatric disabilities. The modification of the medical establishment rules in the workforce arena so that these psychiatric disabilities of the workforce or adequately taken care of on par with the best benchmark global practices available in the Scandinavian countries is needed.

22 Leadership needs to be provided in every aspect and the best possible leadership is the best insurance against insanity. Leadership and governance are correlated. In the Cross Border Mergers and Acquisition environment, the sales side may be in the denial mode on the engagement front while the buy-side was maybe over-optimistic in thinking that when once the process of acquisition is complete, they can satisfy the disgruntled labour with a magic wand and do enough of the cultural detoxification. Leadership plays a vital role in Cross-Border Mergers and Acquisitions not only from the point of the industry but also from the point of government. Otherwise, it becomes blind leading the blind. The government and industry must have good communication available always among them. The leadership gap is fatalistic to any CBMA activity. Leadership ensures engagement through motivation and a feeling of belongingness among the workers. It must be made mandatory for the welfare officers in both the target and acquired companies to do an engagement survey beforehand to know the positioning and the ideological comfort of the stakeholders to the challenge of the prospective cross-border merger and acquisition activity affecting their future.

23 Dysfunctional leadership is found to be dangerous. This functionality is reflected in the following matrix:

1 Decline rates of productivity
2 A huge number of complaints kept pending
3 Lack of successor planning
4 High turnover rate
5 Dis-harmony between compensation system and corporate objectives
6 Lack of innovation
7 Lack of feedback loop.

Making proper modifications in the syllabus of management studies to include the above-mentioned errors and possible solutions arising is needed, therefore. Just by asking the right questions, more transparency is ensured.

Just by asking questions right to transparency is initiated. Silence in questioning is a sure way to slavery. There is a need for modification of the law relating to the Whistle blowers' Protection Act in that adequate protection must be given to those who dare to ask questions and more production to those who dare to ask the right questions.

24 Disengagement at the bottom coupled with dysfunctionality at the top is the surest sign of the death of the organisation. Disengagement spreads like cancer and dysfunctionality devitalises like diabetes. There is a need for an adequate modification to the service and the conduct rules of the government servants as well as the labour law of industrial disputes act and other acts in back the organisations of both the government and industry must be granted enough freedom to recognise the cancerous cells and deal with them properly to protect the body politic of the organisational core competency.

25 Skills and behaviour attitude and aptitude are important ingredients of leadership. Proper leadership is the catalyst for the culture of the company. There is a need for incubating hence suggests that the rules and regulations of best HR practices be modified to take initiatives of recognising the proper qualities of leadership and incubate the same to convert them into the real Assets of the nation.

Eighty-eight per cent of the brand value in any organisation is made up of intangible assets; quality of leadership and labour are the main ingredients of such intangible assets.

Intellectual Capital is equal to the Summation of Human Capital (HC) and Innovation Capability (I).

$$IC = HC + I$$

The Non-Last Word

The ultimate aim of any state is the welfare of its citizens. Democracy is a means and not an end. Law is the arm of Democracy. The credibility of the State as a democratic institution internationally and nationally is the result of its chronological implementation of the Rule of Law. Rule of law, internationally in the context of cross-border mergers and acquisitions, means certainty and executability of contracts, in a mutually trustworthy environment of legal arbitration and adjudication in case of any dispute in transactions. Predictability is part of certainty. Mature democracies do not happen in a day. Legal incubation of democratic values both in economics and in politics defines the signature of the functionality of the State. India, that is Bharat, is a maturing democracy on its way to gain its lost place in the comity of nations.

8 Recent Reforms in Law in India

Law in general and corporate law in particular, in any country, require a level playing field for its compliance and its credibility. Corporate law under the Companies Act 2013 in India is a progressive step when compared to its former version of 1956. Certain non-compliances in the matters of mandatory filing of information, timely adjudication of disputes used to be penal offenses earlier. Since no company or corporation logically would be intentionally non-compliant with the provisions of the Companies Act, de-criminalising certain non-compliances and changing the name of non-compliances-offenses to matters of routine functions with additional costs to be paid for a delay is the norm of the day across the world. India, in order to further ease the process of doing business, de-criminalised many erstwhile offenses under the Companies Act 2013. This effort is in continuation with the Companies Amendment Act, 2019 in which 16 out of the 81 compoundable offenses were re-categorised as civil defaults.

The Company Law Committee 2019 was constituted by the Ministry of Corporate Affairs to review the mechanisms in a comprehensive manner. A new provision in the name of *in-house adjudication mechanism (IAM) was incorporated to avoid dilatory adjudication by the courts. By means of this new mechanism, the adjudicating officer shall impose penalties for 23 compoundable civil offenses, and in case of any dispute, an appeal can be made to the regional director*.

Seven compoundable offenses were removed since they have a remedy under other laws.

Issues like non-maintenance of books of accounts at the Register Office, non-compliance and contravention of public-offer and due to buy-back requirements etc were criminal offenses earlier and under the new Act, 11 of such compoundable offenses are no longer offenses and the penalty is a levy of fine now. There has been an inordinate framework for five offenses which include non-cooperation by promoters, directors with the company liquidator since a countervailing provision already exists in the IBC. Under the new Companies Act 2013, even one-person companies are possible. Lesser penalties are deemed for certain companies which include one-person companies, small companies, start-up companies or producer companies.

DOI: 10.4324/9781003396987-8

Reclassification of the 46 offenses under the Companies Act, as recommended by the high-level panel, would be able to reduce the number of comparable offenses under the Companies Act which earlier used to attract criminal penalties by around 70%. The following graphic illustrates the above initiative. The committee headed by the then Corporate Affairs Secretary Mr I. Srinivas recommended that 23 out of 66 comparable offenses under the Companies Act may be dealt with in house adjudication framework.

All the above initiatives are parts of the reforms to reduce the load on the National Company Law Tribunal so that smaller issues can be adjudicated smoothly without involving larger legal fora. The principle underlying the above initiatives is a test of objective determination versus subjective assessment.

A civil wrong is an offense that comes out of procedural error or lapses on technical grounds. The determination of such default should be objective and should not be viewed with suspicion of fraud when such lapse is not in conflict with the public interest. For instance, so-called offenses relating to non-compliance of orders of NCLT, which include matters concerning winding up of companies, default in the publication of NCLT orders relating to the reduction of share capital, the rectification of registers of security holders, variation of rights of shareholders, and payment of interest and redemption of debentures, etc. are removed from the list of the offenses of the Companies Act 2013. Interestingly, 23 compoundable offenses which used to be having imprisonment as punishment are totally removed and imprisonment has been replaced by a fine and thus a criminal offense has been amended to look like a civil penalty. Notable among them include violations regarding Corporate Social Responsibility (CSR) issues related to party transactions, defaults in the submission of material data or statistics to the Central Government.

India recently attained the status of the fifth largest economy in the world and is about to become the fourth largest one with its $ 5,000,000,000,000 GDP dream. Dreams become reality when policies become practices. The level playing field demands moving with the times and the ease of doing business should not remain as a mere slogan. Section 26(9) and section 40(5) of SEBI Act, in relation to the contravention of the provisions relating to the public offering of securities by company and matters related to the differences of dealing the treatment of application money received pursuant of a public offer, are now decriminalised. With the deletion of the imprisonment part of the popular sections, while retaining the pecuniary penalty, this step is considered to be in the right direction. The provisions related to the procedure regarding buyback of securities also do not draw imprisonment-related provisions of punishment in case of violation.

The provisions relating to significant beneficial owners underwent a change. Contraventions of the provisions relating to financial statements by the companies no longer attract punishment of imprisonment. The violations of the Corporate Social Responsibility contributions used to attract

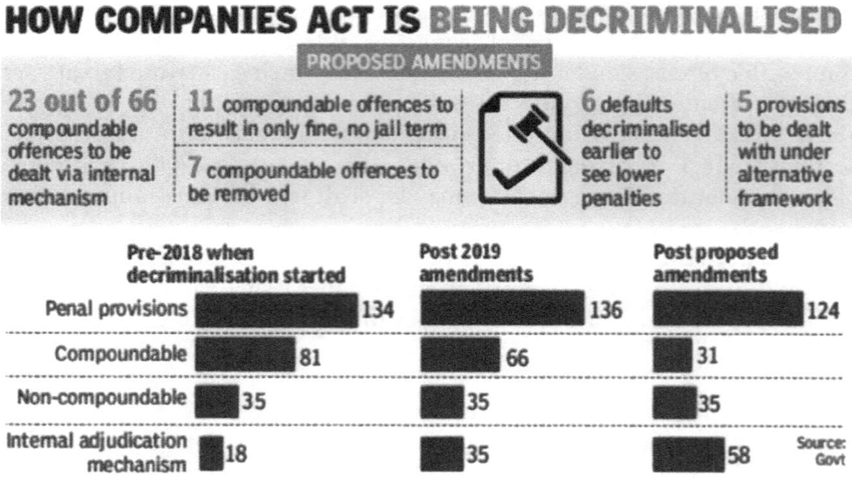

280 Recent Reforms in Law in India

HOW COMPANIES ACT IS BEING DECRIMINALISED

PROPOSED AMENDMENTS

- **23 out of 66** compoundable offences to be dealt via internal mechanism
- **11** compoundable offences to result in only fine, no jail term
- **7** compoundable offences to be removed
- **6** defaults decriminalised earlier to see lower penalties
- **5** provisions to be dealt with under alternative framework

	Pre-2018 when decriminalisation started	Post 2019 amendments	Post proposed amendments
Penal provisions	134	136	124
Compoundable	81	66	31
Non-compoundable	35	35	35
Internal adjudication mechanism	18	35	58

Source: Govt

Figure 8.1 De criminalising of Company Act, 2016.

imprisonment punishments. The imprisonment is now replaced by a monetary fine. Similar provisions have been made in the case of matters related to the appointment and qualification of directors.

Related-party transactions of listed companies and unlisted companies need to be prohibited and in case, they occur, punishment should be stringently enforced. However, in the case of listed companies, in place of imprisonment, the fine art of the penalty has been made manifold. In the case of unlisted companies, a minimum prescribed fine has been imposed in case of occurrence of any violation.

Any organisation including a start-up company requires goodwill to survive in an increasingly competitive environment. The criminalisation of violations of avoidable transactions will undoubtedly tarnish the image of the company in the long run. The Law Committee Report observed that criminal sanctions are more gregarious and permanent; the cost of civil penalties may be absorbed as part of running a business in the ordinary course.

CBMA and UNICORNS

Eighty-six per cent of the successful unicorn owners (a unicorn start-up is worth more than $ 1.0 billion) are from IITs (Indian Institute of Technology). By the year 2025, from the current 44, unicorns are likely to reach 100. Some known Unicorns brands are InMobi, Zomato, Swiggy, Razorpay, Cars24 and BYJU's. At US$ 104.00 billion, the 44 Unicorns created 1.4 million direct and indirect jobs. Swati Bhargava of Cash Karo and Falguni Nair of Nykaa inspire women entrepreneurs.

The common and unique fact between successful CBMA and Unicorn is that both are (a) Disrupters. (b) Both use first user familiarity (c) Strong executive leadership (d) Digital technology platforms (e) Innovation, IT, IOT, AI and ML (f) Financial technology (g) Ease of Transactions.

The unique factors for the rise of unicorns include:

i   Private Equity Funds(PEFs),
ii Internet Usage,
iii Digitised Commerce,
iv Availability of skilled talent, and
v   Compensation by foreign funds in trust when locals are afraid to invest.

Two success stories in 2020 during the COVID-19 Pandemic are (i) Innovaccer and (ii) Digit Insurance. FB, Google, Microsoft, as technological giants, entered the Indian unicorn Space. The regulatory environment must be facilitative than obstructive. De-risking start-up needs a massive joint effort by IITs, IIMs, governments and private companies.

Anil Chawla, the Co-Founder of Clix Capital, feels, "By providing our mini corns and sooni corns the right regulatory ambience and local sources of funding, India can create a truly innovative and resilient economy"; Mini Corns is a start-up with a US$ 1 million-plus valuation. Sooni corn is the one that is soon likely to become a unicorn.

National Asset Reconstruction Company Limited (NARCL), also called the BAD BANK, is another innovative measure by the Government of India, in the current year 2021, to which the SBI transferred Rupees 20,000 crores, including NPAs of Essar Power- Gujarat, Reliance Naval. Twenty-two NPAs worth Rs 89000 crores were to be transferred to NARCL.

The budget for FY 2021–2022 mentioned significant changes in the corporate law arena. Changes have been proposed to decriminalise the LLP Act, 2008 and to increase the threshold of the definitions of small companies, the introduction of a new version of MCA, coupled with desirable changes in the one-person company framework and an increase in the foreign direct investment limits in the Insurance Company Sector.

The Finance Minister of India announced that the changes in the Limited Liability Act 2008 are needed because similar changes have already been brought in the Companies Act 2013. The CLC (Company Law Committee) already proposed decriminalisation of the Limited Liability Partnership Act 2008 of certain compoundable offenses and shifting them to the in-house adjudication mechanism. The CLC report had been kept for public recommendations till February 2, 2021. Twelve offenses and one penal provision have been proposed to be omitted. The purpose is to lessen the burden on NCLT. There are provisions for issuance of secured nonconvertible debentures by the LLP's and also provisions for restricting the merger of LLPs with the companies apart from the introduction of accounting standards for certain classes of LLPs.

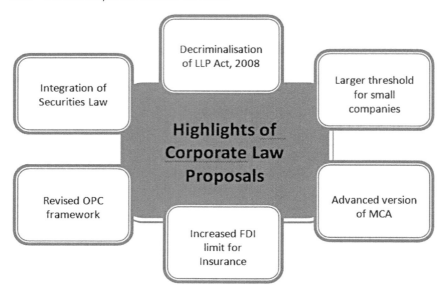

Figure 8.2 Important proposed modifications of Corporate Law in India.

The definition of the small company has been changed from the paid-up capital being increasing from Rs 50 lakhs to Rs 2 crores. For small companies, it is further proposed that they need not submit the cash flow statement as part of the financial statements and the necessity of four board meetings has been done away with by replacing it with only one meeting in a calendar year. This step is likely to bring more than Two lakh additional companies under the definition of the small company which can have a lower compliance burden including lower penalties for violations and over filing requirements. This is the right step in the direction of an easier way of doing business in India.

One-Person Company Framework (OPC)

The present limitation of two years mandatory period before converting the one-person company to other kinds has been done away with in the new budget. The purpose is to motivate the growth of OPCs and in that process to encourage start-ups. The residential requirement of eligibility of the persons for starting the OPCs stands reduced from 182 days to 120 days. Even Non-Resident Indians also can operate OPCs in India.

MCA

21 Version 3.0

The Ministry of Corporate Affairs portal, namely, MCA 21 version 3.0, according to the new budget, will be utilising Data Analytics, Artificial Intelligence and Machine Learning. E-Scrutiny, E-Consultation and E-Adjudication as part of Compliance Management are vital parts of MCA now.

NCLT Framework Strengthening

The National Company Law Tribunal is overburdened and in order to reduce the workload, E-Courts have been proposed to be implemented in the budget. This is part of the initiative for Digital India.

Foreign Direct Investment in Insurance Companies

The FDI limits have been increased from the current 49% to 74%. However, the majority of the directors on the board and keep managerial persons have to be residents in India. At least 50% of the directors ought to be independent directors and a specified percentage of the profits need to be retained a general reserve. In other words, adequate safeguards have been kept to prevent any mismanagement.

Securities Market Code

Presently, the operative laws in the market of securities in India are as follows.

1. SEBI Act 1992.
2. Depositories Act 1996.
3. Securities Contracts (Regulation) Act 1956.
4. Government Securities Act 2007.

In line with the labour code, the present budget proposes to combine the above four Acts into one consolidated rationalised single code, namely the Securities Market Code.

Exemption of Stamp Duty in Government Sale Transactions

The Stamp Act 1899 is applicable for transactions involving the sale or disinvestment or the merger of all companies. The budget 2021–2022 proposes to do away with the applicability of the provisions of the above-said Act towards government transactions which include asset transfer among public sector enterprises.

There are proposals to reduce the tax disputes in India. Approximately Rs 6 trillion is stuck in direct tax litigation in courts and tribunals across India. There is a need to provide a mediation framework towards a negotiated settlement rather than dragging it inordinately in the legal fora. The budget has proposals for reducing the period of reopening the past tax assessments, incentivising digital business and start-ups, extending faceless assessment at an appellate level also insofar as the tax complaints are concerned.

Mergers—Acquisitions Vis-à-vis Budget 2021–2022

Hitherto, any transaction of business transfer for an agreed consideration is taxable as capital gains in the hands of the seller. The confusion arose over the concept of slump sales. The definition of the slump sale gave rise to an interpretation that whenever authorities reject cash transactions in terms of slump sale only, then the taxing provisions of the slump sale arose. Presently, in order to solve the above dispute, the definition of slump sale has been widened to include all types of transfers and in that process making all exchange transactions taxable. Goodwill is no longer a depreciable asset. The Supreme Court of India accepted the position of goodwill under the business restructuring exercise. In the present budget, it has been proposed that goodwill shall not be considered as a depreciable asset and therefore is no longer eligible for a claim of tax depreciation. There is a possibility of a genuine hardship to investors because of the above change and hence there is a need to look at it afresh from the point of view of the interest of the investors.

Public sector companies will have relief whenever there is an amalgamation. Strategic disinvestment of the PSUs is one of the key focus areas of the Government of India.

Latest Developments (till June 24, 2021)

The Technical Advisory Committee (TAC) of the National Financial Reporting Authority (NFRA) suggested the introduction of policy for deciding the finalisation of disciplinary matters against auditors. NFRA was created under sub-section (1) of section 132 of C. A., 2013. The parallel institution in the USA is the Public Company Accounting Oversight Board (PCAOB). The aim of National Financial Reporting Authority (NFRA) is to protect the public interest, interest of investors and creditors by establishing quality standards in auditing, accounting with effective supervision of the accounting function of companies. NFRA can take up investigations in matters relating to auditors of listed, unlisted companies of capital not less than Rs 50 crores, in insurance, banking and electricity. NFRA deals with notifications related to, Company Act (Amendment 2019), Company Act 2013, Limited Liability Partnership Act, 2008, Charter Accountants Act, 1949, Banking Regulating Act, 1949, Insurance Act, 1938.

The National Financial Reporting Authority (NFRA) has the mandate to check the functioning of accounting/auditing by a certain class of companies called Public Interest Entities. Hence, the database is being prepared currently, which includes Company Identification Number (CIN). NFRA is closely and conjointly working with Ministry of Corporate Affairs (MCA), Corporate Data Management (CDM) of Division and their recognised National Stock Exchanges. Database of 5300 listed and 1000 unlisted companies were completed by June 2019 and 200 insurance companies also figure in this list. The TAC is headed by Prof. R. Narayana Swamy of IIM,

Bangalore. TCA's main task was to advise on (i) Quality of audit (ii) Promotion of awareness in Audit/Accounting standards and role of NFRA. Auditee company pays the auditor, and thus there is an inherent contradiction in the aims and process of auditing. Accounting scams globally necessitated the creation of PCAOB in the USA and the Financial Reporting Council (FRC) in the UK.

SEBI took the professional services of an international consultant to recommend modification in the structure and organisation issues. The consultant opined that the ICAI has been passive in its oversight and less active on the investigation, and hence Satyam Scam, bank scams, etc. happened. There are 1,500 auditors in India compared to 3,000 in the USA. "In the lay term, we recommend that SEBI drive the case for establishing a separate regulation (NFRA) which is independent of audit profession." ICAI is a regulator. NFRA too is a regulator. The Disciplinary Committee of the Institute of Chartered Accountants of India (ICAI) takes four years to dispose of a case. ICAI covers other companies and recommends action to NFRA. The TAC pointed out that like in any other disciplinary matters of any other profession, enforcing, adjudicating disciplinary matters consumes time and often is frustrating as it takes efforts, resources and litigations before tribunals, courts, appeals, etc. and before the NCLAT. There is above all the spectre of uncertainty. NFRA needs a comprehensive standalone law covering litigant aspects. The law should provide for "institutional, functional and financial autonomy of NFRA" apart from empowering NFRA to fill out "the operational details and requirement within the overall framework."

Prevention of Scams/Frauds in CBMAs

Role of NFRA (India), PCAOB (USA)

Comparative Infrastructure in the USA and Lessons to Be Learned

PCAOB is the creation under the SEC of the legal requirement for audit and accounting inspection to prevent fraud under the Sarbanes- Oxley Act 2002 (S.O. Act 2002). Prevention of fraud concerns the protection of American Investors. When a legal body, under the Sovereign Authority of the USA, as third party expresses studied and informed opinion on the health and integrity of financial statements of companies, the general investors can make investment decisions. Accuracy, honesty and integrity are essential not only in the published reports which happen on quarter-to-quarter basis but in the process of making such reports.

Fudging of figures of a company will not confine its damage to that company's financial health and hence prolonged survival, but a ripple effect poisons the whole economy, severally blowing the confidence of investors and all stakeholders in the economy itself. The Supreme Court of USA in the case of *US vs Arthur Young* accords vitality to the auditor in being a public watchdog demanding total imperviousness from clients and total adherence to public trust.

The evaporation of US$ 7 trillion from the years 1990 to 2001, through fraudulent gimmickry of financial figures at Enron and WorldCom resulted in the necessity that Sarbanes-Oxley Act, 2002 (S.O. Act 2002) was passed and PCAOB became a powerful watchdog institution.

Protecting investors would remain a pipe dream if the accuracy and reliability of corporate disclosures are not ensured. Section 101 of the Act states that the PCAOB oversees the audits of public companies "in order to protect the interests of investors and further the public interest in the preparation of informative, accurate, and independent audit reports."

The Big Four audit firms in the USA acquired 160 consulting firms by the year 2015 alone. They became an oligopoly in the global auditing profession. The Big Four are no longer mere audit firms. They have advertising, consulting, legal service provisions as adjunct functions. Before the SO Act, 2002, some of these firms were part independent auditors and consultant defendants! Twenty years of PCAOB did not prevent the damage to auditor independence. Instead of being a sole independent auditor, Big Four wear caps like "Strategic Partner" and "Trusted Advisor." If the same firm is paid more as a trusted advisor, how can be auditing be independent?

The PCAOB, in the year 2018, introduced, as a check, the new Audit Participant Form. This Form is expected to disclose how much the so-called independent audit was actually conducted by the so-called independent firm. Auditors were also expected to issue an "Early Warning" about the financial health of the company in the near future.

The Financial Accounting Standards Board (FASB) established fresh conditions for Chief Financial Officers (CFOs) of a firm to disclose the ongoing concern matters. The PCAOB contemplates repeating a similar feat. Lobbying is another strategy by Big Four; 80% of the responses came from these Big Four for a new initiative by PCAOB, while only 8% came from investors.

The Board of Directors should be diverse. Diversity is both at once business indispensability and business convenience. The audit firms may be encouraged to have better professionals on their boards.

The Environment Social and Governance (ESG) matters now are a concern for global investors as 89% of investors look into ESG matters closely. The need of the hour is integration of functioning of SEC, FASB and PCAOB in sustainability matters.

PCAOB

The new Chairman Gary Gensler of SEC removed the current head of PCAOB and overhauled the Board, in the month of June 2021. The critics pointed out the dysfunction of PCAOB, its inability to protect the interest of investors and in ensuring the independence of audit firms. In the light of the KPMG–PCAOB cheating scandal in the year 2017, the then SEC Chairman installed new Board members in the PCAOB. The critics pointed (1) the infrequency of Board meetings, (2) failure to seek public consent on the revision of rules, (3) failure to act on recommendations regarding reforms in the areas of disclosure of audit quality metrics, auditing non-compliance with laws and regulations, going concern audit opinions and need of auditors filings with other mandatory filings with SEC, (4) the 40 % fall of activity of PCAOB in the year 2020 compared to the year 2019.

Professor Shiva Raj Gopal, the Kester and Byrnes Professional of Columbia Business School, feels that the SEC of the USA should expand its watchdog focus to protect the interests of American investors throughout the world. PCAOB expressly articulated its regretful inability in not having access to the working paper of audits of the Chinese listed companies on the US stock exchanges, with 217 such companies exceeding the US$ 2 trillion combined market cap. These facts were revealed by the U.S.–China Economy Security Review Commission.

Audit transparency is essential in the CBMA framework. In a communication on June 15, 2021, the Columbia-based professor Shiva Raj Gopal felt that While the U.S. Securities and Exchange Commission (SEC) is beginning to take action, under the recently passed Holding Foreign Companies Accountable Act of 2020, to address issues with the auditing practices of PCAOB-registered firms in emerging markets, including China, we think a more strategic focus is warranted to fulfill the SEC's mandate to protect investors, maintain orderly markets, and facilitate capital formation. Capital markets were not as globalized as they are today when the SEC was established in 1934. A global approach, suitable for the 21st century, is necessary.

Foreign missions jointly are required to be set up under the Office of the International Affairs (OIA) of SEC and PCAOB. If SEC, PCAOB and FASB are to protect the avowed American interests in investments, prevent frauds in CBMAs and deliver as "eyes and ears" of America, and the SEC shall cover (a) the Asia Pacific from Singapore, (b) EU from London, (c) Latin America from Sao Paulo, as the extension of the soft power of the USA's new Monroe Doctrine. Professor Shiva Raj Gopal adds: "A defining feature of soft power is that it is not coercive, and the currency of soft power includes culture, political values, and foreign policies." Soft power needs to be complemented with hard power. Therefore, it is also recommend tasking the overseas SEC and PCAOB missions with local inspections of audit firms and of companies based in the region and cross-listed in the U.S.

In the case of non-compliance, the threat of the cessation of diplomatic ties and ban on foreign markets is a viable option. The professor feels, "It is time for the SEC and the PCAOB to invest in expanding their international footprint if they want to effectively safeguard the interests of American investors in overseas companies."

Some important ruling of courts related to CBMAs are vital in guiding the course of action for future. In *Re Kiloskar Electric Co. Ltd.*[1] it was held that the Court has neither the expertise nor the jurisdiction to delve deep into the commercial wisdom exercised by the creditors and members of the Company who have ratified the scheme by the requisite majority. To that extent the jurisdiction of the Company Court is peripheral and supervisory and not appellate. The supervisory jurisdiction of the Company Court can also be culled out from the provisions of Section 392 of the Act.

Sec 392 of the Companies Act refers to Companies Act 1956. The following guidelines were given by honourable Supreme Court of India through *Mihir H. Mafatlal vs Mafatlal Industries Ltd.*[2]

In *Miheer H. Mafattal v. Mafatlal Industries Ltd.*, the Supreme Court has laid down certain guidelines to be followed by the Court while sanctioning a merger. The guidelines are as follows:

1. The statutory procedures such as the requisite meeting of the creditors or class of creditors, or of the members or class of members and backing up by majority vote should be complied with.[3]
2. The meetings of the creditors should have the relevant information[4] so that the voters could arrive at an unbiased and an informed decision with respect to the scheme of merger and the decision should be just and fair.
3. The court should be satisfied that the applicant seeking approval of a merger has provided all the relevant information under proviso of Section 391(2).
4. The proposed scheme should not be contrary to any provision of law and public policy. The scheme should be just, fair and reasonable. The valuation of shares and the share exchange ratio should be fair and reasonable.
5. The creditors, members or class of members should act bona fide and should not coerce the minority and compromise their interests.

Under the Companies Act 1956, winding up of a company means any company. "Any company liable to be wound up under the Act" means all companies to which the provisions relating to winding up apply.[5]

All foreign Companies are included in the Body corporates. "A foreign company is included in the expression 'body corporate'.[6] The provisions of section 390 enable unregistered companies and foreign companies to invoke the provisions of the Act pertaining to mergers.[7]

Cross-Border Mergers and Acquisitions and Jurisdiction

Under the 1956 Act, a foreign company having a place of business in India shall get themselves registered with the Registrar of Companies at New Delhi, though the principal office might be situated somewhere else.[8]

In *Re Bank of Muscat*,[9] the Court was faced with a question as to which court would have jurisdiction to sanction a merger in cases where the principal office and the place of ROC is different. Bank of Muscat had its branch office in Bangalore, and being a foreign company it filed its registration papers with the ROC according to Section 592 read with Section 597 of the 1956 Act. The foreign company proposed a merger with an Indian banking company, i.e. Centurion Bank Ltd.

The Karnataka High Court observed that according to the language of Section 10[10] it is that court where its principal place of business is situated which has the jurisdiction, because its principal place of business is deemed to be a registered office of the foreign company. So, it was held that the merger scheme presented before the High Court of Karnataka was correct and the court has the relevant jurisdiction to sanction the merger.

United States and the Doctrine Effect

The US Supreme Court in *American Banana Co.v. United Fruit Co.*[11] was of the opinion that "where the acts in restraint of trade were committed outside its territorial jurisdiction, such acts would not fall under the prohibitions of the Sherman Act."

The Doctrine became relayed subsequently through the *U.S. vs Aluminium Company of America*. Subsequently in *United States v. Aluminium Company of America*,[12] the U.S. Supreme Court was of the opinion that the domestic courts will assume jurisdiction if an activity has an effect to restrain trade and commerce in the country, irrespective of the fact whether the activity has no taken place within the territorial jurisdiction of the USA.

In *Timberlane Lumber Co. v. Bank of America National Trust & Savings Association*,[13] the Court opined that it had jurisdiction over alleged anti-competitive activities; however, it restricted itself from applying extra-territorial jurisdiction.

Notes

1. (2003) 116 Comp Cas 413 (Kar).
2. (1997) 1 SCC 579.
3. See Companies Act, (1956). Section 391.
4. Ibid. Section 393(1)(a).
5. Re Khandelwal Udyog Ltd & ACME Mfg Ltd, (1977) Comp Cas 503 (Bom).
6. Companies Act, (1956). Section 394(4)(b). Section 2(7).
7. Bank of India Ltd v. Ahmedabad manufacturing & Calico Printing Company Ltd (1972) 42 Comp Case.
8. Companies Act, (1956). Section 597.
9. 60 CLA 325 (Kar).
10. "The Court having jurisdiction under this Act shall be - (a) the High Court having jurisdiction in relation to the place at which the registered office of the company concerned is situate…"
11. 213 U.S. 347 (1909).
12. 377 U.S. 271 (1964).
13. 749 F.2d 1378.

9 Kaizen for Global Excellence

Recent amendments to various legal provisions and implications for CBMAs indicate that the whole world is getting ready to face the new Omicron variety of the COVID virus. As on December 19, 2021, it would be relevant to review the amendments in law both in the USA and India along with important judicial pronouncements. Unicorns, new start-ups and the practical implications of global announcements by the Prime Minister of India to reduce the carbon imprint assume importance not merely in energy sector but in economic coordination among the leaders in green energy and major consumers of energy, like India. The new automobile policy of scrapping of old vehicles, building new express ways, corridors and the initiatives like Production Linked Incentives (PLIs), the initiative for new chip production in India itself, the globally relevant fact of India emerging as manufacturing hub of hardware related to Communication Industries and a host of such initiatives became relevant issues for present situation and further growth of CBMAs in India.

Initiatives are on the anvil to amend the Income Tax Act, 1961 as to make it more pro-business organisations and less cumbersome for businessmen. Due diligence is learnt the hard way, and democratic governments prefer constant Kaizen. The Arbitration Council rulings on global companies of communications with reference to retrospective taxation became a truly learning opportunity for India. When the word "transfer" becomes legal in the CBMA framework, it implies a merger, amalgamation demerger or any combination of asset reconstruction of corporation becomes a taxable entity. Legitimacy of transactions is the purpose of accounting standards both in India and in the USA.

Transfer of assets can call for tax man's review interest of capital growth tax.[1] So are the provision in relation to (a) amalgamation,[2] (b) Slump sales,[3] (c) setoff and carry-forward of losses,[4] (d) demerger,[5] (e) capital gains,[6] (f) security transaction tax.[7] Relaxations in legal provisions through amendments of scrapping of old irrelevant, obstructions obscurantist law like an albatross and replacing it with flexibility inbuilt and expiry date mentioned provision are the need of the day. For example, if a foreign company holds shares of Indian companies, then in the instance of merger, demerger acquisition of either domestic or cross-border of such company with another

DOI: 10.4324/9781003396987-9

foreign company, the capital gains tax is exempted,[8] under certain conditions. There are many instances when companies gained through diligent compliance with the above provision.

Recent Examples of Implementation of Legal Provisions in India

Videocon Industries, led by Venugopal Dhoot, became the main contributor of NPAs to public sector banks Union Bank and the Dena Bank. Recently, SEBI slapped a fine of Rs 7.50 million on him and two others, Videocon Realty, Infrastructures and Electro Parts (India). SEBI said, "Notices being insiders had executed off market transactions while in possession of Unpublished Price Sensitive Information (UPSI).[9] The positive examples include industries like Infosys.

> Infosys, post Covid Pandemic utilized digital initiatives and modernised all consultancy platform by utilising the technology related to artificial intelligence.

The Enforcement Directorate attached assets worth Rs 578 crores in the UK of Wadhwans, the former DHFL promoter, under the provisions of Prevention of Money Laundering Act (PMLA).

Post-COVID Pandemic Changes, Threats and Opportunities

Consumer Packaged Goods (CPG) need Key Performance Indicators (KPI) in real time, in turn requiring in place a resilient supply chain. Business to Consumer (BTC) activity need omni channel experience, customer fruitful across channels, customer visit conversion and customer hyper personalisation. For being more efficient, less costly and differentially competent, the new adoption through Artificial Intelligence, Cloud capability utility and ingenious application become factors of sustainable winning in the digital market domains.

The National Crime Record Bureau of India in its report post-COVID pandemic mentioned that more entrepreneurs and employees than farmers committed suicide in the past year. The COVID-19 pandemic-induced trauma is real. Ensuring mental well-being and reduction of stress from uncertainty are the objectives. Ninety-two per cent of Indians feel that "robots can help them advance their careers better than humans."[10]

Management decision-making is critical in the pandemic era. Documentation and financial judgements occupy this specific deliverable conditionalities bordering on survival of both organisational vitality and employee retention. AI and robotics are playing important role in these challenging environments, across many industries including those going for CBMAs. Pandemic, according to 96% of survey respondents from India,[11] changed the definition of success which now is more aligned with achieving work–life balance, prioritising mental health and having flexibility over when and where they work being the key.

The COVID-19 pandemic made cloud computing relevant for banking in both performance improvement and digital financial inclusion spaces helping in greater visibility, isolation of data and control. It reduces time to take decisions and errors in processes too so that implementation can be at a greater speed.

IBBI Regulatory Framework Changed Mandate

To avoid delay in the CIRP (Corporate Insolvency Resolution Process), the Standing Committee of Finance of IBBI recommended making a framework with the power of law to bring the COC (Committee of Creditors) under the regulatory framework of IBBI. The purpose of the amendment is to bring the C.O.C. also under regulatory frame to avoid duplication, delay and even derailment of the IBC framework. The other purpose of the amendment, as of the first week of October 2021, is to stream live the CIRP through more certainty and improved objectivity. New initiatives include, apart from establishing a bank for dealing with NPAs, establishing the National Financial Reporting Authority. The purpose is to bring in standardisation in accounting procedures. Institutional vitality ultimately works for better enforcement of contracts, in turn helping to confidence building in global investor community to invest in India. An improved rank on Ease of Doing Business Index is a positive sign.

The reform agenda has another initiative on the anvil for implementation from January 1, 2021, called the Prompt Correction Action (PCA) of the Reserve bank of India (RBI). RBI issued a notification, mentioning,

> The objective of the PCA framework is to enable supervisory intervention at appropriate time and require the supervised entity to initiate and implement remedial measures in a timely manner so as to restore its financial health. The PCA framework is also intended to act as a tool for effective market discipline. The PCA framework does not preclude the Reserve Bank of India from taking any other action as it deems fit at any time, in addition to the corrective actions prescribed in the frame work.[12]

The PCA evaluations are on capital, profitability, leverage and asset quality. The new changes include removal of the criteria of return on asset as an indicator to qualify for PCA.

The COVID-19 pandemic forced the Government of India to suspend certain sections of IBC from March 25 2020 (Sec. 7, 9 and 10 of IBC, 2016). The latest amendment by the government was the "Insolvency and Bankruptcy Code, Ordinance, 2020," through which section 10(A) and section 66(3) were inserted. The addition of section 66(3) of IBC is for the protection of partner/director of a corporate debtor from any liability in case any default occurs when Corporate Insolvency Resolution Process

(CIRP) gets suspended u/s 10 A of IBC. Further, regulation 40 C was also introduced in IBBI Regulations, 2016, for providing exemption from the lockdown period.[13]

NCLT Chennai Bench held that "the ordinance shall have retrospective applicability to all applications irrespective of their date u/s 7, 9, & 10 of IBC."[14] However Kolkata NCLT made a contradictory order.[15]

Evaluation of Initiatives and Implications for Further Action

The Insolvency and Bankruptcy Code completed a five-year period in the year 2021. No law is absolute and an economic reformist law is much less from its embryonic form of reflecting the intentions of the makers and experiences of peers abroad. The economic law becomes a formidable ally in nation's development through enterprise calibration and continuous improvement influencing and being influenced by global, national, local factors. IBC underwent six legislative operations to be part of the overall economic reform agenda of democratic government of India. The three objectives of IBC respectively are:

i   Resolution of insolvency which is a nature business.
ii Maximisation of net asset value of insolvent firm.
iii Recreation through optimised entrepreneurship. Safeguard of stakeholders' interest through a time-bound enforcement of agreements.

Creative destruction through protection of viable firm and wading act of redundant dead wood is the philosophy behind IBC initiative. Apart from inbuilt in-efficiency, better competencies from market, newer products, other causes for insolvencies and bankruptcies include pandemic-induced credit crisis, operational logistics, demand crunch and decimated investments for crucial expansions or diversification of product mixes. The COVID-19 pandemic unfailingly repeated its expected impact, worse in quantum than a 2008 global financial crisis. Some remedies, learnt hard from past came to rescue in saving firms going en masse insolvent/bankrupt, include (a) flexibility in loan repayment (b) reduction or cancelation of interest rates, (c) no penalty claiming, (d) extension of time frame, (e) infusion of fresh capital in banks for disbursement, (f) modification in asset classification, (g) ordinance keeping stringent sections of law in abeyance and (h) freedom to decision makers to be empathetic from mere tool boxes for adherence agenda. A 100-year-old lesson of the Great Depression and the Spanish flu was not forgotten.

Pandemic liquidation infuses premature death of even healthy firms, compelling a distress sale if any. Suspensions of certain provision of IBC are well-crafted strategy to keep a competent industry live than to liquidate a problematic one. March 25, 2020 is a crucial date in IBC's history for, on that day, the Government of India, through an ordinance, performed a "Key hole surgery."[16]

Suspending a Tiny Part of IBC

Through proactive, cautions watch, the Finance Ministry did not wait longer to send a correct message. The initial six-month period covered all three lockdowns, and the extension was necessary due to the unabated wrath that the COVID-19 pandemic created, leaving no company/organisation/individual unaffected. The suggestion was aimed at equality and balancing of interests of both debtors and creditors. A mere 2% of insolvency proceedings were self-initiated in the past. Checks were inbuilt to detect useful defaulter strategic exploitation of ordinance, under section 29A of IBC, 2016.

Certain views were critical with reference to sub-section 31 of Sec. 66 of IBC, 2016 in alleging that it may encourage fraudulent activity by unethical directors of a certain category of company due to protection, through liability protection under sub-section (2). This critical view is redundant is the light of sub-section (1) of the same provision and also due to section 166 of the Companies Act, 2013.

IBBA, the Insolvency and Bankruptcy Board of India assessed the performance of the IBC for five years in June 2021. Miss Medha Shekar, Assistant Manager IBBA, writes,

> Today, the Code is a well-oiled apparatus, buttressed by a thriving ecosystem comprising of about 3500 Insolvency Professionals, three Insolvency Professional Agencies, about 80 Insolvency Professional Entities, one Information Utility, 16 Registered Valuer Organisations, more than 3900 Registered Valuers, several benches of the Adjudicating Authority with pan India presence and a massive volume of jurisprudence that has facilitated the cause of the Code time and again. The Code has rescued 348 CDs till March, 2021 through resolution plans, one third of which were in deep distress. On the flip side, it has referred 1277 CDs for liquidation, three-fourth of which were either sick or defunct. The CDs rescued had assets valued at Rs. 1.11 lakh crore, while the CDs referred for liquidation had assets valued at Rs. 0.46 lakh crore when they were admitted to corporate insolvency resolution process (CIRP) under the Code. Thus, in value terms, around three fourth of distressed assets were rescued on account of the Code. The Code has also facilitated recovery of non-performing assets by banks. RBI data indicates that as a percentage of claims, scheduled commercial banks have been able to recover 45.5 per cent of the amount involved through IBC for the financial year 2019–2020, which is the highest as compared to recovery under other modes and legislations.

The former Chairman of SBI Mr Kumar too expressed that IBC brought a behavioural change in all stakeholders. Distress, when seen in early stages, like cancer be cured before it became default and ultimately a disaster on doing up in bankruptcy. IBC works like an early warning alerting acoustic accountability/accountancy ecosystem. IBBA mentions that, "till March, 2021, 17,305 applications for initiation of CIRPs of CDs having underlying default of Rs. 5,33,145 crore were resolved before their admission," and reduced time from 43 years (according to Doing of Business reports of World Bank), to 406 days. IBBA adds,

> till March, 2021, resolution of about 322 CIRPs (for which data was available) costed on an average 0.92 per cent of liquidation value and 0.49 per cent of resolution value. This is a significant improvement in comparison to the erstwhile regime that entailed a cost of almost 9 per cent of estate value.[17]

The latest amendment is the introduction of pre –packaged insolvency resolution processes for MSMF, India's rank moved up from 136 to 52 in terms of "resolving insolvency" in the last three years in the World Bank Group's Doing Business Reports. In the Global Innovation Index, India's rank improved from 111 in 2017 to 47 in 2020 in "Ease of Resolving Insolvency."

The challenges of cross-border insolvency and enterprise group insolvency are being looked into now.

Lessons of the Pandemic—2nd Annum in the Year 2021

The COVID-19 pandemic continues to teach the globally active population lessons of adjustment towards the emerging trends while surviving the pandemic and modifying the transactions environment in minimising the risks of pandemic origin. The online community is in education, conferences and business deals, monitoring, meeting clients and even delivering judgements after online arguments and telecasting the same like that of the Gujarat High Court. Law emerges to conduct the transactions within the framework of ethical principles, among others notably the doctrine of natural justice and fundamental principles of Equality, Freedom and Justice. There are uncertainties in the following areas.

Role of AI (Artificial Intelligence) and ML (Machine Learning) in the Corporate Sector

AI and ML are now substitutes for the human face. Computer-trained voice recognition software, drones, driverless cars, robotic surgeries and websites as marketing tools, social media dominating the business cycles, transactions, project design, project management, etc. are increasingly replacing human labour. At the moment, one broad law, namely the Information Technology Act, covers the above-mentioned areas. While Rupay, PayPal, etc. dominate the payments market, the world is emerging towards a paperless currency. Digitalisation is the new mantra, and the law needs to catch up to fill up the huge gap. If the law is inadequate, and cannot anticipate the frauds that currency can create, the disaster Germany suffered in post-First World War, and some Latin American countries suffered now, would be repeated. At this moment, the world witnesses the crisis in Afghanistan too glaring to inform the inadequacies of the global issues related to the foreign exchange rates, falling currencies and the new words like "Bit Coins."

Exposure of New Sectors to Competition and Predation

Competition works against monopoly and the spirit behind the competition is freedom at the level of individual and accountability for fair play at the level of the organisation. The ultimate institution in any country is the Government, the working arm of a Sovereign State. When competition is neither respected nor secured, the level playing field is replaced by the project redesigns of bureaucratic-political-criminal mafia (vide the Vohra Committee report). Companies are either destroyed or there would be hostile takeovers and harassment to the honest law-abiding businessmen. This has been the global trend and is factored in the Ease of Doing Business Rankings. It is also part of the Corruption Perception Index.

The takeovers through genuine mergers and acquisitions are part of natural growth and are a vital play of market dynamics. However, legal loopholes, either in deliberate policy or in implementation or through commercial gerrymandering, are unhealthy in the short run and disastrous in the long run. Global capital chases fair opportunities and never false/fraudulent assurances of the import dictators or terrorist regimes under autonomy mask. Countries as a whole or regions within countries of federal set up would compete for the global financial and FDI enabled capital. Law provides the risk assessment criteria to teams of expert investment advisor firms across the globe. Opportunity for profit and assessment of risk is dynamic and, like foreign exchange rates, changes frequently. Stable economies are symbolically expressed through stable currencies and stable legal institutional setup.

Law is an institution, interpretation and assurance against uncertainty.

The Dangers of Living with Obsolescence

Throwing out toxic substances is an essential ingredient of life preservation systems in all organic life forms. So is the case of organisations and law for organisations. The Companies Act, 1956 India was so obsolete that it required a complete overhaul, and so the Government of India brought a new Act, namely the Companies Act, 2013. Secondly, the MRTP Act outlived its purpose, and the Competition Act, 2002 replaced it rightly so. Reform in existing law through legislation and through ordinances is part of governance in a democracy. However, the main purpose of overhauling the entire system is to ensure that the system remains always healthy, and dynamic rather than rusting and collapsing due to (1) Irrelevance, (2) Incompetence, (3) Lethargy, (4) Non-farsightedness and (5) Indifference.

Disruptions, Hacking, Cyber Threats and Fraud

Corporate law operates in the corporate environment and disruptions, hacking, and cyber threats galore. Cyber threats and hacking are not confined to geographies. Handling cyber threats requires a coordinated response. It is CERT-IN in India, and the National Security Council is aware of the threats and so are the dedicated workforce teams of experts in the RBI, DRI, ED, IB, RAW and the CBI. The law needs to guide the available talent ordinate with the best talent available anywhere including fellow Democratic establishments like those of the USA, Israel, the UK or France, Japan, and Australia. Law enforcers' accountability and performance analytics can be overseen by a single-window cabinet like the CFIUS of the USA or any such new body in India.

Cost of Repetition and the Question of Legitimacy and Intention of Enforcement

Where things can go wrong, things will go wrong. Eternal vigilance is the price for liberty. If duplications in operations galore, confusion rather than fusion would be the end result. A single window system is preferred to multiple windows for (1) Speedy disposal, (2) Accountability, (3) Timely management, (4) Co-ordination and (5) Anticipation of troubles and timely response.

Multiple enforcement agencies need to be brought under a single roof for better Coordination, Commands, Control, Communication, Care, Caution, Concern, Corroboration, Co-option and Competence (C^{10}). The Indian Railways is now attempting the same. Many public sector banks witnessed mergers so that duplication would not become a loophole for fraudsters. The recent PNB scam fraudster gang exploited the loopholes in public sector banks raised huge loans against the same security. To prevent a repetition of such duplication, due diligence in critical functions is needed. The author studied the inventory of the issues and systems and would venture to suggest remedial measures. The intention of enforcement is always and should always be the spirit and the letter of the law of the land and the enforcement authorities should be capable of answering any question about their intention through accountable actions through the judiciary.

Law is meant to be equal in the application and is impartial in effect. Audit means hearing. The basic doctrine of rights of natural justice is expressed in the famous Latin maxim, "Audi Alteram Partem." Whistle blower protection law needs more teeth and a timely response mechanism in place without delay on one hand and derailment on the other. This research would aim to examine and suggest remedies.

Kaizen in the Economy, Law and Integration of Technologies vs Increasing Redundancy of Differentials

Economy and law travel together and reinforce each other. Any disturbance would delay the moment of both of them. Kaizen is a Japanese word, signifying constant learning for the betterment.

Coding as a new skill is being taught online to even children. The new literacy is in computeronomics. The new languages are no longer English, German but Python and Java. Applications of technologies are wide and in varied fields. The world is increasingly becoming a unique place of Production Consumption and Transaction (PCT) aided by ICTs. The Internet of Things (IOT) and virtual reality with 3-D printing, telecasting, holograms is no longer in science fiction. All are realities today. Space travel is no longer a subsidised activity either of NASA or of ISRO, but now many enthusiastic businessmen tour the space with their teams.

Law needs support at the grassroots areas in India. The Internet made information availability easy and websites provide data. Search engines allow initial access to the important discoveries and success stories.

Current Reforms in India

Labour law, security law and corporate law and communication law are important parts of the economic legislation, and the current reforms are efforts towards simplification and suitability of the new emerging global compulsions.

The gap between capacity and aspiration is physical at the individual and organisational levels. The impact of the gap is almost like the law of Boyle in connection with the relationship between the pressure on the temperature in that while other factors remaining constant, the proportionality is direct. The more the gap between capacity and aspiration, the more would be the gap at the individual level. At the institutional level, it is extremely difficult to identify the gap. However, when a neighbouring country grows four times bigger than our country at the same time, this is lethal for the survival of the country itself. Ethics are the first casualty in real politics and as Morgenthau so famously opined, international political economy is essentially a power game.

The suitable law enables a level playing field and the recent discovery of the manipulation of Business Ease rankings is another eye-opener of the vitality of being fair and ethical in investment decisions. Corporate law reform started in India in the year 2013 and new additions are made as per requirement. Unicorns of India are a force to reckon with today. Still, gaps abound between propaganda and practice ground. Law should not leave discretion at any level: (1) the draft, (2) the making, (3) the implementation, (4) the adjudication, (5) the feedback, (6) the amendment, (7) the inclusiveness, (8) the open-mindedness, (9) transparency and (10) alertness.

Non-Performing Assets and the Banking Law

Banking law has its origins almost nine decades ago and recent changes/reforms aim to reduce the non-performing assets, estimated to be Rs 12,00,000 crore. There are major mergers and banks. Auditing by professional organisations is part of the new reform agenda and the establishment of the Financial Service Regulation Authority under the chairmanship of Shri Injeti Srinivas is in tune with similar initiatives in the USA. The recent establishment of "Bad Bank" with this unit capital of Rs 36,000 crore is another initiative that has the potential promise to handle the non-performing assets and prevent the crisis from becoming out of control.

Non-performing assets are assets only notionally. IBC's effort also had a haircut of nearly 92% in certain cases. Declaring losses and liabilities as potential profits and future assets is criminal activity, if the intention is to defraud the regulators, shareholders, investors and other stakeholders. Here, the role of the Indian Penal Code assumes relevance because according to the IPC, crime is both intention and action, namely mens rea and actus reus.

The action on big four audit groups globally and in India is a step to prevent the fraudulent postponement of a looming crisis. India saw the big scams in the previous decades of the 21st century in the form of 2G spectrum auction, Satyam Ramalinga Raju case and the PNB scam. There are many administrative changes in the regulatory bodies in the USA that also check up the connivance of fraudulent accounting violations to cover up the wrongs and the wrongdoings. Timely response is essential in every crisis. Procrastination is a sure disaster, be it with ontological diagnosis or with forensic accounting/audit activity.

IBC, IBBA and Specific Law for the Prevention of Insolvency

Insolvency and Bankruptcy Code, 2016 and the institutional setup IBBA completed five years in operation in 2021. While expectations are many, the performance leaves much to be desired as was felt by many independent observers. Insolvency is not avoidable as it is part of the risk, which any business can and may undergo, sometimes for man-made reasons and sometimes through disruptions that technology brings no one buys a non-smartphone of days, whereas 25 years ago, even a pager has many takers. However, when public money is given in loans to private companies through public sector banks, accountability is at stake. Unfortunately, this chronic insolvency is a fraud to go scot-free in the name of "labour welfare." Private sector banks are no saints as fraudulent activity is caused by many private sector banks, finally leading to the collapse of such banks the world over. The Government in India, being the supreme regulator aided by the Reserve Bank of India, promulgated a law called the Banking Regulation Act to guide the activities of the banks and hence cannot escape the responsibility in curbing the trends of insolvency either in the public sector or in the private sector or the cooperative sector. The creation of Co-Operatives Ministry in India is a case in point.

The law needs specific support from technology like financial technologies. If private organisations like Bajaj Auto Finance or Muthoot Finance company can generate profits, and if HDFC Bank can never see red in the profit and loss account, the government-controlled sectors can learn and adapt to avoid these pitfalls.

The Role of Enforcement

Law originates in intention and when it is passed as Act, it must lead to action. Without proper implementation, the law loses its very purpose of itself, of its origin. The proper, sincere and serious implementation only would enable the handlers of law to know the loopholes and rectify the same in time. Law does not operate in a vacuum and loopholes in law would not remain of the same size and emerge as cancerous, questioning the very credibility of law first as an instrument and the law as the institution. Implementation needs training to those who are in charge and stability of tenure logically improves ability, provided tangible result-oriented accountability remains as the vital link between the stability of official tenure and ability of delivery of officials.

Lobbies, Pressure Groups, Publicity and Public Interest Litigation Policy

Corporates appoint lobbyists transparently in the USA and indirectly in India. There are federations, trade promotion bodies, professional groups. Most prominent are chartered accountants, auditors, chambers of commerce, transporters, exporters. Recently, a trend has been observed regarding public interest litigation. Social media groups and paid media coverages are not new in corporate battles. Law enforcers need to keep a watch on lobbies. Freedom of expression cannot be allowed to masquerade as a strategic tool in business rivalry warfare. Competition is natural in business. All parties should be made to follow the rules of the game and when the umpire fails, Empire too follows.

Indexes of Governance—Ease of Doing Business, Arbitration, Redressal of Disputes, ADRs

Governments are the services through various departments of the government delivered according to the law. Objectivity is impartial, transparent and scientific. Indexes should be developed legally with transparent analysis and objective analytics to measure effectiveness. The code, when effective obviates the court.

Corporate legal problems are repetitive and issues like tax disputes contractual obligations, recoveries of receivables, damage recoveries enforcement of promises made require not the subjective legal eagles but objective of factual and legal analytics. When indexes are developed, traffic is regulated. Every violation is visited with a fine, and recidivism will surely cause expulsion from the vocation. Indexes are interlinked and hence coordination needs to be inbuilt. Corruption would be minimal when objectives of law are transparently enforced.

Regulatory Authorities and Enforcement

Enforcement authorities implement the law and regulatory authorities within a profession apply the rules and regulations to their stipulated functional jurisdictional activities. RERA (Real Estate Regulatory Authority), for instance, applies the provisions of the Real Estate Act within the activities of the stakeholders of the segmented profession. The spirit behind every rule, code, regulation, sub-rules, explanation, the exception is that the law and the articles of the Constitution sanction legitimacy to all the laws through their upholding through initial scrutiny, application, interpretation and review. The judicial review is a salient feature and part of the basic structure of the conference of India, as expressed in the famous *Keshevananda Bharathi* judgement case. Whenever there is a missing link, noises rightly are heard and timely replies should reasonably address such questions.

Law should address the procedural aspect also as part of the anticipatory function. One view is that regulatory authorities should not be allowed to have their key positions filled up by the former bureaucrats.

Credibility of the State through Performance of Government

State means four elements—population, territory, Government and Sovereignty. State enforces the writ through Government and expresses its internal and external Sovereignty as the supreme authority. Law is the main instrument and the voice of the Government. Government operates through the effective implementation of law. When law fails, State too fails and nations get split. Law hence is the supreme command of the State and an expression of its Sovereignty. Rule of law is the rule of the State in its ultimate manifestation of virtue.

Seamless Connectivity from Military, Medicine and Management (M^3) for Diagnosis, Delivery and Diligence (D^3)

Enormous progress is being made when this sentence is being written in all the above-mentioned fields. Cross-functional applications can be developed from space science, nanotechnology to the forensic audit, software architecture. Law is specific to functional areas like maritime law, space law, biotechnology law, pollution law. However, lawyers must be encouraged to study these fields by consultant groups and professionals in the emerging areas may be co-opted as expert members for making law by the Law Commission and various parliamentary committees. The task, being vital, can be handled only by the Law Ministry in the case of India and by the Department of Justice in the case of the USA.

9/11, 26/11, the Taliban march to Kabul, COVID-19's third wave, the collapse of Lehman Brothers in the year 2008, the balance of payments crisis for India in the year 1991—all are threats in the guise of opportunities for students of law, to learn, unlearn and relearn. The law was inadequate at some stage—maybe the domestic law, the National Law or the International trust or goodwill. Rogue states and terrorist states are impervious to any or all the above. Some nations learned the hard lessons and did not allow the repetition of 9/11. In the USA, Homeland Security emerged as a preventive instrument against possible terrorist attacks.

Law should not be a knee-jerk response. Law may not prevent an earthquake, but it should ensure equal relief to all the victims. Law is the ultimate hope of the entire people—rich, poor, mighty, unassuming, influential or persona non grata. Earthquakes, pandemics and terrorist attacks do not discriminate among the victims. So should be the law. Law, as in a learning institution, needs to be open, alert, simulated, free, equal and just before it offers similar promises to the followers of law. Law is an impersonal permanent guardian yesterday, today and hence tomorrow. The faith in law is the signature of its identity and the strength at the same time.

Law as a Link from the Past, through Present for Future and Perspectives of Law

Certainty and predictability are two dimensions in the time framework. Certainty is the past, present and hence is predictable in the future, other conditions remaining unchanged. Law, as expected by the followers needs to be certain and predictable so that the followers of law seek the support of law whenever they face trouble.

When corporate law acquires the essential qualities of certainty and predictability, businesses will be sustainable and wasteful expenditure would be minimal. Lobbies, speed money, contingency expenditure, relationship management expenditure, hospitality overheads-type expenses would disappear from the accounts of the businesses. Ethics would be administered as standard operating procedure. Law and scams should be mutually exclusive and not strange partners.

Students of law should be sensitive to the emerging technologies, discoveries, disruptions and trend settings. Law should go hand-in-hand with the technology, and seamless connectivity is a link that is vital both for technology and for the law. Technology itself is multidimensional. So should be the law. However, the common interests of both the law and technology are human welfare and sustainable equilibrium in gradual happiness of all living that inherits this universe and the space.

Law as a Fair Elixir of Tri Virtues—Equality, Freedom and Justice

The law provides level playing field among all stakeholders with three essential features, namely, Equality, Freedom and Justice. Fair play in the redressal of grievance requires the presence of the above ingredients. The doctrine of natural justice points out the essential upholding of the right to be hard before being punished.

Corporate Justice, Civil Justice, Criminal Justice and Governance

Corporate Justice essentially portrays fairness in business transactions and the delivery of justice without delay. In corporate parlance, delay means loss and derailment of opportunities. It may result in the destruction of the credibility and creditworthiness of the business organisation. Civil justice in India takes decades to be dispensed, and before the era of NCLT or IBC, corporate disputes were no different from civil disputes. The resolution of disputes needs a disposal framework, reasonably acceptable to all litigants. When fraud with the intention to cause wrongful loss/gain is mixed with seemingly harmless corporate transactions, the criminal justice system takes over. This situation deserves special attention. Justice is unpartitionable. Law of the land, hence, needs to address possible contradictions.

Global Trade, Export Import 2021 and International Trade in Goods and Services in India

Domestic Trade Policy

India's economic growth levels have been lower in 2020 primarily due to the effects of the 2019 novel corona virus disease (COVID-19) pandemic. The UN World Economic Situation and Prospects 2021 report states that India's economy shrank by 9.6% in 2020. In response to the effects of the pandemic, the Prime Minister of India announced the launch of the Self-reliant India Campaign (Atmanirbhar Bharat Abhiyaan) on May 12, 2020, which is a special economic and comprehensive package of Rs 20 billion (equivalent to 10% of India's GDP). In keeping with this, the Government's Budget in 2021 included various stimulus and incentive schemes that aim to revive growth. There is an increased focus on indigenisation with a view of making India a global manufacturing hub and increasing its competitiveness globally.

Trade Negotiations: The Department of Commerce (DoC) of the Ministry of Commerce and Industry is primarily responsible for negotiating trade agreements. Within the DoC, the Trade Policy Division (TPD), particularly Services-I, Services-II and Services-III desks, are responsible for negotiating trade agreements.

It takes on average 18 to 20 months to negotiate trade agreements with India. However, this is not indicative of a trend. For example, India has been negotiating trade agreements with the EU and Australia for several years.

Financial Services

The financial services sector can be broadly divided into the banking, securities and insurance sectors. India has made certain commitments on financial services to the WTO under the General Agreement on Trade and Services (GATS). India's Schedule of Specific Commitments (GATS/SC/42/Suppl.4) can be accessed at: WTO: Schedules of specific commitments and lists of Article II exemptions.

Suppliers of Financial Services Must Comply with the Requirements Set Out in the Relevant Legislation

Banking

The banking sector is regulated by the Reserve Bank of India (RBI), which is India's central bank. Some of the key laws applicable to the banking sector include the:

- Reserve Bank of India Act 1934.
- Banking Regulation Act 1949.
- Foreign Exchange Management Act 1999 (FEMA).
- Securitisation and Reconstruction of Financial Assets and Enforcement of Security Interest Act 2002.
- Recovery of Debts Due to Banks and Financial Institutions Act 1993.
- Prevention of Money Laundering Act 2005.
- Factoring Regulation Act 2011.

The RBI issues regulations, notifications, directions and circulars governing the conduct of banks and financial institutions.

Securities

The securities sector is primarily regulated by the Securities and Exchange Board of India (SEBI) under the Securities and Exchange Board of India Act 1992. The RBI, the Forward Markets Commission and the Pension Fund Regulatory and Development Authority, among others, also regulate the securities market.

Insurance

The insurance and reinsurance sector is regulated by the Insurance Regulatory and Development Authority. The main statutes include the following:

- Insurance Act 1938.
- Insurance Regulatory and Development Authority Act 1999.
- Life Insurance Corporation Act 1956.
- General Insurance Business Act 1972.

Main Requirements:
Only advocates are entitled to practise law in India. To be eligible for enrolment as an advocate, a candidate must:

- Be a citizen of India.
- Have reached the age of 21.
- Have a degree in law from a university as provided under the Advocates Act 1961.

A foreign national can be admitted as an advocate, subject to the condition of reciprocity. Therefore, if duly qualified Indian citizens are allowed to practise law in a foreign country, nationals of that country must be permitted to practise law in India, subject to certain conditions laid down by the BCI. There are currently no conditions prescribed by the BCI in this regard.

DIPP and FDI

The FDI Policy issued by the Department of Industrial Policy and Promotion (DIPP) sets out sector-specific conditions and caps on FDI. Up to 100% FDI is permitted in sectors and activities that are not listed in the FDI Policy, subject to the applicable laws and regulations. Further, Chapter 5 of the FDI Policy lists prohibited sectors and permitted sectors The FDI Policy 2020 (effective from October 15, 2020) lists several services sectors that are subject to specific FDI caps and conditions, including:

- Broadcasting.
- Telecoms.
- Print media.
- Civil aviation.
- Banking.
- Insurance.
- Pensions.
- Non-banking financial services.
- Construction.
- E-Commerce.
- Trading.

Notes

1. Sec. 47 9(IV) of I. T. Act 1961.
2. Sec. 2 (1B) of I. T. Act 1961.
3. Sec. 50 (B) of I. T. Act 1961.
4. Sec. 71–79 of I. T. Act 1961.
5. Sec. 2 (19A) of I. T. Act 1961.
6. Sec. 47–54 of I. T. Act 1961.
7. Sec. 96–105 of I. T. Act 1961.
8. Sec. 47 of I. T. Act 1961.
9. Financial Express Page No-09, 29.09.2021, India.

10 Financial Express Page No-08, 08.11.2021, India – career journeys, Tapping tech to retain and grow talent.
11 A.I. at work survey conducted by Oracle and Work Place Intelligence (08.11.2021, P-08, Financial Express).
12 The Hindu November 7, 2021, P-11.
13 https://ibbi.gov.in//uploads/legalframwork/741059f0d8777f311ec76332ced1e9cf.pdf
14 Arrow line Organic Products Private Limited v. M/s Rockwell Industries Limited
15 Foseco India Limited v. Om Boseco Rail Products Limited.
16 Shri M.S. Sahoo, in Chairman's report access on December 12, 2021.
17 As per World Bank's Doing Business Reports.

Index

Ability: of a company to surpass its previous guidance 51; of buyers in having acquisition financing 221; of financial resources at a lower cost 66; of parties to seek damages 134; of the US to compete with China 55; operational 235; resolving, of the companies 235; stability of tenure logically improves 300; to compete in global markets 5; to perform better 270; to utilise an emerging opportunity 218
Accountability 26, 43–46, 85, 109, 142, 160–161, 165, 184, 187, 216, 235, 261
Accountancy Council of India 190
Agriculture 22, 70
Amalgamation 2, 8, 9, 11, 31, 94, 96, 100, 137, 140, 145, 146, 151, 152, 187, 193, 234, 262, 270, 290
Amalgamation Rules 146
Amendment: Banking Regulation Act, 1949 219; Companies Act, 2013 246; Companies Act, 2013 6, 67; Cost and Works Accountants Act, 1959 143; Dodd-Frank Act (USA) 255; FEMA, 1999 35; Indian Partnership Act, 1932 246; Insolvency and Bankruptcy Code 181, 234, 244; Limited Liability Partnership Act, 2008 246; Maharashtra Stamp Act, 1993 151; Prevention of Corruption Act, 1988 94; SARFAESI Act, 2002 246; sector-specific 35; Sick Industrial Companies Repeal Act, 2003 246; Specific Relief Act, 1963 153–157; Stamp Act, 1899 15, 116; The Chartered Accountants Act, 1949 143; The Company Secretaries Act, 1980 143; to make entry easier for private sector 269; to procedures 34; to several other laws 147; Trade and Competitive Act (USA) 47, 49
Anti-Corruption 43, 99, 163, 164, 167–170, 184, 255
Anti-trust Law 43, 45, 46, 48, 53, 128, 129, 131, 133, 221, 225, 266
Artificial Intelligence 207, 211–212, 219, 256–257, 270–271, 282, 291

Backward Integration 4, 218
Bank for International Settlement (BIS) 8
Banking Law Reforms Committee (BLRC) 185
Banking Regulation Act 6, 35, 95, 151, 187–188, 192–194, 219, 253, 267, 299
BRICS 59, 63, 65
Brooke Bond India Limited (BBIL) 108
Business Sustainability 248
Bad Bank 64, 266, 281, 299
Bankruptcy Law 243, 245
Banking Reforms 15, 29, 187, 191, 219, 249

Cabinet Committee on Economic Affairs (CCEA) 6
Central Government 8, 9, 114, 183, 186, 234, 279
Competition Commission of India (CCI) 8, 15, 37, 116, 136, 141, 161, 262, 263
Clayton Act 51, 128, 129, 223, 224
Companies Amendment Act 144, 278
Compensatory Forestation Act 17
Competition Controller of India Rules 17
Competition Act 2, 15, 30, 37, 94, 100, 116, 128, 136, 137, 138, 139, 141, 144, 150, 262, 264

308 *Index*

Competition Law 3, 15, 37, 116, 127, 221, 262, 266
Compliance 2, 9, 12, 30, 31, 33, 43, 48, 83, 92–96, 99, 101, 104, 114, 115, 127, 155, 159, 164, 165, 183, 199, 219, 220, 223, 230, 232, 251, 253–256, 278, 279, 282, 283
Comptroller and Auditor General (CAG) 160, 240
Contract Act 7, 94, 154, 156, 199
Corporate Data Management (CDM) 284
Corporate Governance 6, 12, 37, 43, 47, 109, 110, 160
Corruption 24, 44, 72, 94, 100, 120, 122, 157, 161–164, 166, 167, 169, 172, 173, 180, 192
Corruption Perception Index (CPI) 164
Covid-19 1, 3, 32, 35, 42, 67, 136, 190, 205, 207, 209–214, 216, 220, 222, 223, 225, 227, 230, 232, 233, 239, 243, 246, 248, 250, 253, 257
Criminal Culpability 255
Criminal Liability 164, 167
Crisis Management 119, 212, 220
Cross Border Mergers and Acquisition (CBMA) 1–7, 10–28, 30–38, 40–46, 48–51, 53, 55, 57, 59–60, 65, 68, 79–106, 107–123, 145–147, 150, 172, 181, 208, 252
Culpability 255
Culture 11, 37, 44, 45, 65, 79, 80, 108, 110, 111, 117, 121, 166, 168, 240, 263, 272, 274, 277, 287
Cyber Business 72

Data Security Council of India (DSCI) 258
Demerger 72, 96, 100, 115, 127–174, 234, 264, 290
Demonetisation 3, 24, 85
Department of Industrial Policy and Promotion (DIPP) 94, 95, 100, 305
Department of Justice (DOJ) 12, 39, 41, 44, 45, 49, 51, 53, 120, 129–133, 163, 222, 228–229, 302
Developed Economies 34, 62, 66, 67, 161, 203
Developed Market (DM) 26, 34, 32, 102
Director of Revenue Intelligence (DRI) 237
Doctrine 228, 287, 289, 295
Dodd-Frank Act 48, 254, 255
Due Diligence 3, 5, 37, 42–46, 80, 83, 95–98, 101, 114, 117, 121, 123, 167–168, 180, 197, 203, 206–207, 209, 211, 213, 217, 220, 221, 231, 237, 256, 258, 265, 269, 274, 290, 297

Ease of Doing Business 9, 11, 23, 67, 83, 84, 138, 150, 153, 155, 156, 157, 184, 198, 199, 215, 233, 240, 245, 249, 250, 251, 252, 253, 256, 260
Ease of Doing Business Index (EDBI) 83, 84, 138, 150, 153, 155, 184, 198, 199, 215, 233, 240
Emerging Economies 34, 65, 67, 72, 187
Emerging Market 2, 3, 18, 21, 26, 29, 33, 34, 52, 67, 70, 112, 113, 287
Employee Accountability 213
Environment Protection Act 17
Environment Social and Governance (ESG) 286

Fast-Track Merger 9
Federal Bureau of Investigation (FDI) 101
Federal Trade Commission (FTC) 12, 39, 49–51, 53–54, 86, 116, 117, 122, 126, 129–130, 133, 135, 197, 199, 202, 204, 222, 237, 238, 266
Financial Action Task Force (FATA) 8
Financial Management 145, 227
Financial viability 221
FIRPTA 40
Foreign Account Tax Compliance Act (FATCA) 180
Foreign Corrupt Practice Act (FCPA) 45, 162
Foreign Direct Investment (FDI) 6, 15, 34, 66, 84, 94, 95, 100, 101, 110, 200, 225, 267, 283
Foreign Exchange Management Act 9, 31, 34, 94, 150
Foreign Exchange Regulation Act (FERA) 31
Foreign Investment Promotion Policy (FIPP) 66
Foreign trade 22, 133, 134, 267
Foreign Trade Antitrust Improvements Act (FTAIA) 133
FPI 191, 208

Generally Accepted Accounting Principle (GAAP) 108, 168
Global Compliance 165
Global Economy 3, 24, 71, 200, 211, 217

Index 309

Global Innovation Index 295
Goods and Service Tax (GST) 18, 23, 34, 92, 226
Governance 29, 37, 38, 43, 47, 109, 110, 160, 173, 187, 215, 219, 227, 286
Government of India (GoI) 6, 17, 31, 32, 84, 86, 92, 95, 104, 138, 196, 199, 200, 206–209, 215, 216, 218, 227, 233, 240, 242, 256, 265, 275, 292, 296
Gross Domestic Product (GDP) 24, 66, 111, 113, 155, 191, 216, 238, 256

Haryana-Delhi Chamber of Commerce and Industry (PHDCCI) 90
Herfindahl-Hirschman Index (HHI) 3
High Court 8, 16, 38, 116, 138, 141, 149, 151, 188, 193, 236, 251, 289, 295
Hindustan Lever limited (HLL) 108
HSR Act 46, 130, 223
Human resource 34, 119, 165, 184, 273, 274
Human Rights Act 199, 273

IBC (Insolvency and Bankruptcy Code) 14, 31, 32, 34, 86, 90, 91, 100, 147, 150, 161, 181, 182, 186, 187, 194, 195, 197, 198, 232–235, 238, 241, 243, 259, 264
Implementation 7, 17, 30, 32, 37, 44, 48, 62–64, 68, 86, 112, 150, 167, 173, 184, 196, 198, 200, 233, 237, 246, 257, 277, 291
Implication(s) 81, 98, 136, 146, 150, 153, 155, 157, 218, 220, 221, 231, 290, 293
Inability 128, 156, 209, 228, 286
Inbound Merger 9, 102, 145, 146
Income Tax Act (IT Act) 2, 3, 7, 15, 16, 31, 57, 58, 94, 100, 290
Indian Penal Code (IPC) 99, 249, 299
Innovation 10, 56, 80, 91, 105, 117, 131, 212, 218, 225, 226, 229, 248, 251, 257, 258, 262, 267
Innovation Management Office (IMO) 117
Insider Trading 35, 95–98, 115, 116, 199
Insolvency and Bankruptcy Board of India (IBBI) 90, 238, 240, 294
Insurance Regulatory Development Authority (IRDA) 15, 248
Integration 2, 4, 12, 18, 67, 79, 80, 105, 109, 117, 119, 123, 167, 218, 220, 272, 274, 286, 298

Internal Revenue Code (IRC) 12, 41
Internal Revenue Service (IRS) 41
International Bank for Reconstruction and Development (IBRD) 67, 164
International Finance of Reporting Standards (IFRS) 108
International Monetary Fund (IMF) 26, 62
International Law 42, 58

Jiangling Motor Company Group (JMCG) 5
Judicial review 38, 39, 49, 116, 129, 301

Kaizen 33, 290
Kellogg School of Management 82
Kubota Agriculture Commissioner India Pvt Ltd 264

Labour Law 59, 94, 96, 121, 198, 202, 220, 250, 271
Legal Due Diligence 43–46, 95, 96, 97, 123
Legal Innovation 251
Less Developed Country (LDC) 67
Liability 5, 40, 43–48, 56, 94, 135, 152, 158, 160, 164, 167, 216, 232, 234
Liberalization 2, 66, 139, 147, 235
Limited Liability Act 94, 281
Limited Liability Company (LLC) 185, 264
Limited Liability Limited Partnership (LLLP) 160
Limited Liability Partnership (LLP) 143–145, 185
Litigation 30, 31, 98, 131, 134, 136, 137, 150, 154, 155, 167, 184, 217, 220, 221, 229, 232, 234, 236, 239, 244, 246, 254, 255, 283, 285
Lok Sabha (People's House) 6, 153

Mahindra and Mahindra Limited (M&M) 5
Management 5, 7, 16, 39, 58, 65, 70, 79, 81, 83, 90, 104, 110, 113, 114, 117, 119, 141, 145, 158, 165, 171, 181, 184, 189, 202, 206, 209, 212, 219, 221, 224, 227, 231, 234, 235, 244, 246, 250, 255, 268, 270, 272, 273
Marketing Management 82
Ministry of Corporate Affairs (MCA) 17, 90, 95, 143, 150, 161, 240, 252, 278

Index

Ministry of Finance (MoF) 92, 216
Misgovernance 122, 236
Mismanagement 117, 182, 267, 283
Money Laundering 8, 31, 99, 113, 172, 180, 235, 249
Monopoly Restrictive Trade Practices (MRTP) Act 15, 30, 37, 116, 137, 296
Multilateral Memorandum of Understanding (MOU) 8
Multinational Corporations (MNC) 22, 26, 28, 29, 61, 128, 191, 192

National Democratic Alliance (NDA) 23, 63
National Financial Reporting Authority (NFRA) 284
National Security 47, 49–50, 54–55
National Security Act 44, 49, 54
NCLT (National Company Law Tribunal) 2, 4, 8, 14, 38, 86, 100, 147, 149, 186, 192, 194, 195, 238, 242, 259, 279, 283
NPA (Non-Performing Asset) 34, 64, 84, 91, 191, 197, 235, 236, 238, 241, 265, 266, 281
Non-liability 47, 159

Organization of American States (OAS) 104, 164
Outbound Merger 8, 10, 95, 112, 145, 146, 147

Parliament 5, 6, 86, 145, 155, 156, 272
Partnership Act 17, 143–145, 159, 246
Pollution Control Act 17
Political reforms 22
Predictability 122, 234, 253
Pre-pack 90–92, 243, 260, 264
Prevention of Corruption Act 17, 94, 99
Prevention of Money Laundering Act 31, 99, 249, 291
Prevention of Sexual Harassment at Workplace 17
Protectionism 1, 55, 82, 214, 215, 225
Public Company Accounting Oversight Board (PCAOB) 38, 284
Public Sector Banks (PSB) 104

Rajya Sabha (Upper House) 6
RBI Act 35
RCEP 215
RDDBFI Act 244
Real Estate 14, 38, 39, 41, 55, 85, 93, 99, 120, 132, 152, 156, 159, 181, 200, 209, 236, 272, 301

Real Estate Regulation Act (RERA) 93
Regulatory Law 43, 199, 223
Reliability 43, 226, 269
Reserve Bank of India (RBI) 6, 16, 95, 147, 187, 189, 192, 194, 195, 196, 199, 219, 242, 252, 265, 268, 269, 292
Resolvability 241
Revenue 31, 41, 56, 72, 92, 153, 160, 169, 190, 192, 221, 224, 232, 251
Right to Accountability 273
Risk Management 7, 113, 165, 181, 184, 219
R N Malhotra Committee 15

Sarbanes Oxley Act 38
Securitisation and reconstruction of Financial Asset and Enforcement of Security Interest (SARFAESI) Act 104, 186, 235, 304
Security and Exchange Board of India (SEBI) 2, 7, 8, 15, 16, 22, 23, 27, 35, 36, 58, 67, 94, 95–98, 100, 112, 115, 116, 120, 147, 150, 161, 187, 196–198, 201, 203, 210, 221, 235, 254, 264, 274, 279
Security Exchange Commission (SEC) 48, 169
Serious Fraud Investigation Office (SFIO) 171, 182
Special Purpose Vehicle (SPV) 112, 222
Specific Relief Act 94, 100, 153, 156, 157
Stamp duty 15, 94, 117, 151–153, 200, 283
Stamp Duty Act 37, 116, 150, 200
Stamp Law 151, 216, 235, 236, 296
Strategic Mangement 58, 65, 81
Suitability 7, 42
Supply Chain Management 207, 213, 216, 231, 250, 269
Supreme Court of India (SCI) 85, 91, 116, 220, 236, 284
Synergy 5, 32, 68, 109, 120, 121, 187

Taxability 57
Tax Compliance 83, 114, 232
Tax Hikes Act (THA) 41
Tax Liability 158, 232
Trade Union Act 17, 250
Transnational Corporations (TNC) 29, 56
Technical Advisory Committee (TAC) 284

UIDAI 26
United Nations Conference on Trade and Development (UNCTAD) 22, 66, 104
United States Internal Revenue Code (USIRC) 41
Unlimited Liability 158, 159

Vicarious Liability 167

World Bank 30, 65, 84, 91, 164, 184, 233, 238, 253, 255, 295
Work from Home (WFH) 224, 232, 257, 259
World Trade Organization (WTO) 104